MW00998004

# ON THE HEROIC FRENZIES

THE DA PONTE ITALIAN LIBRARY

Giordano Bruno

# ON THE HEROIC FRENZIES

## A Translation of
## DE GLI EROICI FURORI

by Ingrid D. Rowland
Text edited by Eugenio Canone

Published in Collaboration with
the UCLA Centre for Medieval and Renaissance Studies

UNIVERSITY OF TORONTO PRESS
Toronto  Buffalo  London

© University of Toronto Press 2013
Toronto Buffalo London
www.utppublishing.com
Printed in Canada

ISBN 978-1-4426-4389-5

Printed on acid-free paper

The Lorenzo Da Ponte Italian Library

---

**Library and Archives Canada Cataloguing in Publication**

Bruno, Giordano, 1548–1600
[De gli eroici furori. English & Italian]
On the heroic frenzies : a translation of De gli eroici furori (1585) /
by Ingrid D. Rowland ; text edited by Eugenio Canone.

Translated from the Italian.
Includes bibliographical references and index.
Text in English and Italian.
ISBN 978-1-4426-4389-5

1. Philosophical anthropology – Early works to 1800.   2. Philosophy,
Renaissance – Early works to 1800.   I. Canone, Eugenio   II. Rowland,
Ingrid D. (Ingrid Drake)   III. Title.   IV. Title: De gli eroici furori. English & Italian

BD450.B7413 2013      128      C2013-900019-4

---

Publication of this book has been assisted by the Istituto Italiano di Cultura, Toronto.

This book has been published under the aegis and with the financial assistance of:
Fondazione Cassamarca, Treviso; the National Italian-American Foundation; Ministero
degli Affari Esteri, Direzione Generale per la Promozione e la Cooperazione Culturale;
Ministero per i Beni e le Attività Culturali, Direzione Generale per i Beni Librari e gli
Istituti Culturali, Servizio per la promozione del libro e della lettura.

University of Toronto Press acknowledges the financial assistance to its publishing
program of the Canada Council for the Arts and the Ontario Arts Council.

University of Toronto Press acknowledges the financial assistance to its publishing
program of the Canada Book Fund.

*To the memory of Enzo Crea*

# Contents

# Acknowledgments

This translation was completed in its initial phases during fellowships at the Getty Research Institute and the Rockefeller Foundation Study Center at Bellagio. Thanks especially to Michael Roth, President of Wesleyan University and former Associate Director of the Getty Research Institute, to Gianna Celli, Director Emerita at Bellagio, and to the following: Eugenio Canone, Brian Copenhaver, Karen De Leon-Jones, Paul Elie, Germana Ernst, Jonathan Galassi, Hilary Gatti, Wouter Hanegraff, David Marsh, Marco Pasi, Walter Stephens, Haris Vlavianos, and an anonymous reader.

The Department of Special Collections at Glasgow University Library provided generous help with the emblems in this book. Particular thanks to Nicola Russell of the Department of Special Collections and David Weston, Keeper of Special Collections and Assistant Director.

The book is dedicated to the memory of Enzo Crea, whose readings of Bruno with Lucio Mariani gave the philosopher of Nola such fitting voice.

# Introduction

The little love-god lying once asleep
Laid by his side his heart-inflaming brand,
Whilst many nymphs that vowed chaste to keep
Came tripping by; but in her maiden hand
The fairest votary took up that fire
Which many legions of true hearts had warmed,
And so the general of hot desire
Was sleeping by a virgin hand disarmed.
This brand she quenched in a cool well by,
Which from love's fire took heat perpetual,
Growing a bath and healthful remedy
For men diseased; but I, my mistress' thrall,
Came there for cure; and this by that I prove:
Love's fire heats water, water cools not love.

William Shakespeare, Sonnet 154

Between 1584 and 1585, the London press of John Charlewood printed a series of six philosophical dialogues, written in Italian by a man who called himself Giordano Bruno Nolano, Giordano Bruno of Nola. At the time, Bruno lived in the house of Michel de Castelnau, the French ambassador to the Court of St James. His position was something like that of a resident scholar; he had originally hoped to find work at Oxford, but his experiences there had been disastrous.

Bruno's dialogues were Charlewood's first venture into Italian publishing, but far from his last; London, as he well knew, was filled with people who either knew Italian or were Italian, from the bankers who gave

their name to Lombard Street to Queen Elizabeth and her courtiers, for whom Italian art, literature, and music represented the pinnacle of refinement. In Elizabethan London, even an offering as sophisticated as a philosophical work in Italian could sell well enough to make its publication a worthwhile project for author and printer alike.

But Bruno's dialogues were more than sophisticated; they were revolutionary. The first of them, *The Ash Wednesday Supper* (*La cena de le ceneri*), took the Copernican theory of a Sun-centred universe as its starting point, proceeding onward to show that Copernicus and his theory were as obsolete as the Old World of three continents, for now Giordano Bruno of Nola had come on the scene to act as philosophy's version of Christopher Columbus. Bruno proclaimed that the universe was infinitely huge, filled with solar systems beyond number, in a dialogue that mixed moments of high comedy with flights of sublime poetry and deep thought – all of it peppered by a redolent vocabulary of insults, together with damning caricatures of Oxford dons and London riffraff. Readers were both appalled and fascinated. Bruno claimed that his savage description of Cockneys in *The Ash Wednesday Supper* so angered Londoners that he was forced to live thereafter as a prisoner in his own house – fortunately for him, a house large enough to serve as an embassy.

Before the controversies raised by *The Ash Wednesday Supper* could settle, Bruno and Charlewood had produced another long dialogue, *On the Cause, Principle, and One* (*De la causa, principio, e Uno*), followed not long afterward by *On the Infinite, Universe, and Worlds* (*Dell'infinito universo e mondi*). In all of these works (whose titles are eternally ambiguous because we can never know quite where the commas should or should not be placed in them), Bruno seemed to be struggling to find the right words to express his revolutionary philosophy, not least because the implications of that philosophy were apparently opening out to him as quickly as he could write them down. Thus, the infinite universe he presented in *The Ash Wednesday Supper* required him to explain God's place within this new system – and Bruno obliged by describing God as the causal agent for the cosmos, and therefore its beginning (the word *principio* in his title *De la causa, principio, e Uno* could mean either 'beginning' or 'principle'). But God was also the unifying ingredient (the One, the *Uno*) of this infinitely vast, infinitely variegated expanse of space. Bruno argued further that a universe so boundless must also contain other solar systems, and other inhabitants – how could it not? He wrote a third dialogue, *Dell'infinito universo e mondi* to explain his position. A comma would let us decide whether the dialogue's title is meant to be

*On the Infinite, Universe, and Worlds,* or *On the Infinite Universe, and Worlds,* but Charlewood's cheap, quick edition is too slipshod to be a completely trustworthy on this point. Bruno's original manuscript, for this and all his other English dialogues, is lost; we cannot settle the question by going back to his own written text.

The discussions in these first three dialogues always revolve around a character who must be an alter ego of Bruno himself. This personage is named either Theofilo or Philotheo – each means "beloved by God" in Greek – and the connection with Bruno is clinched by several title pages describing him as "Philotheo Giordano Bruno." *The Ash Wednesday Supper* and *On the Cause, Principle, and One* also make use of a friendly, but decidedly less flashy figure to act as a foil to Theofilo/Philotheo's scintillating presentation of Bruno's Nolan philosophy. Bruno seems to have drawn the models for both these characters from his group of London friends: for *The Ash Wednesday Supper,* 'Smitho' may possibly be identified as John Smith, dedicatee of a 1597 textbook called *The Italian Schoole-master.* The second partner in the dialogue *On the Cause, Principle, and One* has a more distinctive name: "Dicsono," in fact, is clearly the Scotsman Alexander Dicson, one of Bruno's closest followers in Britain. *On the Infinite Universe and Worlds,* on the other hand, sets Philotheo alongside a distinguished kindred soul who has already accepted the Nolan philosophy: a gentleman of Verona, the poet and physician Girolamo Fracastoro. Fracastoro is best known now for his poem *Syphilis,* which gave both a name and a description to a new disease that had begun to ravage Europe in the late fifteenth century, but he also wrote poetry on astronomical themes; Bruno must already have been thinking of the elder poet as a model for his own work. Each of these three dialogues also included an opponent, a personage set in his ways and pedantic in his manner, who finds the Nolan philosopher's ideas repugnantly novel, but is too slow-witted to keep up with the fast pace of debate. *The Ash Wednesday Supper* adds a fourth character to a mix that already includes the pedant Prudenzio, the well-meaning Smitho, and the brilliant Theofilo: a clownish servant, Frulla (roughly, "Lightweight"), whose tongue is nearly as quick and sharp as Theofilo's own, as is his eye for human frailty. What Frulla lacks is an education, and the social status an education brings. The fact that he can follow the discussion as well as he does makes pedantic Prudenzio look all the more stupid.

In 1585, however, Bruno abruptly changed his style of writing. He still composed dialogues, but their form became increasingly experimental. *Expulsion of the Triumphant Beast* (*Spaccio della bestia trionfante*), his fourth

London dialogue, features a cast of mythological figures rather than contemporaries. These timeless immortals plan to redesign the constellations so that they will illustrate myths more edifying than the classical stories about the gods on Mount Olympus. The old gods' rivalries, love affairs, and interference in human events, after all, exhibit the worst qualities of human nature among divinities who ought to know better. At the time, of course, Bruno was engaged in redesigning the shape of the universe in far more radical terms. He seems to be suggesting that the supply of stories to attach to the stars is as infinite as the potential of our imagination, that we, in our own minds, are as unlimited in our possibilities as the universe in which we live – a daunting prospect for people who had been accustomed since ancient times to living in a neat, spherical cosmos with definite limits.

With *Expulsion of the Triumphant Beast*, Bruno begins to suggest that his own endeavour will extend beyond revolutionizing natural philosophy to revolutionizing human behaviour as well. The infinitely expanded universe requires a new kind of moral and religious conduct. As biting in its tone as ever, *Expulsion of the Triumphant Beast* contains another, separate dialogue, the devastatingly satirical *Kabbalah of the Horse Pegasus* (*Cabala del cavallo pegaseo*), which acts as a kind of comic coda to the larger work.

Bruno would continue to investigate the relationship between cosmology and individual behaviour in the last and most complex of his London dialogues, *On the Heroic Frenzies*. By the time he and Charlewood had set the *Heroic Frenzies* to print, he must have known that his sponsor, the French ambassador Michel de Castelnau, was in serious financial and political trouble in London. In fact, Bruno dedicated his first three dialogues to his French host, but addressed *Expulsion of the Triumphant Beast* to Sir Philip Sidney in a conspicuous change of strategy. Bruno must have been on the lookout for potential sponsors in England rather than facing a return to Paris with Castelnau's entourage. For all his troubles in England, the country brought him relief from the struggle between Catholic and Protestant that had driven him from Paris in the first place.

Sidney, however, did not respond to either of these remarkable, and remarkably aggressive, efforts. Instead, shortly after publishing *On the Heroic Frenzies*, Giordano Bruno of Nola prepared his return to Paris with Castelnau and his family. He arrived there in 1586, thus ending an extraordinarily creative period of his eventful life.

The circumstances that brought an Italian philosopher to the French embassy in London were complicated, to say the least. Bruno, born in

1548, began his life in the small city of Nola, in the hinterlands of Mount Vesuvius, the son of a professional soldier who maintained some illustrious connections among Neapolitan nobles and *litterati*. The boy was christened Filippo, possibly as tribute to King Philip II of Spain, his father's ultimate employer, for at the time the Kingdom of Naples was ruled by a Spanish viceroy. Filippo Bruno moved as a teenager to Naples itself, first as a student (in about 1563) and then as a novice in the Dominican convent of San Domenico Maggiore.[1] At the time (as indeed for several centuries before), the friars of San Domenico belonged to the most powerful religious congregation in the Kingdom of Naples. Their college, which admitted ten students a year, was the most selective university in the Kingdom, and had once boasted Thomas Aquinas as one of its professors. Along with the Dominican college, both the royal university and the Neapolitan offices of the Inquisition were also housed within the vast premises of San Domenico Maggiore. The congregation's sponsors included many of the most powerful families of the realm, including both sons of the local barons and members of the Spanish court, groups that were often at odds with one another. On shelves set high in the sacristy of San Domenico Maggiore the bodies of the Aragonese royal family that had ruled Naples from 1441 to 1503 lay (and still lie) in lead-lined sarcophagi. With connections like these, the friars were famous for their freedom from outside control, by the pope, the viceroy, the nobles, or their own order. They were a power unto themselves.

In this august place, in this august company, Filippo Bruno entered the Dominican order with the religious name Giordano (a tribute to his professor of metaphysics, Giordano Crispo) and was ordained as a priest in 1572; in the same year he gained admission, at last, to the Dominican college. He took his degree in theology three years later, in 1575. In 1576, during a visit to Rome, he learned that the Inquisition in Naples had found the copy of Erasmus he had stashed in the latrine; the Dutchman's works had been placed on the *Index of Prohibited Books* and could be read only with special permission. In his ten years at San Domenico, Bruno had already come to the Inquisition's attention twice before, and he decided to run away rather than face close examination back in Naples.

From 1576 to 1579, Bruno wandered from one town to another in northern Italy, teaching astronomy, working as a copy editor, living sometimes as Filippo, sometimes as Giordano, sometimes dressing as a layman, and sometimes as a Dominican, although the order had officially defrocked and excommunicated him in absentia shortly after his flight from Rome. Finally, in 1579, unable to find a steady job, he moved

to Calvinist Geneva. Before he could teach in the city, he was required
to convert to Calvinism (which he must have done) and take instruc-
tion in proper doctrine at the local university. Unfortunately, however,
Bruno, as an experienced teacher, had scant patience for student life or
for incompetent professors. When he published a little pamphlet noting
twenty errors his professor had made in a single lecture, the Genevan
authorities threw him into jail, and then tried him in a Calvinist court,
where he was convicted and excommunicated. Before he could serve
his sentence, Bruno moved on again, this time to the south of France.
At the University of Toulouse, he spent two happy years from 1580 to
1582 as a professor of philosophy, until local political strife between
Catholics and Protestant Huguenots threatened to break out into war
(ten years earlier Huguenots all over France had been slaughtered in
the St Bartholomew's Day Massacre). Bruno moved on to Paris, where
in 1582 he became a royal lecturer and confidante of King Henri III.
His excommunication as a Catholic prevented his being hired at the
Sorbonne, and this may be one of the reasons for Bruno's move to England in 1583. His original hope, clearly, had been to join the faculty at
Oxford, but he failed dramatically in that aim. His initial lectures at the
university quoted the Italian philosopher Marsilio Ficino so closely that
he was eventually accused of plagiarism, and his ideas about cosmology,
conveyed with voluble Neapolitan gestures in his Italian-accented Latin,
seemed crazier to his hearers than those of Copernicus. After deliver-
ing three lectures at Oxford, and hearing the charges of plagiarism, he
withdrew to the French embassy in London, where he earned his keep
by providing the ambassador with learned companionship. His remarkable literary output shows how fervently he hoped that he could convey
by pen what he had failed to convey in person; for someone who had
always been a successful teacher before, and in both Italy and France,
this failure to get through to English audiences must have been a ter-
rible blow.

### The *Eroici furori*

The sheer variety of Bruno's writings shows how difficult he found it
to express his ideas about the universe in a way that satisfied him completely. Leonardo and Galileo would both declare that the language of
nature was mathematics, but sixteenth-century mathematics could barely be distinguished from arithmetic and geometry. Bruno understood
enough about the universe, and about contemporary mathematics, to

realize that all the planetary systems propounded in his day, no matter whether they centred on earth or sun, were only models; the real movements of the heavens took place on a much larger scale where, in the ancient formula repeated by Augustine and the fifteenth-century German cardinal Nicholas of Cusa, "the centre was everywhere and the circumference nowhere."

Bruno tried to convey his philosophy through pictures, both geometrical diagrams and the mental images that he and his contemporaries used as aids to memory. For the diagrams, there were always insurmountable limitations imposed by the size of a printed page and his own lack of experience as an engraver – he seems to have made all his own illustrations for his books, and they are fascinating but by no means professional. As for memory images, he could only suggest possibilities and ways to combine them, but in the end mental images always stayed hidden away within the heads of his hearers and readers. As a philosophical writer, Bruno used every kind of language at his disposal, poetry and prose, Italian and Latin, high rhetoric, expository prose, ribald vulgarity.

He faced another set of problems because he believed that his findings about the universe should have consequences for human behaviour. He began to outline those consequences first in his comedy of 1582, *The Candlemaker* (*Candelaio*), and then in his Italian dialogues. Living out the Nolan philosophy meant accepting the world as it was, which in turn implied accepting a much larger definition of life in which the earth, stars, and planets were also living things, infused with divinity. At the same time, Bruno still believed that the universe demanded moral behaviour: no matter how huge and abstract its movements might seem, the world's pervasive goodness demanded a matching goodness from all its creatures. The cosmos was not simply a huge mechanical system, but a living being that he could only describe through a series of profoundly emotional metaphors: a mother, a nursemaid, a wellspring, light, love, a creation truly worthy of an omnipotent God.

The Inquisition would eventually condemn Bruno as a heretic in 1600, but he never saw his beliefs as heretical; the Nolan philosophy, he would tell his Venetian examiners in 1592, was actually a help to faith:[2]

> I hold that there is an infinite universe, that is, an effect of the infinite divine power ... so that I have declared that there are infinite particular worlds like this Earth of ours, which, like Pythagoras, I understand to be a heavenly body, like the Moon, the other planets, and the stars, which are infinite, and that all these bodies are worlds and without number, and they

constitute an infinite universality in an infinite space, and this is called the
infinite universe, in which there are innumerable worlds …

Furthermore, in this universe I put a universal providence, by virtue of
which every thing lives, moves, and has its being in its own perfection. And
I understand this in two ways: one, in the way that the soul is present in the
body, all in the whole, and all in every individual part, and this I call the
nature, shadow, and trace of divinity; the other, in the ineffable sense in
which God, by essence, presence, and power, is present in everything and
over everything, not as a part, not as a soul, but in a way that cannot be explained.

Then, within divinity I understand that all its qualities are really the same
thing, along with the theologians and the greatest philosophers: I accept
three qualities: power, wisdom, and goodness, or mind, intellect, and love,
with which all things first have their being by reason of the Mind, then their
orderly being distinguished by the intellect, and their concord and symmetry through love. This I understand to be in everything and over everything.

Bruno, therefore, did not describe any part of this Creation as radically
evil; he spent much more time denouncing irritants like asinine pedants and rude Englishmen than he ever did inveighing against Satan.
Although he had seen his share, and perhaps more than his share, of
poverty, disease, bad government, cruelty, prejudice, intrigue, and religious hatred, he ascribed most of these calamities to the changeability
inherent in the structure of the cosmos rather than to any immanent
principle of evil. Many of our problems, he maintained, were as self-
inflicted as the agonies of lovers. And thus, in order to account for his
philosophy, he turned, like Plato before him, to the ancient analogy
between human love and the love of wisdom, and created the longest
and most complex of his Italian dialogues. He dedicated it to Sir Philip
Sidney in 1585.

The dedication to Sidney takes a peculiar form; rather than a "Lettera
dedicatoria," a dedicatory letter like the ones Bruno attached to the be-
ginnings of his first three dialogues and addressed to his patron Castelnau, he calls this letter to Sidney an *Argomento* – an *Argument*. As Eugenio
Canone has pointed out,[3] Bruno normally uses this term to describe the
synopses he attaches to his works of poetry, and to his play, *The Candlemaker*, in order to ensure that readers will fully grasp the philosophical
points he intends to make. "Program" is a roughly equivalent term for
"Argomento" in general, but in the case of this large, complex work, the
*Argument* is distinctly and aggressively, argumentative.

Like Plato's dialogue on the subject of love, the *Symposium*, the *Heroic Frenzies* presents love from a series of viewpoints, ranging from the most physical to the most sublimely spiritual. Like Plato, Giordano Bruno believed that spiritual, philosophical love could be as disruptive of normal human existence as raving madness, and he called this love a *furore*. The Italian philosopher Marsilio Ficino (the same Ficino he was accused of plagiarizing in Oxford) had first used *furore* to translate *mania*, the term Plato in turn had used to describe the divine possession that affects madmen ("maniacs"), but also prophets, poets, healers, and lovers, especially lovers of wisdom – philosophers. Bruno carefully specified that the *furori* he would treat in his own dialogue were "heroic" cases of divine possession, preparing his readers for a dialogue that, like Plato's *Symposium*, aimed to bring them closer and closer to understanding the joys of a love that took wisdom as its object – an eternal principle rather than a single individual. Nothing in the restrained, elegant Plato can compare, however, with the bitter impetus Bruno puts into his *Argument*. As he tells Sidney:

> It is truly, O most generous Sir, the work of a low, filthy, animal nature to have made oneself the constant admirer, and to have fixed a solicitous attachment upon or around the beauty of a woman's body. Good God! What more vile and ignoble sight can present itself to a clear-sighted eye than a man, brooding, afflicted, tormented, sorry, melancholy; who waxes now cold, now hot, now boiling, now trembling, now pale, now blushing, now in a pose of perplexity, now in the act of decisiveness, a man who spends the best season and the choicest fruits of his life distilling the elixir of his brain toward putting into thought and writ and sealing in public monuments those endless tortures, those grave torments, those reasoned arguments, those laborious thoughts and those bitter desires addressed to the tyranny of an unworthy, imbecilic, foolish and sordid smut?

The violent denunciation of women that begins this letter is one of the most conspicuous and problematic aspects of the *Heroic Frenzies* (and may not have been the most effective way for Bruno to ingratiate himself with a potential patron). Bruno tries to make it clear in the course of his onslaught that his real objective is to exalt the love of wisdom, which is really the love of God. Surely, he urges, this is a more worthy subject for poetry than physical eros, especially when a higher philosophical purpose may add some fresh new metaphors to the hackneyed evocation of the beloved's "eyes ... cheeks ... bosom ... white ... crimson ... tongue

... tooth ... lip ... hair ... dress ... mantle ... glove ... slipper ... empty window." Bruno takes his own list from Petrarch's fourteenth-century *Canzoniere* (which drew itself from conventions of troubadour poetry); the images are as old as chivalry, and many go back as far as ancient Greece and Rome.

Events in Sir Philip Sidney's own life may have prompted Bruno to counsel the erudite lord away from sexual love and towards philosophy; Sidney had been betrothed for several years to Penelope Devereux, daughter of the Earl of Essex, but in 1581 the beautiful eighteen-year-old had been married instead, against her own objections, to Robert Rich, Earl of Warwick. In the following year, Sidney had begun to circulate, in manuscript, a sequence of sonnets and songs, *Astrophel and Stella*, that told the story of his love and its inevitable frustration (Astrophel means "Star-lover" in Greek, and Stella is "star" in Latin). By 1583, Sidney had married, and extremely well: his wife, Frances Walsingham, was the daughter of Sir Francis, Queen Elizabeth's head of secret services. *Astrophel and Stella*, however, continued to circulate among his friends for its purely poetic value.

Two years later, Bruno has taken it upon himself to tell Sidney, the author of a highly successful book of love poetry, that the love of God is the only love worth enshrining in verse. As a diplomatic letter, the dedication to the *Eroici furori* was anything but diplomatic, and its timing something less than timely.

As Bruno acknowledges, explicitly in the dialogue itself and implicitly in its *Argument*, some of his pronouncements about love and custom inevitably reflect the vast difference in mores between Naples and London. Naples, founded by Greeks and governed by Spaniards with a significant cultural legacy from the Arab world, maintained a tradition in which women were kept secluded, physically, socially, and intellectually. As a group, English aristocratic women were far better educated and far more emancipated than their Neapolitan counterparts, and within that group Queen Elizabeth, who adamantly refused to marry, and Penelope Devereux, who eventually left her dullard husband Sir Robert Rich to live openly with a lover, were more emancipated still. Bruno's letter to Sidney reflects his bemusement at such goings on, and such women: "for they are not females, they are not women; but rather (compared with the others) they are nymphs, they are goddesses, they are made of celestial substance."

Bruno may have grown up in the company of his mother and his female cousins in their hamlet outside Nola, but from the age of seventeen

onward he had spent most of his time in the society of men, in an order, the Dominicans, that took a more severe view of womanhood than many others. The Jesuits of Naples were openly courting the sponsorship of wealthy women, and promoting (as the Franciscans had for centuries) the doctrine of the Immaculate Conception, which held that Mary, like Jesus, had been born without sin. The Dominicans, heirs to Aristotle's view that women were defective versions of men, maintained (in what was increasingly a losing battle) that only Christ had been sinless. However enthusiastically Bruno rebelled against Aristotle, scholasticism, and the Dominicans, the *Eroici furori* shows how completely his experience as a friar and priest – and a Neapolitan – had shaped his thoughts, attitudes – even his philosophy, which retained a strong scholastic streak.

This last and most complex of Bruno's London dialogues may also be his most intimately biographical. From a whole series of indications, we are led to understand that Bruno himself has pursued the heroic quest for divine love whose progress he, too, has "inscribed on paper, enclosed in books, set before the eyes and intoned in the ears, a noise, a commotion, a clash of devices, of emblems, of mottoes, of epistles, of sonnets, of epigrams, of books." He is not describing a progress that he can easily envision being made by women readers, in part because he is so involved in his own quest that he cannot really imagine how to adjust his ideas to any other viewpoint, in part because by the time his discussion passes beyond the body to treat the infinite universe, the distinction between man and woman no longer matters.

In fact, however, Bruno's view of women may not have been as entirely negative as it sounds in his *Argument*. His play *The Candlemaker, Candelaio*, published three years earlier than the *Heroic Frenzies* in Paris, but set in Naples, portrays its female characters with great sympathy, showing the real effects of a strict, often hypocritical Neapolitan society on their lives. And he clearly appreciates the effect of education and emancipation on those nymph-like Englishwomen, not just their fair skins.

Furthermore, on occasion Bruno, like Plato before him and Tommaso Campanella afterward (another product of that remarkable convent, San Domenico Maggiore, and briefly Bruno's fellow inmate in the prison of the Holy Office in Rome), makes a concerted effort to show that the universe is not simply and exclusively male. One of his tools in this effort is language itself. In Latin, nouns could be male, female, or neuter; in Italian vernacular, every noun that Bruno used was either male or female. His world, therefore, was divided into genders to a degree that his English contemporaries and his English-speaking readers in any period

may never entirely grasp. In the *Eroici furori*, with its incessant emphasis on opposites, the polarity between male and female words and ideas added yet another level of expressive power to his writing. The universe, *universo*, was male by definition; the world-soul, *anima*, feminine; hence his choice in the course of the dialogue to call infinity by the name of Amphitrite, the wife of Neptune, is a deliberate action to ensure that the highest principle of his philosophy, the realm that he ascribes to God, will be seen as essentially female.

To a Sir Philip Sidney newly (and by all accounts happily) married, the *Heroic Frenzies* argues that the love of God is the only love worth pursuing to the point of extreme self-denial and the only love worth writing about; sexual love can be fulfilled physically; hence, it is much more efficient simply to deal with it on this level. (Bruno may have taken a vow of celibacy as a young friar, but he seems not to have kept it. He would tell the Inquisition that he found it strange that so pleasantly natural an activity could be considered a sin.) As a literary production, the *Heroic Frenzies* is much more than a philosophical dialogue; it is also a veritable anthology of love poetry: a massive collection of sonnets, emblems, versicles, and songs, some of them borrowed from other writers, most of them Bruno's own. Their widely differing tones and qualities suggest that he must have been writing poetry most of his life (and that some of it may indeed have been inspired, for all that, by the passions of the unworthy flesh).

Any writer of Italian vernacular sonnets looked back to one supreme master, the fourteenth-century writer Francesco Petrarca, known to his English admirers, like Sidney, as Petrarch. Bruno's admiration for Petrarch's verse, and his liberal borrowings from it, did not prevent his harsh disapproval of the fact that these poems were inspired by their author's obsessive, unrequited love for the woman he called Laura. As Bruno declared to Sidney, such self-denying "courtly" love was an absurd waste of time:

> I mean for the world to be certain of one thing, namely that the purpose for which I agitate myself in this prefatory outline, where I speak individually to you, excellent Lord, and in the Dialogues created around the following articles, sonnets, and verses, is that I want everyone to know that I would hold myself as most unworthy and beastly if with great expenditure of thought, desire and labour I would ever have been satisfied with imitating (as they say) Orpheus in the worship of a living woman, and after death, if it were possible, retrieving her from Hell ...

Bruno's own poetry is shot through with echoes of Petrarch, along with a host of other poets, in Latin and vernacular, ranging from the exalted ranks of Vergil and Dante to popular songs. It is complex, learned, and technically sophisticated. Like the rest of his writing, it is best at its extremes: when it praises the sublime beauties of Creation or when it zeroes in to insult an adversary.

The whole dialogue, although it is also a treatise on cosmology and ethics, is one long, intense discussion about poetry. Bruno begins by setting the action in his native Nola, with two friends of his father's, the poet Luigi Tansillo and the officer Odoardo Cicala, discussing a series of sonnets, four of them Tansillo's own. Their conversations, five in all, take up the first half of the *Eroici furori*. With great immediacy, they bring in a third participant, because all the while the reader is handling and pondering the same texts as Tansillo and Cicada.

Plato's dialogues used real people, including his teacher, Socrates, and his brothers, Glaucon and Adeimantus (while Plato, interestingly, kept himself carefully out of the picture). The conversations these real people recount, however, are always remembered conversations, remote, not immediate, and possibly distorted by faulty recall. Plato reminds his readers at every turn that true reality is not of this world around us; it lies somewhere else. Bruno, however, is trying to convey the opposite conviction: that true reality really is all around us, and God, in all his immortality, is inside us as well as above us. Tansillo and Cicada and their counterparts, then, are not talking some time long ago (even if they are far away from Bruno's London): they are talking now, and, to the extent that Bruno's writing can make it possible, talking with us.

Tansillo, a soldier-poet and friend of the Spanish soldier-poet Garcilaso de la Vega, is the most clearly developed character among the conversationalists in the *Heroic Frenzies*. He must have exerted great influence on the young Bruno, at the very least in his capacity as a poet, for echoes of his work show up throughout *Eroici furori* in addition to the four poems that Bruno quotes outright. There is nothing in Tansillo's flowing, polished occasional verse to indicate that his love sonnets are any different from Petrarch's; like Petrarch's *Songbook*, they seem to tell a biographical tale, in his own case about his love for Laura Monforte, his travels abroad, his final break with her, and his eventual marriage to Luisa Puccio. But Bruno presents Tansillo without hesitation as a writer of allegory, whose love poetry is really, like Bruno's, poetry about the love of wisdom. And certainly, Tansillo is present when Giovanni Bruno,

"father of the Nolan," begins to discuss his own philosophy of life in the anecdote he relates to Cicada (see part 1, dialogue 2).

The four sonnets that Bruno chooses from Tansillo certainly fit well with an allegorical interpretation. In them, God is light and warmth, inflaming the soul with desire for wisdom; vice, stupidity, laziness and ignorance are dark, heavy, and cold.

Thus, as Bruno alerts his readers, the love poems of *the Heroic Frenzies* –including Tansillo's – only appear to form a collection of conventional love poetry. In fact, as he notes to Sidney in his *Argument*, he has arranged them so that they will convey the same divine message as the erotic poetry of the biblical *Song of Songs*, however great their differences of form or content:

> Finally, I mean to say that these heroic frenzies achieve a heroic subject and object, and for that reason they can no more be reduced to consideration as common and natural loves than dolphins can be seen in the trees of the forest, or wild boars beneath the sea cliffs. Therefore, in order to liberate them all from such a suspicion I first thought of giving this book a title similar to that of Solomon, who under the cover of ordinary love and emotion contains similar divine and heroic passions, as the mystical and cabalistic doctors interpret them. I wanted, that is to say, to call it *Canticles*.

The *Song of Songs*, like Dante's *Vita nuova* and Petrarch's *Songbook*, presents a series of love poems in a sequence that seems to tell a story. The Bible, however, does not go in for unrequited love: the *Song of Songs* tells of lovers who keep one another waiting expectantly, meet, make love, separate, suffer, and describe each other in an extravagant series of metaphors; the biblical poetry is exquisitely sensuous.

> Behold, thou art fair, my love; behold, thou art fair; thou hast doves' eyes within thy locks: thy hair is as a flock of goats, that appear from mount Gilead.
> Thy teeth are like a flock of sheep that are even shorn, which came up from the washing; whereof every one bear twins, and none is barren among them.
> Thy lips are like a thread of scarlet, and thy speech is comely: thy temples are like a piece of a pomegranate within thy locks.
> Thy neck is like the tower of David builded for an armoury, whereon there hang a thousand bucklers, all shields of mighty men.

Until the day break, and the shadows flee away, I will get me to the mountain
   of myrrh, and to the hill of frankincense.
Thy lips, O my spouse, drop as the honeycomb: honey and milk are under
   thy tongue; and the smell of thy garments is like the smell of Lebanon.
Thou hast ravished my heart, my sister, my spouse; thou hast ravished my
   heart.

In the same Italian vernacular verse form as Petrarch's *Songbook* and
Tansillo's *Songbook* (not to mention, in English, Sidney's *Astrophel and
Stella*), *the Heroic Frenzies* therefore expounds, in the language appropriate to Bruno's own place and time, the same truths that Solomon expounded in his *Song*, and Plato in dialogues like *Symposium* and *Phaedrus*.
Bruno's sequence of dialogues and poems, like those he has taken as
his models, lays out the path from bewilderment to understanding, of
alienation from divinity to all-enveloping oneness with divinity. As with
most of Bruno's works, the course he sets centres on himself. *The Heroic
Frenzies* is a biography, less of events than of stages in Bruno's own understanding of the world. With great affection, he recalls them one by one,
and then, still affectionately, he leaves them behind for the supreme
beauty of his new vision.
   That vision requires a whole new genre of literature, but also of poetry; the *Heroic Frenzies* combines poetry and prose, like Boëthius's *Consolation of Philosophy*, Dante's *Vita nuova*, but also more recent allegories
like Jacopo Sannazaro's Neoplatonic pastoral romance *Arcadia* (1504),
which is set, like Bruno's dialogue, in the region around Naples. Tansillo
and Cicada are both convinced that the number of potential poetic genres is as great as the number of poets, and that rules about genres must
bend to the force of inspiration. If the *Eroici furori* is like a Petrarchan
*Songbook* set within a Platonic dialogue, so be it. Tansillo and Cicada are
willing to accept new forms of self-expression:

CICADA There are some poetic rule-makers who barely accept Homer as a
   poet, and relegate Virgil, Ovid, Martial, Hesiod, Lucretius, and many others to the rank of mere versifiers, grading them by the rules of Aristotle's
   *Poetics.*
TANSILLO Know for certain, my brother, that these people are real beasts, for
   they forget that such rules principally serve to illustrate facets of Homeric
   poetry or its genre, and sometimes to use a heroic poet like Homer as an
   example, but they do not instruct other authors whose different wits, arts,

and inspirations could make them equal, similar, or superior in different genres.

In the *Heroic Frenzies*, therefore, more than anywhere else in his extensive legacy, Giordano Bruno reveals himself as a writer, as ardently committed to the peculiar demands and disciplines of writing as he was to the demands and disciplines of philosophy. As he tells Sidney, Solomon wrote the *Song of Songs* to express many of the same ideas that drive him to passionate inspiration, but their own times require a different kind of expression: "Because just as the passions of that wise Jew have their own style, order, and title, which no one could understand or better explain than he himself, were he present, so too these *Canticles* have their own proper title, order and style." Nonetheless, the "order and style" that Bruno has imposed on his *Heroic Frenzies* assigns the figure of Luigi Tansillo, graceful poet of love, only to the first half of the work. He is thus a dominant, but not definitive figure, a figure who marks the initial stages in the heroic lover's passage from passionate raving to calm enlightenment. Part 1 of the *Heroic Frenzies* concentrates on the lover's interior development, whereas part 2 will thrust him into the surrounding world. In a general sense, then, Tansillo, like Plato's Socrates, serves as the teacher who begins to nurture a philosophical spirit, but must inevitably then send that spirit on its way, the "lonely sparrow" of the poem Tansillo and Cicada examine in part 1, dialogue 3:

> Go forth, then: I hope you find
> A nobler fate, and have a god to guide you:
> The one the sightless dare to say is blind.
>
> Go; and find beside you
> Each deity of this masterful design;
> And don't return to me unless you're mine.

However emphatically Tansillo and Cicada may rail against poetic rules, Giordano Bruno wants his readers to know that his rebellion is not a matter of his own technical incompetence: he will show his readers that he has mastered the intricacies of the Petrarchan sonnet, and therefore qualifies as a true poet both by his own terms – as an inspired writer – and by the reductive terms of his pedantic contemporaries. His sonnets seek out unusual rhymes and experiment with some of the form's most demanding strictures. However little he thought of contemporary

rhetorical manuals, he knew what they were about. He experiments with repetition, with the "dramatic" sonnet (a sonnet in dialogue), with strange rhymes. His poetry echoes his wide reading and his capacious memory, with clear traces of classic authors like Horace, Vergil, Lucan, Seneca, Dante, and Petrarch, as well as recent authors like Tasso, Boiardo, Ariosto, Folengo, Tansillo, and the fifteenth-century songwriter Serafino Aquilano. He professed not to know English in *The Ash Wednesday Supper*, but that work was written earlier in his English stay. Could he read Sir Philip Sidney's sonnets, and is that one reason for his choosing Sidney as the addressee of his *Argument*?

The second half of the *Heroic Frenzies* abandons the sequential structure of part 1. If the poems of part 1 form an extended sequence of sonnets, a *Canzoniere*, part 2 is eclectic, and its cast of characters changes along with the types of poetry it contains. Most of the participants in these later dialogues can still be traced to Nola. Most, like Tansillo and Cicada, are also gentleman soldiers and presumably Giovanni Bruno's former comrades-in-arms. But not all; two are unknown, and the final two are women.

The first pair, however, Cesarino and Maricondo (who becomes Mariconda in part 2, dialogue 2), are literary-minded military men just like Tansillo and Cicada. In the first dialogue of the second part of the *Heroic Frenzies*, they also take up an activity that has already occupied Tansillo and Cicada: describing and explaining a series of *imprese*, the riddling pictures with explanatory mottoes that were such a popular amusement in sixteenth-century Italy. Many people adopted an *impresa*, or a whole set of *imprese*, as a personal sign: Lorenzo de' Medici, an early admirer of the game, chose a diamond ring with the motto SEMPER – "always," an image of the loyalty he wanted to project. Unlike emblems, which are meant to be clear rather than riddling, a well-conceived *impresa* only made complete sense when its image and its motto were examined together, and even then its meaning was meant to be obscure to all but an inner circle of friends. Bruno also gives each of his *imprese* a sonnet as well, so that short text, poetic text, and image form a three-way system of allusions. By extending the series of *imprese* from the last dialogue of the first part of the *Heroic Frenzies* into the first dialogue of the second part, Bruno exemplifies another recurrent motif in this work: the ending that becomes a beginning, a literal embodiment of the Gospel's assertion that "the last shall be first."

Bruno's *imprese* also recall, deliberately, the images he uses in his art of memory, and in the biography of the heroic philosophical lover they

represent the stage of mental discipline where he is learning to govern, and then to deploy, his thoughts. There are thirty-two in all, each with a picture, a motto, a sonnet, and an explanation in prose. Even then, frequently, the participants in the dialogue insist that the true meaning behind all these different forms of communication must be pondered privately, in each reader's innermost mind and heart.

In the second dialogue of the second part, Cesarino and Mariconda take up a different sequence of sonnets: a series of set pieces addressed by the eyes to the heart and vice versa. Some critics believe that this dialogue may have been an early exercise that Bruno incorporated entire into his larger, later work. The poems themselves exploit a highly restricted repertory of images as a way of intensifying the depth of their significance – spinning an infinity of meanings off four images: heart, eyes, fire, water. Here, especially, Bruno deliberately transforms a series of Petrarchan conceits into a philosophical discussion, not only of philosophical love, but also, importantly, about the way in which every phenomenon in the material world eventually turns into its opposite: water becomes fire, fire becomes water, asses become kings, kings become asses.

The last three dialogues in part 2 of the *Eroici furori* abandon Petrarch for another model, an allegorical poem, really a drama in verse, by the Neapolitan Marcantonio Epicuro, called *Cecaria*, "Blindness." It was published in Naples in 1543, but also circulated in manuscript, and one of the manuscripts in which it appears includes the poem among a collection of Neoplatonic texts, both prose and poetry. *Cecaria*, like so many sixteenth-century works, is an allegory: Epicuro uses the blindness of a frustrated lover, and his eventual cure, to stand in for the blindness of a benighted soul that finds illumination; the poem, like the *Heroic Frenzies*, is an allegory of divine love. Bruno multiplies the number of blind men to nine; not simply lost souls, they may also be wandering planets in a universe whose infinity they only gradually come to understand.

If Tansillo, Cicada, Cesarino, and Maricondo/a can be identified with local Nolan gentlemen, the figures of Liberio and Laodonio, who introduce us to the blind men, are completely elusive. Their story continues in the fourth dialogue with Severino and Minutolo, two more Nolan gentlemen-at-arms, Giambattista Severino and Giovanni Geronimo Minutolo. The fifth and final section of the dialogue is turned over to two young women of Nola, Laodomia and Giulia – probably Bruno's cousins Laodomia and Giulia Savolino, who lead the blind men to their final release from blindness – when they finally grasp the essentials of the Nolan

philosophy, and recognize that the universe is endless, but that within that endless expanse, God, and God's love, are with us and within us, inseparably and forever.

Aside from its debt to Nola, the *Heroic Frenzies* owes a fundamental debt to Plato and to Neoplatonic philosophy, despite the fact that Bruno's reality is here and now, whereas Plato sets reality in a remote place far beyond. Plato's writings, in their versions by Marsilio Ficino, were fundamental to Bruno's development as a philosopher, as the Oxford dons had been quick to notice. From Plato (or perhaps from Ficino's version of Plato), Bruno has adopted the dialogue as a means of communication, along with the understanding that none of a dialogue's viewpoints are necessarily expressions of ultimate truth, but only attempts to draw closer to truth. From the Neoplatonists, especially a group of Augustinian friars active in Naples in the sixteenth century, Bruno has also taken an extensive metaphor, the image of the material world as a forest. The word that Plato used to describe the stuff of nature, *hyle*, was the word that meant "wood"; Latin *materia* would also come to mean either "wood" or "matter." But one translator of Plato's Greek into Latin, a fourth-century contemporary of St Augustine named Calcidius, employed his own term for *hyle*: *silva*, "woods" or "forest" rather than "wood." And as it happened, Calcidius's peculiar translation of one Platonic dialogue, *Timaeus*, was the single work of Plato to be read continuously throughout the Middle Ages into the fifteenth century.

In the early sixteenth century, an influential Augustinian prelate named Giles of Viterbo (Egidio da Viterbo in Italian) took up the image of a Forest of Matter with vivid intensity in a manuscript that was widely read but never printed. This influential volume made an attempt to reconcile Christian theology with Platonic philosophy, but Giles did so in a curious way. He began with the standard theological textbook of the day, preserving its chapter headings, but entirely rewriting the contents. The textbook itself had been written in the twelfth century by the Dominican Peter Lombard, who called his work *Sentences;* like the catechism, it made its points by a process of endless questions and answers: How are the persons of the Holy Trinity related to one another? What happens when a mouse eats the Host? (For that question, at least, the answer was lapidary: *Deus scit* – "God knows.") This intricate and supremely boring apparatus of argument is what Giles of Viterbo rewrote, using word-pictures, myths, and metaphors drawn from Plato's dialogues, the poetry of Homer and Vergil, and classical mythology. He called the result "The *Sentences* according to the mind of Plato," *Sententiae ad mentem Platonis,* and it is the

one book in which the Forest of Matter figures as prominently as its does in the *Heroic Frenzies.*

Bruno could have read Giles of Viterbo most easily in the Neapolitan convent of San Giovanni a Carbonara, where Giles had stayed on several occasions, and where his protégé, the Neapolitan nobleman Girolamo Seripando, had entered the order. Like Giles himself, Seripando went on to become prior general of the Augustinian order, cardinal, and cardinal protector of the Augustinians. But Seripando and his brother Antonio had also endowed a private library within the convent of San Giovanni, filled with books and manuscripts with a Neoplatonic slant (including the copy of Marcantonio Epicuro's *Blindness* mentioned above), and here, with one of Seripando's students, Fra Teofilo da Vairano, the young Filippo Bruno, not yet a Dominican, came to study logic between 1563 and 1565.

The Forest of Matter is a crucial image for the *Heroic Frenzies.* In the first place, the forest was as immediate an image as any for the world's stubborn impenetrability. It could only be seen clearly from the outside, above the treetops, and Giles used this overview to evoke the way the material world must look from the vantage of Plato's higher world of Ideas. On several occasions Plato himself compared the human search for knowledge to hunting game; by the same figure of speech we still "track down," "approach," and "investigate" what we do not know. Marsilio Ficino, Plato's great explicator in the fifteenth century, took the image of the spiritual hunt a step further, to signify the explicit pursuit of God, an archetypal creator of such brilliance that He was to the sun what the sun is to us: "That hunter is excessively fortunate who has applied himself to pursuing, with all his powers, step by step, the Sun of the sun. He shall have found what he sought, inflamed by its heat, even before he seeks it."[4]

In Giles of Viterbo's hands, the Forest of Matter transformed Platonic philosophy into concrete images by taking words like *silva* and tracking literally: matter, *silva*, became the Forest, in which confused humanity hunted down knowledge of God. He cast the goddess Diana, the huntress, as a model for the searching human soul – a feminine noun in Hebrew, Greek, and Latin (*ruah, psyche, anima*). In the Forest, his Diana sought out tracks or traces, literally footprints, *vestigia*, of God's divine light.

Literary forests were never deserted places in the sixteenth century (in fact, the forest in Ludovico Ariosto's *Orlando furioso* sometimes seems as crowded as an urban piazza.) Giles focused his own attention on the

figure of Actaeon, the hunter of Greek and Roman myth who saw the goddess Diana bathing. The outraged goddess transformed him into a stag, and the poor hero was torn to death almost immediately by his own hounds. Giles wrote of Actaeon not only in his *Sentences*, but also in a vernacular poem, the "Beautiful Hunt of Love," in which he contrasted the living death that earthly love brings on its victims:

> Now some would claim that mine's a lesser grief
> Than Actaeon's, who turned into a stag;
> Yet unlike my misfortune, his was brief
> Despite the fact that he was torn to rags.
> By suffering at last he gained relief;
> Long as I live, my pain will never flag.
> To my annoyance, Death's rejected me,
> And thus in living I die constantly.

In the *Heroic Frenzies*, Bruno used the same image to present an Actaeon who "dies" to earthly goals, and is transported by his sublime vision to seeing both Diana, and his quest, in an entirely new light:

> He saw her; and the hunter turned to prey.
> The stag who sought to bend
> His lightened step toward denser forest depths
> His dogs devoured; they caught him in their trap.
> The thoughts that I extend
> Toward lofty prey recoil and deal me death,
> Rending me in their fell and savage snap.

Unlike the fervently Christian Giles of Viterbo, however, Bruno ultimately urges his readers not to find divinity in a transcendent realm of Ideas, but in the world around them. God, for the Nolan philosopher, is not above the universe, but intimately within it, the matrix that holds all the incessantly active atoms that combine and recombine to create different forms of matter. As Miguel Angel Granada (the erudite commentator on the most recent scholarly edition of the *Eroici furori*) observes, the Diana that Actaeon sees is Nature itself: the stars and planets of the infinite universe.[5] But there is a still more fundamental image of God: for Diana, the Moon, creates no light of her own but only reflects with light of the Sun. The moving force of the universe is its ultimate source of light, the Sun of the Sun, the soul of souls. But Bruno also uses

another image for the principle of divinity that underlies all things, and this image is female: the sea goddess Amphitrite. In God, indeed, he will contend, all extremes become one: there is no male or female, no fire or water, no light or darkness.

Despite profound differences of structure and content, therefore, the *Heroic Frenzies* are to Bruno's Nolan philosophy what the *Symposium* was to the philosophy of Plato, an initiation through the imagery of love, presented first by a father figure (Socrates and Tansillo), and at last, surprisingly, by women. Plato chooses the prophetess Diotima to instruct Socrates in the ultimate mysteries of philosophical love. Bruno entrusts the final section of the *Heroic Frenzies* to his two cousins, Laodomia and Giulia Savolino. When he explains his reasons for doing so to Philip Sidney, he also says a good deal about his own reading of Plato's *Symposium*. Diotima's position of authority within that dialogue was deliberately designed to unsettle Plato's male Athenian readers, who kept their wives carefully secluded at home. Bruno seems to understand Plato's tactic when he adopts it as his own, mindful not of the comparatively emancipated women of England, but of the very different conditions in Spanish-dominated (and Greek-founded) Naples:

> Two women are introduced, for whom (according to the custom of my country) it is inappropriate to comment, argue, decipher, know much and act as professors, as if to usurp a man's prerogative to teach, establish guidelines, rules and teaching; but they may, on the other hand, divine and prophesy whenever the spirit moves their bodies. Let it suffice, therefore, to make them only the players of the allegory, leaving the ideas and the business of declaring the meaning to some masculine wit.

Plato, more enigmatically, has his prophetess Diotima express doubts that Socrates shall be able to understand her completely (many readers believe that this is where Plato draws the line between his teacher's insight and his own):

> These are the lesser mysteries of love, into which even you, Socrates, may enter; to the greater and more hidden ones which are the crown of these, and to which, if you pursue them in a right spirit, they will lead, I know not whether you will be able to attain. But I will do my utmost to inform you, and do you follow if you can.[6]

And yet the final revelation of the *Heroic Frenzies* will also revolve around

a woman who is as capable and enlightened as Diotima, who, unfettered by the custom of her country, may indeed "comment, argue, decipher, know much and act as professors, as if to usurp a man's prerogative to teach, establish guidelines, rules and teaching." The dialogue's final section focuses on nine young men, all of them blinded by love, who have stumbled along together from Naples to arrive at the banks of the Thames, carrying a jar of water given to them by the goddess Circe. If they can open it, the enchantress has told them, they will be cured of their blindness. Laodomia and Giulia, standing at the riverside, help them to open the jar, and at that moment, the nine blind men see "twin lights" – the eyes of the resident nymph of the Thames, and are cured at last, en masse, of their inability to see.

The blind men, as noted above, are a direct borrowing from the Neapolitan poet Marcantonio Epicuro's poem *Cecaria, Blindness*, published in 1543, but also available in Girolamo Seripando's library in manuscript, bound together with Giles of Viterbo's "Love's Beautiful Hunt." Although the swains are nine (and Miguel Angel Granada plausibly suggests that they may well be planetary images as well as types of humanity), they parallel, in their travels and their experience, the single man who once left Circe's lair as a blind lover, only to find full enlightenment in England: Bruno himself. The nymph whose eyes grant the power of sight is naturally Elizabeth, a fine courtly tribute to the queen, but the symbolism does not end there. The fact that there are two eyes, two "lights," two "windows," suggests that there is always more than one path to the final vision: Bruno describes these two guiding beacons elsewhere in the dialogue as "the lights of the twin splendour of divine goodness and beauty." If two can become one, so can infinity.

Like Plato's *Symposium*, the *Heroic Frenzies* are more than a literary tour de force: they are a call to action, an encouragement for Philip Sidney to turn his own poetic talents away from glorifying an individual woman, Penelope Rich née Devereux, to glorifying God, creating not another version of Petrarch's *Songbook*, but rather the sacred love poetry of Solomon's *Song of Songs*, just as Bruno himself has done at impressive length.

Although the *Heroic Frenzies* emphasizes the Nolan's connections to ancient philosophy, the dialogue also points out the novelty of his own convictions. Like hieroglyphs in Egypt, like the *Song of Songs* in Israel, like Plato's *Symposium* in Greece, the dialogue has been written in a combination of imagery and contemporary language, so that the Nolan can share his experience as a philosopher-lover with those, like Sidney, who can understand it without revealing it wholesale to everyone. The Nolan

philosophy requires proclamation to the wise as well as hiding from the ignorant, so that eventually it can redeem the world. Theirs is a time in which the very shape of the heavens has changed: not simply purified, as in Bruno's recent dialogue, *Expulsion of the Triumphant Beast*, but revealed in its full majesty. The Nolan and humanity are on the threshold of something new:

> But here contemplate the harmony and consonance of all the spheres, intelligences, muses, and instruments together, where heaven, the movement of the worlds, the works of nature, the discourses of intellect, the mind's contemplation, the decrees of divine providence, all celebrate with one accord the lofty and magnificent oscillation that equals the lower waters with the higher, exchanges night for day, and day with night, so that divinity is in all things, so that everything is capable of everything, and the infinite goodness communicates itself without end according to the full capacity of all things.

For Bruno himself, this enlightenment came through physical displacement as well as expenditure of time, study, and passionate devotion. The journey that began in Nola in the house of Giovanni Bruno ends on the banks of the Thames, as it does for the blind men, who sing a song to honour their sudden ability to see, not in the old way, but with the eyes of philosophical enlightenment.

The dialogue's closing vision shows Elizabeth as ruler of the heavens and the oceans alike, a goddess on a par with Jove and Neptune, because, as we already know from *The Expulsion of the Triumphant Beast*, she is wiser by far than either of these two ancient gods, and in her the two extremes of sky and sea become one:

> Jove answered: "God who rules the bounding sea,
> My happiness can never be exceeded,
> For so Fate has decreed it,
> But we may share our riches equally.
>
> Among your nymphs the Sun shall take the station
> She held, and by the laws that regulate
> Our kingdoms alternate
> She'll shed her glow among my constellations."

From the invectives against women in his opening letter, Bruno has

moved by the end of his dialogue to a vision in which a woman wields power equal to that of any man; like Plato and St Paul, he occasionally stated, and must have believed on some level, that male and female made no real difference to the potential of an individual soul:

> If my intention is given due consideration, no chaste and honest woman should prefer to take offence at my natural and truthful discourse, and become angry with me rather than endorsing and loving me in return, passively reproving in women's love for men what I actively reprove in men's love for women. With such spirit, talent, opinion, and determination, therefore, I swear that in this composition my intention – first and foremost, central and accessory, ultimate and final – was and is to induce the contemplation of divinity, and to put before the eyes and ears of others not vulgar frenzies, but heroic love,

We should take Giordano Bruno at his word.

## *About the Translation*

The chief challenge that the *Eroici furori* poses for a translator is its mixture of prose and poetry. The poetry, especially, is of widely varying quality, some of it (including Luigi Tansillo's) highly polished, and some much rougher in style and sense. This fact made it easier to contemplate setting the verse in verse; the results did not have to rival Shakespeare. To the greatest extent possible, meter and rhyme mimic that of the original poems. I have not, however, tried to mimic Elizabethan English. On occasion I have slightly adjusted Bruno's long, complicated Renaissance sentences and streamlined his periphrastic circumlocutions.

Wherever possible, I have quoted biblical passages from the King James Version, as this is the English translation of the Bible made closest to Bruno's own time, and nearest the place where Bruno was living in 1585. For biblical books rejected by the Anglican canon (Ecclesiasticus, Wisdom of Solomon), I have used the Douai-Rheims Version.

### Dramatis personae

The participants in the dialogues of the *Eroici furori* are, with one exception (Cicada), all probably to be imagined as citizens of Nola. Bruno's biographer Vincenzo Spampanato made an exhaustive search of census documents from Nola in the sixteenth century and was able to find infor-

mation about most of the possible real-life models for Bruno's interlocutors.[7] Most of them come from the same generation as Bruno's father,
who was still alive at the time that the *Eroici furori* was written. Like Plato,
Bruno chooses characters who will project the conversations back into
an ambiguous time that is neither the present nor a specific moment
in the past, just as the physical setting must be Nola, but an imaginary
remembered Nola rather than the real place. Plato's displacement of
conversations in space and time was meant to underline the feeble, sub-
jective nature of all human understanding, and Bruno seems to be using
Plato's technique to the same ends. At the same time, he may be hoping
that someone in Naples might read his work; in all his years of exile, he
never entirely gave up the hope of returning to Italy, and ultimately did
return, to his tragic misfortune.

### *1.1–1.5 Tansillo, Cicada*

The focus of attention for the first five dialogues is the poet Luigi Tansillo (1510–68), who spent much of his career in Naples, the crowded,
dangerous city that made the poet long for tranquil Nola. To judge from
the report that Bruno's Tansillo makes of a conversation in dialogue
1.4, the real Tansillo must have known Bruno's father, Giovanni Bruno,
who served the Spanish viceroy of Naples as a soldier in the same company as Luigi's cousin Cola (Nicola) Tansillo. (Another member of the
company was Cola Antonio Santoro, whose brother Giulio, as cardinal
inquisitor, would one day supervise Bruno's trial for heresy and execution in Rome.) Luigi Tansillo also did military service as a courtier of
Don Garzia de Toledo, son of the Spanish viceroy, Don Pedro de Toledo. He composed his first major work, a ribald poem "The Vintner"
("Il Vendemmiatore"), in 1532. Thereafter he dedicated himself to the
kinds of poetry appropriate to a sixteenth-century courtier, including
occasional pieces and love poetry in the tradition of Petrarch. These col-
lected poems were eventually gathered, like Petrarch's, into a *Canzoniere*
(*Songbook*), arranged in a vaguely biographical order, ostensibly to tell
the story of Tansillo's love for Laura Monforte, his travels abroad, his
break with her, and his eventual marriage to Luisa Puccio. Bruno, however, presents Tansillo's love poetry here in the *Eroici furori* as motivated
by a higher philosophical purpose. The poet's philosophical quest dominates the first five dialogues, where Tansillo remains the dominant interlocutor. Once the heroic philosopher has transformed his interior life
and is ready, with his new insights, to interact with the external world,

Bruno shifts the conversation from Tansillo and Cicada to new pairs of interlocutors. Tansillo was also an elegant, restrained stylist, and it seems clear from the *Heroic Frenzies* that Bruno greatly admired the poet's mastery of language.

Cicada is probably modelled on the Odoardo Cicala who appears in Bruno's earlier dialogue *On the Cause, Principle, and One*, a naval officer and scholar based in Naples, probably a friend of Tansillo's in real life. (Bruno and his contemporaries used the forms "cicada" and "cicala" indiscriminately, with examples in the *Eroici furori*.) Although Cicala was not Nolan by birth, his surname has the same root as Monte Cicala, the hill outside Nola where Giordano Bruno's immediate family lived.

### 2.1 Cesarino, Maricondo

Cesarino and Maricondo also seem to have been drawn from Bruno's childhood memories of Nola. Giandomenico Cesarino retired from military service in 1563, and presumably knew Giovanni Bruno from their years of service. Angelo and Francesco Maricondo were two of Nola's more prominent citizens; it is not clear which of the two Bruno has chosen as his interlocutor, but they belonged, like Tansillo and Cicada, to the generation of Bruno's father.

### 2.2 Mariconda, Cesarino

The switch between Maricondo and Mariconda, like that between Cicala and Cicada, is typical of sixteenth-century usage. These are presumably still the same people as the interlocutors of the previous dialogue.

### 2.3 Liberio, Laodonio

These two characters are not as easily associated with real Nolans as those in the other dialogues; the local census documents from Nola show no one with these classical names. However, Liberi or Liveri was the name of a village near Nola; hence "Liberio" may evoke the same suggestions of place as "Cicada." At the same time, it also suggests Liber, one of the names of Bacchus, and one clearly evocative of the freedom from inhibition that wine brings on (and may also be connected to Luigi Tansillo's earliest poem, "Il Vendemmiatore," "The Vintner"). Laudonio, in turn, is the masculine form of Laudomia, the name of one of Bruno's cousins, Laudomia Savolino, who is commemorated in dialogue 2.5. Derived from

Greek (it means "tamer of the people"), it is one of the classical names that were especially popular among sixteenth-century Italians despite continued laments against "pagan" names on the part of the Church.

## 2.4 Severino, Minutolo

These characters are once again probably based on residents of Nola who were contemporaries of Bruno's father. The Severino family were wealthy and well-educated landed gentry in the area of Nola; this Severino might be Francesco or Orazio. Gian Geronimo Minutolo was a nobleman of Nola who owned property on Monte Cicala that bounded on the property of Bruno's maternal relatives, the Savolino.

## 2.5 Giulia, Laodomia, the Nine Blind Men

Bruno's biographer Vincenzo Spampanato notes that Giordano Bruno had two cousins named Giulia and Laodomia Savolino, born in 1544 and 1550 (Bruno himself was born in 1548).[8] These participants in his dialogue have been given the same treatment that Bruno reserved for Englishwomen: "They are not women; they are nymphs, they are goddesses, they are made of divine substance." Like Plato in the *Symposium*, Bruno uses women to express the highest truths of his philosophy.

The Nine Blind Men are inspired by the blind man who appears in Marcantonio Epicuro's philosophical poem *Cecaria* ("Blindness"). This philosophical poem was published in 1543, but it was also available in manuscript in a library where Bruno may have gone to study in his earliest years as a student in Naples: a special collection that had once belonged to the Neapolitan cardinal Girolamo Seripando.

It is difficult, however, not to imagine the Blind Men in conjunction with a stunning painting by Pieter Brueghel the Elder (now in the National Museum of Capodimonte in Naples) that shows a series of blind men tumbling into a ditch – an image evoked also in dialogue 1.3. Brueghel's work belonged to the Neapolitan royal collection, but did not arrive in Naples until 1734.

## Notes

1 Though colloquial English usually uses "convent" to mean a nunnery, the term actually refers to any Catholic religious community for men or women.

Mendicant orders like the Dominicans, because of their preaching and involvement in the community at large, do not adhere entirely to the monastic ideal of retreat from the world; hence their members are termed friars rather than monks, and their communities are called convents rather than monasteries or abbeys (which are monasteries administered by an abbot or abbess).

2 Bruno's third interrogation by the Inquisition, 3 June 1592; see Luigi Firpo, ed., *Giordano Bruno, Oeuvres complètes, Documents I, Le Procès* (Paris: Les Belles Lettres, 2000), 65–9.

3 Eugenio Canone, *Giordano Bruno, De gli Eroici furori* (Milan: Silvio Berlusconi Editore, 2011), 287–8.

4 Marsilio Ficino and Giovanni Cavalcanti, Letter to Giorgio Antonio Vespucci, in Marsilio Ficino, *Opera omnia* (Turin: Bottega d'Erasmo, 1959), vol. 1.2.631: "Fortunatus nimium venator, qui solis Solem passim sibi sectandum totis viribus proposuerit. Nempe prius etiam quaerat, hunc facillime reperit, quem non nisi eiusdem calore accensus quaesivit."

5 Miguel Angel Granada, ed., *Giordano Bruno, Oeuvres complètes, vol. VII, Des fureurs héroïques* (Paris: Les Belles Lettres, 1999; rev. ed. 2008), xcvii, 555–8; 605–7

6 Plato, *Symposium* 209e–210a, trans. Benjamin Jowett (*The Dialogues of Plato*), Oxford: The Clarendon Press, 1871, vol. 1: 525–6.

7 Vincenzo Spampanato, *Vita di Giordano Bruno*, Messina: Giuseppe Principato, 1927, vol. 1, 64–5.

8 Ibid., 64.

# The *Imprese* of the
# *Eroici furori*

The central section of the *Eroici furori*, comprising dialogue 5 of part 1 and dialogue 1 of part 2, describes a cavalcade of knights (who are really aspiring philosophers) carrying banners with their insignia or *imprese*. John Charlewood's cheap printed edition of the *Eroici furori* did not include images of the *imprese* Bruno describes within his text: commissioning an artist to engrave these complex miniatures would have cost much too much, and in any event talented engravers were hard to find in London. Even royal commissions were published on the cheap: the commemorative booklet describing Henry VIII's famous "Field of Gold" tournaments in 1520 has no more than a crude woodcut on the title page showing two jousting knights. Even the "festival books" commemorating the most powerful monarch of the sixteenth century, Holy Roman Emperor Charles V, have illustrations only on the title page (as in his 1549 entry into Mantua). Bruno himself sometimes provided woodcut illustrations for his own works, but his skills were not sufficient for the specialized task of emblem-making. As a result, his readers have always been compelled to use their imaginations.

Many of the images Bruno describes are strikingly similar to actual published emblems and *imprese* (personal emblems), both Italian and French, and in one case his idea probably draws from a painting by Titian, which he must have seen on display in Venice. It is not surprising to find similarities to French emblems in his dialogue; by the time he reached London in 1583, Bruno had spent several years in France, first as a professor at the University of Toulouse, and then in Paris, as a special appointee to King Henri III.

The early modern emblems and *imprese* that follow are meant to guide a modern reader's imagination as they once guided the imaginations of Bruno's contemporaries; they are not exact illustrations of Bruno's imagery (though Eugenio Canone's recent reconstruction of the *imprese* of the *Eroici furori* are often strikingly similar).[1]

The twenty-seven engravings reproduced here and, in Bruno's words, "drawn up like an army in marching order" (p. 143), are provided by courtesy of the Department of Special Collection of the University of Glasgow Library; Titian's *Allegory of Prudence* is reproduced by courtesy of the National Gallery of Art, London c/o Art Resource.

## Part 1, Dialogue 5

1. "Now here is the first, which bears a shield divided into four colours. The crest shows a flame beneath a brazen jar; a gust of vapour rushes forth from its opening, and around it is written: BUT THEY SAW THREE KINGDOMS [SED TRIA REGNA VIDERUNT]."

Georgette de Montenay, *Emblemes ou devises chrétiennes* (1571), "Qui se exaltat humiliabitur" ("Whoever puffs himself up will be humiliated" – or deflate like a pot that boils over).

2. "The next insignia has a shield divided into four colours, and on its crest there is a sun spreading its rays over the face of the earth. And there is a motto that says: EVER THE SAME, EVERYWHERE ENTIRE [IDEM SEMPER UBIQUE TOTUM]."

Guillaume La Perrière, *Le theatre des bon engins* (1544), LXXII: a sun ripening fruit.

3. "The third shows a naked boy on its shield, reclining in a green mead-ow, who props his raised head on his arm with his eyes turned heav-enward towards certain buildings with chambers, towers, fields, and gardens above the clouds; and there is a castle made of fire. In between them is the motto, which says: WE SUPPORT EACH OTHER [MUTUO FULCIMUR]."

Guillaume La Perrière, *Le theatre des bon engins* (1544), XXIX: A dreaming knight, faced with the choice between worldly power (in the net) and heavenly virtue.

4. "What is the meaning of that insect, that flies around the flame and is on the verge of burning itself up, and what does that motto mean: THE ENEMY IS NO ENEMY [HOSTIS NON HOSTIS]?"

Gilles Corrozet, *Hecatomgraphie* (1540), "La guerre doulce aux inexperimentez" ("War is sweet to the inexperienced").

5. "Fine, but what is the meaning of that palm branch surrounded by the motto: CAESAR IS HERE [CAESAR ADEST]?"

Roman coins minted in Judaea show a single palm branch and the motto CAESAR in Greek, but an elaborate palm branch also features in:

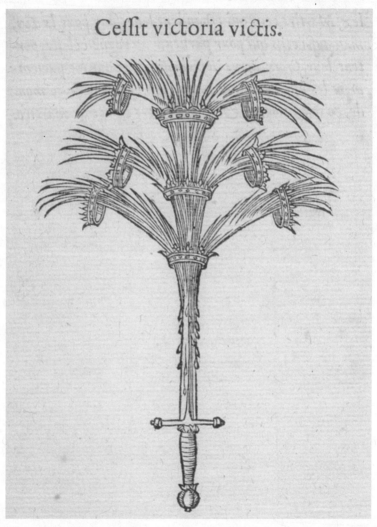

Claude Paradin, *Devises héroïques* (1557), "Cessit victoria victis" ("Victory gives in to the vanquished"). This is a bloody sword that gives way to the crowned palms of Christian martyrdom.

6. "Next we see the figure of a flying Phoenix, to whom a lad turns who is burning in the flames, with the motto: THE FATES STAND IN THE WAY [FATA OBSTANT]."

Claude Paradin, *Devises héroïques* (1557), "Unica semper avis" ("This bird is forever unique").

7. "But what is the meaning of that image of the Sun with one circle inside it and one outside, with the motto: IT CIRCLES [CIRCUIT]?"

Claude Paradin, *Devises héroïques* (1557), "Haec conscia numinis aetas" ("This age
is aware of [Christian] God").

8. "The crest of the next emblem shows a full moon with the motto: EVER THUS FOR ME AND FOR THE STAR [TALIS MIHI SEMPER ET ASTRO]."

Paolo Giovio, *Dialogo dell'imprese* (1574) [SM 520], Emblem 22: the *impresa* of Signor Mortier, ambassador of France, with the motto "When it is full it rivals the Sun."

9. "And it seems to me that the emblem I now see on the next shield has a certain consequence and symbolic force in terms of what we have just said; there a gnarled oak with many branches stands rooted, with the wind blowing against it, and around it is inscribed the motto: STRENGTH LIKE THE OAK [UT ROBORI ROBUR]."

The image of the mighty oak that withstands every storm because it is so deeply rooted in the soil comes from Vergil's *Aeneid*, 4.441–9, where the poet describes the hero Aeneas resisting the pleas of his spurned lover Dido (the translation here is John Dryden's):

> As, when the winds their airy quarrel try,
> Justling from ev'ry quarter of the sky,
> This way and that the mountain oak they bend,
> His boughs they shatter, and his branches rend;
> With leaves and falling mast they spread the ground;
> The hollow valleys echo to the sound:
> Unmov'd, the royal plant their fury mocks,
> Or, shaken, clings more closely to the rocks;
> Far as he shoots his tow'ring head on high,
> So deep in earth his fix'd foundations lie.
> No less a storm the Trojan hero bears;
> Thick messages and loud complaints he hears,
> And bandied words, still beating on his ears.
> Sighs, groans, and tears proclaim his inward pains;
> But the firm purpose of his heart remains

Andrea Alciati, *Emblemata* (1584), "The Oak"

10. "Look, this emblem contains the design of a hammer and anvil, around which is the motto FROM AETNA [AB AETNA]."

Girolamo Ruscelli, *Imprese illustri* 1584 [SM 1462], Impresa 8: The *impresa* of Cardinal Innocenzo Cybò, with the motto DURABO ("I will last").

11. Here is a golden apple, richly enamelled with different precious gems, and around it is the motto: [LET IT BE GIVEN] TO THE FAIREST [PULCHRIORI DETUR]."

Andrea Alciati, *Emblemata* (Augsburg, 1534), "In studiosum captum amore" ("Against a Scholar captivated by Love").

12. "The next [emblem] bears a head with four faces that blow towards the four corners of the heavens; thus there are four winds in a single subject. Above this are two stars, and in between a motto that says: NEW-BORN AEOLIANS [NOVAE ORTAE AEOLIAE]."

Georgette de Montenay, *Emblemes ou devises chrétiennes* (1571), "Venite" ("Come" – the summons of Christ).

13. "Then let us see the meaning of this burning torch, with the inscription around it: FOR LIFE, NOT FOR THE HOUR [AD VITAM NON AD HORAM]."

Hadrianus Junius, *Emblesmes* (1567), "Amour perpetuel" ("Perpetual Love": "Close up, I burn; at a distance, I suffer").

14. "But what is the meaning of that fiery bolt that has flames in place of a steel point, and around it is a cord, and it bears the motto: AN IN-STANT LOVE INSISTS [AMOR INSTAT UT INSTANS]."

Paolo Giovio, *Dialogo dell'imprese* (1574) [SM 520], Emblem 98: the *impresa* of Ippolito de' Medici, with a Greek motto, βάλλ᾿ οὕτως, "Strike like this."

15. "Here you see a serpent that languishes on the snow where a plough-man has thrown it, and a naked boy burning in the middle of a flame, with certain other details and circumstances, and a motto that says: THE SAME, THE VERY SAME, NOT THE SAME [IDEM ITIDEM NON IDEM]."

Gilles Corrozet, *Hecatomgraphie* (1540), "La voye de jeunesse incognue" ("Youth's unknowable path").

**Part 2, Dialogue 1**

16. "This figure [is] taken from the antiquities of the Egyptians. They made this type of statue in which, above a torso resembling all three, they placed three heads: one of a wolf who looked backward, another of a lion who had its face turned towards the centre, and the third of a dog who looked ahead, to signify that things past trouble our thoughts, but not as much as present things, which effectively torment us, but always promise better for the future. Thus, it is the wolf back there who howls, the lion here who roars, and next it will be the dog who applauds ... above the wolf is ALREADY, above the lion, NOW, above the dog, ANON; these inscriptions signify the three parts of time [IAM MODO PRAETEREA]."

Titian's *Allegory of Prudence* (painted between 1550 and 1565) was still in Venice when Bruno lived there in 1577. It is now in the National Gallery of Art, London.

17. "Here I see a smoking censer held up by an arm, and a motto that says, HIS ALTAR [ILLIUS ARA]."

Georgette de Montenay, *Emblemes ou devises chrétiennes* (1571), "Abundabit iniquitas – refrigescet Charitas" ("Iniquity will abound – Charity will provide relief").

18. "Now let's discuss this next image, of a Phoenix that burns in the Sun, whose smoke almost succeeds in obscuring the splendour of that star whose heat has set it afire. The motto alongside it says NEITHER LIKE NOR EQUAL [NEC SIMILE NEC PAR]."

Barthélemy Aneau, *Picta poesis*, "Unius Dei Aeternitas" ("The Eternity of the One God").

19. "Tell me, have you already seen and pondered the meaning of this heart-shaped fire with four wings, two of which have eyes, and the entire composition is encircled by luminous rays? Around it is inscribed the question: DO WE STRIVE IN VAIN? [NITIMUR IN CASSUM?]."

Georgette de Montenay, *Emblemes ou devises chrétiennes* (1571), "Dominus custodiat introitum tuum" ("The Lord shall guard your coming in").

20. "Here stands the wheel of time, rotating around its own centre, and here is the motto: I MOVE IN PLACE [MANENS MOVEOR]."

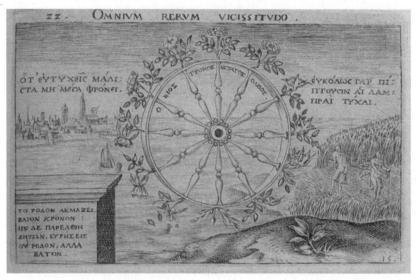

This emblem is as close to Bruno's own thinking as any: Jean de Boissard, *Emblèmes latins* (1588), "Omnium rerum vicissitudo" ("The alternation of all things").

21. "I see a ship inclined above the waves, its lines attached to the shore, with the motto: TEMPEST-TOSSED IN PORT [FLUCTUAT IN PORTU]."

Andrea Alciati, *Livret des emblemes* (1536), "Spes proxima" ("Hope is near").

22. "Here are two stars in the form of two shining eyes, with a motto that says: DEATH AND LIFE [MORS ET VITA]."

Pierre Cousau, *Le pegme* (1560), "Sur Castor et Pollux" ("Brotherly Love").

23. "Here is an eagle who flies towards heaven on two wings, but is held back, I know not how or why, by the weight of a stone tied to one of its feet. And it has the motto: THE UNCERTAIN IS SPLIT [SCINDITUR INCERTUM]."

Johannes Sambucus, *Les emblemes* (1567), "Moderata conditio" ("A balanced state").

24. "Now let us see what is presented us by these two shining arrows above a target, around which is written: THE INSTANT WON INSIS-TENT [VICIT INSTANS]."

Gilles Corrozet, *Hecatomgraphie* (1540), "Parler peu et venir au poinct" ("Speaking little and getting right to the point").

25. "Now let's look at this quiver and bow, which belong to Love, as the sparks around them show, and the knot in the hanging cord, with the motto: SUDDENLY, SECRETLY [SUBITO CLAM]."

Andrea Alciati, *Emblemes* (1549) "Vis Amoris" ("The Power of Love").

26. "Now let's see what the meaning might be of that flaming arrow, with the motto wrapped around it: WHERE THE NEW WOUND? [CUI NOVA PLAGA LOCO?]"

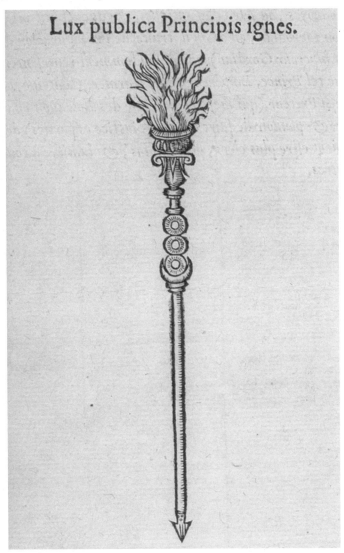

Claude Paradin, *Devises héroïques* (1557), "Lux publica Principis ignes" ("The fires of the Prince are the Public's Light").

27. "Now here is a boy in a boat, who is about to be engulfed by stormy waves at any moment, and yet, all languid and inert, he has abandoned his oars. And around him is the motto: NO FAITH IN FACES [FRONTI NULLA FIDES]."

Gilles Corrozet, *Emblemes in Cebes* (1543), "Peril inopine" ("Unexpected danger").

## Part 2, Dialogue 2

28. "Here you see a flaming yoke wrapped in cords; around it is written LIGHTER THAN THE BREEZE [LEVIUS AURA]."

Paolo Giovio, *Dialogo dell'imprese* (1574) [SM 520], Emblem 34: the *impresa* of Pope Leo X, with the motto "SUAVE" – "Gentle," from Matthew 11:30, "For my yoke is easy and my burden is light."

## Note

1  Eugenio Canone, *Giordano Bruno. De gli Eroici Furori*, ed. with intro. and commentary by Eugenio Canone, Biblioteca dell'Utopia (Milan: Silvio Berlusconi Editore, 2011), lxvii–lxxvi.

DE GLI EROICI FURORI /
ON THE HEROIC FRENZIES

GIORDANO BRUNO, NOLAN

*On the Heroic Frenzies*
*To the most illustrious and excellent Gentleman, Sir Philip Sidney*
*Paris, Antonio Baio [London: John Charlewood], in the year 1585*

# ARGOMENTO DEL NOLANO SOPRA GLI EROICI FURORI

*Scritto al molto illustre signor Filippo Sidneo*

È cosa veramente, o generosissimo Cavalliero, da basso, bruto e sporco ingegno, d'essersi fatto constantemente studioso, et aver affisso un curioso pensiero circa o sopra la bellezza d'un corpo femenile. Che spettacolo (o Dio buono) più vile et ignobile può presentarsi ad un occhio di terso sentimento, che un uomo cogitabundo, afflitto, tormentato, triste, maninconioso: per dovenir or freddo, or caldo, or fervente, or tremante, or pallido, or rosso, or in mina di perplesso, or in atto di risoluto; un che spende il meglior intervallo di tempo, e gli più scelti frutti di sua vita corrente, destillando l'elixir del cervello con mettere in concetto, scritto, e sigillar in publici monumenti, quelle continue torture, que' gravi tormenti, que' razionali discorsi, que' faticosi pensieri, e quelli amarissimi studi destinati sotto la tirannide d'una indegna, imbecille, stolta e sozza sporcaria?

Che tragicomedia? che atto, dico, degno più di compassione e riso può esserne ripresentato in questo teatro del mondo, in questa scena delle nostre conscienze, che di tali e tanto numerosi suppositi fatti penserosi, contemplativi, constanti, fermi, fideli, amanti, coltori, adoratori e servi di cosa senza fede, priva d'ogni costanza, destituta d'ogni ingegno, vacua d'ogni merito, senza riconoscenza e gratitudine alcuna, dove non può capir più senso, intelletto e bontade, che trovarsi possa in una statua, o imagine depinta al muro? e dove è più superbia, arroganza, protervia, orgoglio, ira, sdegno, falsitade, libidine, avarizia, ingratitudine et altri crimi eximii, che avessero possuto uscir veneni e instrumenti di morte dal vascello di Pandora, per aver pur troppo largo ricetto dentro il cervello di mostro tale? Ecco vergato in carte, rinchiuso in libri, messo avanti gli occhi, et intonato a gli orecchi un rumore, un strepito, un fracasso d'insegne, d'imprese, de motti, d'epistole, de sonetti, d'epigrammi, de libri, de prolissi scartafazzi, de sudori estremi, de vite consumate, con strida ch'assordiscon gli astri, lamenti che fanno ribombar gli antri infernali, doglie che fanno stupefar l'anime viventi, suspiri da far exinanire e compatir gli dèi, per quegli occhi, per quelle guance, per quel busto, per quel bianco, per quel vermiglio, per quella lingua, per quel dente, per quel labro, quel crine, quella veste, quel manto, quel guanto, quella scarpetta, quella pianella, quella parsimonia, quel risetto, quel sdegnosetto, quella vedova

# THE NOLAN'S ARGUMENT[1] OF THE HEROIC FRENZIES

*Addressed to the most Noble Gentleman, Sir Philip Sidney*

It is truly, O most noble Sir, the work of a low, brutish, and filthy nature to become the constant admirer, to have attached a devoted thought to or around the beauty of a woman's body. Good God! What more vile and ignoble sight can present itself to a clear-sighted eye than a man, brooding, afflicted, tormented, sorry, melancholy, who waxes now cold, now hot, now boiling, now trembling, now pale, now blushing, now in a pose of perplexity, now in the act of decisiveness, a man who spends the best season and choicest fruits of his life distilling the elixir of his brain towards putting into thought and writ and etching on public monuments those endless tortures, those grave agonies, those reasoned arguments, those laborious thoughts and those bitter desires, addressed to the tyranny of feckless, feeble-minded, stupid, and sordid smut?

What tragicomedy, what recital, I say, more deserving of pity and laughter, could be produced in this theatre of the world, on this stage of our perceptions,[2] than all these characters rendered pensive, contemplative, constant, steadfast, faithful, lovers, devotees, and slaves of a thing that is lacking in faith, bereft of all constancy, destitute of intelligence, empty of all merit, void of any acknowledgment or gratitude, from whom no more sense, intellect, or goodness are to be obtained than might be found in a statue or a painting on a wall? And in whom there abound more disdain, arrogance, effrontery, vainglory, rage, scorn, perfidy, lust, greed, ingratitude, and other mortal vices than the poisons and instruments of death that could have issued forth from Pandora's Box, all to find, alas, such ample refuge within the brain of such a monster? Behold, inscribed on paper, enclosed in books, set before the eyes and intoned in the ears, a noise, a commotion, a clash of devices, of emblems, of mottoes, of epistles, of sonnets, of epigrams, of books, of long-winded scribblings, of terminal sweats, of lives consumed, with cries that deafen the stars, laments that make Hell's caverns reverberate, aches that strike the living dumb, sighs that exhaust the pity of the gods, for those eyes, for those cheeks, for that bosom, for that white, for that crimson, for that tongue, for that tooth, for that lip, for that hair, that dress, that mantle, that glove, that little shoe, that slipper, that avarice, that giggle, that scorn,

fenestra, quell'eclissato sole, quel martello; quel schifo, quel puzzo, quel sepolcro, quel cesso, quel mestruo, quella carogna, quella febre quartana, quella estrema ingiuria e torto di natura: che con una superficie, un'ombra, un fantasma, un sogno, un circeo incantesimo ordinato al serviggio della generazione, ne inganna in specie di bellezza. La quale insieme insieme viene e passa, nasce e muore, fiorisce e marcisce; et è bella cossì un pochettino a l'esterno, che nel suo intrinseco vera e stabilmente è contenuto un navilio, una bottega, una dogana, un mercato de quante sporcarie, tossichi e veneni abbia possuti produre la nostra madrigna natura; la quale dopo aver riscosso quel seme di cui la si serva, ne viene sovente a pagar d'un lezzo, d'un pentimento, d'una tristizia, d'una fiacchezza, d'un dolor di capo, d'una lassitudine, d'altri et altri malanni che son manifesti a tutto il mondo; a fin che amaramente dolga, dove suavemente proriva.

Ma che fo io? che penso? son forse nemico della generazione? ho forse in odio il sole? Rincrescemi forse il mio et altrui essere messo al mondo? Voglio forse ridur gli uomini a non raccòrre quel più dolce pomo che può produr l'orto del nostro terrestre paradiso? Son forse io per impedir l'instituto santo della natura? Debbo tentare di suttrarmi io o altro dal dolce amaro giogo che n'ha messo al collo la divina providenza? Ho forse da persuader a me et ad altri, che gli nostri predecessori sieno nati per noi, e noi non siamo nati per gli nostri successori? Non voglia, non voglia Dio che questo giamai abbia possuto cadermi nel pensiero. Anzi aggiongo che per quanti regni e beatitudini mi s'abbiano possuti proporre e nominare, mai fui tanto savio o buono che mi potesse venir voglia de castrarmi o dovenir eunuco. Anzi mi vergognarei se cossì come mi trovo in apparenza, volesse cedere pur un pelo a qualsivoglia che mangia degnamente il pane per servire alla natura e Dio benedetto. E se alla buona volontà soccorrer possano o soccorrano gl'instrumenti e gli lavori, lo lascio considerar solo a chi ne può far giudicio e donar sentenza. Io non credo d'esser legato: perché son certo che non bastarebbono tutte le stringhe e tutti gli lacci che abbian saputo e sappian mai intessere et annodare quanti furo e sono stringari e lacciaiuoli (non so se posso dir) se fusse con essi la morte istessa, che volessero maleficiarmi. Né credo d'esser freddo, se a refrigerar il mio caldo non penso che bastarebbono le nevi del monte Caucaso o Rifeo. Or vedete dumque se è la raggione o qualche difetto che mi fa parlare.

Che dumque voglio dire? che voglio conchiudere? che voglio determinare? Quel che voglio conchiudere e dire, o Cavalliero illustre, è che

that empty window, that eclipse of the sun, that throbbing, that disgust, that stench, that sepulchre, that cesspit, that menstruation, that carrion, that quartan fever,[3] that uttermost insult and lapse of nature, that with a surface, a shadow, a phantasm, a dream, a spell of Circe[4] placed in the service of reproduction, should deceive us in the semblance of beauty, which at once comes and goes, issues and dies, flowers and rots, and is pretty enough on the outside, but inside truly and enduringly harbours a shipyard, a workshop, a customs-house, a marketplace of very foulness, toxin and poison that our stepmother Nature has managed to produce: and once the seed she requires has been paid out, she repays it often with a stench, a remorse, a sadness, a flaccidity, a headache, a lassitude, this and that distemper known to all the world, so that every place aches bitterly where it itched so sweetly before.

But what am I doing? What am I thinking? Am I perhaps an enemy of reproduction? Do I perhaps hate the sun? Do I resent perhaps my own birth and that of others? Do I wish, perhaps, to keep humankind from picking the sweetest apple that the garden of our earthly paradise can possibly produce? Do I mean, perhaps, to block the holy establishment of Nature? Dare I try to extract myself or someone else from the bittersweet yoke that divine providence has fixed around our necks? Do I mean perhaps to persuade myself and others that our ancestors were born for us, but that we are not born for our descendants? God forbid and forfend that such a thought should cross my mind! Indeed, I will add that for every kingdom and happiness that could be named and offered me, I have never been either so wise or so virtuous that I could conceive the desire to castrate myself or to become a eunuch. Indeed, I would be ashamed, such as I seem to be, to yield up one hair of myself to any mortal who worthily eats his bread, in order to serve Nature and blessed God. As for whether tools and hard work can come to the aid of goodwill, I leave that to the sole consideration of those who are qualified to pass judgment and render an opinion.[5] I do not believe that I am bound, because I am certain that all the strings and laces that the purveyors of strings and laces have ever contrived to weave and knot would not suffice to bind me with their black magic – not even (dare I say it?) if Death itself were on their side. Nor do I believe that I am cold, not when the snows of the Caucasus and the Rhipaean mountains[6] would not suffice to cool my heat. So judge, then, whether it be reason or some defect that urges me to speak.

What, then, do I mean to say? What do I mean to prove? What I mean to prove and say, illustrious Sir, is that what belongs to Caesar should

quel ch'è di Cesare sia donato a Cesare, e quel ch'è de Dio sia renduto a Dio. Voglio dire che a le donne, benché talvolta non bastino gli onori et ossequii divini, non perciò se gli denno onori et ossequii divini. Voglio che le donne siano cossì onorate et amate, come denno essere amate et onorate le donne; per tal causa dico, e per tanto, per quanto si deve a quel poco, a quel tempo e quella occasione, se non hanno altra virtù che naturale, cioè di quella bellezza, di quel splendore, di quel serviggio: senza il quale denno esser stimate più vanamente nate al mondo che un morboso fungo, qual con pregiudicio de meglior piante occupa la terra; e più noiosamente che qualsivoglia napello o vipera che caccia il capo fuor di quella. Voglio dire che tutte le cose de l'universo, perché possano aver fermezza e consistenza, hanno gli suoi pondi, numeri, ordini e misure, a fin che siano dispensate e governate con ogni giustizia e raggione. Là onde Sileno, Bacco, Pomona, Vertunno, il dio di Lampsaco, et altri simili che son dèi da tinello, da cervosa forte e vino rinversato, come non siedeno in cielo a bever nettare e gustar ambrosia nella mensa di Giove, Saturno, Pallade, Febo et altri simili: cossì gli lor fani, tempii, sacrificii e culti denno essere differenti da quelli de costoro.

Voglio finalmente dire che questi furori eroici ottegnono suggetto et oggetto eroico: e però non ponno più cadere in stima d'amori volgari e naturaleschi, che veder si possano delfini su gli alberi de le selve, e porci cinghiali sotto gli marini scogli. Però per liberare tutti da tal suspizione, avevo pensato prima di donar a questo libro un titolo simile a quello di Salomone, il quale sotto la scorza d'amori et affetti ordinarii, contiene similmente divini et eroici furori, come interpretano gli mistici e cabalisti dottori: volevo (per dirla) chiamarlo *Cantica*. Ma per più caggioni mi sono astenuto al fine: de le quali ne voglio referir due sole. L'una per il timor ch'ho conceputo dal rigoroso supercilio de certi farisei, che cossì mi stimarebono profano per usurpar in mio naturale e fisico discorso titoli sacri e sopranaturali; come essi sceleratissimi e ministri d'ogni ribaldaria si usurpano più altamente che dir si possa gli titoli de sacri, de santi, de divini oratori, de figli de Dio, de sacerdoti, de regi: stante che stiamo aspettando quel giudicio divino che farà manifesta la lor maligna ignoranza et altrui dottrina, la nostra simplice libertà e l'altrui maliciose regole, censure et instituzioni. L'altra per la grande dissimilitudine che si vede fra il volto di questa opra e quella, quantumque medesimo misterio e sustanza d'anima sia compreso sotto l'ombra dell'una e l'altra: stante che là nessuno dubita che il primo instituto del sapiente fusse più

be rendered unto Caesar, and what belongs to God should be rendered unto God. I mean to say that, although at times for women divine honours and obsequies are insufficient, they should not for that reason arrogate to themselves such honours and obsequies. I mean that women should be honoured and loved as women should be honoured and loved: for that reason, I say, and to the extent that they deserve, for that trifle, for that moment, and on that occasion, if they have no other quality than what is natural – namely that beauty, that splendour, that service, without which they should be counted as more useless to the world than a toadstool, which occupies the earth in place of a better plant, and more annoying than an asp or viper that pokes its head forth from the soil. I mean to say that all things in the universe, to give them solidity and consistency, have their own weight, number, order, and measure, so that they will be administered and governed with all justice and reason.[7] Therefore just as Silenus, Bacchus, Pomona, Vertumnus, the god of Lampsacus [Priapus], and others like them, who are gods of the dining room, of strong beer and spilled wine, do not sit in Heaven sipping nectar and tasting ambrosia at the table with Jove, Saturn, Pallas, Phoebus, and the like – so, too, their shrines, temples, sacrifices, and rituals must be different from those of the others.

Finally, I mean to say that these heroic frenzies achieve a heroic subject and object, and for that reason they can no more sink to the level of common and natural loves than dolphins can been seen in the trees of the forest, or wild boars beneath the sea cliffs. Hence, to free them all from such a suspicion, I first thought of giving this book a title like that of Solomon, who under the cover of ordinary love and emotion contains similar divine and heroic frenzies, as the mystical and cabalistic doctors interpret them. I wanted, that is to say, to call it *Canticles*. But in the end I resisted, for several reasons, of which I will note only two. First of all, because of the fear that I have conceived of the disapproval of certain Pharisees,[8] who would regard me as profane for usurping sacred and supernatural titles for my natural and physical discourse, whereas they, criminals and ministers of every ribaldry, usurp more profoundly than one can say the titles of holy men, of saints, of divine orators, of sons of God, of priests, of kings; while we await that divine judgment that will make plain their malign ignorance and our own learning, our simple liberty and their malicious rules, censures, and institutions. Second, because of the great difference evident between this work and that one, although the same mystery and substance of soul lie concealed beneath the shadows of the one and the other. For in that case no one doubts that

tosto di figurar cose divine che di presentar altro; perché ivi le figure sono aperta e manifestamente figure, et il senso metaforico è conosciuto di sorte che non può esser negato per metaforico: dove odi quelli occhi di colombe, quel collo di torre, quella lingua di latte, quella fragranzia d'incenso, que' denti che paiono greggi de pecore che descendono dal lavatoio, que' capelli che sembrano le capre che vegnono giù da la montagna di Galaad. Ma in questo poema non si scorge volto che cossì al vivo ti spinga a cercar latente et occolto sentimento: atteso che per l'ordinario modo di parlare e de similitudini più accomodate a gli sensi communi, che ordinariamente fanno gli accorti amanti, e soglion mettere in versi e rime gli usati poeti, son simili a i sentimenti de coloro che parlarono a Citereida, a Licori, a Dori, a Cinzia, a Lesbia, a Corinna, a Laura et altre simili: onde facilmente ogn'uno potrebbe esser persuaso che la fondamentale e prima intenzion mia sia stata addirizzata da ordinario amore che m'abbia dettati concetti tali; il quale appresso per forza de sdegno s'abbia improntate l'ali e dovenuto eroico; come è possibile di convertir qualsivoglia fola, romanzo, sogno e profetico enigma, e transferirle in virtù di metafora e pretesto d'allegoria a significar tutto quello che piace a chi più comodamente è atto a stiracchiar gli sentimenti: e far cossì tutto di tutto, come tutto essere in tutto disse il profondo Anaxagora. Ma pensi chi vuol quel che gli pare e piace, ch'alfine o voglia o non, per giustizia la deve ognuno intendere e definire come l'intendo e definisco io, non io come l'intende e definisce lui: perché come gli furori di quel sapiente Ebreo hanno gli proprii modi ordini e titolo che nessuno ha possuto intendere e potrebbe meglio dechiarar che lui se fusse presente; cossì questi Cantici hanno il proprio titolo ordine e modo che nessun può meglio dechiarar et intendere che io medesimo quando non sono absente.

D'una cosa voglio che sia certo il mondo: che quello per il che io mi essagito in questo proemiale argomento, dove singularmente parlo a voi eccellente Signore, e ne gli Dialogi formati sopra gli seguenti articoli, sonetti e stanze, è ch'io voglio ch'ogn'un sappia ch'io mi stimarei molto vituperoso e bestialaccio, se con molto pensiero, studio e fatica mi fusse mai delettato o delettasse de imitar (come dicono) un Orfeo circa il culto d'una donna in vita; e dopo morte, se possibil fia, ricovrarla da l'inferno: se a pena la stimarei degna, senza arrossir il volto, d'amarla sul naturale di quell'istante del fiore della sua beltade, e facultà di far figlioli alla natura e dio; tanto manca che vorrei parer simile a certi poeti e versificanti in far trionfo d'una perpetua perseveranza di tale amore, come d'una cossì pertinace pazzia, la qual sicuramente può competere con tut-

the primary intention of Wise [Solomon] was to represent divine matters above all else, for there the images are openly and manifestly images, and the metaphorical sense is so well known that it cannot be denied as a metaphor: as when you hear about those dove's eyes, that neck like a tower, that tongue of milk, that fragrance of frankincense, those teeth that are like flocks of sheep come up from the washing, that hair like the goats which appear from Mount Gilead.[9] In this poem, however, you will not discern a face that so vividly urges you to look for hidden and occult sentiment, as its ordinary manner of speech and its comparisons – which are more attuned to the common images that lovers use and which the usual poets put in verse and rhyme – resemble the feelings of those who spoke to Cythereis, or Lycoris, to Doris, to Cynthia, to Lesbia, to Corinna, to Laura, and the like.[10] For which reason it would be easy to believe that my primary and basic intention had been guided by an ordinary love that inspired me to such conceits, which, on being rejected, had borrowed wings and become heroic.[11] In just this way, it is possible to transform any ballad, romance, dream, and prophetic riddle and adapt it, through the power of metaphor and the pretext of allegory, to mean whatever anyone likes who is better able to stretch his emotions to the point that everything can mean anything – just as the wise Anaxagoras said, "All is in all."[12] But let everyone think whatever he likes and pleases, because in the end, like it or not, in all fairness every one of them should understand and define it as I understand and define it, and not as *they* would understand or define it. For just as the frenzies of that wise Jew have their own style, order, and title, which no one could understand or explain better than he himself, were he present, so, too, these *Canticles* have their own proper title, order, and style, that no one can explain and understand better than I myself, if I am not absent.

I want the world to be certain of one thing, namely, that the purpose for which I bestir myself in this prefatory outline, where I speak individually to you, excellent Lord, and in the Dialogues, shaped around the poems, sonnets, and stanzas that follow, is this: I want every one to know that I would deem myself most disgraceful and brutish if with great thought, desire, and labour I had ever delighted, or delight now, in imitating (as they say) an Orpheus by worshipping a living woman, and, after death, if it were possible, by retrieving her from Hell, when on the contrary I could scarcely regard her as worthy, without blushing, of loving physically, even at that momentary height of her beauty and her capacity to beget children according to God and nature. And how much less would I want to appear to resemble certain poets and versifiers in parading the

te l'altre specie che possano far residenza in un cervello umano: tanto, dico, son lontano da quella vanissima, vilissima e vituperosissima gloria, che non posso credere ch'un uomo che si trova un granello di senso e spirito, possa spendere più amore in cosa simile che io abbia speso al passato e possa spendere al presente. E per mia fede, se io voglio adattarmi a defendere per nobile l'ingegno di quel tosco poeta che si mostrò tanto spasimare alle rive di Sorga per una di Valclusa, e non voglio dire che sia stato un pazzo da catene, donarommi a credere, e forzaròmmi di persuader ad altri, che lui per non aver ingegno atto a cose megliori, volse studiosamente nodrir quella melancolia, per celebrar non meno il proprio ingegno su quella matassa, con esplicar gli affetti d'un ostinato amor volgare, animale e bestiale, ch'abbiano fatto gli altri ch'han parlato delle lodi della mosca, del scarafone, de l'asino, de Sileno, de Priapo, scimie de quali son coloro ch'han poetato a' nostri tempi delle lodi de gli orinali, de la piva, della fava, del letto, delle bugie, del disonore, del forno, del martello, della caristia, de la peste; le quali non meno forse sen denno gir altere e superbe per la celebre bocca de canzonieri suoi, che debbano e possano le prefate et altre dame per gli suoi.

Or (perché non si faccia errore) qua non voglio che sia tassata la dignità di quelle che son state e sono degnamente lodate e lodabili: non quelle che possono essere e sono particolarmente in questo paese Britannico, a cui doviamo la fideltà et amore ospitale: perché dove si biasimasse tutto l'orbe, non si biasima questo che in tal proposito non è orbe, né parte d'orbe: ma diviso da quello in tutto, come sapete; dove si raggionasse de tutto il sesso femenile, non si deve né può intendere de alcune vostre, che non denno esser stimate parte di quel sesso: perché non son femine, non son donne: ma (in similitudine di quelle) son nimfe, son dive, son di sustanza celeste; tra le quali è lecito di contemplar quell'unica Diana, che in questo numero e proposito non voglio nominare. Comprendasi dumque il geno ordinario. E di quello ancora indegna et ingiustamente perseguitarei le persone: perciò che a nessuna particulare deve essere improperato l'imbecillità e condizion del sesso, come né il difetto e vizio di complessione: atteso che se in ciò è fallo et errore, deve essere attribuito per la specie alla natura, e non per particolare a gl'individui. Certamente quello che circa tai supposti abomino è quel studioso e disordinato amor venereo che sogliono alcuni spendervi, de maniera che se gli fanno servi con l'ingegno, e vi vegnono a cattivar le potenze et atti più nobili de l'anima intellettiva. Il qual intento essendo

perpetual duration of such love, as if of an insanity so chronic that it could certainly rival all the other kinds that might take up residence in the human brain. I am so far, I say, from that vain, vile, and vituperated glory, that I cannot believe that any man with a grain of sense or spirit could expend more love on such an object than I have spent myself in the past, or could spend in the present. And by my faith, if I am going to try to defend as noble the wit of that Tuscan poet[13] who displayed such throes of agony along the banks of the Sorgue for a certain lady of Vaucluse, rather than choosing to say that he was a raving lunatic, then I shall have to make myself believe, and force myself to persuade others of this: that for lack of a talent equal to higher matters, he studiously nourished that melancholy in order to exercise his wit on that tangled skein, and by unravelling the emotions of an obsessive love that was vulgar, animal, and bestial, he did what others have done, who have spoken in praise of the fly, of the cockroach, of the ass, of Silenus, of Priapus; and these last have been aped by others who have written poems in our time, in praise of urinals, of chamber pots, of fava beans, of their beds, of lies, of dishonour, ovens, hammers, famine, and plague – which, perhaps, should travel no less proudly and haughtily on the illustrious mouths of their troubadours, than those ladies, and others, can and should on theirs.

Now let there be no mistake about it: I do not wish to detract here from the dignity of those ladies who are and were rightly praised and praiseworthy – and especially not those who might and do inhabit this Britannic nation, to whom I owe the fidelity and love of a guest. For one might blame all the world, but one cannot blame what is not the world in this respect, nor part of it, but is entirely separate from it in every way, as you know.[14] And whenever the entire female sex is discussed, one need not and should not construe it as a reference to any of yours, who should not be regarded as part of that sex; for they are not females, they are not women; but rather (compared with the others) they are nymphs, they are goddesses, they are made of celestial substance, among whom we may contemplate that one and only Diana,[15] whom I choose not to name among their number and in this context. So let the reader understand that I mean the ordinary kind [of women]. And within that category it would be unworthy and unjust for me to persecute individual persons, as no woman in particular should stand accused of the weakness and condition of her sex as if it were a flaw and vice in her individual makeup. For if there be a fault and error to be found, if should be attributed to nature according to species and not by particulars to individual persons. Certainly what I abominate in this regard is that obsessive and disorderly

considerato, non sarà donna casta et onesta che voglia per nostro naturale e veridico discorso contristarsi e farmisi più tosto irata, che sotto-
scrivendomi amarmi di vantaggio, vituperando passivamente quell'amor
nelle donne verso gli uomini, che io attivamente riprovo ne gli uomini
verso le donne. Tal dumque essendo il animo, ingegno, parere e determinazione, mi protesto che il mio primo e principale, mezzano et
accessorio, ultimo e finale intento in questa tessitura fu et è d'apportare
contemplazion divina, e metter avanti a gli occhi et orecchie altrui furori
non de volgari, ma eroici amori, ispiegati in due parti: de le quali ciascuna è divisa in cinque dialogi.

## ARGOMENTO DE' CINQUE DIALOGI
## DE LA PRIMA PARTE

Nel primo dialogo della prima parte son cinque articoli, dove per ordine:
nel primo si mostrano le cause e principii motivi intrinseci sotto nome
e figura del monte, e del fiume, e de muse che si dechiarano presenti,
non perché chiamate, invocate e cercate, ma più tosto come quelle che
più volte importunamente si sono offerte: onde vegna significato che la
divina luce è sempre presente; s'offre sempre, sempre chiama e batte a
le porte de nostri sensi et altre potenze cognoscitive et apprensive: come
pure è significato nella *Cantica* di Salomone dove si dice: *En ipse stat post
parietem nostrum, respiciens per cancellos, et prospiciens per fenestras.* La qual
spesso per varie occasioni et impedimenti avvien che rimagna esclusa fuori e trattenuta. Nel secondo articolo si mostra quali sieno que' suggetti,
oggetti, affetti, instrumenti et effetti per li quali s'introduce, si mostra
e prende il possesso nell'anima questa divina luce: perché la inalze e la
converta in Dio. Nel terzo il proponimento, definizione e determinazione che fa l'anima ben informata circa l'uno, perfetto et ultimo fine. Nel
quarto la guerra civile che séguita e si discuopre contra il spirito dopo
tal proponimento; onde disse la *Cantica: Noli mirari quia nigra sum: de-
coloravit enim me sol, quia fratres mei pugnaverunt contra me, quam posuerunt
custodem in vineis.* Là sono esplicati solamente come quattro antesignani:
l'Affetto, l'Appulso fatale, la Specie del bene, et il Rimorso; che son se-
guitati da tante coorte militari de tante, contrarie, varie e diverse potenze, con gli lor ministri, mezzi et organi che sono in questo composto. Nel
quinto s'ispiega una naturale contemplazione in cui si mostra che ogni

venereal love that some expend in such a way as to enslave their minds, until they render captive the most noble actions and potentials of their intellective souls.[16] If my intent is given due consideration, no chaste and honest woman should prefer to take offense at my natural and truthful discourse, and become angry with me rather than endorsing and loving me in return, passively reproving in women's love for men what I actively reprove in men's love for women. With such spirit, talent, opinion, and determination, therefore, I swear that in this composition my intent – first and foremost, central and accessory, ultimate and final – was and is to induce the contemplation of divinity, and to put before the eyes and ears of others not vulgar frenzies, but heroic love, which is explained in two parts, each divided into five dialogues.

## CONTENT OF THE FIVE DIALOGUES OF THE FIRST PART

In the first dialogue of the first part there are five sections[17] in this order: in the first, the causes and intrinsic motivating principles are revealed in the word and image of the mountain and the river, and of Muses who declare themselves present, not because they have been summoned, invoked, and sought after, but rather have offered themselves insistently time and again; on this basis it is shown that the divine light is always present, always offers itself, always calls out and knocks at the door of our senses and our other powers to learn and know:[18] just as the same idea is signified in the Canticle of Solomon where it says: *He standeth behind our wall, he looketh forth at the windows, shewing himself through the lattice.*[19] Often, because of various incidents and impediments, it happens that the light is shut out and held back. The second section reveals the subjects, objects, affections, instruments, and effects by which this divine light introduces itself, reveals itself, and takes possession of the soul in order to raise it up and turn it towards God. In the third are revealed the proposition, definition, and determinations that the well-informed soul makes about its one, perfect, and ultimate purpose. In the fourth is revealed the ensuing war that breaks out with the spirit after such a proposal; for which reason the *Canticle* says: *Look not upon me, because I am black, because the sun hath looked upon me; my mother's children were angry with me; they made me the keeper of the vineyards.*[20] There Affection, Fatal Impulse, the Species of Good, and Remorse are simply presented as four standard-bearers, who are followed by vast troops of many, contrary, various, and diverse

contrarietà si riduce a l'amicizia: o per vittoria de l'uno de' contrarii, o per armonia e contemperamento, o per qualch'altra raggione di vicissitudine; ogni lite alla concordia, ogni diversità a l'unità: la qual dottrina è stata da noi distesa ne gli discorsi d'altri dialogi.


Nel secondo dialogo viene più esplicatamente descritto l'ordine et atto della milizia che si ritrova nella sustanza di questa composizione del furioso; et ivi: nel primo articolo si mostrano tre sorte di contrarietà: la prima d'un affetto et atto contra l'altro, come dove son le speranze fredde e gli desiderii caldi; la seconda de medesimi affetti et atti in se stessi, non solo in diversi, ma et in medesimi tempi; come quando ciascuno non si contenta di sé, ma attende ad altro: et insieme insieme ama et odia; la terza tra la potenza che séguita et aspira, e l'oggetto che fugge e si suttrae.

Nel secondo articolo si manifesta la contrarietà ch'è come di doi contrarii appulsi in generale; alli quali si rapportano tutte le particolari e subalternate contrarietadi, mentre come a doi luoghi e sedie contrarie si monta o scende: anzi il composto tutto per la diversità de le inclinazioni che son nelle diverse parti, e varietà de disposizioni che accade nelle medesime, viene insieme insieme a salire et abbassare, a farsi avanti et adietro, ad allontanarsi da sé e tenersi ristretto in sé. Nel terzo articolo si discorre circa la conseguenza da tal contrarietade.

Nel terzo dialogo si fa aperto quanta forza abbia la volontade in questa milizia, come quella a cui sola appartiene ordinare, cominciare, exeguire e compire; cui vien intonato nella *Cantica: Surge, propera, columba mea, et veni: iam enim hiems transiit, imber abiit, flores apparuerunt in terra nostra; tempus putationis advenit.* Questa sumministra forza ad altri in molte maniere, et a se medesima specialmente quando si reflette in se stessa, e si radoppia; all'or che vuol volere, e gli piace che voglia quel che vuole; o si ritratta, all'or che non vuol quel che vuole, e gli dispiace che voglia quel che vuole: cossì in tutto e per tutto approva quel ch'è bene e quel tanto che la natural legge e giustizia gli definisce: e mai affatto approva quel che è altrimente. E questo è quanto si esplica nel primo e secondo articolo. Nel terzo si vede il gemino frutto di tal efficacia, secondo che (per consequenza de l'affetto che le attira e rapisce) le cose alte si fanno basse, e le basse dovegnono alte; come per forza de vertiginoso appulso

powers, along with the ministers, means, and tools that belong to this great host. In the fifth a natural contemplation is expounded in which it is shown that every opposition can be reduced to friendship either by the victory of one or the other parties, or by harmony and tempering, or by some other principle of alternation:[21] every rivalry to concord, every diversity to unity: and this doctrine has been expounded by us in the discussions of the other dialogues.

The second dialogue describes more explicitly the order and action of the army that is found in the substance of this compound that is the frenzied hero, to wit: in the first section are revealed three types of conflict: first, that of one affection and action against another, as when hopes are cold and desires hot; second, between the affections and actions in themselves, not only in different times, but also simultaneously, as when someone is dissatisfied with himself and so decides to devote his attention to something else, and hates and loves at the same time; and third, between the power that follows and aspires, and the object that flees and escapes.

In the second section we show the conflict that arises as if between two impulses that are contrary in a general sense, and within which all the particular and subordinate contraries find their place, while one goes up and the other goes down as if to two opposite positions or locations. Indeed, each compound impulse, according to the diversity of the inclinations within its diverse parts, and the variety of the dispositions found within it, uniformly rises or falls, goes forward or recedes, moves away from itself or closes in on itself. The third section discusses the result of such a conflict.

The third dialogue makes plain how much power the will of this army can muster, for it alone has the right to order, undertake, execute, and complete. To it the Canticle intones: *Rise up, my dove, my fair one, and come away: For lo, the winter is past, the rain is over and gone; The flowers appear on the earth; the time of the singing of birds is come.*[22] It delegates power to others in many ways, and especially to itself, when it reflects and redoubles itself, for then it desires to desire, and takes pleasure in desiring what it desires – or it retracts itself, when it does not desire what it desires, and is displeased that it desires what it desires. Thus, it approves, entirely and thoroughly, what is beneficial and what natural law and justice ascribe to it: and never approves what is otherwise. And this is what is explained in the first and second sections. In the third is seen the double benefit of such power to act (as a consequence of the affection that attracts and captures it), through which lofty things are laid low, and base things are

e vicissitudinal successo dicono che la fiamma s'inspessa in aere, vapore et acqua; e l'acqua s'assottiglia in vapore, aere e fiamma.

In sette articoli del quarto dialogo si contempla l'impeto e vigor de l'intelletto, che rapisce l'affetto seco, et il progresso de pensieri del furioso composto, e delle passioni de l'anima che si trova al governo di questa Republica cossì turbulenta. Là non è oscuro chi sia il cacciatore, l'ucellatore, la fiera, gli cagnuoli, gli pulcini, la tana, il nido, la rocca, la preda, il compimento de tante fatiche, la pace, riposo e bramato fine de sì travaglioso conflitto.

Nel quinto dialogo si descrive il stato del furioso in questo mentre, et è mostro l'ordine, raggione e condizion de studii e fortune. Nel primo articolo per quanto appartiene a perseguitar l'oggetto che si fa scarso di sé. Nel secondo quanto al continuo e non remittente concorso de gli affetti. Nel terzo quanto a gli alti e caldi, benché vani proponimenti. Nel quarto quanto al volontario volere. Nel quinto quanto a gli pronti e forti ripari e soccorsi. Ne gli seguenti si mostra variamente la condizion di sua fortuna, studio e stato, con la raggione e convenienza di quelli, per le antitesi, similitudini e comparazioni espresse in ciascuno di essi articoli.

## ARGOMENTO DE' CINQUE DIALOGI
### DELLA SECONDA PARTE

Nel primo dialogo della seconda parte s'adduce un seminario delle maniere e raggioni del stato dell'eroico furioso. Ove nel primo sonetto vien descritto il stato di quello sotto la ruota del tempo. Nel secondo viene ad iscusarsi dalla stima d'ignobile occupazione et indegna iattura della angustia e brevità del tempo. Nel terzo accusa l'impotenza de suoi studi gli quali quantumque all'interno sieno illustrati dall'eccellenza de l'oggetto, questo per l'incontro viene ad essere offoscato et annuvolato da quelli. Nel quarto è il compianto del sforzo senza profitto delle facultadi de l'anima mentre cerca risorgere con l'imparità de le potenze a quel stato che pretende e mira. Nel quinto vien rammentata la contrarietà e domestico conflitto che si trova in un suggetto, onde non possa intieramente appigliarsi ad un termine o fine. Nel sesto vien espresso l'affetto aspirante. Nel settimo vien messa in considerazione la mala corrispondenza che si trova tra colui ch'aspira, e quello a cui s'aspira. Nell'ottavo è messa

made lofty; thus, by the power of headlong impulse and alternating succession, they say that fire condenses into air, vapour and water, and water is rarefied into vapour, air, and flame.[23]

The seven sections of the fourth dialogue contemplate the drive and vigour of the intellect, which sweeps up affection along with it, and the progression of thought in the frenzied individual, and of the frenzies of the soul that finds itself in charge of this turbulent republic. There it will not be unclear who is meant by the hunter, the fowler, the wild creature, the dogs, the chicks, the den, the nest, the crag, the prey, or what the completion means of so many labours, the peace, repose, and longed-for end of such an arduous conflict.

The fifth dialogue describes the state of the frenzied hero in such circumstances, and shows the order, method, and condition of his exertions and fortune. The first section concerns the pursuit of an object that makes itself scarce; the second the continuous and unremitting rivalry of the affections; the third, the lofty and fiery proposals that lack all substance; the fourth, the willing will, the fifth, ready defences and stout reinforcements. Thereafter, in various ways, we see the condition of his fortune, exertion, and state, each with its reasons and opportunities, through the antitheses, similes, and comparisons expressed in each of these sections.

## CONTENT OF THE FIVE DIALOGUES OF THE SECOND PART

The first dialogue of the second part introduces a seminar on the kinds and causes of the frenzied hero's [frenzied] state. Here the first sonnet describes his state beneath the wheel of time. In the second he defends himself against a reputation for ignoble concerns and worthless waste of his brief, limited time. In the third he acknowledges the futility of his efforts, for no matter how brightly they may be lit inwardly by the excellence of their object, the latter, on the contrary, is dimmed and obscured by them. The fourth is a lament for the fruitless effort of the soul's faculties while it struggles to rise again, with its inadequate powers, to that state towards which it aims and aspires. The fifth calls to mind the opposition and internal conflict that is found within an individual, so that he cannot devote himself to a single end or purpose. The sixth expresses the feeling of aspiration. The seventh considers the lack of connection between the aspirant and the object of his aspiration. The eighth sets

avanti gli occhi la distrazzion dell'anima, conseguente della contrarietà
de cose esterne et interne tra loro, e de le cose interne in se stesse, e de
le cose esterne in se medesime. Nel nono è ispiegata l'etate et il tempo
del corso de la vita ordinarii all'atto de l'alta e profonda contemplazione: per quel che non vi conturba il flusso o reflusso della complessione
vegetante: ma l'anima si trova in condizione stazionaria e come quieta.
Nel decimo l'ordine e maniera in cui l'eroico amore tal'or ne assale, fere
e sveglia. Nell'undecimo la moltitudine delle specie et idee particolari
che mostrano l'eccellenza della marca dell'unico fonte di quelle, mediante le quali vien incitato l'affetto verso alto. Nel duodecimo s'esprime la
condizion del studio umano verso le divine imprese, perché molto si pre-
sume prima che vi s'entri, e nell'entrare istesso: ma quando poi s'ingolfa
e vassi più verso il profondo, viene ad essere smorzato il fervido spirito
di presunzione, vegnono relassati i nervi, dismessi gli ordegni, inviliti
gli pensieri, svaniti tutti dissegni, e riman l'animo confuso, vinto et exi-
nanito. Al qual proposito fu detto dal sapiente: *qui scrutator est maiestatis,
opprimetur a gloria*. Nell'ultimo è più manifestamente espresso quello che
nel duodecimo è mostrato in similitudine e figura.


Nel secondo dialogo è in un sonetto, et un discorso dialogale sopra di
quello, specificato il primo motivo che domò il forte, ramollò il duro, et
il rese sotto l'amoroso imperio di Cupidine superiore, con celebrar tal
vigilanza, studio, elezione e scopo.
Nel terzo dialogo in quattro proposte e quattro risposte del core a gli
occhi, e de gli occhi al core, è dechiarato l'essere e modo delle potenze
cognoscitive et appetitive. Là si manifesta qualmente la volontà è risve-
gliata, addirizzata, mossa e condotta dalla cognizione; e reciprocamente
la cognizione è suscitata, formata e ravvivata dalla volontade, procedendo or l'una da l'altra, or l'altra da l'una. Là si fa dubio se l'intelletto o
generalmente la potenza conoscitiva, o pur l'atto della cognizione, sia
maggior de la volontà o generalmente della potenza appetitiva, o pur
de l'affetto: se non si può amare più che intendere, e tutto quello ch'in
certo modo si desidera, in certo modo ancora si conosce, e per il roverso;
onde è consueto di chiamar l'appetito 'cognizione', perché veggiamo
che gli Peripatetici nella dottrina de quali siamo allievati e nodriti in gioventù, sin a l'appetito in potenza et atto naturale chiamano 'cognizione';
onde tutti effetti, fini e mezzi, principii, cause et elementi distinguено in
prima, media, et ultimamente noti secondo la natura: nella quale fanno
in conclusione concorrere l'appetito e la cognizione. Là si propone in-

before our eyes the distraction of the soul occasioned by the conflict between external and internal factors, as well as among the internal factors themselves, and among the external factors themselves. The ninth describes the age and season in the course of life that are proper to the act of lofty and profound contemplation: when the ebb and flow of our vital humours no longer creates a disturbance, and the soul instead finds itself in a stationary, and, as it were, quiet condition. The tenth describes the order and manner in which heroic love sometimes attacks, wounds, and arouses; the eleventh, the multitude of particular species and forms by which the emotions are incited upward, each revealing the excellence and the telltale sign of their one and only source. The twelfth expresses the condition of human striving towards divine undertakings, for it requires great presumption before entering upon them, and in the very act of entering – but afterward, when one has been engulfed and goes ever deeper, the fervent spirit of presumption is muted, one's muscles go slack, the artillery is dismissed, one's thoughts disheartened and plans dispelled, and the spirit remains confused, conquered, and emptied. On this topic, the Wise Man said: *Whoever inquires into majesty shall be crushed by glory.*[24] The last expresses more openly what had been shown in the twelfth though simile and imagery.

The second dialogue, in a sonnet and an explanatory discourse in dialogue, identifies the first cause that conquered the strong man, softened his toughness, and improved him under the amorous command of Cupid, by celebrating his vigilance, aspiration, choice, and purpose.

In the third dialogue four proposals of the heart to the eyes, and four replies of the eyes to the heart reveal the essence and mode[25] of the powers of knowledge and desire. It is made manifest how the will is revived, directed, moved and guided by the desire to know, and how knowledge is sparked, formed, and given life by the will, each proceeding from the other in turn. Then doubt arises whether the intellect – or more generally the power to know, or rather the act of knowing – is greater than the will, or the power of desire in general, or of emotion: whether it is possible to love more than to know, and whether everything that is in some way desired, is also in some way known, and vice versa. Hence it is customary to call the appetite "knowledge," because we see that the Peripatetics,[26] in whose teachings we were raised and nurtured in our youth,[27] apply the term "knowledge" to the appetite in both potentiality and actuality. Thus, they distinguish every effect, purpose, and means, principle, cause, and element as known, first, intermediately, or last according to nature, in which they make appetite and knowledge eventual-

finita la potenza della materia, et il soccorso dell'atto che non fa essere la potenza vana. Laonde cossì non è terminato l'atto della volontà circa il bene, come è infinito et interminabile l'atto della cognizione circa il vero: onde 'ente', 'vero' e 'buono' son presi per medesimo significante, circa medesima cosa significata.

Nel quarto dialogo son figurate et alcunamente ispiegate le nove raggioni della inabilità, improporzionalità e difetto dell'umano sguardo e potenza apprensiva de cose divine. Dove nel primo cieco, che è da natività, è notata la raggione ch'è per la natura che ne umilia et abbassa. Nel secondo cieco per il tossico della gelosia è notata quella ch'è per l'irascibile e concupiscibile che ne diverte e desvia. Nel terzo cieco per repentino apparimento d'intensa luce si mostra quella che procede dalla chiarezza de l'oggetto che ne abbaglia. Nel quarto, allievato e nodrito a lungo a l'aspetto del sole, quella che da troppo alta contemplazione de l'unità, che ne fura alla moltitudine. Nel quinto che sempre mai ha gli occhi colmi de spesse lacrime, è designata l'improporzionalità de mezzi tra la potenza et oggetto che ne impedisce. Nel sesto che per molto lacrimar have svanito l'umor organico visivo, è figurato il mancamento de la vera pastura intellettuale che ne indebolisce. Nel settimo cui gli occhi sono inceneriti da l'ardor del core, è notato l'ardente affetto che disperge, attenua e divora tal volta la potenza discretiva. Nell'ottavo, orbo per la ferita d'una punta di strale, quello che proviene dall'istesso atto dell'unione della specie de l'oggetto; la qual vince, altera e corrompe la potenza apprensiva, che è suppressa dal peso, e cade sotto l'impeto de la presenza di quello; onde non senza raggion talvolta la sua vista è figurata per l'aspetto di folgore penetrativo. Nel nono, che per esser mutolo non può ispiegar la causa della sua cecitade, vien significata la raggion de le raggioni, la quale è l'occolto giudicio divino che a gli uomini ha donato questo studio e pensiero d'investigare, de sorte che non possa mai gionger più alto che alla cognizione della sua cecità et ignoranza, e stimar più degno il silenzio ch'il parlare. Dal che non vien iscusata né favorita l'ordinaria ignoranza; perché è doppiamente cieco chi non vede la sua cecità: e questa è la differenza tra gli profettivamente studiosi, e gli ociosi insipienti: che questi son sepolti nel letargo della privazion del giudicio di suo non vedere, e quelli sono accorti, svegliati e prudenti giudici della sua cecità; e però son nell'inquisizione, e nelle porte de l'acquisizione della luce: delle quali son lungamente banditi gli altri.

ly concur. In the dialogue, the potentiality of matter is posited as infinite, as is the assistance of actuality, which does not render potentiality vain. Hence, the act of willing what is good cannot be limited, just as the act of knowing what is true is infinite and limitless. Therefore, being, truth, and goodness are taken as meaning, and referring to, the same thing.

In the fourth dialogue are symbolized, and to some extent explained, the nine reasons for the incapacity, disproportion, and deficiency of human thought and learning when directed towards divinity. The first blind man, who is blind from birth, presents the first reason: nature, which humiliates and degrades us. The second blind man, who is blind from the toxin of jealousy, presents the second reason: the anger and lust that deflect and distract us. The third blind man, blinded by a sudden flash of intense light, presents the third reason: the brightness of the object that dazzles. The fourth, long raised and nurtured in the light of the sun, presents the fourth reason: excessive contemplation of the One robs attention from the Many. The fifth, who always has his eyes overflowing with tears, symbolizes the disproportion that interferes between potentiality and its object, which thwarts us. The sixth, who has exhausted his physical supply of tears through constant weeping, symbolizes the lack of genuine intellectual nourishment, which enfeebles us. The seventh, whose eyes have been burnt away by the ardour of his heart, signifies the fiery emotion that disperses, attenuates, and sometimes devours our power of discernment. The eighth, blinded by the point of an arrow, suffers the blindness that comes from the very act of union with the sight of the desired object, which vanquishes, alters, and corrupts our power to perceive. This power is overwhelmed by the object's weight, and falls before the onslaught of its presence – hence, not without reason, it is symbolized in the form of a penetrating thunderbolt. The ninth, who cannot explain the cause of his blindness because he is also mute, signifies the reason of all reasons: the secret divine judgment that has granted humankind this zeal and urge for investigation, but in such a way that we can never reach higher than the realization of our own blindness and ignorance, and must therefore regard silence as more worthy than speech. Still, we should not excuse or promote ordinary ignorance, for whoever fails to see his own blindness is doubly blind. And there is this difference between the profitably zealous and the stupidly idle: the latter are buried in lethargy by the failure to understand their own sightlessness, whereas the former are informed, alert, and prudent judges of their own blindness, and therefore are engaged in the quest, and stand on the verge of attaining that light from which the others have been banished far away.

## ARGOMENTO ET ALLEGORIA
## DEL QUINTO DIALOGO

Nel quinto dialogo, perché vi sono introdotte due donne, alle quali (secondo la consuetudine del mio paese) non sta bene di commentare, argumentare, desciferare, saper molto, et esser dottoresse per usurparsi ufficio d'insegnare e donar instituzione, regola e dottrina a gli uomini; ma ben de divinar e profetar qualche volta che si trovano il spirito in corpo: però gli ha bastato de farsi solamente recitatrici della figura lasciando a qualche maschio ingegno il pensiero e negocio di chiarir la cosa significata. Al quale (per alleviar overamente tòrgli la fatica) fo intendere qualmente questi nove ciechi, come in forma d'ufficio e cause esterne, cossì con molte altre differenze suggettive correno con altra significazione, che gli nove del dialogo precedente: atteso che secondo la volgare imaginazione delle nove sfere, mostrano il numero, ordine e diversità de tutte le cose che sono subsistenti infra unità absoluta, nelle quali e sopra le quali tutte sono ordinate le proprie intelligenze che secondo certa similitudine analogale dependono dalla prima et unica. Queste da Cabalisti, da Caldei, da Maghi, da Platonici e da cristiani teologi son distinte in nove ordini per la perfezzion del numero che domina nell'università de le cose, et in certa maniera formaliza il tutto: e però con semplice raggione fanno che si significhe la divinità, e secondo la reflessione e quadratura in se stesso, il numero e la sustanza de tutte le cose dependenti. Tutti gli contemplatori più illustri, o sieno filosofi, o siano teologi, o parlino per raggione e proprio lume, o parlino per fede e lume superiore, intendeno in queste intelligenze il circolo di ascenso e descenso. Quindi dicono gli Platonici che per certa conversione accade che quelle che son sopra il fato si facciano sotto il fato del tempo e mutazione, e da qua montano altre al luogo di quelle. Medesima conversione è significata dal pitagorico poeta, dove dice:

> Has omnes ubi mille rotam volvere per annos
> Lethaeum ad fluvium deus evocat agmine magno:
> rursus ut incipiant in corpora velle reverti.

Questo (dicono alcuni) è significato dove è detto in revelazione che il drago starà avvinto nelle catene per mille anni, e passati quelli sarà disciolto. A cotal significazione voglion che mirino molti altri luoghi dove il millenario ora è espresso, ora è significato per uno anno, ora

## OUTLINE AND ALLEGORY
## OF THE FIFTH DIALOGUE[28]

In the fifth dialogue, two women are introduced, who (according to the custom of my country) cannot appropriately comment, argue, decipher, know much, or act as professors – as if to usurp a man's prerogative to teach, establish guidelines, rules, and teachings – but who may rather divine and prophesy whenever the spirit moves their bodies.[29] It has sufficed, therefore, to make them only the players of the allegory, leaving to some male intelligence the care and business of expounding its meaning. And to lighten this fellow's task, or rather to eliminate it, I make clear that these nine blind men – by their apparent function and outward circumstance, as well as by many other personal differences – have a different meaning than the nine from the preceding dialogue: for according to our common notion of the nine spheres, they represent the number, order, and diversity of all the things that exist within an absolute unity, and within and over them are ordered the individual intelligences that, by a certain analogy, depend upon the First and Sole Intelligence.[30] These are divided by the Cabalists, the Chaldeans, the Magi, the Platonists, and the Christian theologians into nine orders, according to the perfection of the number [3] that reigns over the material universe, and in a certain fashion gives form to the whole. Therefore, by a simple reckoning they make it signify divinity, which, being reflected and squared, constitutes the number and substance of all dependent things. All the most illustrious contemplators – whether philosophers or theologians, whether they speak by the light of their own reason or speak by faith and a higher light – perceive a cycle of ascent and descent among these intelligences. Hence, the Platonists say that by a certain rotation, those that have risen above fate must submit themselves to the fate of time and change, while others ascend to replace them. The same rotation is noted by the Pythagorean poet[31] when he says:

> All of the souls who revolved one thousand years on the wheel, now
> God summons, in a great troop, up to the river of Lethe,
> So they begin once again desiring return to their bodies.

This, some say, is what is meant in *Revelation*,[32] where it is said that the dragon will be bound in chains for a thousand years, after which it shall be released. They maintain that many other passages point to the same meaning, in which the millennium is either named explicitly, or signi-

per una etade, ora per un cubito, ora per una et un'altra maniera. Oltre che certo il millenario istesso non si prende secondo le revoluzioni definite da gli anni del sole, ma secondo le diverse raggioni delle diverse misure et ordini con li quali son dispensate diverse cose: perché cossì son differenti gli anni de gli astri, come le specie de particolari non son medesime.

Or quanto al fatto della revoluzione, è divolgato appresso gli cristiani teologi, che da ciascuno de' nove ordini de spiriti sieno trabalzate le moltitudini de legioni a queste basse et oscure regioni; e che per non esser quelle sedie vacanti, vuole la divina providenza che di queste anime che vivono in corpi umani siano assumpte a quella eminenza. Ma tra filosofi Plotino solo ho visto dire espressamente come tutti teologi grandi, che cotal revoluzione non è de tutti, né sempre: ma una volta. E tra teologi Origene solamente come tutti filosofi grandi, dopo gli Saduchini et altri molti riprovati, have ardito de dire che la revoluzione è vicissitudinale e sempiterna; e che tutto quel medesimo che ascende ha da ricalar a basso: come si vede in tutti gli elementi e cose che sono nella superficie, grembo e ventre de la natura. Et io per mia fede dico e confermo per convenientissimo, con gli teologi e color che versano su le leggi et instituzioni de popoli, quel senso loro: come non manco d'affirmare et accettar questo senso di quei che parlano secondo la raggion naturale tra' pochi, buoni e sapienti. L'opinion de quali degnamente è stata riprovata per esser divolgata a gli occhi della moltitudine; la quale se a gran pena può essere refrenata da vizii e spronata ad atti virtuosi per la fede de pene sempiterne, che sarrebe se la si persuadesse qualche più leggiera condizione in premiar gli eroici et umani gesti, e castigare gli delitti e sceleragini? Ma per venire alla conclusione di questo mio progresso: dico che da qua si prende la raggione e discorso della cecità e luce di questi nove, or vedenti, or ciechi, or illuminati; quali son rivali ora nell'ombre e vestigii della divina beltade, or sono al tutto orbi, ora nella più aperta luce pacificamente si godeno. All'or che sono nella prima condizione, son ridutti alla stanza di Circe, la qual significa la omniparente materia, et è detta figlia del sole, perché da quel padre de le forme ha l'eredità e possesso di tutte quelle le quali con l'aspersion de le acqui, cioè con l'atto della generazione, per forza d'incanto, cioè d'occolta armonica raggione, cangia il tutto, facendo dovenir ciechi quelli che vedeno: perché la generazione e corrozzione è causa d'oblio e cecità, come esplicano gli antichi con la figura de le anime che si bagnano et inebriano di Lete.

fied by a year, by an era, by a cubit, or in one way or another (aside from
the fact that the millennium itself is certainly not to be taken according
to the revolutions defined by solar years, but rather according to the different reckonings of the different measures and orders by which different things are portioned out: for the years of the stars are different, just
as their individual species are not the same).[33]

Now as for the fact of revolution, it is widely said among the Christian
theologians that from each one of nine orders of spirits, multitudes of
legions have plummeted downward towards our low and obscure regions,
and so that their thrones will not remain empty, Divine Providence wills
it that those souls who live in human bodies should be assumed up to
that height. But among philosophers I have only seen Plotinus declare
expressly, like all the great theologians, that such a revolution is not for
everyone, nor everlasting, but for one time only.[34] And among the theologians, only Origen,[35] like all the great philosophers, has dared to say, following the Sadducees and many other censured sects, that the revolution
is recurrent, reciprocal, and perpetual, and that everything that ascends
must drop back down, as can be seen with all the elements and things that
are found on the surface, in the lap, and in the womb of Nature. Now I,
by my faith, acknowledge and confirm the former sense of the matter
as eminently appropriate among theologians and those concerned with
the laws and institutions of people, just as I do not hesitate to affirm and
accept the latter sense among those who speak of natural reason among
the few, the good, and the wise. Their opinion was justly censured for
having been disclosed to the eyes of the masses. For if these are barely
restrained from vice and spurred to acts of virtue by faith and fear of
eternal punishment, what would happen if they were persuaded that heroic and humane deeds were rewarded, and crimes and misdeeds chas-
tised on more lenient terms? But, to come to the end of my digression,
I maintain that we may glean from it the meaning and exposition of the
blindness and light of these nine, who are by turns clairvoyant, blind, and
illumined. First, they are rivals among the shadows and vestiges of divine
beauty;[36] then they are completely blind, and at last, they bask peacefully
in the clear light. While they are in the first condition, they are led into
the chamber of Circe, who signifies all-generating matter, and is called
the daughter of the Sun,[37] for she has obtained the rights and possession
of every shape from the father of them all, and through them – with the
sprinkling of water, that is, with the act of generation, and by the force
of enchantment, that is, by occult harmonic principle – she transforms
everything, blinding those who see. (For generation and corruption are

Quindi dove gli ciechi si lamentano dicendo: «Figlia e madre di tenebre et orrore», è significata la conturbazion e contristazion de l'anima che ha perse l'ali, la quale se gli mitiga all'or che è messa in speranza di ricovrarle. Dove Circe dice «Prendete un altro mio vase fatale», è significato che seco portano il decreto e destino del suo cangiamento, il qual però è detto essergli porgiuto dalla medesima Circe; perché un contrario è originalmente nell'altro, quantumque non vi sia effettualmente: onde disse lei, che sua medesima mano non vale aprirlo, ma commetterlo.

Significa ancora che son due sorte d'acqui: inferiori sotto il firmamento che acciecano, e superiori sopra il firmamento che illuminano: quelle che sono significate da Pitagorici e Platonici nel descenso da un tropico et ascenso da un altro. Là dove dice «Per largo e per profondo peregrinate il mondo, cercate tutti gli numerosi regni», significa che non è progresso immediato da una forma contraria a l'altra, né regresso immediato da una forma a la medesima: però bisogna trascorrere, se non tutte le forme che sono nella ruota delle specie naturali, certamente molte e molte di quelle.

Là s'intendeno illuminati da la vista de l'oggetto, in cui concorre il ternario delle perfezzioni, che sono beltà, sapienza e verità, per l'aspersion de l'acqui che negli sacri libri son dette acqui de sapienza, fiumi d'acqua di vita eterna. Queste non si trovano nel continente del mondo, ma *penitus toto divisim ab orbe*, nel seno dell'Oceano, dell'Amfitrite, della divinità, dove è quel fiume che apparve revelato procedente dalla sedia divina, che have altro flusso che ordinario naturale. Ivi son le Ninfe, cioè le beate e divine intelligenze che assisteno et amministrano alla prima intelligenza, la quale è come la Diana tra le nimfe de gli deserti. Quella sola tra tutte l'altre è per la triplicata virtude, potente ad aprir ogni sigillo, a sciòrre ogni nodo, a discuoprir ogni secreto, e disserrar qualsivoglia cosa rinchiusa. Quella con la sua sola presenza e gemino splendore del bene e vero, di bontà e bellezza appaga le volontadi e gl'intelletti tutti: aspergendoli con l'acqui salutifere di ripurgazione.

Qua è conseguente il canto e suono, dove son nove intelligenze, nove muse, secondo l'ordine de nove sfere; dove prima si contempla l'armo-

the cause of forgetfulness and blindness, as the ancients explain through the image of the souls that bathe and grow drunk in the waters of Lethe.)

Therefore, the complaint of the blind men, saying "child and dam of dark and gloomy arts,"[38] signifies the disturbance and dejection of the soul that has lost its wings, which is alleviated as soon as she conceives the hope of recovering them. Circe's words, "Receive from me this strangely destined jar,"[39] mean that each of them has carried with him the decree and destiny of his own transformation (provided him by Circe herself, because every extreme exists from the outset within its opposite, although it may not be present effectually. Thus, she says that she cannot open [the jar], but only hand it over.)[40]

It also means that there are two kinds of waters: the lower ones beneath the firmament, which are blinding, and the upper ones above the firmament, which illuminate, the ones that are mentioned by the Pythagoreans and Platonists in the descent from one tropic and the ascent to another.[41] When she says, "wander all the earth / Deeply and widely, search / In all the many kingdoms you may find," it means that no form moves forward directly to become its opposite; neither does it regress immediately from its opposite condition. It may not need to pass through every single shape to be found on the wheel of natural species, but it will nevertheless pass through a great many of them.

At last the blind men will perceive themselves as illuminated by the sight of the object, in which the trinity of perfections coexists, which are beauty, wisdom, and truth,[42] through the sprinkling of the waters that in the Holy Books are called the waters of wisdom, the rivers of the water of eternal life.[43] These waters are not to be found on the surface of the world, but "within everything, yet divided from the globe," *penitus toto divisim ab orbe*,[44] in the bosom of the Ocean, of Queen Amphitrite, of divinity, where there appeared that river which revealed itself as proceeding from the divine throne, with a course unlike that of any ordinary natural river.[45] In it are Nymphs, who are the divine and blessed intelligences that assist and minister to that Prime Intelligence who resembles Diana among the nymphs of the desert.[46] She alone among all the others is able, by her threefold virtue, to open every seal, to unravel every knot, to disclose every secret and to unlock everything that is shut away. By her sole presence, and by her twin splendour of goodness and truth, she rewards all wills and intellects with goodness and beauty, sprinkling them with the healing waters of purification.[47]

There follows the song and music of the nine intelligences or nine Muses, according to the order of the nine spheres, in which we con-

nia di ciascuna, che è continuata con l'armonia de l'altra; perché il fine
et ultimo della superiore è principio e capo dell'inferiore, perché non
sia mezzo e vacuo tra l'una et altra: e l'ultimo de l'ultima per via de circolazione concorre con il principio della prima. Perché medesimo è più
chiaro e più occolto, principio e fine, altissima luce e profondissimo abisso, infinita potenza et infinito atto, secondo le raggioni e modi esplicati
da noi in altri luoghi.

Appresso si contempla l'armonia e consonanza de tutte le sfere, intelligenze, muse et instrumenti insieme; dove il cielo, il moto de' mondi,
l'opre della natura, il discorso de gl'intelletti, la contemplazion della
mente, il decreto della divina providenza, tutti d'accordo celebrano l'alta e magnifica vicissitudine che agguaglia l'acqui inferiori alle superiori,
cangia la notte col giorno, et il giorno con la notte, a fin che la divinità
sia in tutto, nel modo con cui tutto è capace di tutto, e l'infinita bontà
infinitamente si communiche secondo tutta la capacità de le cose.

Questi son que' discorsi, gli quali a nessuno son parsi più convene-
voli ad essere addirizzati e raccomandati che a voi, Signor eccellente: a
fin ch'io non vegna a fare, come penso aver fatto alcuna volta per poca
advertenza, e molti altri fanno quasi per ordinario, come colui che presenta la lira ad un sordo et il specchio ad un cieco. A voi dumque si pre-
sentano, perché l'Italiano raggioni con chi l'intende; gli versi sien sotto
la censura e protezzion d'un poeta; la filosofia si mostre ignuda ad un
sì terso ingegno come il vostro; le cose eroiche siano addirizzate ad un
eroico e generoso animo, di qual vi mostrate dotato; gli officii s'offrano
ad un suggetto sì grato, e gli ossequii ad un signor talmente degno qualmente vi siete manifestato per sempre. E nel mio particolare vi scorgo
quello che con maggior magnanimità m'avete prevenuto ne gli officii,
che alcuni altri con riconoscenza m'abbiano seguitato. Vale.

## AVERTIMENTO A' LETTORI

Amico lettore, m'occorre al fine da obviare al rigore d'alcuno a cui
piacesse che tre de' sonetti che si trovano nel primo dialogo della
seconda parte de' *Furori eroici*, siano in forma simili a gli altri, che sono
nel medesimo dialogo: voglio che vi piaccia d'aggiongere a tutti tre

template the harmony of each as contained in the harmony of the next (indeed, the final terminus of the highest is the initial starting point of the lowest), for there is no intermediary or vacuum between one and the other. And the last line of the last verse, by way of circulation, coincides with the beginning of the first line of the first, because the greatest brightness and the deepest darkness are one and the same, beginning and end, loftiest light and deepest abyss, infinite potentiality and infinite actuality, according to the principles and methods that we have explained in other dialogues.[48]

At last, we contemplate the harmony and consonance of all the spheres, intelligences, Muses, and instruments together, where heaven, the movement of worlds, the works of nature, the discourses of intellect, the mind's contemplation, the decrees of divine providence, together celebrate the lofty and magnificent alternation that equals the lower waters with the higher, exchanges night for day, and day for night, so that divinity is in all things, so that everything is capable of everything, and the infinite goodness conveys itself endlessly to all things in their full measure.

These are the remarks that seemed most fitly addressed to you, excellent Sir. I hope that I have not acted (as I have inadvertently done on occasion, and as many seem to do as a matter of course) by presenting a lyre to a deaf man and a mirror to a blind one. They are presented to you so that this Italian may converse with someone who understands him, that his verses may stand under the scrutiny and protection of a poet, that his philosophy may show herself naked to a mind as lucid as your own, that these heroic matters may address a heroic and noble spirit, with which you are clearly endowed, these favours may be offered to so gracious a subject, and these honours to a lord so dignified, as you have always shown yourself to be. As for myself, I acknowledge that you have come forward with greater generosity than others, in gratitude, have shown by following behind. Farewell.

## NOTE TO MY READERS

Dear Reader, to satisfy the demands of any who would prefer that three of the sonnets appearing in the first dialogue of the second part of the *Heroic Frenzies* have the same form as the others in that same dialogue, I'd like you please to add the final tercet to each of them [this has already

gli suoi tornelli. A quello che comincia *Quel ch'il mio cor*, giongete in fine:

> Onde di me si diche:
> costui or ch'hav'affissi gli occhi al sole,
> che fu rival d'Endimion si duole.

A quello che comincia *Se da gli eroi*, giongete in fine:

> Ciel, terr', orco s'opponi;
> s'ella mi splend'e accende et èmmi a lato,
> farammi illustre, potente e beato.

A quello che comincia *Avida di trovar*, giongete al fine:

> Lasso, que' giorni lieti
> troncommi l'efficacia d'un instante,
> che femmi a lungo infortunato amante.

## ISCUSAZION DEL NOLANO ALLE PIÙ VIRTUOSE E LEGGIADRE DAME

> De l'Inghilterra o vaghe Ninfe e belle,
> non voi ha nostro spirt' in schif', e sdegna;
> né per mettervi giù suo stil s'ingegna,
> se non convien che femine v'appelle.

> Né computar, né eccettuar da quelle,
> son certo che voi dive mi convegna:
> se l'influsso commun in voi non regna,
> e siete in terra quel ch'in ciel le stelle.

> De voi, o Dame, la beltà sovrana
> nostro rigor né morder può, né vuole,
> che non fa mira a specie sopr'umana.

> Lungi arsenico tal quindi s'invole,
> dove si scorge l'unica Diana,
> qual è tra voi quel che tra gli astri il sole.

been done in the translation]. To the one that begins *What my heart opens outward*, please add these lines at the end:

> Let it be said indeed:
> Now that he's set his sights upon the Sun
> He's sorry to have trailed Endymion.

To the one that begins *If by the gods, the heroes, and the nations*, add:

> Let Heav'n, Earth, Hell dissent;
> If she shine forth, inflame, and stand by me
> Then splendid, powerful and blest I'll be.

To the one that begins *The avid eagle*, add:

> Alas, my happy tales
> Were stopped by an instant's efficacy
> That made a luckless lover out of me.

## APOLOGY OF THE NOLAN TO THE MOST VIRTUOUS AND GENTLE LADIES

> Ye fair and lovely English nymphs, our soul
> Would spare you its revulsion, nor disdain you;
> Its wits are gathered not to lay you low,
> For "women" it could hardly bear to name you.
>
> To count you as distinct from them, I'm sure,
> Is, goddesses, my proper duty given.[49]
> For nothing common moves you, shining pure
> On Earth, as do the stars above in Heaven.
>
> Your sovereign beauty, Ladies, can't be blighted,
> Our rigor has been aimed another way;
> No superhuman species stands indicted.
>
> Such arsenic as this shall fall away
> When once that sole Diana has been sighted,
> The Sun among your stars, your nighttime's day.

L'ingegno, le parole
el mio (qualumque sia) vergar di carte
faranv' ossequios'il studio e l'arte.

My wit and what I say,
And all I write (whatever it may be)
To you, in art and ardor, bend their knee.

# PRIMA PARTE

# FIRST PART

## DIALOGO PRIMO

*Interlocutori*: TANSILLO, CICADA

TANSILLO: Gli furori dumque atti più ad esser qua primieramente locati e considerati, son questi che ti pono avanti secondo l'ordine a me parso più conveniente.

CICADA: Cominciate pur a leggerli.

TANSILLO:

〜

> 1  Muse che tante volte ributtai,
> importune correte a' miei dolori,
> per consolarmi sole ne' miei guai
> con tai versi, tai rime e tai furori,
> con quali ad altri vi mostraste mai,
> che de mirti si vantan et allori;
> 2  or sia appo voi mia aura, àncora e porto,
> se non mi lice altrov'ir a diporto.
>
> 3  O monte, o dive, o fonte
> ov'abito, converso e mi nodrisco;
> dove quieto imparo et imbellisco;
>
> alzo, avviv', orno, il cor, il spirto e fronte:
>   morte, cipressi, inferni
> cangiate in vita, in lauri, in astri eterni.

〜

1. È da credere che più volte e per più caggioni le ributtasse, tra le quali possono esser queste. Prima perché, come deve il sacerdote de le muse, non ha possut'esser ocioso: perché l'ocio non può trovarsi là dove si combatte contra gli ministri e servi de l'invidia, ignoranza e malignitade. Secondo, per non assistergli degni protectori e defensori che l'assicurassero, *iuxta* quello:

# FIRST DIALOGUE

*Interlocutors*: TANSILLO, CICADA

TANSILLO: The frenzies, then, most suitable to be placed and considered here at the outset are those that I set before you, in the order that has seemed to me most appropriate.

CICADA: Well, start reading them.[1]

TANSILLO:

✧

> Muses, whom I've so often pushed aside,
> Come running now to soothe me; you alone
> Console me in my pain's contrary tide
> With verses, rhymes, and frenzies never shown
> Before to men who boasted, in their pride,
> Of myrtles or of laurels as their crown.[2]
> Now be my breeze, my anchor, and my port,
> Unless there's someplace else I might resort.
>
> O mount, O goddesses, O fountainhead[3]
> Where I dwell, linger, find my sustenance,
> I rest, I learn, in beauty I advance,
>
> Arise, revive, crown heart, spirit and head –
> Cypresses, Hell, and death
> Become laurels, eternal stars, life's breath.

✧

It is likely that he[4] has rebuffed them many times and for many reasons, among which may be the following. First, he has had none of the free time proper to the priest of the Muses, because there is no free time to be found on the field of combat against the ministers and servants of Envy, Ignorance, and Malice. Second, for the lack of worthy protectors and defenders to stand by him, as in:

Non mancaranno, o Flacco, gli Maroni,
se penuria non è de Mecenati.

Appresso per trovarsi ubligato alla contemplazion, e studi de filosofia: li quali se non son più maturi, denno però come parenti de le Muse esser predecessori a quelle. Oltre perché traendolo da un canto la tragica Melpomene con più materia che vena, e la comica Talia con più vena che materia da l'altro, accadeva che l'una suffurandolo a l'altra, lui rimanesse in mezzo più tosto neutrale e sfacendato, che comunmente negocioso. Finalmente per l'autorità de censori che ritenendolo da cose più degne et alte, alle quali era naturalmente inchinato, cattivavano il suo ingegno: perché da libero sotto la virtù lo rendesser cattivo sott'una vilissima e stolta ipocrisia. Al fine nel maggior fervor de fastidi nelli quali incorse, è avvenuto che non avend'altronde da consolarsi, accettasse l'invito di costoro, che son dette inebriarlo de tai furori, versi e rime, con quali non si mostraro ad altri: perché in quest'opra più riluce d'invenzione che d'imitazione.

CICADA: Dite: che intende per quei che si vantano de mirti et allori?

TANSILLO: Si vantano e possono vantarsi de mirto quei che cantano d'amori: alli quali (se nobilmente si portano) tocca la corona di tal pianta consecrata a Venere, dalla quale riconoscono il furore. Possono vantarsi d'allori quei che degnamente cantano cose eroiche, instituendo gli animi eroici per la filosofia speculativa e morale, overamente celebrandoli e mettendoli per specchio exemplare a gli gesti politici e civili.

CICADA: Dumque son più specie de poeti e de corone?

TANSILLO: Non solamente quante son le muse, ma e di gran numero di vantaggio: perché quantumque sieno certi geni, non possono però esser determinate certe specie e modi d'ingegni umani.

CICADA: Son certi regolisti de poesia che a gran pena passano per poeta Omero, riponendo Vergilio, Ovidio, Marziale, Exiodo, Lucrezio et altri molti in numero de versificatori, examinandoli per le regole de la *Poetica* d'Aristotele.

O Flaccus, we shall never lack for Vergils,
If patrons like Maecenas don't run out.[5]

Or then again, because he finds himself committed to contemplation and philosophical studies that may be less venerable than the Muses, but, as related concerns, must come before them. Or else, because tragic Melpomene tugged him to one side with more substance than wit, and comic Thalia tugged to the other with more wit than substance, with the result that as each tried to steal him from the other, he lingered in the middle, more neutral and idle than engaged with either side. Or, finally, because of the authority of censors who reined him back from the more worthy and lofty matters to which his talent was naturally inclined, and confined his wit, so that they could transform him, a free man guided by virtue, into the captive of vile and stupid hypocrisy. In the end, in the chaos of all the disturbances he faced, it so happened that, lacking any other consolation, he accepted the invitation of those he describes as making him drunk on such *frenzies, verses, and rhymes* as they had never shown anyone else. For in this work, invention outshines imitation.

CICADA: Tell me, what does he mean by *those who boast of myrtle and laurel?*

TANSILLO: Those who sing of love can and do boast of myrtle; if they live nobly, they earn a crown of that plant, which is consecrated to Venus, whose inspiration they acknowledge. Those who worthily sing of heroic matters may boast of laurels, either by instructing heroic spirits in speculative and moral philosophy, or by celebrating them and holding them up as a mirror and example of political and civil achievement.

CICADA: And so there are different kinds of poets and crowns?

TANSILLO: Not only are there as many as there are Muses, but there are many more besides. For there may be definite genres of poetry, but some species[6] and modes of human genius[7] cannot be so defined.

CICADA: There are some poetic rule-makers who barely accept Homer as a poet, and relegate Vergil, Ovid, Martial, Hesiod, Lucretius, and many others to the rank of mere versifiers, grading them by the rules of Aristotle's *Poetics.*

TANSILLO: Sappi certo, fratel mio, che questi son verè bestie: perché non considerano quelle regole principalmente servir per pittura dell'omerica poesia o altra simile in particolare; e son per mostrar tal volta un poeta eroico tal qual fu Omero, e non per instituir altri che potrebbero essere, con altre vene, arti e furori, equali, simili e maggiori, de diversi geni.

CICADA: Sì che come Omero nel suo geno non fu poeta che pendesse da regole, ma è causa delle regole che serveno a coloro che son più atti ad imitare che ad inventare; e son state raccolte da colui che non era poeta di sorte alcuna, ma che seppe raccogliere le regole di quell'una sorte, cioè dell'omerica poesia, in serviggio di qualch'uno che volesse doventar non un altro poeta, ma un come Omero: non di propria musa, ma scimia de la musa altrui.

TANSILLO: Conchiudi bene, che la poesia non nasce da le regole, se non per leggerissimo accidente; ma le regole derivano da le poesie: e però tanti son geni e specie de vere regole, quanti son geni e specie de veri poeti.

CICADA: Or come dumque saranno conosciuti gli veramente poeti?

TANSILLO: Dal cantar de versi: con questo, che cantando o vegnano a delettare, o vegnano a giovare, o a giovare e delettare insieme.

CICADA: A chi dumque serveno le regole d'Aristotele?

TANSILLO: A chi non potesse come Omero, Exiodo, Orfeo et altri poetare senza le regole d'Aristotele; e che per non aver propria musa, vuolesse far l'amore con quella d'Omero.

CICADA: Dumque han torto certi pedantacci de tempi nostri, che excludeno dal numero de poeti alcuni, o perché non apportino favole e metafore conformi, o perché non hanno principii de libri e canti conformi a quei d'Omero e Vergilio, o perché non osservano la consuetudine di far l'invocazione, o perché intesseno una istoria o favola con l'altra, o perché non finiscono gli canti epilogando di quel ch'è detto e proponendo per quel ch'è da dire; e per mille altre maniere d'examine, per censure e regole in virtù di quel testo. Onde par che vogliano conchiudere che essi loro a un proposito (se gli venesse de

TANSILLO: Know for certain, my brother, that these people are real beasts, for they forget that such rules principally serve to present Homeric poetry or its like in detail, and sometimes to identify a poet as heroic in the way that Homer was, but not to guide other poets who might become, in other veins, by other arts, or frenzies, the equal, the like, or the superior of these various genres.

CICADA: So Homer, in his genre, was not a poet who depended on rules, but he is the source of rules useful for poets who are better at imitating than inventing; rules compiled, moreover, by someone who was no poet at all, who only knew how to codify rules for this one genre, that is, for Homeric poetry, for the benefit of anyone who wanted to become – not an original poet, but a Homeric one – not thanks to his own muse, but thanks to the ape of another's muse.

TANSILLO: You conclude well: that poetry does not arise from rules except by the merest coincidence; but rules derive from poetry, and hence there are as many genera and species of true rules as there are genera and species of true poets.

CICADA: How, then, will we recognize true poets?

TANSILLO: By singing their verses, and by this: whether, in the singing, they delight us, instruct us, or do both at once.

CICADA: Then who needs the rules of Aristotle?

TANSILLO: Anyone who (unlike Homer, Hesiod, Orpheus, and others) cannot compose poetry without Aristotle's rules, and anyone who, for lack of a personal Muse, would rather court Homer's.

CICADA: Then certain wretched pedants of our time are wrong to exclude some from the rank of poets, either because they neglect to bring in the appropriate tales and metaphors, or because their books or poems fail to begin in the way that Homer or Vergil do, or because they omit the customary invocation of the Muses, or because they combine one story or tale with another, or because they end their poems by summarizing what has been said and anticipating what remains to be said, and for a thousand other sorts of criteria for criticisms and rules that might apply to a text. Apparently, therefore, they mean to

fantasia) sarrebono gli veri poeti, et arrivarebbono là, dove questi si forzano: e poi in fatto non son altro che vermi che non san far cosa di buono, ma son nati solamente per rodere, insporcare e stercorar gli altrui studi e fatiche; e non possendosi render celebri per propria virtude et ingegno, cercano di mettersi avanti o a dritto o a torto per altrui vizio et errore.

TANSILLO: Or per tornar là d'onde l'affezzione n'ha fatto alquanto a lungo digredire: dico che sono e possono essere tante sorte de poeti, quante possono essere e sono maniere de sentimenti et invenzioni umane, alli quali son possibili d'adattarsi ghirlande non solo da tutti geni e specie de piante, ma et oltre d'altri geni e specie di materie. Però corone a' poeti non si fanno solamente de mirti e lauri: ma anco de pampino per versi fescennini, d'edera per baccanali, d'oliva per sacrifici e leggi; di pioppa, olmo e spighe per l'agricoltura; de cipresso per funerali: e d'altre innumerabili per altre tante occasioni. E se vi piacesse anco di quella materia che mostrò un galant'uomo quando disse:

> O fra Porro poeta da scazzate,
> ch'a Milano t'affibbi la ghirlanda
> di boldoni, busecche e cervellate.

CICADA: 2. Or dumque sicuramente costui per diverse vene che mostra in diversi propositi e sensi, potrà infrascarsi de rami de diverse piante, e potrà degnamente parlar con le «Muse»: perché sia appo loro sua «aura» con cui si conforte, «àncora» in cui si sustegna, e «porto» al qual si retire nel tempo de fatiche, exagitazioni e tempeste. 3. Onde dice: «O monte» Parnaso dove «abito», Muse con le quali «converso», «fonte» eliconio o altro dove mi «nodrisco»: monte che mi doni quieto alloggiamento, Muse che m'inspirate profonda dottrina, fonte che mi fai ripolito e terso; monte dove ascendendo «inalzo» il core; Muse con le quali versando «avvivo» il «spirito»; fonte sotto li cui arbori poggiando adorno la «fronte»; «cangiate» la mia «morte» in «vita», gli miei «cipressi» in «lauri», e gli miei «inferni» in cieli: cioè destinatemi immortale, fatemi poeta, rendetemi illustre, mentre canto di morte, cipressi et inferni.

conclude that they themselves (if the fancy took them) would be the real poets in the matter, and would reach the goal towards which the others are struggling; and yet in fact they are nothing but worms, incapable of doing anything worthwhile. Instead, they are born to gnaw, soil, and shit upon the study and labour of others; unable to achieve fame by their own qualities and talents, they try to push ahead by fair means or foul, through other people's deficiencies or mistakes.

TANSILLO: Now to return to the point from which our enthusiasm has made us digress at some length, I declare that there are, and can be, as many varieties of poets as there are and can be varieties of emotions and human creations, to which it is possible to attach garlands, not only of every genus and species of plant, but also of other genera and species of matter. Thus, poets' crowns are made not only of myrtle and laurel, but also of vine-leaves for Fescennine verses,[8] of ivy for bacchanals, of olive for sacrifices and laws, of poplar, elm, and tufts of wheat for eclogues, of cypress for elegies, and of countless others for many other occasions, and, if you please, also from that material a gentleman displayed when he declared:[9]

> O brother Leek, thou bard of boxer's blows,
> Who in Milan dost fasten on the wreath
> Of sausage, tripe, and fricassee of brain.

CICADA: Well, then, for all the different poetic veins he uses in different subjects and senses, this fellow may wreathe himself in the fronds of different plants, and may worthily speak of the *Muses*, because they own the *breeze* with which he consoles himself, the *anchor* by which he is sustained, and the *port* into which he withdraws in times of travail, turmoil and tempest. Hence, he says, O *Mount* Parnassus, where *I dwell; Muses*, with whom I *linger;* Heliconian *fountainhead*, and so forth, where *I find my sustenance; mountain* that gives me peaceful shelter, *Muses*, who inspire profound *learning* in me, *fountainhead* that makes me clean and clear, *mountain* whence I *arise*, lifting up my heart ascending; *Muses* in whose company I *revive* my spirit; *fountainhead* under whose trees I recline and *crown* my head, transform my *death* into *life's breath*, my *cypresses* into *laurels*, and my *hell* into *eternal stars*: that is, destine me to immortality, make me a poet, render me famous, while I sing of *cypresses, hell, and death*.

TANSILLO: Bene, perché a color che son favoriti dal cielo, gli più gran mali si converteno in beni tanto maggiori: perché le necessitadi parturiscono le fatiche e studi, e questi per il più de le volte la gloria d'immortal splendore.

CICADA: E la morte d'un secolo, fa vivo in tutti gli altri. Séguita.

TANSILLO: Dice appresso:

༄

1   In luogo e forma di Parnaso ho 'l core,
dove per scampo mio convien ch'io monte;
son mie muse i pensier ch'a tutte l'ore
mi fan presenti le bellezze conte;
onde sovente versan gli occhi fore
lacrime molte, ho l'Eliconio fonte:
per tai montagne, per tai ninfe et acqui,
com'ha piaciut' al ciel poeta nacqui.

2   Or non alcun de reggi,
non favorevol man d'imperatore,
non sommo sacerdot' e gran pastore,
mi dien tai grazie, onori e privileggi;
    ma di lauro m'infronde
mio cor, gli miei pensieri, e le mie onde.

༄

1. Qua dechiara: prima qual sia il suo monte, dicendo esser l'alto affetto del suo «core»; secondo, quai sieno le sue «muse», dicendo esser le «bellezze» e prorogative del suo oggetto; terzo, quai sieno gli fonti, e questi dice esser le «lacrime». In quel monte s'accende l'affetto; da quelle bellezze si concepe il furore; e da quelle lacrime il furioso affetto si dimostra. 2. Cossì se stima di non posser essere meno illustremente coronato per via del suo core, pensieri e lacrime, che altri per man de «regi», imperadori e papi.

CICADA: Dechiarami quel ch'intende per ciò che dice: «il core in forma di Parnaso».

TANSILLO: Well said. Those who are favored by Heaven find the greatest evils converted into good that is all the greater, for constraints give birth to work and study, and these most often give birth to the glory of immortal splendour.

CICADA: And to die in one century means to live in all the others. Go on.

TANSILLO: After that he says:

ॐ

> My heart's Parnassus in its form and place
> And there to flee the world I make my climb.
> I think about my Muses all the time
> Remembering their myriad forms of grace,
> Until abundant tears shed down my face –
> A very Heliconian spring is mine.
> Through such a mountain, such nymphs, such a source
> The heavens would make a poet of me perforce.
>
> Therefore no royal might,
> No Emperor's indulgent, generous hand
> No supreme pontiff, high priest of the land
> Can grant such grace, such honour, such a right
> As can a laurel prize
> Wreathed by my heart, my thoughts, my weeping eyes.

ॐ

Here, he first explains what his *mountain* is, saying that it is the lofty feeling of his heart; who his *Muses* are, saying that they are the beauties and attractions of his object; third, what the *springs* are, which he says are his *tears*. On that mountain his emotions catch fire, by those beauties the frenzy is conceived, and in those tears his frenzied emotion reveals itself. Thus, he reckons that he cannot be crowned any less brilliantly by his heart, worries, and tears, than others may be by the hands of *kings, emperors,* and *popes.*

CICADA: Explain what he means by the passage that says: *my heart's Parnassus in its form.*

TANSILLO: Perché cossì il cuor umano ha doi capi che vanno a terminarsi a una radice, e spiritualmente da uno affetto del core procede l'odio et amore di doi contrarii: come have sotto due teste una base il monte Parnaso.

CICADA: A l'altro.

TANSILLO: Dice:

ॐ

    1.  Chiama per suon di tromb' il capitano
    tutti gli suoi guerrier sott'un'insegna;
    dove s'avvien che per alcun in vano
    udir si faccia, perché pronto vegna,
    qual nemico l'uccide, o a qual insano
    gli dona bando dal suo camp' e 'l sdegna:
    cossì l'alm' i dissegni non accolti
    sott'un stendardo, o gli vuol morti, o tolti.

    2.  Un oggetto riguardo,
    chi la mente m'ingombr', è un sol viso,
    ad una beltà sola io resto affiso,

    chi sì m'ha punt' il cor è un sol dardo,
      per un sol fuoco m'ardo,
    e non conosco più ch'un paradiso.

ॐ

1. Questo «capitano» è la voluntade umana che siede in poppa de l'anima, con un picciol temone de la raggione governando gli affetti d'alcune potenze inferiori, contra l'onde de gli émpiti naturali. Egli con il «suono de la tromba», cioè della determinata elezzione, chiama «tutti gli guerrieri», cioè provoca tutte le potenze (le quali s'appellano guerriere per esserno in continua ripugnanza e contrasto) o pur gli effetti di quelle, che son gli contrarii pensieri; de quali altri verso l'una, altri verso l'altra parte inchinano: e cerca constituirgli tutti «sott'un'insegna» d'un determinato fine. Dove s'accade ch'alcun d'essi vegna chiamato in vano a farsi prontamente vedere ossequioso (massime quei

TANSILLO: Just as the human heart has two peaks that end in a single root, and spiritually the hatred and love of two extremes proceed from a single emotion of the heart, so Mount Parnassus has one base beneath two peaks.

CICADA: On to the next.

TANSILLO: He says:

ॐ

> By bugle blast the captain summons all
> His warriors beneath a single standard.
> Should any of them have chanced to miss the call
> To hurry, if attention may have wandered,
> He kills them like his foes, or lets them fall
> Like madmen, prey to exile, shamed and slandered.
> The soul, for any thoughts that can't be sent
> To serve her flag, seeks death, or banishment.
>
> One object I desire;
> A single face preoccupies my mind;
> A single beauty's all I hope to find.
>
> A single bolt has pierced my heart entire;
> I burn with but one fire,
> The paradise I know is but one kind.

ॐ

This *captain* is the human will, which sits at the helm of the soul, piloting the emotions of the lower powers by the little tiller of reason amid the waves of natural impulse. By the sound of the *bugle*, that is, of determined choice, he summons all his *warriors*, that is, he calls up all the powers (which are called warriors because they are in continual strife and conflict), or their effects, which are contrary thoughts that incline in this direction or that; and he tries to muster them under the *single standard* of one determined purpose. When it happens that some of these ignore the command to present themselves at his service (especially those that proceed from the natural powers, which show little if

che procedeno dalle potenze naturali quali o nullamente o poco ubediscono alla raggione), al meno forzandosi d'impedir gli loro atti, e
dannar quei che non possono essere impediti, viene a mostrarsi come
uccidesse quelli, e donasse bando a questi: procedendo contra gli altri
con la spada de l'ira, et altri con la sferza del sdegno.

2. Qua un «oggetto riguarda», a cui è volto con l'intenzione. Per
«un viso» con cui s'appaga «ingombra la mente». «In una sola beltade» si diletta e compiace; e dicesi «restarvi affiso», perché l'opra d'intelligenza non è operazion di moto, ma di quiete. E da là solamente
concepe quel «dardo» che l'uccide, cioè che gli constituisce l'ultimo
fine di perfezzione. «Arde per un sol fuoco», cioè dolcemente si consuma in uno amore.

CICADA: Perché l'amore è significato per il fuoco?

TANSILLO: Lascio molte altre caggioni, bastiti per ora questa: perché cossì la cosa amata l'amore converte ne l'amante, come il fuoco tra tutti
gli elementi attivissimo è potente a convertere tutti quell'altri semplici
e composti in se stesso.

CICADA: Or séguita.

TANSILLO: «Conosce un paradiso»: cioè un fine principale, perché paradiso comunmente significa il fine, il qual si distingue in quello ch'è
absoluto, in verità et essenza, e l'altro che è in similitudine, ombra e
participazione. Del primo modo non può essere più che uno, come
non è più che uno l'ultimo et il primo bene. Del secondo modo sono
infiniti.

&

Amor, sorte, l'oggetto e gelosia,
m'appaga, affanna, content' e sconsola;
il putto irrazional, la cieca e ria,
l'alta bellezza, la mia morte sola:
mi mostr' il paradis', il toglie via,
ogni ben mi presenta, me l'invola;
tanto ch'il cor, la mente, il spirto, l'alma,
ha gioia, ha noia, ha refrigerio, ha salma.

any obedience to reason), then, at the very least, in an effort to block their actions and to inflict damage on those that cannot be blocked, he acts as if he would kill the former and banish the latter, proceeding against the former with the sword of his wrath, and the others with the lash of his contempt.

Here he *desires one object* to which he has turned his attention. Through *one face* from which he derives fulfilment he *preoccupies his mind*. In a *single beauty* he delights and takes pleasure, and says that he fixes his sole *hope*, because the work of understanding is not an operation of motion, but of repose. And from that alone does he conceive the *bolt* that kills him, namely, that constitutes for him the ultimate extreme of perfection. He *burns with but one fire*, that is, he is sweetly consumed by one love.

CICADA: Why is love signified by fire?

TANSILLO: I will pass over many other reasons; for now let this one suffice for you: because love transforms the beloved into the lover, just as fire among all the elements has the power to transform all the others, whether simple or compound, into itself.

CICADA: Go on.

TANSILLO: *The paradise he knows is but one kind*, that is, [he knows] but one chief purpose, because paradise commonly signifies ultimate purpose, which can be subdivided into a paradise that exists absolutely in its truth and essence, and another that exists in likeness, shadow, and participation.[10] Of the first sort there cannot be more than one, just as there is no more than one prime and ultimate Goodness. Of the second sort there are infinite numbers.

ꜱ

> Love, destiny, the Object, Jealousy
> Fulfils me, frets me, sates me, makes me languish.
> The crazy cherub, blind delinquency,
> Exalted beauty, death in greatest anguish
> Discloses Paradise; removes it whole;
> Presents me every goodness; steals it back.
> So that my heart, my mind, spirit, and soul
> Rejoices, broods, restores itself, goes slack.

Chi mi torrà di guerra?
Chi mi farà fruir mio ben in pace?
Chi quel ch'annoia e quel che sì mi piace
..............................
    farà lungi disgionti,
per gradir le mie fiamme e gli miei fonti?

Mostra la caggion et origine onde si concepe il furore e nasce l'en-
tusiasmo, per solcar il campo de le muse, spargendo il seme de suoi
pensieri, aspirando a l'amorosa messe, scorgendo in sé il fervor de gli
affetti in vece del sole, e l'umor de gli occhi in luogo de le piogge. Mette quattro cose avanti: l'«amore», la «sorte», l'«oggetto», la «gelosia».
Dove l'amore non è un basso, ignobile et indegno motore, ma un eroico signor e duce de lui; la sorte non è altro che la disposizion fatale et
ordine d'accidenti alli quali è suggetto per il suo destino; l'oggetto è
la cosa amabile, et il correlativo de l'amante; la gelosia è chiaro che sia
un zelo de l'amante circa la cosa amata, il quale non bisogna donarlo a
intendere a chi ha gustato amore, et in vano ne forzaremo dechiararlo
ad altri. L'amore «appaga»: perché a chi ama, piace l'amare; e colui
che veramente ama non vorrebbe non amare. Onde non voglio lasciar
de referire quel che ne mostrai in questo mio sonetto:

Cara, suave et onorata piaga
del più bel dardo che mai scelse amore;
alto, leggiadro e precioso ardore,
che gir fai l'alma di sempr'arder vaga:

    qual forza d'erba e virtù d'arte maga
    ti torrà mai dal centro del mio core,
    se chi vi porge ogn'or fresco vigore
    quanto più mi tormenta, più m'appaga?

    Dolce mio duol, novo nel mond' e raro,
    quando del peso tuo girò mai scarco,
    s'il rimedio m'è noia, e 'l mal diletto?

    Occhi, del mio signor facelle et arco,

Who'll free me from this warfare?
Who'll leave me peace to revel in my pleasure?
Who'll make what I abhor and what I treasure
.............................[11]
Two widely distant things
To gratify my blazes and my springs?

He indicates the cause and origin by which his frenzy was conceived and his enthusiasm born, to plough the field of the Muses, sowing the seed of his thoughts, anticipating the lovesome harvest, discovering that inside him the fervour of his emotions takes the part of the Sun, and the moisture of his eyes takes the place of the rain. He sets forth four things: *Love, Destiny, the Object, and Jealousy*. Here Love is not a base, ignoble, and unworthy engine, but his heroic lord and leader. Destiny is nothing other than the fated arrangement and order of accidents to which he is subjected as his lot. The Object is the thing that is lovable and the counterpart of the lover. As for Jealousy, clearly it is the lover's zeal for the thing beloved, which need not be explained to anyone who has tasted love, and making the effort to explain it to anyone else is pointless. Love fulfils, because whoever loves enjoys loving, and he who truly loves would never wish not to love. Hence I would not like to leave out what I showed in this sonnet of mine:

Beloved, sweet and honored wound, of bolt
More beautiful than love e'er chose before,
Exalted, gracious, precious heat, you jolt
A soul that yearns to blaze forevermore.

What potent herb, what magic art or power
Could draw you from my heart's innermost core,
If what renews your vigour hour by hour
Torments me, and yet satisfies me more?

My sweet distress, new to the world and rare,
When shall I be unburdened of your woe,
If solace is my pain, and grief is rest?

Two eyes, my sovereign Cupid's torch and bow,

doppiate fiamme a l'alma e strali al petto,
poich'il languir m'è dolce e l'ardor caro.

La sorte «affanna» per non felici e non bramati successi, o perché faccia stimar il suggetto men degno de la fruizion de l'oggetto, e men proporzionato a la dignità di quello; o perché non faccia reciproca correlazione, o per altre caggioni et impedimenti che s'attraversano. L'oggetto «contenta» il suggetto, che non si pasce d'altro, altro non cerca, non s'occupa in altro, e per quello bandisce ogni altro pensiero. La gelosia «sconsola», perché quantumque sia figlia dell'amore da cui deriva, compagna di quello con cui va sempre insieme, segno del medesimo, perché quello s'intende per necessaria consequenza dove lei si dimostra (come sen può far esperienza nelle generazioni intiere, che per freddezza di regione, e tardezza d'ingegno, meno apprendono, poco amano, e niente hanno di gelosia), tutta volta con la sua figliolanza, compagnia e significazione vien a perturbar et attossicare tutto quel che si trova di bello e buono nell'amore. Là onde dissi in un altro mio sonetto:

O d'invidia et amor figlia sì ria,
che le gioie del padre volgi in pene,
caut'Argo al male, e cieca talpa al bene,
ministra di tormento, gelosia;

Tisifone infernal fetid'Arpia,
che l'altrui dolce rapi et avvelene,
austro crudel per cui languir conviene
il più bel fior de la speranza mia;

fiera da te medesma disamata,
augel di duol non d'altro mai presago,
pena, ch'entri nel cor per mille porte:

se si potesse a te chiuder l'entrata,
tant'il regno d'amor saria più vago,
quant'il mondo senz'odio e senza morte.

Giongi a quel ch'è detto che la gelosia non sol tal volta è la morte e ruina de l'amante, ma per le spesse volte uccide l'istesso amore, massime

> Doubly inflame my blazing soul and pierce my breast
> Longing is sweet to me, and ardour fair.[12]

Destiny *frets* at unfortunate and unwanted events, either because she makes the subject seem less worthy of attaining the Object and less equal to its dignity, or because she fails to bring about a complementary match, or for other reasons and impediments that block the way. The Object *satisfies* the subject, who feeds on nothing else, seeks nothing else, cares for nothing else, and for it banishes every other thought. Jealousy *dismays*, for although she is daughter of that Love from which she derives, and his constant companion, and the sign of his presence – because we can deduce that Love is present as a necessary consequence wherever Jealousy appears (as can be proved by experience among those entire populations, who, for the coldness of their regions and the slowness of their minds, learn little, love less, and feel jealousy not at all)[13] – nonetheless, through her descent from Love, her constant companionship, and her status as his signal, she succeeds in upsetting and poisoning all that is beautiful and good about Love. For which reason I said in another of my sonnets:

> Felonious child of Love and Rivalry
> Who turns her father's raptures to distress,
> Alert to evil, blind to happiness,
> The Minister of Torture, Jealousy.
>
> Hell's Fury, fetid Harpy, born to swindle
> And poison other people's sweet delight;
> Cruel as a southern gale, before whose blight
> My hope's most lovely flower is bound to dwindle.
>
> Brute hateful to yourself, fell bird of fate
> With omens of distress your only screed,
> You find a thousand ways to penetrate
>
> The heart; but were you driven from the gate,
> Love's kingdom would be lovelier indeed,
> Sweet as a world released from death and hate.

To what has been said let me add that Jealousy is not only on occasion the death and ruin of the lover, but that on many occasions she kills

quando parturisce il sdegno: percioché viene ad essere talmente dal suo figlio affetta, che spinge l'amore e mette in dispreggio l'oggetto, anzi non lo fa più essere oggetto.

CICADA: Dechiara ora l'altre particole che siegueno, cioè perché l'amore si dice putto irrazionale?

TANSILLO: Dirò tutto. «Putto irrazionale» si dice l'amore non perché egli per sé sia tale; ma per ciò che per il più fa tali suggetti, et è in sugetti tali: atteso che in qualumque è più intellettuale e speculativo, inalza più l'ingegno e più purifica l'intelletto facendolo svegliato, studioso e circonspetto, promovendolo ad un'animositate eroica et emulazion di virtudi e grandezza: per il desio di piacere e farsi degno della cosa amata. In altri poi (che son la massima parte) s'intende pazzo e stolto, perché le fa uscir de proprii sentimenti, e le precipita a far delle extravaganze, perché ritrova il spirito, anima e corpo mal complessionati, et inetti a considerar e distinguere quel che gli è decente da quel che le rende più sconci: facendoli suggetto di dispreggio, riso e vituperio.

CICADA: Dicono volgarmente e per proverbio, che l'amor fa dovenir gli vecchi pazzi, e gli giovani savii.

TANSILLO: Questo inconveniente non accade a tutti vecchi, né quel conveniente a tutti giovani; ma è vero de quelli ben complessionati, e de mal complessionati quest'altri. E con questo è certo, che chi è avezzo nella gioventù d'amar circonspettamente, amarà vecchio senza straviare. Ma il spasso e riso è di quelli alli quali nella matura etade l'amor mette l'alfabeto in mano.

CICADA: Ditemi adesso, perché cieca e ria se dice la sorte o fato?

TANSILLO: «Cieca» e «ria» si dice la sorte ancora, non per sé, perché è l'istesso ordine de numeri e misure de l'universo; ma per raggion de suggetti si dice et è cieca: perché le rende ciechi al suo riguardo, per esser ella incertissima. È detta similmente ria, perché nullo de mortali

Love itself, especially when she gives birth to disdain, for she comes to be so affected by her offspring that she forces Love and puts the Object to scorn; indeed, makes the Object no longer the Object.

CICADA: Now explain the next phrases; why, for instance, is Love called the *crazy cherub?*

TANSILLO: I'll tell you everything. Love is called a *crazy cherub* not because he is one himself, but because of what he usually does to his subjects, and with his subjects: with anyone who is more intellectual and speculative, he elevates the mind still higher and purifies the intellect still more, making that person alert, studious, and discreet, and urging him on towards a heroic enthusiasm and emulation of the virtues and greatness, all for the desire to please and make himself worthy of the thing he loves.[14] But among the others (who are the greatest number) Love is seen as crazy and foolish, because he makes them take leave of their own feelings and rushes them off to commit extravagant acts, because he exposes their disorderly spirit, soul and body, unsuited to considering what is appropriate for them and distinguishing it from what will increase their instability, and make them the subject of scorn, ridicule, and blame.

CICADA: They say in a popular proverb that Love makes old men crazy and young men wise.

TANSILLO: Not every old man encounters such misfortune, nor every young man such fortune; in fact [good fortune] happens only to those [young men] who are well balanced, and [misfortune] to ill balanced [elders]. And hence it is certain that whoever learns in his youth to love discreetly, will also love as an old man without losing his way. The mockery and ridicule are for those to whom, at a mature age, Love begins teaching the ABCs.

CICADA: Now tell me why Destiny or Fate is called *blind delinquency.*

TANSILLO: Again, Fortune is called *blind delinquency* not on her own account, as she is the very order governing number and measure in the universe.[15] Rather, she is called blind herself on account of her subjects, because she makes them blind in her regard, being herself

è che in qualche maniera lamentandosi e querelandosi di lei, non la incolpe. Onde disse il pugliese poeta:

> Che vuol dir, Mecenate, che nessuno
> al mondo appar contento de la sorte,
> che gli ha porgiuta la raggion o cielo?

Cossì chiama l'oggetto «alta bellezza», perché a lui è unico e più eminente, et efficace per tirarlo a sé; e però lo stima più degno, più nobile, e però sel sente predominante e superiore: come lui gli vien fatto suddito e cattivo. «La mia morte sola» dice de la gelosia, perché come l'amore non ha più stretta compagna che costei, cossì anco non ha senso di maggior nemica: come nessuna cosa è più nemica al ferro che la ruggine, che nasce da lui medesimo.

CICADA: Or poi ch'hai cominciato a far cossì, séguita a mostrar parte per parte quel che resta.

TANSILLO: Cossì farò. Dice appresso de l'amore: «mi mostra il paradiso»; onde fa veder che l'amore non è cieco in sé, e per sé non rende ciechi alcuni amanti, ma per l'ignobili disposizioni del suggetto: qualmente avviene che gli ucelli notturni dovegnon ciechi per la presenza del sole. Quanto a sé dumque l'amore illustra, chiarisce, apre l'intelletto e fa penetrar il tutto e suscita miracolosi effetti.

CICADA: Molto mi par che questo il Nolano lo dimostre in un altro suo sonetto:

> Amor per cui tant'alto il ver discerno,
> ch'apre le porte di diamante nere,
> per gli occhi entra il mio nume, e per vedere
> nasce, vive, si nutre, ha regno eterno;
>
> fa scorger quant' ha 'l ciel, terr', et inferno;
> fa presenti d'absenti effiggie vere,
> repiglia forze, e col trar dritto, fere;
> e impiaga sempr'il cor, scuopre l'interno.

so very uncertain. Likewise, she is called *delinquency* because there is nothing among mortals for which they will not blame her in the laments and complaints they address to her. For which reason the Apulian poet said:

> Maecenas, why is no one in the world
> Apparently contented with the Fate
> That Reason or Heaven have handed them to date?[16]

Therefore he calls the Object *exalted beauty*, because for him it is unique, and more lofty and effective at pulling him towards itself, and hence he regards it as more worthy and more noble, and hence he perceives it as dominant and superior, just as he himself is made subordinate and base. He says *my* own *sole undoing* of Jealousy, because just as Love has no more intimate companion than she, so, too, he senses that there is no greater enemy, just as there is no greater enemy to iron than rust, which derives from iron itself.

CICADA: Now that you have begun in this fashion, continue to explain the rest, phrase by phrase.

TANSILLO: So I shall. He next says of Love: *discloses Paradise*, by which means he shows that Love is not blind in itself, and does not blind any lover by itself, but rather by the subject's own ignoble disposition; just as it happens that night birds are blinded by the sun. With regard to itself, then, Love illuminates, clarifies, and opens the intellect, penetrates everything, and achieves miraculous effects.

CICADA: I am quite convinced that the Nolan makes the same point in another sonnet of his:

> Love, by whom I discern the truth sublime,
> Who opens the black diamond-studded gates;
> My little god through my eyes penetrates:
> Of sight is born, lives, feeds, reigns for all time.
>
> He shows the span of heaven, earth, and Hell,
> Makes images within my mind grow real.[17]
> He gathers strength and aiming straight, strikes well,
> Pierces the heart, and lays bare what I feel.

> O dumque volgo vile, al vero attendi,
> porgi l'orecchio al mio dir non fallace,
> apri, apri, se puoi, gli occhi, insano e bieco:
>
> fanciullo il credi perché poco intendi,
> perché ratto ti cangi ei par fugace,
> per esser orbo tu lo chiami cieco.

Mostra dumque il paradiso amore, per far intendere, capire et effettuar cose altissime; o perché fa grandi almeno in apparenza le cose amate. «Il toglie via», dice de la sorte: perché questa sovente, a mal grado de l'amante, non concede quel tanto che l'amor dimostra, e quel che vede e brama, gli è lontano et adversario. «Ogni ben mi presenta», dice de l'oggetto: perché questo che vien dimostrato da l'indice de l'amore, gli par la cosa unica, principale, et il tutto. «Me l'invola», dice della gelosia, non già per non farlo presente togliendolo d'avanti gli occhi; ma in far ch'il bene non sia bene, ma un angoscioso male; il dolce non sia dolce, ma un angoscioso languire. «Tanto ch'il cor», cioè la volontà, «ha gioia» nel suo volere per forza d'amore, qualumque sia il successo. «La mente», cioè la parte intellettuale, «ha noia», per l'apprension de la sorte, qual non aggradisce l'amante. «Il spirito», cioè l'affetto naturale, «ha refrigerio», per esser rapito da quell'oggetto che dà gioia al core, e potrebbe aggradir la mente. «L'alma», cioè la sustanza passibile e sensitiva, «ha salma», cioè si trova oppressa dal grave peso de la gelosia che la tormenta.

Appresso la considerazion del stato suo, soggionge il lacrimoso lamento, e dice: «Chi mi torrà di guerra», e metterammi in pace; o chi disunirà quel che m'annoia e danna, da quel che sì mi piace et apremi le porte del cielo, perché gradite sieno le fervide fiamme del mio core, e fortunati i fonti de gli occhi miei? Appresso continuando il suo proposito soggionge:

৵

> Premi (oimè) gli altri, o mia nemica sorte;
> vatten via, gelosia, dal mondo fore:
> potran ben soli con sua diva corte
> far tutto nobil faccia e vago amore.

O therefore, lowly mob, behold the truth;
And lend your ears to my unerring fable.
Open your eyes, dour madman, if you're able –

In ignorance, you take him for a youth;
He seems erratic to your fickle mind;
Your lack of vision makes you call him blind.

Therefore, Love *discloses Paradise* to make it possible to intend, understand, and effect the loftiest matters, or because it makes the things that are beloved great, at least in appearance.[18] He says that Destiny *removes it whole,* because fate often refuses to concede what love discloses, in spite of the lover, so that what he sees and longs for becomes distant and hostile. He says of the Object that it *presents me every goodness,* because what has been pointed out to him by Love's finger seems to him the only and principal thing, the all in all. He says that Jealousy *steals it back,* not making goodness disappear by removing it from view, but rather by making it so that goodness is no longer good, but an anguished sickness, and sweetness no longer sweet, but an anguished languishing. So that the *heart,* that is, the will, *rejoices* in its desire by virtue of love, no matter what the outcome. The *mind,* that is, the intellectual part, *broods,* because of its apprehension about its fate should the lover not find favour. The *spirit,* that is, natural emotion, *restores itself,* because it has been captivated by that object that grants joy to the heart, and might possibly please the mind. The *soul,* that is the receptive and sensitive substance, *goes slack,* that is, it finds itself oppressed by the heavy burden of the jealousy that torments it.

After considering his state, he adds the tearful lament and says, "*Who'll free me from this warfare?*" and set me at peace, or who will separate *what I abhor* and injures me from *what I treasure,* and fling open the gates of heaven for me, so that the fervid flames of my heart are gratifying to me, and my eye's wellsprings are the source of good fortune? Next, continuing his topic, he adds:

Oppress another, O my hostile Fate
And Jealousy, out of this world begone;
A noble face, joined in celestial state
By pretty Love, can do all things alone.

Lui mi tolga de vita, lei de morte;
lei me l'impenne, lui brugge il mio core;
lui me l'ancide, lei ravvive l'alma;
lei mio sustegno, lui mia grieve salma.

Ma che dich'io d'amore?
se lui e lei son un suggetto o forma,
se con medesm' imperio et una norma
fann' un vestigio al centro del mio core?
Non son doi dumque: è una
che fa gioconda e triste mia fortuna.

∽

Quattro principii et estremi de due contrarietadi vuol ridurre a doi
principii et una contrarietade. Dice dumque: «Premi (oimè) gli altri»,
cioè basti a te, o mia sorte, d'avermi sin a tanto oppresso, e (perché
non puoi essere senza il tuo essercizio) volta altrove il tuo sdegno. E
«vatten via» fuori del mondo, tu gelosia: perché uno di que' doi altri
che rimagnono potrà supplire alle vostre vicende et offici; se pur tu,
mia sorte, non sei altro ch'il mio amore, e tu gelosia, non sei estranea
dalla sustanza del medesimo. Reste dumque lui per privarmi de vita,
per bruggiarmi, per donarmi la morte, e per salma de le mie ossa:
con questo che lei mi tolga di morte, mi impenne, mi avvive e mi
sustente.

Appresso, doi principii et una contrarietade riduce ad un principio
et una efficacia, dicendo: «Ma che dich'io d'amore?». Se questa faccia, questo oggetto è l'imperio suo, e non par altro che l'imperio de
l'amore; la norma de l'amore è la sua medesima norma; l'impression
d'amore ch'appare nella sustanza del cor mio, non è certo altra impression che la sua: perché dumque dopo aver detto «nobil faccia»,
replico dicendo «vago amore»?

## DIALOGO SECONDO

TANSILLO: Or qua comincia il furioso a mostrar gli affetti suoi e discuoprir le piaghe che sono per segno nel corpo, et in sustanza o in essenza
nell'anima, e dice cossì:

Let him free me from life, and she from death;
She sets in flight the heart he'd immolate.
He kills my soul; she gives it vital breath;
She's my support; and he's a deadly weight.

Of Love, can I say more
Than this: If he and she share but one form,
And both by equal right and single norm
Have pressed their imprint deep in my heart's core,
They're one, not two; it's she
Alone who cheers and clouds my destiny.

༖

He wants to reduce the four principles and four extreme terms of two contraries to two principles and a single contrary. Therefore he says *Oppress another*, that is, let it be enough, *O! my Fate* to have oppressed me as much as you have already, and turn your disdain elsewhere (as you cannot exist without doing what you do). *Out of this world begone*, you, *Jealousy*, because one of those two who remain can take your place and perform your duties: for you, my Fate, are nothing other than my Love, and you, Jealousy, are no stranger to his same substance. Therefore let him remain, to *free me from life, immolate* me, *kill my soul*, act as the *deadly weight* on my bones, and together with him let her deliver me *from death*, give me wings and *set me in flight*, revive me with *vital breath* and *support* me.

Then, he reduces these two principles and single contrary to one principle and one value, saying: *Of Love can I say more than this?* If this face, this Object, is his domain, and it seems to be nothing other than Love's domain, then the *norm*, the measure, of Love is the same norm as hers, the *imprint* of love that appears on the substance of my *heart* is certainly no other imprint than hers: why, therefore, after having said *noble face*, do I reply by saying *pretty Love?*

## SECOND DIALOGUE

TANSILLO: Now here, the frenzied hero begins to show his emotions and to reveal the wounds that occur as a sign on his body and occur in substance or essence in his soul, and he says:

※

Io che porto d'amor l'alto vessillo,
gelate ho spene, e gli desir cuocenti:
a un tempo triemo, agghiaccio, ardo e sfavillo,
son muto, e colmo il ciel de strida ardenti;

dal cor scintill', e da gli occhi acqua stillo;
e vivo e muoio, e fo ris' e lamenti:
son vive l'acqui, e l'incendio non more,
ch'a gli occhi ho Teti, et ho Vulcan al core,

Altr'amo, odio me stesso:
ma s'io m'impiumo, altri si cangia in sasso;
poggi'altr'al ciel, s'io mi ripogno al basso;
sempr'altri fugge, s'io seguir non cesso;
s'io chiamo, non risponde:
e quant'io cerco più, più mi s'asconde.

※

A proposito di questo voglio seguitar quel che poco avanti ti dicevo: che non bisogna affatigarsi per provare quel che tanto manifestamente si vede, cioè che nessuna cosa è pura e schetta (onde diceano alcuni, nessuna cosa composta esser vero ente: come l'oro composto non è vero oro, il vino composto non è puro vero e mero vino); appresso, tutte le cose constano de contrarii: da onde avviene che gli successi de li nostri affetti per la composizione ch'è nelle cose, non hanno mai delettazion alcuna senza qualch'amaro; anzi dico, e noto di più, che se non fusse l'amaro nelle cose, non sarrebe la delettazione, atteso che la fatica fa che troviamo delettazione nel riposo; la separazione è causa che troviamo piacere nella congiunzione: e generalmente essaminando, si troverà sempre che un contrario è caggione che l'altro contrario sia bramato e piaccia.

CICADA: Non è dumque delettazione senza contrarietà?

TANSILLO: Certo non, come senza contrarietà non è dolore, qualmente manifesta quel pitagorico poeta quando dice:

꒦꒷

As carrier of Love's exalted flag,
I suffer frozen hopes and hot desire
I shiver, freeze, flare up, dissolve in slag
I'm mute, my cries to heaven are all afire.

My heart sheds sparks; water, my streaming eyes
I live and die; I cackle and I smart.
The waters live, the inferno never dies:
My eyes have Thetis; Vulcan's in my heart.[19]

I love someone and hate myself – however
He'll turn to stone if I take wing and soar;
If he's near Heaven, I'll soon touch the floor.
This other flees, and I pursue forever,
Replies not, though I call incessantly.
The more I search, the more he hides from me.

꒦꒷

On this topic, I want to pursue what I just told you, that there is no
need to tire ourselves in proving what can be seen so patently, namely,
that nothing is pure and simple. (Hence, some used to say that no
composite thing can be a real essence, just as alloyed gold is not real
gold, and blended wine is not pure, true, and neat wine.) Moreover,
all things consist of opposites, and thus the events that befall our emotions, because of the compounding that exists in things,[20] cannot provide any enjoyment without some complement of bitterness. Indeed,
I further declare and note that if there were no bitterness in things,
there would be no enjoyment, because our exertions make us take
pleasure in resting, separation is the reason that we enjoy connection,
and, to examine matters in general, it will always be the case that one
extreme provides the reason that its opposite becomes the object of
longing and the source of pleasure.

CICADA: So there is no enjoyment without opposition?

TANSILLO: Certainly not, just as there is no pain without opposition, as
the Pythagorean poet shows when he says:[21]

Hinc metuunt cupiuntque, dolent gaudentque, nec auras
respiciunt, clausae tenebris et carcere caeco.

Ecco dumque quel che caggiona la composizion de le cose. Quindi
aviene che nessuno s'appaga del stato suo, eccetto qualch'insensato
e stolto, e tanto più quanto più si ritrova nel maggior grado del fosco
intervallo de la sua pazzia: all'ora ha poca o nulla apprension del suo
male, gode l'esser presente senza temer del futuro; gioisce di quel
ch'è e per quello in che si trova, e non ha rimorso o cura di quel ch'è
o può essere, et in fine non ha senso della contrarietade la quale è
figurata per l'arbore della scienza del bene e del male.

CICADA: Da qua si vede che l'ignoranza è madre della felicità e beatitudine sensuale, e questa medesima è l'orto del paradiso de gli animali;
come si fa chiaro nelli dialogi de la *Cabala del cavallo Pegaseo*, e per
quel che dice il sapiente Salomone: «chi aumenta sapienza, aumenta
dolore».

TANSILLO: Da qua avviene che l'amore eroico è un tormento, perché
non gode del presente come il brutale amore; ma e del futuro e de
l'absente; e del contrario sente l'ambizione, emulazione, suspetto e
timore. Indi dicendo una sera dopo cena un certo de nostri vicini:
«Giamai fui tanto allegro quanto sono adesso», gli rispose Gioan Bruno padre del Nolano: «Mai fuste più pazzo che adesso».

CICADA: Volete dumque che colui che è triste sia savio, e quell'altro ch'è
più triste sia più savio?

TANSILLO: Non, anzi intendo in questi essere un'altra specie di pazzia,
et oltre peggiore.

CICADA: Chi dumque sarà savio, se pazzo è colui ch'è contento, e pazzo
è colui ch'è triste?

TANSILLO: Quel che non è contento né triste.

CICADA: Chi? quel che dorme? quel ch'è privo di sentimento? quel ch'è
morto?

Thus do they fear and desire, lament and rejoice without seeing
Daylight, enclosed as they are in the dark of their windowless prison.

This, then, is what causes things to be mixtures. Thus no one is satisfied with his state, except for some senseless fool, who will be all the more satisfied the more he becomes mired in the murky depths of his insanity; then he has little or no awareness of his illness, enjoys being in the present without fearing the future, delights in what he is and in what he finds, and lacks all remorse or worry about what is or could be; in short, he lacks all awareness of the opposition that is symbolized by the tree of the knowledge of good and evil.

CICADA: Plainly, then, ignorance is the mother of happiness and sensual bliss, and this is precisely what the garden of paradise is for animals, as is made clear in the dialogues of the *Kabbalah of the Horse Pegasus*,[22] and in the saying of wise Solomon: *He that increaseth knowledge increaseth sorrow.*[23]

TANSILLO: It follows from this that heroic love is torment, because, unlike animal love, it takes no joy in the present, but rather in the future and in what is absent; and it feels the ambition, envy, suspicion, and fear of its opposite. Thus, when a certain neighbour of ours said one evening after dinner, "I was never as merry as I am tonight," Giovanni Bruno, the father of the Nolan, replied, "Then you were never as crazy as you are at this moment."

CICADA: Then you mean to say that a gloomy man is a wise man, and a gloomier man is wiser still?

TANSILLO: No, in fact I think he has a different kind of craziness, a worse one.

CICADA: Who, then, would be wise, if the happy man is crazy and the gloomy one is crazy as well?

TANSILLO: The one who is neither happy nor sad.

CICADA: Who is that? The one who's asleep? The one who's unconscious? The one who's dead?

TANSILLO: No: ma quel ch'è vivo, vegghia et intende; il quale considerando il male et il bene, stimando l'uno e l'altro come cosa variabile e consistente in moto, mutazione e vicissitudine (di sorte ch'il fine d'un contrario è principio de l'altro, e l'estremo de l'uno è cominciamento de l'altro), non si dismette, né si gonfia di spirito, vien continente nell'inclinazioni e temperato nelle voluptadi: stante ch'a lui il piacere non è piacere, per aver come presente il suo fine. Parimente la pena non gli è pena, perché con la forza della considerazione ha presente il termine di quella. Cossì il sapiente ha tutte le cose mutabili come cose che non sono, et afferma quelle non esser altro che vanità et un niente: perché il tempo a l'eternità ha proporzione come il punto a la linea.

CICADA: Sì che mai possiamo tener proposito d'esser contenti o mal contenti, senza tener proposito de la nostra pazzia, la qual espressamente confessiamo; là onde nessun che ne raggiona, e per consequenza nessun che n'è participe, sarà savio: et infine tutti gli omini saran pazzi.

TANSILLO: Non tendo ad inferir questo, perché dirò massime savio colui che potesse veramente dire talvolta il contrario di quel che quell'altro: «Giamai fui men allegro che adesso» over «Giamai fui men triste che ora».

CICADA: Come non fai due contrarie qualitadi dove son doi affetti contrarii? perché, dico, intendi come due virtudi, e non come un vizio et una virtude, l'esser minimamente allegro, e l'esser minimamente triste?

TANSILLO: Perché ambi doi li contrarii in eccesso (cioè per quanto vanno a dar su quel più) son vizii, perché passano la linea; e gli medesimi in quanto vanno a dar sul meno, vegnono ad esser virtude, perché si contegnono e rinchiudono intra gli termini.

CICADA: Come l'esser men contento e l'esser men triste non son una virtù et uno vizio, ma son due virtudi?

TANSILLO: Anzi dico che son una e medesima virtude: perché il vizio è là dove è la contrarietade; la contrarietade è massime là dove è l'estremo; la contrarietà maggiore è la più vicina all'estremo; la minima o nulla è nel mezzo, dove gli contrarii convegnono e son uno et indifferente:

TANSILLO: No, rather it's the one who is alive, who sees and understands, and who, taking good and evil into consideration, regards each of them as variable, consisting of motion, change, and alternation (so that the end of one opposite is the beginning of the other, and the endpoint of one is the other's inception). Therefore, he neither despairs nor puffs up his spirit, and becomes restrained in his inclinations and temperate in his pleasures: for him pleasure is no pleasure, because its Object is in the present. Likewise, pain for him is no pain, because by force of reasoning he is mindful of its end. Thus, the wise man regards all changeable things as non-existent, and affirms that they are nothing but vanity, and nothingness, because time has the same ratio to eternity that a point has to a line.

CICADA: Hence, we can never regard ourselves as contented or discontented without also taking account of our insanity, openly confessing it. In that case, no thinking person, and consequently no person of any awareness, will be wise, and in the end all men will be crazy.

TANSILLO: I'm not inclined to infer anything of the sort, because I maintain that the wisest man can at times truly declare the opposite of the statement "I was never less happy than now": namely, "I was never less unhappy than now."

CICADA: How can you not see two opposing qualities where there are two conflicting emotions? Why, I ask you, do you regard as two virtues, rather than a vice and a virtue, being minimally happy and being minimally unhappy?

TANSILLO: Because both opposites in their excess – that is, insofar as they reach the point of excess – are vices, because they cross the line, and the same opposites – insofar as they begin to decrease – turn into virtues, because they are contained and enclosed within their boundaries.

CICADA: So that being less content and being less unhappy are not a virtue and a vice, but rather two virtues?

TANSILLO: Indeed, I would say that they are one and the same virtue, because vice exists where there is opposition, and opposition occurs most intensely where there are extremes; the greatest opposition is the closest to the extreme, the least, or non-existent opposition occurs in

come tra il freddissimo e caldissimo è il più caldo et il più freddo; e nel mezzo puntuale è quello che puoi dire o caldo e freddo, o né caldo né freddo, senza contrarietade. In cotal modo chi è minimamente contento e minimamente triste, è nel grado della indifferenza, si trova nella casa della temperanza, e là dove consiste la virtude e condizion d'un animo forte, che non vien piegato da l'Austro né da l'Aquilone. – Ecco dumque (per venir al proposito) come questo furor eroico, che si chiarisce nella presente parte, è differente da gli altri furori più bassi, non come virtù dal vizio: ma come un vizio ch'è in un suggetto più divino o divinamente, da un vizio ch'è in un suggetto più ferino o ferinamente. Di maniera che la differenza è secondo gli suggetti e modi differenti, e non secondo la forma de l'esser vizio.

CICADA: Molto ben posso da quel ch'avete detto conchiudere la condizion di questo eroico furore che dice «gelate ho spene, e li desir cuocenti»; perché non è nella temperanza della mediocrità, ma nell'eccesso delle contrarietadi ha l'anima discordevole: se triema nelle gelate speranze, arde negli cuocenti desiri; è per l'avidità stridolo, mutolo per il timore; sfavilla dal core per cura d'altrui, e per compassion di sé versa lacrime da gli occhi; muore ne l'altrui risa, vive ne' proprii lamenti; e (come colui che non è più suo) altri ama, odia se stesso: perché la materia (come dicono gli fisici) con quella misura ch'ama la forma absente, odia la presente. E cossì conclude nell'ottava la guerra ch'ha l'anima in se stessa; e poi quando dice ne la sestina «ma s'io m'impiumo, altri si cangia in sasso» e quel che séguita, mostra le sue passioni per la guerra ch'essercita con li contrarii esterni. Mi ricordo aver letto in Iamblico, dove tratta de gli Egizzii misterii, questa sentenza: *Impius animam dissidentem habet: unde nec secum ipse convenire potest neque cum aliis.*

TANSILLO: Or odi un altro sonetto di senso consequente al detto:

Ahi, qual condizion, natura, o sorte:
in viva morte morta vita vivo.

the middle where the extremes converge and become one and indistinguishable. Thus, between the extremes of hottest and coldest there are degrees of hotter and colder, and right in the middle is what you could call either hot or cold, or neither hot nor cold, without contradiction. In the same way, whoever is minimally content and minimally happy is in a condition of indifference, and finds himself in the house of temperance, and this is where the quality and condition of a strong spirit reside, buffeted by neither the South Wind nor the North.

You see, then, to return to our topic, how the heroic frenzy that is described in the present section differs from the other lower passions, not as virtue differs from vice, but in the way that a vice that exists in a divine subject, or exists more divinely, differs from a vice in a more bestial subject, or that exists in a more bestial manner. Therefore, the difference occurs according to different subjects and degrees rather than according to the form of vice itself.

CICADA: From what you have said, I can easily deduce the condition of this heroic frenzy that says, "I have *frozen hopes* and *seething desires*," because it is not in the temperance of moderation but in the excess of extremes that he has a discordant spirit. If he *shivers* from his *frozen hopes*, he *burns* from his *hot desires*; he is *strident* in his zeal and *timid* in his fear. He burns away in his heart for desiring another, and in pity for himself his eyes shed tears. He dies at the laughter of others, lives on his own laments, and (like someone who is no longer in control of himself) loves another and hates himself; for inasmuch as matter (so the physicists tell us) loves an absent form, it hates its present condition. Thus, in the octave he describes the war that he conducts within himself. When he then says in the sestet, *He'll turn to stone if I take wing and soar* and so on, he presents his frenzies through the war that he conducts with the contradictions outside himself. I remember having read in Iamblichus, where he writes about the Egyptian Mysteries, the following sentence:[24] *The unbeliever has a conflicted soul, so that he can never agree with himself, let alone with others.*

TANSILLO: Now listen to another sonnet, whose meaning follows from what we have just said:

ॐ

What a condition, destiny or state
This living death and deathly life bestow!

Amor m'ha morto (ahi lasso) di tal morte,
che son di vit' insiem' e morte privo.
Vòto di spene, d'inferno a le porte,
e colmo di desio al ciel arrivo:
talché suggetto a doi contrarii eterno,
bandito son dal ciel e da l'inferno.

Non han mie pene triegua,
perch' in mezzo di due scorrenti ruote,
de quai qua l'una, là l'altra mi scuote,
qual Ixion convien mi fugga e siegua:
perché al dubbio discorso
dan lezzion contraria il sprone e 'l morso.

Mostra qualmente patisca quel disquarto e distrazzione e in se medesimo: mentre l'affetto lasciando il mezzo e meta de la temperanza, tende a l'uno e l'altro estremo; e talmente si trasporta alto o a destra, che anco si trasporta a basso et a sinistra.

CICADA: Come con questo che non è proprio de l'uno né de l'altro estremo, non viene ad essere in stato o termine di virtude?

TANSILLO: All'ora è in stato di virtude quando si tiene al mezzo declinando da l'uno e l'altro contrario: ma quando tende a gli estremi inchinando a l'uno e l'altro di quelli, tanto gli manca de esser virtude, che è doppio vizio, il qual consiste in questo che la cosa recede dalla sua natura, la perfezzion della quale consiste nell'unità: e là dove convegnono gli contrarii, consta la composizione, e consiste la virtude. Ecco dumque come è morto vivente, o vivo moriente; là onde dice: «in viva morte morta vita vivo». Non è morto, perché vive ne l'oggetto; non è vivo, perché è morto in se stesso: privo di morte, perché parturisce pensieri in quello; privo di vita, perché non vegeta o sente in se medesimo. Appresso è bassissimo per la considerazion de l'alto intelligibile e la compresa imbecillità della potenza; è altissimo per l'aspirazione dell'eroico desio che trapassa di gran lunga gli suoi termini, et è altissimo per l'appetito intellettuale che non ha modo e fine di gionger numero a numero; è bassissimo per la violenza fattagli dal contrario sensuale che verso l'inferno impiomba. Onde trovandosi talmente

Love's struck me down (alas) with such a fate
That neither death nor life is mine to know.
Bereft of hope at Hell's infernal gate,
And brimming with desire, to Heaven I go.
Therefore, as contradiction's constant slave
I'm exiled both from Heaven and the grave.

My woes grant no reprieve
Because at two wheels' whirling intersection,
Each knocks me in the opposite direction.
Ixion-like,[25] I come and yet I leave:
Ambiguous proceedings
Where spur and rein inspire contrary readings.

*෨*

The poet shows how he suffers internal discord and distraction; in the meantime, his emotion, leaving the centre and mean of temperance, seeks one extreme and then the other, transported as high, or as far to the right, as it is brought low, or to the left.[26]

CICADA: But if [his emotion] belongs to neither extreme, why does it not come to rest within the state or bounds of virtue?

TANSILLO: Well, it is in a state of virtue when it keeps to the mean, avoiding both extremes. But when it tends to the extremes, inclining to one or the other, it strays so far from virtue that it becomes a double vice. Vice consists in this: when a thing retreats from its nature, whose perfection consists in unity; but when opposites converge, there reconciliation comes about, there virtue abides. You see, then, how he is dead while living and alive while dying, so that the poet says "*This living death and deathly life.*" He is not dead, because he lives in the Object [of his quest]; he is not alive, because he is dead to himself. Death "*is not his to know,*" because in love he gives birth to thoughts;[27] life "*is not his to know,*" because in and of himself he neither thrives nor feels. Moreover, when he considers the loftiness of what he would understand and the feebleness of his own powers, he sinks to the bottom; he rises to the summit for aspiring with a heroic desire that greatly surpasses its own limits. He rises high for his intellectual appetite, whose means and Objects are not simply to add one number to another; he sinks

poggiar e descendere, sente ne l'alma il più gran dissidio che sentir si possa; e confuso rimane per la ribellion del senso, che lo sprona là d'onde la raggion l'affrena, e per il contrario. – Il medesimo affatto si dimostra nella seguente sentenza dove la raggione in nome de Filenio dimanda, et il furioso risponde in nome di Pastore, che alla cura del gregge o armento de suoi pensieri si travaglia; quai pasce in ossequio e serviggio de la sua ninfa, ch'è l'affezzione di quell'oggetto alla cui osservanza è fatto cattivo:

*F.* Pastor.

  *P.* Che vuoi?

    *F.* Che fai?

      *P.* Doglio.

        *F.* Perché?

*P.* Perché non m'ha per suo vita, né morte.

*F.* Chi fallo?

  *P.* Amor.

    *F.* Quel rio?

      *P.* Quel rio.

        *F.* Dov'è?

*P.* Nel centro del mio cor se tien sì forte.

*F.* Che fa?

  *P.* Fere.

    *F.* Chi?

      *P.* Me.

        *F.* Te?

          *P.* Sì.

            *F.* Con che?

*P.* Con gli occhi, de l'inferno e del ciel porte.

*F.* Speri?

  *P.* Spero.

    *F.* Mercé?

      *P.* Mercé.

        *F.* Da chi?

*P.* Da chi sì mi martóra nott'e dì.

low when its opposite, his sensual appetite, does him violence and plunges him towards Hell. Thus, finding himself rising and falling, he feels the greatest possible discord within his soul. And he remains confused by the rebellion of the senses that spurs him on when reason reins him in, and vice versa.

The same point is made in the following sonnet, in which Reason, under the name of Filenio, asks questions, and the frenzied hero answers in the guise of a Shepherd, engaged in caring for the flock or herd of his thoughts, which he pastures in homage to and service of his nymph, which is the affection for that Object in whose observance he is made so ill tempered:[28]

ᘐ

F. Shepherd –
  S. What?
    F. How d'you do?
      S. I'm sore.
        F. Why now?
S. Why? Neither life nor death will take my part.
F. The reason?
  S. Love.
    F. That rogue?
      S. That rogue.
        F. Where's he?
S. His stronghold's in the centre of my heart.
F. And there?
  S. He strikes –
    F. Who?
      S. Me.
        F. You?
          S. Yes.
            F. But how?
S. With eyes that open Heaven and Hell to me.
F. You hope?
  S. I hope.
    F. For?
      S. Mercy.
        F. In whose sight?
S. The one who makes me suffer day and night.

    *F.* Hanne?
      *P.* Non so.
        *F.* Sei folle.
    *P.* Che, se cotal follia a l'alma piace?
    *F.* Promette?
      *P.* Non.
        *F.* Niega?
          *P.* Nemeno.
            *F.* Tace?
    *P.* Sì, perché ardir tant'onestà mi tolle.
    *F.* Vaneggi.
      *P.* In che?
        *F.* Nei stenti.
    *P.* Temo il suo sdegno, più che miei tormenti.

꒳

Qua dice che spasma: lamentasi dell'amore, non già perché ami (atteso che a nessuno veramente amante dispiace l'amare), ma perché infelicemente ami: mentre escono que' strali che son gli raggi di quei lumi, che medesimi secondo che son protervi e ritrosi, overamente benigni e graziosi, vegnono ad esser porte che guidano al cielo, overamente a l'inferno. Con questo vien mantenuto in speranza di futura et incerta mercé, et in effetto di presente e certo martìre. E quantumque molto apertamente vegga la sua follia, non per tanto avvien che in punto alcuno si correga, o che almen possa conciperne dispiacere; perché tanto ne manca, che più tosto in essa si compiace, come mostra dove dice:

    Mai fia che dell'amor io mi lamente,
    senza del qual non vogli' esser felice.

Appresso mostra un'altra specie di furore parturita da qualche lume di raggione, la qual suscita il timore, e supprime la già detta, a fin che non proceda a fatto che possa inasprir o sdegnar la cosa amata. Dice dumque la speranza esser fondata sul futuro, senza che cosa alcuna se gli prometta o nieghe: per che lui tace, e non dimanda, per téma d'offender l'onestade. Non ardisce esplicarsi e proporsi, onde fia o con ripudio escluso, overamente con promessa accettato: perché nel suo pensiero più contrapesa quel che potrebbe esser di male in un caso, che bene in un altro. Mostrasi dumque disposto di suffrir più presto

F. And she?
  S. Who knows?
    F. You're crazy.
S. And if insanity's my soul's release?
F. She's promised?
  S. No.
    F. Refused?
      S. No.
        F. Held her peace?
S. Well yes; before that grace ambition fails me.
F. You're wasting time.
  S. With what?
    F. With your delusion.
S. I fear her scorn more than my own confusion.

॰৵৹

Here he says that he is in agony, and bewails that love, not because he loves (for no lover truly dislikes loving), but because he loves unhappily, and all the while the beams shine forth that are the rays of those two lights which – being stubborn and reluctant, or benign and gracious – become the gates that lead to Heaven, or to Hell. With this he dwells in the hope of an uncertain future reward, and in the condition of a present and certain torment. And although he openly perceives his own insanity, he does not therefore correct it in any way, or feel the slightest displeasure at it. Far from it – he enjoys it, as is shown where it says:

> O may I never come to rue the love
> Without which I've no wish for happiness!²⁹

Next he reveals another kind of frenzy, born of a certain light of reason, which awakens fear and suppresses the previous passion, so that he will not proceed in any sense to embitter or provoke the beloved. He therefore says that his hope lies in the future, although nothing is promised or denied him, because he is silent and asks nothing lest he insult her honour. He dares not offer explanations or proposals that would leave him dismissed with a rejection or welcomed with promises. For in his own mind the possible harm outweighs the good that might result from the other. He therefore shows himself more willing

per sempre il proprio tormento, che di poter aprir la porta a l'occasione per la quale la cosa amata si turbe e contriste.

CICADA: Con questo dimostra l'amor suo esser veramente eroico: perché si propone per più principal fine la grazia del spirito e la inclinazion de l'affetto, che la bellezza del corpo, in cui non si termina quell'amor ch'ha del divino.

TANSILLO: Sai bene che come il rapto platonico è di tre specie, de quali l'uno tende alla vita contemplativa o speculativa, l'altro a l'attiva morale, l'altro a l'ociosa e voluptuaria: cossì son tre specie d'amori; de quali l'uno dall'aspetto della forma corporale s'inalza alla considerazione della spirituale e divina; l'altro solamente persevera nella delettazion del vedere e conversare; l'altro dal vedere va a precipitarsi nella concupiscenza del toccare. Di questi tre modi si componeno altri, secondo che o il primo s'accompagna col secondo, o che s'accompagna col terzo, o che concorreno tutti tre modi insieme: de li quali ciascuno e tutti oltre si moltiplicano in altri, secondo gli affetti de furiosi che tendeno o più verso l'obietto spirituale, o più verso l'obietto corporale, o equalmente verso l'uno e l'altro. Onde avviene che di quei che si ritrovano in questa milizia e son compresi nelle reti d'amore, altri tendeno a fin del gusto che si prende dal raccòrre le poma da l'arbore de la corporal bellezza, senz'il qual ottento (o speranza al meno) stimano degno di riso e vano ogn' amoroso studio: et in cotal modo corrono tutti quei che son di barbaro ingegno, che non possono né cercano magnificarsi amando cose degne, aspirando a cose illustri, e più alto a cose divine accomodando gli suoi studi e gesti, a i quali non è chi possa più ricca e commodamente suppeditar l'ali, che l'eroico amore. Altri si fanno avanti a fin del frutto della delettazione che prendeno da l'aspetto della bellezza e grazia del spirito che risplende e riluce nella leggiadria del corpo; e de tali alcuni benché amino il corpo e bramino assai d'esser uniti a quello, della cui lontananza si lagnano, e disunion s'attristano, tutta volta temeno che presumendo in questo non vegnan privi di quell'affabilità, conversazione, amicizia et accordo che gli è più principale: essendo che dal tentare non più può aver sicurezza di successo grato, che gran téma di cader da quella grazia qual come cosa tanto gloriosa e degna gli versa avanti gli occhi del pensiero.

to suffer his own torment forever than to open the door to the occasion for which his beloved disturbs or saddens him.

CICADA: By this he shows that his love is truly heroic, for it puts forth as its principal Object the grace of her spirit and the benevolence of her affection, rather than the beauty of her body, in which divine love cannot reach its fulfilment.

TANSILLO: You well know that just as Platonic rapture is of three kinds – one tending towards the contemplative and speculative life, one to the active moral life, and one to the languid life of pleasure – so, too, there are three kinds of love.[30] Of these, one elevates itself from concern with bodily form to contemplation of divine and spiritual form; one persists in the enjoyment of looking and conversing, and one descends from pleasure at looking into the craving to touch. From these three kinds, others are composed, to the extent that the first kind is combined with the second, or the third, or all three coexist together. And each one of these in turn multiplies into others, to the extent that the emotions of the frenzied lovers tend more towards a spiritual Object, or a bodily Object, or equally towards both. Hence, among those who find themselves in this army, ensnared in the nets of love, (1) some seek the gratification that can be gotten by plucking the fruit of the tree of physical beauty, without which attainment (or at least the hope of it) they regard every amorous impulse as fit for ridicule and scorn. That is the direction in which everyone runs who is of unrefined nature, who cannot and will not improve themselves by loving worthy things, aspiring towards illustrious things and, higher still, towards divinity, adjusting their desires and actions, to which none is more generous and effective at supplying wings than heroic love. (2) Some reach after the fruit of the pleasure they take from looking upon the beauty and grace of the spirit that shines forth in physical charm. And (3) others of this kind, although they love the body and greatly desire to be united with it, and bewail their separation from it, and regret their disunion, nonetheless they fear that by insisting on physical pleasure they will deprive themselves of that affability, company, friendship, and accord that are more fundamental, for the effort is no more certain to produce the joy of success than it is an enormous fear of falling from that grace which they keep before their mind's eye as a grand and glorious thing.

CICADA: È cosa degna, o Tansillo, per molte virtudi e perfezzioni che quindi derivano nell'umano ingegno, cercar, accettar, nodrire e conservar un simile amore: ma si deve ancora aver gran cura di non abbattersi ad ubligarsi ad un oggetto indegno e basso, a fin che non vegna a farsi partecipe della bassezza et indignità del medesimo; in proposito de quali intendo il conseglio del poeta ferrarese:

> Chi mette il piè su l'amorosa pania,
> cerchi ritrarlo, e non v'inveschi l'ali.

TANSILLO: A dir il vero, l'oggetto ch'oltre la bellezza del corpo non hav'altro splendore, non è degno d'esser amato ad altro fine che di far (come dicono) la razza: e mi par cosa da porco o da cavallo di tormentarvisi su; et io (per me) mai fui più fascinato da cosa simile, che potesse al presente esser fascinato da qualche statua o pittura, dalle quali mi pare indifferente. Sarebbe dumque un vituperio grande ad un animo generoso, se d'un sporco, vile, bardo et ignobile ingegno (quantumque sotto eccellente figura venesse ricuoperto) dica: «Temo il suo sdegno più ch'il mio tormento».

## DIALOGO TERZO

TANSILLO: Poneno, e sono più specie de furori, li quali tutti si riducono a doi geni: secondo che altri non mostrano che cecità, stupidità et impeto irrazionale, che tende al ferino insensato; altri consisteno in certa divina abstrazzione per cui dovegnono alcuni megliori in fatto che uomini ordinarii. E questi sono de due specie perché: altri per esserno fatti stanza de dèi o spiriti divini, dicono et operano cose mirabile senza che di quelle essi o altri intendano la raggione; e tali per l'ordinario sono promossi a questo da l'esser stati prima indisciplinati et ignoranti, nelli quali come vòti di proprio spirito e senso, come in una stanza purgata, s'intrude il senso e spirto divino; il qual meno può aver luogo e mostrarsi in quei che son colmi de propria raggione e senso, perché tal volta vuole ch' il mondo sappia certo che se quei non parlano per proprio studio et esperienza come è manifesto, séguite che parlino et oprino per intelligenza superiore: e con questo la moltitudine de gli uomini in tali degnamente ha maggior admirazion e fede. Altri, per

CICADA: It is a worthy thing, Tansillo, in light of the many virtues and perfections that originate from that source in the human spirit, to seek, accept, nurture, and preserve such a love. But great care should be taken not to waste effort pledging oneself to an unworthy or base object, to avoid taking part in its baseness and indignity. It is in this context that I interpret the advice of the poet from Ferrara:[31]

> Whoever sets foot on the swamp of love,
> Try to withdraw it; and don't wet your wings.

TANSILLO: To tell the truth, an object that has no other splendour than physical beauty is unworthy of being loved to any other end than, as they say, to propagate the race, and it seems to me the work of a pig or a horse to torment oneself over it. As for myself, I was never more fascinated by such a thing than I was by some statue or painting – which to me seem no different. Therefore, it would be a great reproach to a generous spirit, if one said of a filthy, base, slothful, and ignoble spirit (however excellent the shape in which it were enclosed): *I fear her scorn more than my own confusion.*

## THIRD DIALOGUE

TANSILLO: There are said to be – and are – several species of frenzy, all of which can be reduced to two kinds: one displays nothing but blindness, stupidity, and an irrational impulse that tends towards senseless bestiality, and the other consists in a certain divine rapture by which some individuals become superior, in fact, to ordinary people. And these individuals, in turn, are of two species: some, because they have come to harbour gods or divine spirits, say and do marvellous things without knowing the reasons why. Such people have usually been promoted to their condition from a state of uneducated ignorance; into them, as if they lacked their own spirit or sense, a divine spirit or sense may enter as if into an empty chamber. This spirit is less able to find room to manifest itself in those who are already filled with their own spirit and sense, for sometimes, indeed, it wants the world to know securely that if such people do not speak from their own study and experience – as is obvious – then they must be speaking and acting by

essere avezzi o abili alla contemplazione, e per aver innato un spirito
lucido et intellettuale, da uno interno stimolo e fervor naturale su-
scitato da l'amor della divinitate, della giustizia, della veritade, della
gloria, dal fuoco del desio e soffio dell'intenzione acuiscono gli sensi,
e nel solfro della cogitativa facultade accendono il lume razionale con
cui veggono più che ordinariamente: e questi non vegnono al fine a
parlar et operar come vasi et instrumenti, ma come principali artefici
et efficienti.

CICADA: Di questi doi geni quali stimi megliori?

TANSILLO: Gli primi hanno più dignità, potestà et efficacia in sé: perché hanno la divinità. Gli secondi son essi più degni, più potenti et
efficaci, e son divini. Gli primi son degni come l'asino che porta li
sacramenti: gli secondi come una cosa sacra. Nelli primi si considera
e vede in effetto la divinità e quella s'admira, adora et obedisce. Ne
gli secondi si considera e vede l'eccellenza della propria umanitade.
– Or venemo al proposito. Questi furori de quali noi raggioniamo, e
che veggiamo messi in execuzione in queste sentenze, non son oblio,
ma una memoria; non son negligenze di se stesso, ma amori e brame
del bello e buono con cui si procure farsi perfetto con transformarsi
et assomigliarsi a quello. Non è un raptamento sotto le leggi d'un fato
indegno, con gli lacci de ferine affezioni: ma un impeto razionale
che siegue l'apprension intellettuale del buono e bello che conosce;
a cui vorrebbe conformandosi parimente piacere, di sorte che della
nobiltà e luce di quello viene ad accendersi, et investirsi de qualitade
e condizione per cui appaia illustre e degno. Doviene un dio dal con-
tatto intellettuale di quel nume oggetto; e d'altro non ha pensiero che
de cose divine, e mostrasi insensibile e impassibile in quelle cose che
comunmente massime senteno, e da le quali più vegnon altri tormen-
tati; niente teme, e per amor della divinitade spreggia gli altri piaceri,
e non fa pensiero alcuno de la vita. Non è furor d'atra bile che fuor
di conseglio, raggione et atti di prudenza lo faccia vagare guidato dal
caso e rapito dalla disordinata tempesta; come quei ch'avendo preva-
ricato da certa legge de la divina Adrastia vegnono condannati sotto la
carnificina de le Furie: acciò sieno essagitati da una dissonanza tanto
corporale per sedizioni, ruine e morbi, quanto spirituale per la iattura
dell'armonia delle potenze cognoscitive et appetitive. Ma è un calor

means of a higher intelligence. In this way, the general population will properly feel greater awe and trust for them.

The others, practised or proficient in contemplation, and born with a lucid and intellectual spirit, are already driven by an inward stimulus and a natural fervour to a love of divinity, of justice, of truth, of glory, and these sharpen their senses in the flames of desire with the bellows of purpose, igniting the light of reason in the crucible of their cognitive faculty, by which they see with greater than usual clarity. These people speak and act not as mere vessels or instruments, but as original creators and achievers.

CICADA: Of these two types, which do you regard as superior?

TANSILLO: The former have greater dignity, power, and effectiveness in and of themselves, because they contain divinity. The second are more worthy, more powerful, and more effective: they are divine. The former are worthy as an ass is worthy who carries the sacraments, the latter are worthy as something sacred.[32] In the former we consider, and see the effects of, divinity, which we admire, adore, and obey. In the second we consider and see the excellence of our own humanity.

Now let us get to the point. These frenzies that we are discussing, and see enacted in these poems, are not forgetfulness, but a memory. They are not self-neglect, but rather the loves and desires for beauty and goodness through which we seek perfection, transforming ourselves in their image. It is not a seizure in the snares of bestial passion, subject to the law of an unworthy fate, but a rational impulse that pursues the intellectual grasp of that goodness and beauty which is knowledge: by imitating them, an individual desires to please them, with the result that he becomes inflamed with their nobility and radiance, and is endowed with such quality and condition as to appear illustrious and worthy. He becomes a god by virtue of intellectual contact with that divinity which is the object of his love, and he has no thought except for divine things, showing himself insensible and imperturbable to the things that are ordinarily felt to the utmost, and by which others are most tormented; he fears nothing, and for love of divinity he disdains all other pleasures, giving not a thought to his life.

This is no frenzy of melancholy that makes him stray from good counsel, reason, and acts of prudence, guided by chance and seized by a chaotic tempest, like those who, having violated certain laws of the divine Adrastia,[33] have been condemned to the butchery of the Furies,

acceso dal sole intelligenziale ne l'anima et impeto divino che gl'impronta l'ali: onde più e più avvicinandosi al sole intelligenziale, rigettando la ruggine de le umane cure, dovien un oro probato e puro, ha sentimento della divina et interna armonia, concorda gli suoi pensieri e gesti con la simmetria della legge insita in tutte le cose. Non come inebriato da le tazze di Circe va cespitando et urtando or in questo, or in quel altro fosso, or a questo or a quell'altro scoglio; o come un Proteo vago or in questa or in quell'altra faccia cangiandosi, giamai ritrova loco, modo, né materia di fermarsi e stabilirsi. Ma senza distemprar l'armonia vince e supera gli orrendi mostri; e per tanto che vegna a dechinare, facilmente ritorna al sesto con quelli intimi instinti, che come nove muse saltano e cantano circa il splendor dell'universale Apolline: e sotto l'imagini sensibili e cose materiali va comprendendo divini ordini e consegli. È vero che tal volta avendo per fida scorta l'amore, ch'è gemino, e perché tal volta per occorrenti impedimenti si vede defraudato dal suo sforzo, all'ora come insano e furioso mette in precipizio l'amor di quello che non può comprendere: onde confuso da l'abisso della divinità tal volta dismette le mani, e poi ritorna pure a forzarsi con la voluntade verso là dove non può arrivare con l'intelletto. È vero pure che ordinariamente va spasseggiando, et or più in una, or più in un'altra forma del gemino Cupido si trasporta; perché la lezzion principale che gli dona Amore è che in ombra contemple (quando non puote in specchio) la divina beltate: e come gli proci di Penelope s'intrattegna con le fante quando non gli lice conversar con la padrona. Or dumque, per conchiudere, possete da quel ch'è detto comprendere qual sia questo furioso di cui l'imagine ne vien messa avanti, quando si dice:

꒰

Se la farfalla al suo splendor ameno
vola, non sa ch'è fiamm' al fin discara;
se quand'il cervio per sete vien meno,
al rio va, non sa della freccia amara;
s'il lioncorno corre al casto seno,

lashed by a discord that is both bodily – suffering, seditions, ruin, and disease – and spiritual – enduring the loss of harmony between the powers of knowledge and desire. No, it is a fervent heat ignited in the soul by the Sun of intelligence, a divine impulse that lends him wings, so that in drawing closer and closer to the Sun of intelligence, shedding the dross of human concerns, he becomes gold proven and pure, he feels divine and internal harmony, he attunes his thoughts and acts to the universal measure of the law that lies innate in all things. He does not, like a man drunk on Circe's cup, go tripping and stumbling into one ditch or another, flinging himself from one precipice or another, or changing his face, like a shifting Proteus, into one form or another, never finding a place, means, or reason to stop and settle.[34] Instead, without disturbing his harmony, he conquers and overcomes dreadful monsters, and whenever he strays, he easily recovers his balance by those innermost instincts that, like nine Muses, dance and sing around the splendour of the universal Apollo; beneath sensible images and material objects, he recognizes divine orders and counsels. It is true that sometimes he is accompanied by love, which is twofold, as his faithful escort,[35] and that sometimes, when faced with obstacles, he finds himself cheated of the reward for his efforts. Then, like a raving madman, he may cast away the love of what he cannot comprehend; confused by the endless depths of divinity, he sometimes throws up his hands, and then returns to forcing himself, by sheer act of will, to aspire towards what he cannot reach with his intellect. It is also true that he ordinarily goes wandering about, and is transported by turns into each of Cupid's two forms, for the principal lesson that Love teaches him is to contemplate the shadows of divine beauty (or its reflection in a mirror), and, like Penelope's suitors, he amuses himself with the maidservants when he is not granted the company of the mistress.[36] Now then, to conclude, from what has been said you may understand what this frenzied lover is, whose image is put before you when the poet says:

〰

The moth in flight towards a pleasing glow
Is unaware that flame will singe its wing.
The panting deer that seeks the river's flow
Knows nothing of an arrow's bitter sting.
The unicorn runs to his lady fair

non vede il laccio che se gli prepara:
i' al lum', al font', al grembo del mio bene,
veggio le fiamme, i strali e le catene.

   S'è dolce il mio languire,
perché quell'alta face sì m'appaga,
perché l'arco divin sì dolce impiaga,
perché in quel nodo è avolto il mio desire:
   mi sien eterni impacci
fiamme al cor, strali al petto, a l'alma lacci.

Dove dimostra l'amor suo non esser come de la farfalla, del cervio
e del lioncorno, che fuggirebono s'avesser giudizio del fuoco, della
saetta e de gli lacci, e che non han senso d'altro che del piacere: ma
vien guidato da un sensatissimo e pur troppo oculato furore, che gli
fa amare più quel fuoco che altro refrigerio, più quella piaga che altra
sanità, più que' legami che altra libertade. Perché questo male non è
absolutamente male: ma per certo rispetto al bene secondo l'opinione, e falso; quale il vecchio Saturno ha per condimento nel devorar
che fa de proprii figli. Perché questo male absolutamente ne l'occhio
de l'eternitade è compreso o per bene, o per guida che ne conduce
a quello; atteso che questo fuoco è l'ardente desio de le cose divine, questa saetta è l'impression del raggio della beltade della superna
luce, questi lacci son le specie del vero che uniscono la nostra mente
alla prima verità: e le specie del bene che ne fanno uniti e gionti al
primo e sommo bene. A quel senso io m'accostai quando dissi:

   D'un sì bel fuoco e d'un sì nobil laccio
beltà m'accende, et onestà m'annoda,
ch'in fiamm' e servitù convien ch'io goda,
fugga la libertade e tema il ghiaccio;

   l'incendio è tal ch'io m'ard' e non mi sfaccio,
el nodo è tal ch'il mondo meco il loda,
né mi gela timor, né duol mi snoda;
ma tranquill' è l'ardor, dolce l'impaccio.

And never sees the cords that set his snare.
In my love's light, her fountains, and her lap,
I see the flame, the arrow, and the trap.

If languishing is kind,
Because that lofty torch fulfils me so,
Because the strike's sweet from that heavenly bow,
Because desire is in those knots entwined,
Be these my endless cares,
My heart's flames, bosom's arrows, spirit's snares.

⌣

Here he shows that his love is not like that of the moth, the deer, or the unicorn, who would flee if ever they had to face the trial of flame, arrow, or snare, and who have no other sensation but that of pleasure. Instead, he is guided by a profoundly felt but all too judicious frenzy, which makes him love that flame more than any other cool solace, that wound more than any other health, those bonds more than any other freedom. For this evil is not absolutely evil, but only evil by the usual standard of what is good, which is a false goodness, like the seasoning that old Saturn used when he devoured his children. For in the absolute sight of eternity, this evil is understood either as good in itself or as a guide that leads to goodness. For this fire is the ardent desire for divinity, this arrow is the imprint of the ray of the supernal light, and these snares are the species of truth that unite our mind to the primal truth, and the species of goodness that unite themselves with the prime and ultimate Goodness. This is the meaning I was arriving at when I said:

With such a pretty blaze, such noble ties
Beauty ignites me, honest virtue binds me
In flames and servitude my pleasure finds me
In flight from liberty, in fear of ice.

The inferno rages; I endure the heat;
The world and I alike admire my noose.
Fear cannot chill me, nor pain set me loose;
The ardour's peaceful, and the bondage sweet.

Scorgo tant'alto il lume che m'infiamma,
el laccio ordito di sì ricco stame,
che nascend' il pensier, more il desio.

Poiché mi splend'al cor sì bella fiamma,
e mi stringe il voler sì bel legame,
sia serva l'ombra, et arda il cener mio.

Tutti gli amori (se sono eroici e non son puri animali, che chiamano naturali e cattivi alla generazione, come instrumenti de la natura in certo modo) hanno per oggetto la divinità, tendeno alla divina bellezza, la quale prima si comunica all'anime e risplende in quelle, e da quelle poi o (per dir meglio) per quelle poi si comunica alli corpi: onde è che l'affetto ben formato ama gli corpi o la corporal bellezza, per quel che è indice della bellezza del spirito. Anzi quello che n'innamora del corpo è una certa spiritualità che veggiamo in esso, la qual si chiama bellezza; la qual non consiste nelle dimensioni maggiori o minori, non nelli determinati colori o forme, ma in certa armonia e consonanza de membri e colori. Questa mostra certa sensibile affinità col spirito a gli sensi più acuti e penetrativi: onde séguita che tali più facilmente et intensamente s'innamorano, et anco più facilmente si disamorano, e più intensamente si sdegnano, con quella facilità et intensione, che potrebbe essere nel cangiamento del spirito brutto, che in qualche gesto et espressa intenzione si faccia aperto: di sorte che tal bruttezza trascorre da l'anima al corpo, a farlo non apparir oltre come gli apparia bello. La beltà dumque del corpo ha forza d'accendere; ma non già di legare e far che l'amante non possa fuggire, se la grazia che si richiede nel spirito non soccorre, come la onestà, la gratitudine, la cortesia, l'accortezza: però dissi bello quel fuoco che m'accese, perché ancor fu nobile il laccio che m'annodava.

CICADA: Non creder sempre cossì, Tansillo; perché qualche volta quantumque discuopriamo vizioso il spirito non lasciamo però di rimaner accesi et allacciati: di maniera che quantumque la raggion veda il male et indignità di tale amore, non ha però efficacia di alienar il disordinato appetito. Nella qual disposizion credo che fusse il Nolano quando disse:

> Above I see the light that draws me higher,
> The cord spun out from such a sumptuous thread
> Gives birth to thoughts, as all desire drops dead.
>
> Within my heart there shines so fair a fire,
> So sweet a shackle's closed around my will,
> My shade's enslaved, my embers smoulder still.

All loves (if they are heroic and they are not those purely animal loves called "natural," and "enslaved to reproduction," serving in a certain [debased] way as nature's tools)[37] have divinity as their goal, and tend towards divine beauty, which first communicates itself through souls and shines forth in them, and from them, or (more accurately) through them, then communicates itself to bodies. Hence, a well-ordered passion loves bodies or physical beauty to the extent that they reflect the beauty of the spirit. Indeed, what we fall in love with in the body is a certain spiritual quality that we perceive in it, called beauty, which does not consist in larger or smaller dimensions, or particular colours or forms, but in a certain harmony and consonance of parts and colours. To the most acute and penetrating senses this beauty shows a certain perceptible affinity with the spirit. Consequently, such people fall in love more easily and more intensely, and also fall out of love more easily, and feel disdain more intensely, with an ease and intensity that may arise from an ugly change in the spirit, which reveals itself in some act or expressed intention, so that this ugliness passes from the soul to the body, which can no longer seem as beautiful as it seemed before. Physical beauty, therefore, has the power to inflame, but not to bind and to prevent the lover's escape, unless it has been reinforced by that grace we seek in the spirit, in the form of honesty, gratitude, courtesy, and discretion. This is why I called the flame that inflamed me *beautiful*, because the bonds that tied me were also noble.

CICADA: Do not believe that this is always the case, Tansillo, because on occasion, even though we have discovered how flawed the spirit is, we are nonetheless unable to give up being inflamed and enthralled by it, so that however clearly reason may see the harm and indignity of such a love, it nonetheless lacks the power to banish that wild desire. I think that the Nolan must have been in such a state when he said:[38]

> Oimé che son constretto dal furore
> d'appigliarmi al mio male,
> ch'apparir fammi un sommo ben Amore.
>
> Lasso, a l'alma non cale
> ch'a contrarii consigli umqua ritenti;
> e del fero tiranno,
> che mi nodrisce in stenti,
> e poté pormi da me stess' in bando,
> più che di libertad' i' son contento.
>
> Spiego le vele al vento,
> che mi suttraga a l'odioso bene:
> e tempestoso al dolce danno amene.

TANSILLO: Questo accade, quando l'uno e l'altro spirto è vizioso, e son tinti come di medesimo inchiostro, atteso che dalla conformità si suscita, accende e si confirma l'amore. Cossì gli viziosi facilmente concordano in atti di medesimo vizio. E non voglio lasciar de dire ancora quel che per esperienza conosco, che quantumque in un animo abbia discuoperti vizii molto abominati da me, com'è dire una sporca avarizia, una vilissima ingordiggia sul danaio, irreconoscenza di ricevuti favori e cortesie, un amor di persone al tutto vili (de quali vizii questo ultimo massime dispiace perché toglie la speranza a l'amante che per esser egli, o farsi più degno, possa da lei esser più accettato), tutta volta non mancava ch'io ardesse per la beltà corporale. Ma che? io l'amavo senza buona volontà, essendo che non per questo m'arrei più contristato che allegrato delle sue disgrazie et infortunii.

CICADA: Però è molto propria et a proposito quella distinzion che fanno intra l'amare e voler bene.

TANSILLO: È vero, perché a molti vogliamo bene, cioè desideramo che siano savii e giusti: ma non le amiamo, perché sono iniqui et ignoranti; molti amiamo perché son belli, ma non gli vogliamo bene, perché non meritano: e tra l'altre cose che stima l'amante quello non meritare, la prima è d'essere amato; e però benché non possa astenersi d'amare, niente di meno gli ne rincresce e mostra il suo rincrescimento: come costui che diceva, «Oimè ch'io son costretto dal furore d'appigliarmi al mio male».

Alas! I'm forced by my insanity
To cling to my delusion
That makes Love seem the highest good to me.

My soul in its confusion
Persists in its conflicting inclinations.
As for the cruel despot
Who feeds me on starvation,
And bans me from myself without a respite:
His rule, not freedom, pleases.

I spread sail to the breezes
That sweep me far away from good I hate,
And toss me towards a sweet but deadly fate.

TANSILLO: This happens where both spirits are flawed, and dyed, as it were, with the same ink, given that love is stimulated, inflamed, and confirmed by such affinity. Thus, those who are vicious easily agree to practise the same vice. I cannot resist making an observation drawn from my own experience: though I have discovered vices that I abominate in a spirit – for example, filthy greed, base craving for money, ingratitude for favours or courtesies received, a love for utterly vile persons (and among such vices this last is the most displeasing, because it deprives the lover of hope that if he were, or became, more worthy, then he might be more acceptable to her) – nonetheless I could not help but burn with desire for physical beauty. But so what? I loved against my will: otherwise, I would have been more upset than overjoyed by her afflictions and misfortunes.

CICADA: For that reason there is a right and proper distinction between loving and liking.

TANSILLO: True. For we like many people; that is, we want them to be wise and just, but we do not love them, because they are unjust and ignorant. We love many people because they are beautiful, but we do not like them, because they do not merit it. And among the things that a lover thinks he does not merit, the first is being loved; hence, even though he cannot abstain from loving, it aggravates him to do so and he shows that aggravation, just as the Nolan did when he said: "*Alas! I'm forced by my insanity / To cling to my delusion.*"

In contraria disposizione fu, o per altro oggetto corporale in similitudine, o per suggetto divino in verità, quando disse:

꒰꒱

> Bench' a tanti martir mi fai suggetto.
> pur ti ringrazio, e assai ti deggio, Amore,
> che con sì nobil piaga apriste il petto,
> e tal impadroniste del mio core,
>
> per cui fia ver ch'un divo e viv'oggetto,
> de Dio più bella imago 'n terra adore;
> pensi chi vuol ch'il mio destin sia rio,
> ch'uccid'in speme, e fa viv'in desio.
>
> Pascomi in alta impresa;
> e bench'il fin bramato non consegua,
> e 'n tanto studio l'alma si dilegua,
> basta che sia sì nobilment'accesa:
>     basta ch'alto mi tolsi,
> e da l'ignobil numero mi sciolsi.

꒰꒱

L'amor suo qua è a fatto eroico e divino, e per tale voglio intenderlo:
benché per esso si dica suggetto a tanti martìri; perché ogni amante
ch'è disunito e separato da la cosa amata (alla quale com'è congionto
con l'affetto, vorrebe essere con l'effetto) si trova in cordoglio e pena,
si crucia e si tormenta: non già perché ami, atteso che degnissima
e nobilissimamente sente impiegato l'amore; ma perché è privo di
quella fruizione la quale ottenerebbe se fusse gionto a quel termine al
qual tende: non dole per il desio che l'avviva, ma per la difficultà del
studio ch'il martora. Stimìnlo dumque altri a sua posta infelice per
questa apparenza de rio destino, come che l'abbia condannato a cotai
pene: perché egli non lasciarà per tanto de riconoscer l'obligo ch'have ad Amore, e rendergli grazie, perché gli abbia presentato avanti
gli occhi de la mente una specie intelligibile, nella quale in questa
terrena vita (rinchiuso in questa priggione de la carne, et avvinto da
questi nervi, e confirmato da queste ossa) li sia lecito di contemplar

But he spoke in quite the opposite frame of mind, either metaphorically about another physical object, or truthfully about a divine subject, when he said:

৵৲

Subject me though you may to deep distress,
I thank you, Love, and note my obligation.
With such a noble wound you pierced my breast,
And put my heart in utter subjugation.

The lively sacred object of my quest,
God's loveliest image, wins my adoration.
Let some regard my destiny as dire,
That kills in hope and lives on in desire.

I feed on a lofty aim
Yet should I never reach my longed-for goal
In which I've spent such efforts of my soul,
It was enough to keep so fine a flame;
It was enough to rise
And free myself from all ignoble ties.

৵৲

Here, as I choose to understand it, his love is completely heroic and divine, even though he declares himself subject to torments on its account. For every lover who is divided and separated from his beloved (to whom he is joined affectively and longs to be joined effectively) finds himself in heartbreak and distress, agonizes and torments himself, not simply because he loves, and feels that his love is most worthily and nobly employed, but because he is deprived of the enjoyment he would attain if he arrived at his intended goal. He suffers not from the desire that animates him, but from the difficulty of his pursuit. So let others regard him as unhappy in his condition, because this apparent ill fortune seems to have condemned him to such misery. Yet he will not on that account fail to acknowledge his debt to Love, and to thank Love for setting before his mind's eye an intelligible image, through which, in this earthly life (while still pent up in this prison of flesh, wrapped in these sinews, and fortified by these bones), he may

più altamente la divinitade, che se altra specie e similitudine di quella
si fusse offerta.

CICADA: Il «divo» dumque «e vivo oggetto», ch'ei dice, è la specie intelligibile più alta che egli s'abbia possuto formar della divinità; e non è
qualche corporal bellezza che gli adombrasse il pensiero come appare
in superficie del senso?

TANSILLO: Vero: perché nessuna cosa sensibile, né specie di quella, può
inalzarsi a tanta dignitade.

CICADA: Come dumque fà menzione di quella specie per oggetto, se
(come mi pare) il vero oggetto è la divinità istessa?

TANSILLO: La è oggetto finale, ultimo e perfettissimo; non già in questo
stato dove non possemo veder Dio se non come in ombra e specchio,
e però non ne può esser oggetto se non in qualche similitudine; non
tale qual possa esser abstratta et acquistata da bellezza et eccellenza
corporea per virtù del senso: ma qual può esser formata nella mente
per virtù de l'intelletto. Nel qual stato ritrovandosi, viene a perder
l'amore et affezzion d'ogni altra cosa tanto sensibile quanto intelligibile; perché questa congionta a quel lume dovien lume essa ancora, e
per consequenza si fa un Dio: perché contrae la divinità in sé essendo
ella in Dio per la intenzione con cui penetra nella divinità (per quanto
si può), et essendo Dio in ella, per quanto dopo aver penetrato viene
a conciperla e (per quanto si può) a ricettarla e comprenderla nel suo
concetto. Or di queste specie e similitudini si pasce l'intelletto umano
da questo mondo inferiore, sin tanto che non gli sia lecito de mirar
con più puro occhio la bellezza della divinitade: come accade a colui
che è gionto a qualch'edificio eccellentissimo et ornatissimo, mentre
va considerando cosa per cosa in quello, si aggrada, si contenta, si
pasce d'una nobil maraviglia; ma se avverà poi che vegga il signor di
quelle imagini, di bellezza incomparabilmente maggiore, lasciata ogni
cura e pensiero di esse, tutto è volto et intento a considerar quell'uno.
Ecco dumque come è differenza in questo stato dove veggiamo la divina bellezza in specie intelligibili tolte da gli effetti, opre, magisteri,
ombre e similitudini di quella, et in quell'altro stato dove sia lecito di
vederla in propria presenza. – Dice appresso: «Pascomi d'alt'impresa»,
perché (come notano gli Pitagorici) cossì l'anima si versa e muove
circa Dio, come il corpo circa l'anima.

yet contemplate divinity more profoundly than through some other appearance or likeness that might be offered him.

CICADA: The *lively sacred object* that he mentions, then, is the highest intelligible image that he has been able to form of divinity. And isn't it some physical beauty that casts its shadow over his thoughts when it appears superficially to his senses?

TANSILLO: True, for no sensible thing, nor its outward appearance, can elevate itself to such dignity.

CICADA: Why, then, does he mention an outward *image* as the Object, when in my view his true Object is divinity itself?

TANSILLO: Divinity is the final Object, the ultimate and wholly perfect Object, but not in this world, where we cannot see God except as if in a shadow or mirror, and hence there cannot be any Object except in some kind of likeness. This is not a likeness that can be abstracted and derived from beauty and physical splendour by the power of the senses; it is one that has been formed within the mind by the power of intellect. When the mind achieves this state, it gradually loses its love and affection for every other sensible or intelligible object. For once joined to that light, the mind becomes a light in itself, and consequently becomes a God, for it contracts[39] divinity into itself; it is already in God because of the purposeful way it penetrates into divinity (to the extent that it can), and God is already in the mind: to the extent that it has penetrated divinity, it has come to understand divinity, and (to the extent that it can) receives and incorporates divinity into its store of ideas. Thus, the human intellect feeds on these outward images and likenesses from the inferior world until it is permitted to gaze with purer eyes upon the beauty of divinity. Imagine a man who comes upon some magnificent and ornate building, and while he considers each detail one by one, takes delight, takes pleasure, and is nourished by a noble sense of wonderment. But if he should happen to see the master plan behind those images, with its incomparably greater beauty, then he would abandon every concern and thought of them, and become entirely rapt and intent on contemplating it alone. You see, then, the difference between this present state – in which we see divine beauty as intelligible images removed from the effects, works, jurisdictions, shadows, and likenesses of divinity – and that other state, in which we may see divine beauty in its own presence.

CICADA: Dumque il corpo non è luogo de l'anima?

TANSILLO: Non: perché l'anima non è nel corpo localmente, ma come forma intrinseca e formatore estrinseco; come quella che fa gli membri, e figura il composto da dentro e da fuori. Il corpo dumque è ne l'anima, l'anima nella mente, la mente o è Dio, o è in Dio, come disse Plotino: cossì come per essenza è in Dio che è la sua vita, similmente per l'operazione intellettuale e la voluntà conseguente dopo tale operazione, si referisce alla sua luce e beatifico oggetto. Degnamente dumque questo affetto del eroico furore si pasce de sì alta impresa. Né per questo che l'obietto è infinito, in atto simplicissimo, e la nostra potenza intellettiva non può apprendere l'infinito se non in discorso, o in certa maniera de discorso, com'è dire in certa raggione potenziale o aptitudinale, è come colui che s'amena a la consecuzion de l'immenso onde vegna a constituirse un fine dove non è fine.

CICADA: Degnamente, perché l'ultimo fine non deve aver fine, atteso che non sarebe ultimo. È dumque infinito in intenzione, in perfezzione, in essenza et in qualsivoglia altra maniera d'esser fine.

TANSILLO: Dici il vero. Or in questa vita tal pastura è di maniera tale, che più accende, che possa appagar il desio, come ben mostra quel divino poeta che disse: «Bramando è lassa l'alma a Dio vivente»; et in altro luogo: *Attenuati sunt oculi mei suspicientes in excelsum*. Però dice: «E bench'il fin bramato non consegua, E 'n tanto studio l'alma si dilegua, Basta che sia sì nobilmente accesa»: vuol dire ch'in tanto l'anima si consola e riceve tutta la gloria che può ricevere in cotal stato, e che sia partecipe di quel ultimo furor de l'uomo in quanto uomo di questa condizione, nella qual si trova adesso, e come ne veggiamo.

CICADA: Mi par che gli Peripatetici (come esplicò Averroe) vogliano intender questo quando dicono la somma felicità de l'uomo consistere nella perfezione per le scienze speculative.

He then says *I feed on a lofty aim*, because (as the Pythagoreans observe) this is how the soul turns and moves about God, as the body does about the soul.

CICADA: Then the body is not the place of the soul?

TANSILLO: No, because the soul is not simply placed in the body, but is present both as an internal form and as an external creator of form, just as the soul forms the parts of the body and shapes its composition from within and without. This is how the body exists in the soul, the soul exists in the mind, and the mind either is God or is in God, as Plotinus said.[40] Just as the soul is in God in its essence, which is its life, so likewise, by its intellectual operation, and by its consequent operation of will, it turns towards its own light and its beatific Object. Worthily, then, this emotion of heroic frenzy *feeds on a lofty aim*. Furthermore, this Object is infinite, utterly simple in its actuality, but our power of understanding cannot grasp infinity except through a discourse, or through a certain kind of discourse, that is to say, by a certain principle of potentiality or aptitude; hence, he is like someone who applies himself to pursuing what is immeasurable, or tries to set an endpoint where there is no endpoint to set.

CICADA: Quite properly, for the ultimate end should have no end; otherwise it would no longer be ultimate. It is therefore infinite in purpose, in perfection, in essence, and in every other aspect by which it constitutes an end.

TANSILLO: You speak truly. Now in this life, such nourishment inflames the desire more than fulfilling it, as the divine poet[41] showed truly when he said, *My soul thirsteth for God, for the living God*; and elsewhere, *Mine eyes fail with looking upward.*[42] For that reason the Nolan says: "*Yet should I never reach my longed-for goal / In which I've spent such efforts of my soul / It was enough to keep so fine a flame*," he means that the soul consoles itself and is filled with all the glory it can receive in such a state, and that it partakes of that ultimate human frenzy available to a man in the condition in which he finds himself, and in which we see him.

CICADA: It seems to me that the Peripatetics (as Averroës explained) mean to say the same thing when they declare that the highest human happiness consists in attaining perfection by means of the speculative sciences.[43]

TANSILLO: È vero, e dicono molto bene: perché noi in questo stato nel
qual ne ritroviamo, non possiamo desiderar né ottener maggior perfezzione che quella in cui siamo quando il nostro intelletto mediante qualche nobil specie intelligibile s'unisce o alle sustanze seperate,
come dicono costoro, o a la divina mente, come è modo de dir de
Platonici. Lascio per ora di raggionar de l'anima o uomo in altro stato
e modo di essere che possa trovarsi o credersi.

CICADA: Ma che perfezzione o satisfazzione può trovar l'uomo in quella
cognizione la quale non è perfetta?

TANSILLO: Non sarà mai perfetta per quanto l'altissimo oggetto possa
esser capito, ma per quanto l'intelletto nostro possa capire: basta che
in questo et altro stato gli sia presente la divina bellezza per quanto
s'estende l'orizonte della vista sua.

CICADA: Ma de gli uomini non tutti possono giongere a quello dove può
arrivar uno o doi.

TANSILLO: Basta che tutti corrano; assai è ch'ognun faccia il suo possibile; perché l'eroico ingegno si contenta più tosto di cascar o mancar degnamente e nell'alte imprese, dove mostre la dignità del suo ingegno,
che riuscir a perfezzione in cose men nobili e basse.

CICADA: Certo che meglio è una degna et eroica morte, che un indegno
e vil trionfo.

TANSILLO: A cotal proposito feci questo sonetto:

> Poi che spiegat'ho l'ali al bel desio,
> quanto più sott'il piè l'aria mi scorgo,
> più le veloci penne al vento porgo:
> e spreggio il mondo, e vers'il ciel m'invio.
>
> Né del figliuol di Dedalo il fin rio
> fa che giù pieghi, anzi via più risorgo;
> ch'i' cadrò morto a terra ben m'accorgo:
> ma qual vita pareggia al morir mio?

TANSILLO: It is true, and they were right to say so. For in our present condition, we can desire or obtain no greater perfection than when our intellect, by means of some noble idea, unites itself either with separate substances, as the Peripatetics say, or with the divine mind, as the Platonists put it. For the moment I will forgo discussing the soul, or the individual, in any other state or mode of existence in which he may find or believe himself to be.

CICADA: But what perfection or satisfaction can we find in imperfect knowledge?

TANSILLO: Knowledge will never mean understanding the Object in a perfect way, but only insofar as our intellect can understand it. Suffice it that in some state or another, divine beauty is perceived by our intellect within the limits of its vision.

CICADA: But not everyone can arrive at that point; only one or two.

TANSILLO: Suffice it that they all make the effort. Suffice it that each one does everything he can. For a heroic spirit will prefer to crash or fall short with dignity in a lofty enterprise that lets him reveal the worth of his spirit, rather than succeed perfectly in things that are less noble and more base.

CICADA: Certainly a worthy and heroic death is better than an unworthy and abject triumph.

TANSILLO: Along those lines I wrote the following sonnet:

> Now that I've spread my wings to sweet desire
> The more I see the air beneath my feet
> I offer to the wind my feathers fleet
> Disdain the world, and to the sky aspire.
>
> The fate of Icarus[44] can never bend
> My course to earth; I rise still higher instead
> All too aware that one day I'll fall dead
> But what life could compare with such an end?

> La voce del mio cor per l'aria sento:
> «Ove mi porti, temerario? china,
> che raro è senza duol tropp'ardimento»;
>
> «Non temer (respond'io) l'alta ruina.
> Fendi sicur le nubi, e muor contento:
> s'il ciel sì illustre morte ne destina».

CICADA: Io intendo quel che dice: «basta ch'alto mi tolsi»; ma non quando dice: «e da l'ignobil numero mi sciolsi», s'egli non intende d'esser uscito fuor de l'antro platonico, rimosso dalla condizion della sciocca et ignobilissima moltitudine; essendo che quei che profittano in questa contemplazione non possono esser molti e numerosi.

TANSILLO: Intendi molto bene; oltre, per «l'ignobil numero» può intendere il corpo e sensual cognizione dalla quale bisogna alzarsi e disciòrsi chi vuol unirsi alla natura di contrario geno.

CICADA: Dicono gli Platonici due sorte de nodi con gli quali l'anima è legata al corpo. L'uno è certo atto vivifico che da l'anima come un raggio scende nel corpo; l'altro è certa qualità vitale che da quell'atto resulta nel corpo. Or questo numero nobilissimo movente ch'è l'anima, come intendete che sia disciolto da l'ignobil numero ch'è il corpo?

TANSILLO: Certo non s'intendeva secondo alcun modo di questi: ma secondo quel modo con cui le potenze che non son comprese e cattivate nel grembo de la materia, e qualche volta come sopite et inebriate si trovano quasi ancora esse occupate nella formazion della materia e vivificazion del corpo; tal'or come risvegliate e ricordate di se stesse riconoscendo il suo principio e geno, si voltano alle cose superiori, si forzano al mondo intelligibile come al natio soggiorno; quali tal volta da là per la conversione alle cose inferiori si son trabalsate sotto il fato e termini della generazione. Questi doi appolsi son figurati nelle due specie de metamorfosi espresse nel presente articolo che dice:

Quel dio che scuot' il folgore sonoro,

Then through the air I hear my heart's voice cry
"Where do you take me, reckless man? Relent!
It's rare that risk not end in desolation."

"Don't fear your sheer destruction," I reply;
"Slice surely through the clouds to die content
If heaven decrees such glorious immolation."

CICADA: I understand the expression *It was enough to rise*, but not the expression *And free myself from all ignoble ties*, unless he means that he has emerged from Plato's cave,[45] and is removed from the condition of the foolish and ignoble masses, given that the people who enjoy this contemplation are few in number.

TANSILLO: You understand it very well. In addition, by *all ignoble ties* he means the body, and sensual knowledge, from which anyone who seeks to bond with a nature of opposite kind must raise and dissociate himself.

CICADA: The Platonists say that there are two kinds of knots that bind the soul to the body. One is a certain vivifying action that descends like a ray of light from the soul to the body; and the other is a certain vital quality that descends from that ray into the body.[46] Now in what way do you understand this most noble motor and number – the soul – to be released from the ignoble number that is the body?

TANSILLO: Certainly they did not mean that it is released in any bodily way, but rather in this way: those powers that are not enclosed and imprisoned in the womb of matter sometimes, as if stunned and inebriated, still busy themselves with forming matter and giving life to the body. But then, as if awakened and brought back to themselves, they recognize their origin and kind, and turn towards higher things, forcing themselves towards the intelligible world as if to their homeland. From that vantage, sometimes, by virtue of their conversion to the lower world, they submit themselves once again to Fate and the limits of reproduction. These two driving forces are embodied in the two species of metamorphosis expressed in the following sonnet, which says:

სპ

That god who wields the lightning's booming bolt

Asterie vedde furtivo aquilone,
Mnemosine pastor, Danae oro,
Alcmena sposo, Antiopa caprone;
fu di Cadmo a le suore bianco toro,
a Leda cigno, a Dolida dragone:
io per l'altezza de l'oggetto mio
da suggetto più vil dovegno un dio.

Fu cavallo Saturno,
Nettun delfin, e vitello si tenne
Ibi, e pastor Mercurio dovenne,
un'uva Bacco, Apollo un corvo furno:
    et io (mercé d'amore)
mi cangio in dio da cosa inferiore.

Nella natura è una revoluzione et un circolo per cui, per l'altrui perfezzione e soccorso, le cose superiori s'inchinano all'inferiori, e per
la propria eccellenza e felicitade le cose inferiori s'inalzano alle superiori. Però vogliono i Pitagorici e Platonici esser donato a l'anima
ch'a certi tempi non solo per spontanea voluntà, la qual le rivolta alla
comprension de le nature, ma et anco della necessità d'una legge interna scritta e registrata dal decreto fatale vanno a trovar la propria
sorte giustamente determinata. E dicono che l'anime non tanto per
certa determinazione e proprio volere come ribelle declinano dalla divinità, quanto per certo ordine per cui vegnono affette verso la materia: onde non come per libera intenzione, ma come per certa occolta
conseguenza vegnono a cadere; e questa è l'inclinazion ch'hanno alla
generazione, come a certo minor bene. (Minor bene dico per quanto
appartiene a quella natura particolare, non già per quanto appartiene
alla natura universale dove niente accade senza ottimo fine che dispo-
ne il tutto secondo la giustizia). Nella qual generazione ritrovandosi
(per la conversione che vicissitudinalmente succede) de nuovo ritor-
nano a gli abiti superiori.

CICADA: Sì che vogliono costoro che l'anime sieno spinte dalla necessità
del fato, e non hanno proprio consiglio che le guide a fatto?

As furtive eagle to Asteria came;
Memory – a shepherd; Danaë – golden rain
Alcmena – her spouse, Antiope – a goat,
Cadmus's sisters saw a snow-white bull,
Leda – a swan, Dolis – a dragon's might.
But through the exaltation of my Goal
I, least of men, become a god outright.


Old Saturn once assumed a stallion's shape,
Neptune a dolphin's, Ibis was a calf,
And Mercury took up a shepherd's staff.
Apollo was a crow, Bacchus a grape;
Yet I (with thanks to Love)
Change from a mortal to a god above.

⤳

In nature, there is one revolution and one cycle by which, for the perfection and improvement of others, superior things bend down towards those inferior to them, and by their own excellence and happiness, inferior things raise themselves to the superior. For this reason the Pythagoreans and Platonists believe that it is granted to souls on occasion, not only by spontaneous will, which consciously directs them towards understanding essential natures, but also by the necessity of an internal law, inscribed and registered by fatal decrees, that they come to achieve the fortune that has been properly determined for them. They say in addition that souls do not turn away from divinity like rebels, by deliberation and individual will,[47] but rather by a certain order of things that inclines them towards the material world; they come to fall, then, not (as it were) by free intention, but by a certain hidden process: and this is the inclination that they have to reproduce, a kind of inclination towards a lesser good. (A lesser good, I mean, in terms of that individual nature, not in terms of universal nature, where nothing happens except for the most excellent purpose of arranging all things justly.) But after finding themselves involved yet again in reproduction (by the reversal of fortune that always follows), they will revert back to their superior habits.

CICADA: And so they remain content with the idea that souls are compelled by the necessity of fate, and make no plans of their own to guide their actions?

TANSILLO: Necessità, fato, natura, consiglio, voluntà, nelle cose giustamente e senza errore ordinate, tutti concorreno in uno. Oltre che
(come riferisce Plotino) vogliono alcuni che certe anime possano fuggir quel proprio male, le quali prima che se gli confirme l'abito corporale, conoscendo il periglio rifuggono alla mente. Perché la mente
l'inalza alle cose sublimi, come l'imaginazion l'abbassa alle cose inferiori: la mente le mantiene nel stato et identità come l'imaginazione
nel moto e diversità; la mente sempre intende uno, come l'imaginazione sempre vassi fingendo varie imagini. In mezzo è la facultà razionale
la quale è composta de tutto, come quella in cui concorre l'uno con
la moltitudine, il medesimo col diverso, il moto col stato, l'inferiore
col superiore. – Or questa conversione e vicissitudine è figurata nella
ruota delle metamorfosi, dove siede l'uomo nella parte eminente, giace una bestia al fondo, un mezzo uomo e mezzo bestia descende dalla
sinistra, et un mezzo bestia e mezzo uomo ascende da la destra. Questa conversione si mostra dove Giove, secondo la diversità de affetti e
maniere di quelli verso le cose inferiori, s'investisce de diverse figure
dovenendo in forma de bestie; e cossì gli altri dèi transmigrano in
forme basse et aliene. E per il contrario, per sentimento della propria
nobiltà, ripigliano la propria e divina forma: come il furioso eroico
inalzandosi per la conceputa specie della divina beltà e bontade, con
l'ali de l'intelletto e voluntade intellettiva s'inalza alla divinitade lasciando la forma de suggetto più basso. E però disse: «Da suggetto più
vil dovegno un Dio, Mi cangio in Dio da cosa inferiore».

# DIALOGO QUARTO

TANSILLO: Cossì si descrive il discorso de l'amor eroico per quanto tende
al proprio oggetto ch'è il sommo bene; e l'eroico intelletto che gionger si studia al proprio oggetto che è il primo vero o la verità absoluta.
Or nel primo discorso apporta tutta la somma di questo, e l'intenzione: l'ordine della quale vien descritto in cinque altri seguenti. Dice
dumque:

৵

Alle selve i mastini e i veltri slaccia

TANSILLO: Necessity, fate, nature, plans, will, among things that are ordered properly and without error, all converge as one. Furthermore
(as Plotinus reports),[48] there are those who claim that certain souls are
able to escape that individual evil: these souls, before their physical
habit has been confirmed, knowing the danger it presents, take refuge
in the mind. And because the mind raises these souls towards sublime
things, just as the imagination lowers them to inferior things, it maintains them in stasis and singleness, just as the imagination keeps them
in motion and diversity; for the mind always tends towards a single
thing, whereas the imagination continually creates various images. In
between lies the rational faculty, which is a composite of everything:
the place, so to speak, where oneness converges with multiplicity,
sameness with diversity, motion with stasis, inferior with superior. Now
this conversion and alternation is symbolized by the Wheel of Metamorphosis, where a man sits on the uppermost part, and a beast lies at
the bottom, as a half-man, half-beast descends to the left, and a half-
beast, half-man ascends to the right. This conversion is shown as well
when Jupiter assumes various shapes according to his various kinds of
affection for inferior things, taking on the form of beasts. The other
gods also transmigrate into base and alien forms. On the other hand,
through a sense of their own nobility they will eventually reassume
their proper and divine form, just as the frenzied hero, by conceiving
the idea of divine beauty and goodness, raises himself on the wings of
intellect and intellective will up towards divinity, abandoning the form
of an inferior subject. And for that reason the Nolan said: *I, least of
men, become a god outright. I ... change from a mortal to a god above.*

## FOURTH DIALOGUE

TANSILLO: This is how the progress of heroic love is described, through
which it turns towards its proper object, which is the ultimate good,
and of the heroic intellect, which strives to join itself to its proper object, which is the prime truth, or truth absolute. Now all of this, and
the point of it, is summed up in the first sonnet; the whole progression
will be described in the other five that follow. This, then, is what the
first one says:

Into the woods young Actaeon released

il giovan Atteon, quand'il destino
gli drizz'il dubio et incauto camino,
di boscareccie fiere appo la traccia.

Ecco tra l'acqui il più bel busto e faccia
che veder poss'il mortal e divino,
in ostro et alabastro et oro fino
vedde: e 'l gran cacciator dovenne caccia.

Il cervio ch'a' più folti
luoghi drizzav'i passi più leggieri,
ratto voraro i suoi gran cani e molti.

I' allargo i miei pensieri
ad alta preda, et essi a me rivolti
morte mi dan con morsi crudi e fieri.

Atteone significa l'intelletto intento alla caccia della divina sapienza, all'apprension della beltà divina. Costui slaccia «i mastini et i veltri»: de quai questi son più veloci, quelli più forti. Perché l'operazion de l'intelletto precede l'operazion della voluntade; ma questa è più vigorosa et efficace che quella: atteso che a l'intelletto umano è più amabile che comprensibile la bontade e bellezza divina, oltre che l'amore è quello che muove e spinge l'intelletto acciò che lo preceda come lanterna. «Alle selve», luoghi inculti e solitarii, visitati e perlustrati da pochissimi, e però dove non son impresse l'orme de molti uomini, «il giovane» poco esperto e prattico, come quello di cui la vita è breve et instabile il furore, «nel dubio camino» de l'incerta e ancipite raggione e affetto designato nel carattere di Pitagora, dove si vede più spinoso, inculto e deserto il destro et arduo camino, e per dove costui slaccia i veltri e mastini appo la traccia di boscareccie fiere che sono le specie intelligibili de concetti ideali, che sono occolte, perseguitate da pochi, visitate da rarissimi, e che non s'offreno a tutti quelli che le cercano: «Ecco tra l'acqui», cioè nel specchio de le similitudini, nell'opre dove riluce l'efficacia della bontade e splendor divino: le quali opre vegnon significate per il suggetto de l'acqui superiori et inferiori, che son sotto e sopra il firmamento; «vede il più bel busto e faccia», cioè

His mastiffs and his hounds, when fateful force
Set him upon the bold incautious course
Of following the track of woodland beasts.

Behold, the sylvan waters now display
The loveliest form that god or man might see;
All alabaster, pearl, and gold is she;
He saw her; and the hunter turned to prey.

The stag who sought to bend
His lightened step towards denser forest depths
His dogs devoured; they caught him in their trap.

The thoughts that I extend
Towards lofty prey recoil and deal me death,
Rending me in their fell and savage snap.

⚬⟩

*Actaeon* signifies the intellect intent on hunting divine wisdom, on grasping divine beauty. He *released / His mastiffs and his hounds,* of whom the latter are swifter, and the former stronger. In the same way, the operation of the intellect precedes the operation of the will, but the will is more vigorous and effective than the intellect, for to the human intellect divine beauty and goodness are more lovable than understandable. Besides, love, like a lantern, moves and drives the intellect to push forward. *Into the woods,* wild and solitary places, visited and traversed by very few, and where for that reason not many human tracks have left their imprint, the *young man,* inexpert and inexperienced, someone, as it were, whose life is brief and whose frenzy is unstable, *set upon the bold incautious course* of the uncertain and ambiguous reasoning and emotion that are depicted in the letter [Y] of Pythagoras,[49] where we see the arduous right-hand road as more thorny, wild, and deserted. This is the direction in which he unleashes his hounds and mastiffs, *following the track of woodland beasts,* which are the intelligible outward images of ideal concepts: for the concepts themselves are hidden, pursued by only a few, visited by fewer still, and do not offer themselves to everyone who seeks them. *Behold the sylvan waters* – that is, the mirror of likenesses, the divine creations through which

potenza et operazion esterna che vedersi possa per abito et atto di contemplazione et applicazion di mente mortal o divina, d'uomo o dio alcuno.

CICADA: Credo che non faccia comparazione, e pona come in medesimo geno la divina et umana apprensione quanto al modo di comprendere, il quale è diversissimo, ma quanto al suggetto che è medesimo.

TANSILLO: Cossì è. Dice «in ostro, alabastro et oro», perché quello che in figura nella corporal bellezza è vermiglio, bianco e biondo, nella divinità significa l'ostro della divina vigorosa potenza, l'oro della divina sapienza, l'alabastro della beltade divina, nella contemplazion della quale gli Pitagorici, Caldei, Platonici et altri al meglior modo che possono s'ingegnano d'inalzarsi. «Vedde il gran cacciator»: comprese quanto è possibile, e «dovenne caccia»: andava per predare e rimase preda, questo cacciator, per l'operazion de l'intelletto con cui converte le cose apprese in sé.

(CICADA: Intendo, perché forma le specie intelligibili a suo modo e le proporziona alla sua capacità, perché son ricevute a modo de chi le riceve.

TANSILLO.) E questa caccia per l'operazion della voluntade, per atto della quale lui si converte nell'oggetto.

CICADA: Intendo: perché lo amore transforma e converte nella cosa amata.

TANSILLO: Sai bene che l'intelletto apprende le cose intelligibilmente, *idest* secondo il suo modo; e la voluntà perseguita le cose naturalmente, cioè secondo la raggione con la quale sono in sé. Cossì Atteone con que' pensieri, que' cani che cercavano estra di sé il bene, la sapienza, la beltade, la fiera boscareccia, et in quel modo che giunse alla presenza di quella, rapito fuor di sé da tanta bellezza, dovenne preda, veddesi convertito in quel che cercava; e s'accorse che de gli suoi cani, de gli

the power of the divine splendour and goodness shines forth, and are represented in the symbol of the higher and lower waters above and beneath the firmament,[50] – *now display / The loveliest form*, that is, the divine power and external operation [of the universe] *that god or man might see*, through the habit or act of contemplation by any mind, divine or mortal, on the part of any god or man.

CICADA: I doubt that he means to compare divine and human perception, in effect putting their ways of understanding in the same category, for these are quite different. Rather, he compares them only in terms of their subject, which is identical.

TANSILLO: Exactly. He says: *All alabaster, pearl, and gold is she*, because what *crimson*, *white*, and *blonde* symbolize on the level of physical beauty is symbolized on the divine level by the *pearl* of divine power, the *gold* of divine wisdom, and the *alabaster* of divine beauty, in the contemplation of which the Pythagoreans, Chaldeans,[51] Platonists, and others contrive to elevate themselves as best they can. *He saw her*: he understood as much as was possible; *and the hunter turned to prey*: he set out to hunt and became the hunted, this young man who hunts by the operation of the intellect, through which he converts the things he perceives into himself.

CICADA: I understand: because he forms intelligible species[52] in his own way and scales them to his capacity – for the manner in which they are received depends entirely on who receives them.

TANSILLO: His hunts his prey, indeed, by the operation of his will, by whose action he converts himself into his own object.

CICADA: I understand; because love transforms and converts the lover into the thing beloved.

TANSILLO: You know, of course, that the intellect perceives things intelligibly, that is, in its own particular way. And the will pursues things naturally, that is, in accordance with the reason for which they exist as they are. Thus, Actaeon with those thoughts – those dogs – who sought outside himself for goodness, wisdom, beauty – the wild creatures – arrived into the presence of that prey, and was enraptured outside himself by such beauty. He became prey himself, and saw himself

suoi pensieri egli medesimo venea ad essere la bramata preda, perché già avendola contratta in sé, non era necessario di cercare fuor di sé la divinità.

CICADA: Però ben si dice il regno de Dio esser in noi, e la divinitade abitar in noi per forza del riformato intelletto e voluntade.

TANSILLO: Cossì è: ecco dumque come l'Atteone, messo in preda de suoi cani, perseguitato da proprii pensieri, corre e drizza i novi passi: è rinovato a procedere divinamente e più leggiermente, cioè con maggior facilità e con una più efficace lena a' luoghi più folti, alli deserti, alla reggion de cose incomprensibili; da quel ch'era un uom volgare e commune, dovien raro et eroico, ha costumi e concetti rari, e fa estraordinaria vita. «Qua gli dan morte i suoi gran cani e molti»: qua finisce la sua vita secondo il mondo pazzo, sensuale, cieco e fantastico; e comincia a vivere intellettualmente: vive vita de dèi, pascesi d'ambrosia et inebriasi di nettare. – Appresso sotto forma d'un'altra similitudine descrive la maniera con cui s'arma alla ottenzion de l'oggetto, e dice:

⁂

Mio pàssar solitario, a quella parte
ch'adombr' e ingombra tutt'il mio pensiero,
tosto t'annida: ivi ogni tuo mestiero
rafferma, ivi l'industria spendi, e l'arte.

Rinasci là, là su vogli allevarte
gli tuoi vaghi pulcini omai ch'il fiero
destin hav'espedit'il cors'intiero
contra l'impres', onde solea ritrarte.

Và: più nobil ricetto
bramo ti godi, e arai per guida un dio
che da chi nulla vede, è cieco detto.

converted into what he sought. He realized then that he himself had turned into the longed-for prey of his own dogs, of his own thoughts, because once he had contracted divinity into himself, he no longer needed to seek it outside himself.

CICADA: And thus it is rightly said that the kingdom of God is within us, and that divinity dwells within us by force of reformed intellect and will.[53]

TANSILLO: Exactly so. See then how Actaeon, preyed upon by his own dogs, persecuted by his own thoughts, runs, and *sought to bend / His lightened step towards denser forest depths*; he has been renewed in order to proceed divinely and more lightly, that is, with greater ease and with more effective energy *towards denser forest depths*, to the deserted places, to the region of things incomprehensible. He may once have been a common and ordinary man, but he has now become rare and heroic; he has uncommon actions and thoughts, and leads an extraordinary life. Here his great and numerous *dogs devoured* him; *they caught him in their trap*: here his life has ended so far as the crazy, sensual, blind, and illusory world is concerned, and he begins to live intellectually, he lives the life of the gods, he feeds upon ambrosia and intoxicates himself on nectar.

Next, in the form of another symbol, he describes how he arms himself to obtain his Object, and says:[54]

My lonely sparrow, in those lofty parts
That cast their weighty shade across my will,
Soon build your nest, confirm your every skill;
There lavish all your industry and art.

Be born again, and there bring up your flock
Of pretty fledglings, now that all the force
Of hostile fate has run its final course
Against the quest to which it posed a block.

Go forth, I hope you find
A nobler fate, and have a god to guide you:
The one the sightless dare to say is blind.

> Và: ti sia sempre pio
> ogni nume di quest'ampio architetto,
> e non tornar a me se non sei mio.

Il progresso sopra significato per il cacciator che agita gli suoi cani, vien qua ad esser figurato per un cuor alato, che è inviato da la gabbia in cui si stava ocioso e quieto, ad annidarsi alto, ad allievar gli pulcini suoi pensieri, essendo venuto il tempo in cui cessano gli impedimenti che da fuori mille occasioni, e da dentro la natural imbecillità subministravano. Licenzialo dumque per fargli più magnifica condizione, applicandolo a più alto proposito et intento, or che son più fermamente impiumate quelle potenze de l'anima significate anco da Platonici per le due ali. E gli commette per guida quel dio che dal cieco volgo è stimato insano e cieco, cioè l'amore: il qual per mercé e favor del cielo è potente di trasformarlo come in quell'altra natura alla quale aspira o quel stato dal quale va peregrinando bandito. Onde disse: «E non tornar a me che non sei mio», di sorte che non con indignità possa io dire con quell'altro:

> Lasciato m'hai, cuor mio,
> e lume d'occhi miei non sei più meco.

Appresso descrive la morte de l'anima, che da Cabalisti è chiamata «morte di bacio» figurata nella *Cantica* di Salomone dove l'amica dice:

> Che mi bacie col bacio de sua bocca,
> perché col suo ferire
> un troppo crudo amor mi fa languire.

Da altri è chiamata «sonno», dove dice il Salmista:

> S'avverrà, ch'io dia sonno a gli occhi miei,
> e le palpebre mie dormitaransi,
> arrò 'n colui pacifico riposo.

> Go forth; and find beside you
> Each deity of this masterful design;
> And don't return to me, unless you're mine.[55]

&#x223f;

The progress signified before by the hunter who stirs up his dogs, is symbolized here as a winged heart, which is sent forth from the cage where it had stayed in quiet leisure, to make its nest on high, to raise the *fledglings* that are its thoughts, for the time has come when all the impediments that have been imposed from outside by a million circumstances, and from within by natural weakness, give way. He releases his heart then, to provide it a *nobler fate*, sending it forth to a greater purpose and intent, now that those powers of the soul, which the Platonists also signify by two wings, are more fully fledged. And he assigns as its guide the god who is considered crazy and blind by the blind masses, that is, Love, who by the mercy and favour of Heaven has the power, as it were, to transform him into that other nature to which he aspires, or (to put it another way) to return him to the state from which he has been wandering in exile. Hence, he has said: *And don't return to me, for you're not mine,*[56] and I am not out of line in saying with that other poet:[57]

> You've left me, heart of mine;
> And you, light of my eyes, are no more with me.

Then he describes the death of the soul, which the Cabalists call the Death of the Kiss, symbolized in the *Canticle* of Solomon when the young woman says:[58]

> Let him kiss me with the kisses of his mouth;
> For with his blow
> A far too cruel love has laid me low.

On other occasions [the death of the soul] is called sleep, as when the Psalmist says:

> I will not give sleep to my eyes
> Or slumber to my eyelids
> Until I find a place for the Lord.

Dice dumque cossì l'alma, come languida per esser morta in sé, e viva ne l'oggetto:

చ

> Abiate cur' o furiosi al core:
> ché tropp'il mio da me fatto lontano,
> condotto in crud' e dispietata mano,
> lieto soggiorn'ove si spasma e muore.
>
> Co i pensier mel richiamo a tutte l'ore:
> et ei rubello qual girfalco insano,
> non più conosce quell'amica mano,
> onde per non tornar è uscito fore.
>
> Bella fera ch'in pene
> tante contenti, il cor, spirt', alma annodi
> con tue punte, tuoi vampi e tue catene,
>
> de sguardi, accenti e modi;
> quel che languisc' et arde, e non riviene,
> chi fia che saldi, refrigere e snodi?

చ

Ivi l'anima dolente non già per vera discontentezza, ma con affetto di certo amoroso martìre parla come drizzando il suo sermone a gli similmente appassionati: come se non a felice suo grado abbia donato congedo al core, che corre dove non può arrivare, si stende dove non può giongere, e vuol abbracciare quel che non può comprendere; e con ciò perché in vano s'allontane da lei, mai sempre più e più va accendendosi verso l'infinito.

CICADA: Onde procede, o Tansillo, che l'animo in tal progresso s'appaga del suo tormento? onde procede quel sprone ch'il stimola sempre oltre quel che possiede?

TANSILLO: Da questo che ti dirò adesso. Essendo l'intelletto divenuto all'apprension d'una certa e definita forma intelligibile, e la volontà all'affezzione commensurata a tale apprension, l'intelletto non si

Then the soul speaks in the following vein, as if she is motionless as death in herself, but alive in the object of her desires:

ॐ

> O lovers, keep watch on the heart you cherish,
> For far away from me I've let mine slip
> To land within a cruel, ruthless grip
> And in that happy haven love and perish.
>
> My thoughts at every moment call him home;
> Like some crazed falcon in rebellious flight
> He shuns the friendly hand where he'd alight
> And off, without a backward look, he's flown.
>
> Harsh beauty, in such pains
> You gloat, the heart, the spirit and soul ensnaring
> Within your talons, in your fires and chains
>
> Of glances, voice, and bearing;
> And they who languish, burn, and run away
> How will you heal them, quench them, make them stay?

ॐ

Here the soul does not really speak from true discontent, but as if she were a martyr for love, addressing her conversation to others who share her passions, as if she had not been perfectly content to bid farewell to her heart, which is rushing where it can never arrive, and longs to embrace what it can never grasp, and because it has departed from her so fruitlessly, it will burn more and more intensely for infinity.

CICADA: Then how, Tansillo, can the heart be fulfilled by its torment? How can that spur prod him on beyond what he already possesses?

TANSILLO: By what I will now reveal to you. Once the intellect has reached the perception of a certain and definite intelligible form, and the will an emotion appropriate to that perception, the intellect does not stop

ferma là: perché dal proprio lume è promosso a pensare a quello che contiene in sé ogni geno de intelligibile et appetibile, sin che vegna ad apprendere con l'intelletto l'eminenza del fonte de l'idee, oceano d'ogni verità e bontade. Indi aviene che qualumque specie gli vegna presentata e da lei vegna compresa: da questo che è presentata e compresa, giudica che sopra essa è altra maggiore e maggiore, con ciò sempre ritrovandosi in discorso e moto in certa maniera. Perché sempre vede che quel tutto che possiede è cosa misurata, e però non può essere bastante per sé, non buono da per sé, non bello da per sé; perché non è l'universo, non è l'ente absoluto: ma contratto ad esser questa natura, ad esser questa specie, questa forma rapresentata a l'intelletto e presente a l'animo. Sempre dumque dal bello compreso, e per conseguenza misurato, e conseguentemente bello per participazione, fa progresso verso quello che è veramente bello, che non ha margine e circonscrizzione alcuna.

CICADA: Questa prosecuzione mi par vana.

TANSILLO: Anzi non, atteso che non è cosa naturale né conveniente che l'infinito sia compreso, né esso può donarsi finito: percioché non sarrebe infinito; ma è conveniente e naturale che l'infinito per essere infinito sia infinitamente perseguitato (in quel modo di persecuzione il quale non ha raggion di moto fisico, ma di certo moto metafisico; et il quale non è da imperfetto al perfetto: ma va circuendo per gli gradi della perfezzione, per giongere a quel centro infinito il quale non è formato né forma).

CICADA: Vorrei sapere come circuendo si può arrivare al centro.

TANSILLO: Non posso saperlo.

CICADA: Perché lo dici?

TANSILLO: Perché posso dirlo, e lasciarvel considerare.

CICADA: Se non volete dire che quel che perséguita l'infinito, è come colui che discorrendo per la circonferenza cerca il centro, io non so quel che vogliate dire.

there, for by its own light it is moved onward to consider that which contains within itself every kind of intelligible and desirable thing, until, with his intellect, the heart comes to perceive the superiority of the wellspring of every idea, the ocean of every truth and goodness. Thereafter, whenever an intelligible species is offered him, and he understands it, then, on the basis of what has been presented and what he has understood, he reckons that above it there must be another and greater species, and in pursuing this activity he finds himself engaged in a certain kind of progress and motion. For he always sees that everything he possesses is a limited quantity, and hence cannot be sufficient in itself, nor good in itself, nor beautiful in itself, for it is not the universe; it is not absolute Being, but only Being contracted into this nature, this species, this form, represented to the intellect and presented to the spirit. And thus he forever progresses from contained, hence limited, beauty, and hence beauty only by participation, to what is truly beautiful, to what has no edge and no limit whatsoever.

CICADA: This pursuit sounds useless to me.

TANSILLO: Not at all, for it is neither natural nor appropriate that infinity be contained, or passed off as finite; otherwise it would not be infinite. On the contrary, it is appropriate and natural that infinity, being infinite, should be infinitely pursued (by a kind of pursuit that has no physical motion, but rather a certain metaphysical motion – not from imperfection to perfection; instead, it circles through the degrees of perfection, to arrive at the infinite centre, which is neither formed, nor form itself).[59]

CICADA: I want to know: how you can arrive at the centre by circling about?

TANSILLO: I cannot know.

CICADA: Why do you say that?

TANSILLO: Because I can say so, and let you think about it.

CICADA: If you do not mean that pursuing infinity is like searching for the centre by circling around the circumference, I have no idea what you mean to say.

TANSILLO: Altro.

CICADA: Or se non vuoi dechiararti, io non voglio intenderti. Ma dimmi, se ti piace: che intende per quel che dice il core esser condotto «in cruda e dispietata mano»?

TANSILLO: Intende una similitudine o metafora tolta da quel, che comunmente si dice crudele chi non si lascia fruire o non pienamente fruire, e che è più in desio che in possessione; onde per quel che possiede alcuno, non al tutto lieto soggiorna, perché brama, si spasma e muore.

CICADA: Quali son quei pensieri che il richiamano a dietro, per ritrarlo da sì generosa impresa?

TANSILLO: Gli affetti sensitivi et altri naturali che guardano al regimento del corpo.

CICADA: Che hanno a far quelli di questo che in modo alcuno non può aggiutargli, né favorirgli?

TANSILLO: Non hanno a far di lui, ma de l'anima: la quale essendo troppo intenta ad una opra o studio, dovien remissa e poco sollecita ne l'altra.

CICADA: Perché lo chiama «qual insano»?

TANSILLO: Perché soprasape.

CICADA: Sogliono esser chiamati insani quei che men sanno.

TANSILLO: Anzi insani son chiamati quelli che non sanno secondo l'ordinario, o che tendano più basso per aver men senso, o che tendano più alto per aver più intelletto.

CICADA: M'accorgo che dici il vero. Or dimmi appresso: quai sono le «punte», gli «vampi» e le «catene»?

TANSILLO: Punte son quelle nuove che stimulano e risvegliano l'affetto

TANSILLO: Something else.

CICADA: Well, if you don't want to tell me what you mean, I don't want to understand you.[60] But tell me, if you please, what does it mean to say that the heart has landed *within a cruel, ruthless grip?*

TANSILLO: It means a simile or metaphor taken from the convention of calling "cruel" a person who rejects, or is reluctant with, a lover, and who exists more in desire than in possession; hence, although the heart may possess something, he does not rest entirely happy *in that happy haven*, because he desires, *loves, and perishes.*

CICADA: What are those *thoughts* that *at every moment call him home* from such a noble quest?

TANSILLO: The sensual emotions and other natural emotions that govern the behaviour of the body.

CICADA: What have they to do with the heart, which cannot help or favour them in any way?

TANSILLO: They have nothing to do with him, but with the soul, which, being too involved with one project or desire, becomes negligent and careless with the others.

CICADA: Why call him "*some crazed falcon*"?

TANSILLO: Because he is too wise.

CICADA: Usually those who aren't wise enough are the ones we call insane.

TANSILLO: In fact, the ones who aren't wise in the ordinary sense are called insane, either because they aim lower for having less sense, or because they aim higher for having more intellect.

CICADA: I realize that you are telling the truth. Next, tell me what are the *talons, fires*, and *chains?*

TANSILLO: The talons are new things that stimulate and arouse the intel-

perché attenda; vampi son gli raggi della bellezza presente che accende quel che gli attende; catene son le parti e circonstanze che tegnono
fissi gli occhi de l'attenzione et uniti insieme gli oggetti e le potenze.

CICADA: Che son gli «sguardi, accenti e modi»?

TANSILLO: Sguardi son le raggioni con le quali l'oggetto (come ne mirasse) ci si fa presente; accenti son le raggioni con le quali ci inspira et
informa; modi son le circonstanze con le quali ci piace sempre et aggrada. Di sorte ch'il cor che dolcemente languisce, suavemente arde
e constantemente nell'opra persevera; teme che la sua ferita si salde,
ch'il suo incendio si smorze e che si sciolga il suo laccio.

CICADA: Or recita quel che séguita.

TANSILLO:

꒰꒱

    Alti, profondi e desti miei pensieri,
ch'uscir volete da materne fasce
de l'afflitt'alma, e siete acconci arcieri
per tirar al versagli' onde vi nasce

l'alto concetto: in questi erti sentieri
scontrarvi a cruda fier' il ciel non lasce.
Sovvengav'il tornar, e richiamate
il cor ch'in man di dea selvaggia late.

    Armatevi d'amore
di domestiche fiamme, et il vedere
reprimete sì forte, che straniere
non vi rendan compagni del mio core.
    Al men portate nuova
di quel ch'a lui tanto diletta e giova.

꒰꒱

Qua descrive la natural sollecitudine de l'anima attenta circa la ge-

lect so that it pays attention. The fires are the rays of present beauty, inflaming whoever pays attention to it. The chains are the parts and circumstances that keep the eyes and the attention concentrated, and the objects and powers united together.

CICADA: What are the *glances, voice, and bearing?*

TANSILLO: The *glances* are the ways in which the Object (as if it were looking) makes its presence known; *voices* are the ways in which it inspires and informs; *bearing* is the circumstance under which it always gratifies and pleases. So that the heart, which languishes sweetly, burns gently, and perseveres faithfully in his enterprise, fears that his wound will heal, that his flame will go out, and that his bonds will come loose.

CICADA: Now read the next sonnet.

TANSILLO:

᳒

> My thoughts, which hope, deep, lofty, and alert,
> To leave the swaddling of the soul in strife;
> Come forth now, dressed as archers fitly girt
> To take aim at the target; bring to life
>
> Sublime Idea; from this sylvan track
> Heaven will turn the savage beasts away.
> Be mindful of returning, summon back
> My heart, now in a cruel goddess's sway.
>
> And arm yourself with love
> Of your domestic fires; repress your vision
> So firmly that you make no rash decision
> To join my heart as sojourners above.
> Return, at least, with this:
> Some news about the reasons for its bliss.

᳒

Here is described the natural care of an attentive soul for the repro-

nerazione per l'amicizia ch'ha contratta con la materia. Ispedisce gli armati pensieri che sollecitati e spinti dalla querela della natura inferiore, son inviati a richiamar il core. L'anima l'instruisce come si debbano portare perché invaghiti et attratti dal oggetto non facilmente vegnano anch'essi sedotti a rimaner cattivi e compagni del core. Dice dumque che s'armino d'amore: di quello amore che accende con domestiche fiamme, cioè quello che è amico della generazione alla quale son ubligati, e nella cui legazione, ministerio e milizia si ritrovano. Appresso li dà ordine che reprimano il vedere chiudendo gli occhi, perché non mirino altra beltade o bontade che quella qual gli è presente, amica e madre. E conchiude al fine che se per altro ufficio non vogliono farsi rivedere, rivegnano al manco per donargli saggio delle raggioni e stato del suo core.

CICADA: Prima che procediate ad altro, vorrei intender da voi che è quello che intende l'anima quando dice a gli pensieri: «il vedere reprimete sì forte».

TANSILLO: Ti dirò. Ogni amore procede dal vedere: l'amore intelligibile dal vedere intelligibilmente; il sensibile dal vedere sensibilmente. Or questo vedere ha due significazioni: perché o significa la potenza visiva, cioè la vista, che è l'intelletto, overamente senso; o significa l'atto di quella potenza, cioè quell'applicazione che fa l'occhio o l'intelletto a l'oggetto materiale o intellettuale. Quando dumque si consegliano gli pensieri di reprimere il vedere, non s'intende del primo modo, ma del secondo; perché questo è il padre della seguente affezzion del appetito sensitivo o intellettivo.

CICADA: Questo è quello ch'io volevo udir da voi. Or se l'atto della potenza visiva è causa del male o bene che procede dal vedere, onde avviene che amiamo e desideramo di vedere? Et onde avviene che nelle cose divine abbiamo più amore che notizia?

TANSILLO: Desideriamo il vedere, perché in qualche modo veggiamo la bontà del vedere; perché siamo informati che per l'atto del vedere le cose belle s'offreno: però desideramo quell'atto, perché desideramo le cose belle.

CICADA: Desideriamo il bello e buono; ma il vedere non è bello, né buo-

duction that occurs because of its friendship with matter. It sends its armed thoughts, which, stirred and driven by the laments of baser nature, are directed to summon back the heart. The soul instructs them about how they should behave, so that, enamoured of and attracted by the Object, they will not themselves so easily be seduced into becoming fellow prisoners of the heart. Hence, she says, *And arm yourself with love*: with the love ignited by *domestic fires*, that is the love that is friendly to reproduction, to which the thoughts are pledged and serve as messengers, ministers, and soldiers. Next she orders them to *repress* their *vision* by closing their eyes, so that they will not admire any goodness or beauty but what is already present before them, as friend and mother. And finally she concludes that if they do not wish to report for any further assignment, they should at least come back to give her some account of her heart's *reasons* and condition.

CICADA: Before moving on, I would like to know from you what the soul means when she tells the thoughts, *repress your vision / so firmly*.

TANSILLO: I'll tell you. All love proceeds from vision: intelligible love from intelligible vision, sensuous love from sensuous vision. Now this vision has two meanings, for it either signifies the power of sight, that is, eyesight, which is the intellect, or sense; or else it signifies the actualizing of that power, namely, the application that the eye or the intellect makes to an object, whether material or intellectual. Thus, when the thoughts are instructed to repress their vision, it is not in the first sense but in the second; because this act of vision is father to the affection that follows on the part of sensual or intellectual desire.

CICADA: This is what I had hoped to hear from you. Now if putting the power to see into action is the cause of whatever evil or good derives from seeing, why is it that we so love and desire to see? And why do we have more love for divinity than knowledge about it?

TANSILLO: We desire to see, because in some way we see the goodness in seeing, for we know that beautiful things are available through the act of seeing; and so we desire to commit that act, because we desire beautiful things.

CICADA: We desire what is good and beautiful, but seeing is neither good

no, anzi più tosto quello è parangone o luce per cui veggiamo non solamente il bello e buono, ma anco il rio e brutto. Però mi pare ch'il vedere tanto può esser bello o buono, quanto la vista può esser bianco o nero: se dumque la vista (la quale è atto) non è bello né buono, come può cadere in desiderio?

TANSILLO: Se non per sé, certamente per altro è desiderata, essendo che l'apprension di quell'altro senza lei non si faccia.

CICADA: Che dirai se quell'altro non è in notizia di senso né d'intelletto? come, dico, può esser desiderato almanco d'esser visto, se di esso non è notizia alcuna, se verso quello né l'intelletto né il senso ha esercitato atto alcuno, anzi è in dubio se sia intelligibile o sensibile, se sia cosa corporea o incorporea, se sia uno o doi o più, d'una o d'un'altra maniera?

TANSILLO: Rispondo che nel senso e l'intelletto è un appetito et appulso al sensibile in generale; perché l'intelletto vuol intender tutto il vero, perché s'apprenda poi tutto quello che è bello o buono intelligibile: la potenza sensitiva vuol informarsi de tutto il sensibile, per che s'apprenda poi quanto è buono o bello sensibile. Indi aviene che non meno desideramo vedere le cose ignote e mai viste, che le cose conosciute e viste. E da questo non séguita ch'il desiderio non proceda da la cognizione, e che qualche cosa desideriamo che non è conosciuta; ma dico che sta pur rato e fermo che non desideriamo cose incognite. Perché se sono occolte quanto all'esser particulare, non sono occolte quanto a l'esser generale: come in tutta la potenza visiva si trova tutto il visibile in attitudine, nella intellettiva tutto l'intelligibile. Però come ne l'attitudine è l'inclinazione a l'atto, aviene che l'una e l'altra potenza è inchinata a l'atto in universale, come a cosa naturalmente appresa per buona. Non parlava dumque a sordi o ciechi l'anima, quando consultava con suoi pensieri de reprimere il vedere, il quale quantumque non sia causa prossima del volere, è però causa prima e principale.

CICADA: Che intendete per questo ultimamente detto?

nor beautiful; instead, it is a touchstone or a light, through which we see not only what is beautiful or good, but also what is bad or ugly. Hence, it seems to me that seeing can no more be beautiful or good than sight can be white or black: now if sight (which is an action) is neither beautiful nor good, how can it be desired?

TANSILLO: Although it may not be desired for itself, it is certainly desired on account of something else that cannot be grasped without being seen.

CICADA: What would you say if that something else is unknown either to the senses or the intellect? I mean, how can something be desired without at least being seen, if we have no knowledge of it whatsoever, if neither intellect nor sense have taken any action towards it, and indeed we have no idea whether it is either perceptible or understandable, whether it is material or immaterial, where it is one or two or many, whether it is of one sort or another?

TANSILLO: My answer is that within the senses and the intellect there is a desire for, and a drive towards, what is perceptible in general. The intellect wants to understand everything that is true, so that it can then perceive every intelligible thing that is beautiful or good. The power of perception wants to know about everything perceptible, so that it can then grasp every perceptible thing that is beautiful or good. Hence, it is no less desirable to see things unknown and unseen than to see things we have already known and seen. This does not mean that desire does not proceed from knowledge, and that whatever we desire is unknown; indeed, I maintain that it is still firmly established that we do not desire unknown things. For they may be hidden as to their particulars, but they are not hidden as to their existence in general, just as our whole power of sight contains everything potentially visible, and our intellect contains everything potentially understandable. It is just like our propensity and inclination to act, when each power inclines towards the act in its universal sense, as something naturally perceived as good. The soul, then, was not speaking to deaf or blind thoughts when she instructed them to repress their vision, which may not be the immediate cause of desire, but is still, after all, its prime and principal cause.

CICADA: What do you mean by what you just said?

TANSILLO: Intendo che non è la figura o la specie sensibilmente o intelligibilmente representata, la quale per sé muove: perché mentre alcuno sta mirando la figura manifesta a gli occhi, non viene ancora ad amare; ma da quello instante che l'animo concipe in se stesso quella figurata non più visibile ma cogitabile, non più dividua ma individua, non più sotto specie di cosa, ma sotto specie di buono o bello, all'ora subito nasce l'amore. Or questo è quel vedere dal quale l'anima vorrebbe divertir gli occhi de suoi pensieri. Qua la vista suole promuovere l'affetto ad amar più che non è quel che vede; perché, come poco fa ho detto, sempre considera (per la notizia universale che tiene del bello e buono) che oltre li gradi della compresa specie de buono e bello, sono altri et altri in infinito.

CICADA: Onde procede che dopo che siamo informati de la specie del bello la quale è conceputa nell'animo, pure desideriamo di pascere la vista esteriore?

TANSILLO: Da quel, che l'animo vorrebbe sempre amare quel che ama, vuol sempre vedere quel che vede. Però vuole che quella specie che gli è stata parturita dal vedere non vegna ad attenuarsi, snervarsi e perdersi. Vuol dumque sempre oltre et oltre vedere, perché quello che potrebe oscurarsi nell'affetto interiore, vegna spesso illustrato dall'aspetto esteriore: il quale come è principio de l'essere, bisogna che sia principio del conservare. Proporzionalmente accade ne l'atto del intendere e considerare: perché come la vista si referisce alle cose visibili, cossì l'intelletto alle cose intelligibili. Credo dunque ch'intendiate a che fine et in che modo l'anima intenda quando dice: «reprimet' il vedere».

CICADA: Intendo molto bene. Or seguitate a riportar quel ch'avvenne di questi pensieri.

TANSILLO: Séguita la querela de la madre contra gli detti figli li quali, per aver contra l'ordinazion sua aperti gli occhi et affissgli al splendor de l'oggetto, erano rimasi in compagnia del core. Dice dumque:

E voi ancor a me figli crudeli,
per più inasprir mia doglia, mi lasciaste;

TANSILLO: I mean that it is not the figure or species represented, perceptibly or intelligibly, that moves of itself. When someone stands gazing at a figure presented before his eyes, he does not yet love, but from the moment in which the spirit conceives that figure within itself, no longer visible but conceivable, no longer divisible but indivisible, no longer a species of thing, but a species of goodness or beauty, love is born in an instant. This is the kind of seeing from which the soul wants to deter the eyes of her thoughts, where sight moves emotion to love best what it does not see, for, as we have just stated, it always believes (on the strength of the knowledge it has of beauty and goodness) that beyond the levels of known species of goodness and beauty, there are more and more, on to infinity.

CICADA: Does it follow, then, that once we have learned about the species of beauty that is conceived in the spirit, we will still long to nourish our outward vision?

TANSILLO: The spirit, because it would like to love what it loves forever, wants to see what it sees forever. Hence, it hopes that the species born from seeing will never fade, or weaken, or be lost. It wants to see farther and farther, so that what may be obscured by inward emotions is more frequently lit by external appearance, which, as a principle of being, must also be a principle of preservation. A similar thing happens in the act of understanding and considering, for just as sight applies itself to visible things, so the intellect applies itself to intelligible things. In any case, I think you must understand what the soul means when she says *repress your vision*, and why she says it.

CICADA: I understand very well. Now report what happened to these thoughts.

TANSILLO: There follows the mother's complaint against those children of hers, who, because they have opened their eyes against her orders, and gazed on the splendour of the Object, have stayed behind to join the heart. And so she says:

ॐ

So once again, my cruel children, you
Desert me, adding to my bitter pain,

e perché senza fin più mi quereli,
ogni mia spene con voi n'amenaste.

A che il senso riman, o avari cieli?
a che queste potenze tronche e guaste,
se non per farmi materia et essempio
de sì grave martir, sì lungo scempio?

Deh (per dio) cari figli,
lasciate pur mio fuoco alato in preda,
e fate ch'io di voi alcun riveda
tornàto a me da que' tenaci artigli.
Lassa, nessun riviene
per tardo refrigerio de mie pene.

✦

Eccomi misera priva del core, abandonata da gli pensieri, lasciata da la speranza, la qual tutta avevo fissa in essi; altro non mi rimane che il senso della mia povertà, infelicità e miseria. E perché non son oltre lasciata da questo? perché non mi soccorre la morte, ora che son priva de la vita? A che mi trovo le potenze naturali prive de gli atti suoi? Come potrò io sol pascermi di specie intelligibili, come di pane intellettuale, se la sustanza di questo supposito è composta? Come potrò io trattenirmi nella domestichezza di queste amiche e care membra, che m'ho intessute in circa, contemprandole con la simmetria de le qualitadi elementari, se mi abandonano gli miei pensieri tutti et affetti, intenti verso la cura del pane immateriale e divino? Su su, o miei fugaci pensieri, o mio rubelle cuore: viva il senso di cose sensibili e l'intelletto de cose intelligibili. Soccorrasi al corpo con la materia e suggetto corporeo, e l'intelletto con gli suoi oggetti s'appaghe: a fin che conste questa composizione, non si dissolva questa machina, dove per mezzo del spirito l'anima è unita al corpo. Come, misera, per opra domestica più tosto che per esterna violenza ho da veder quest'orribil divorzio ne le mie parti e membra? Perché l'intelletto s'impaccia di donar legge al senso e privarlo de suoi cibi? e questo per il contrario resiste a quello, volendo vivere secondo gli proprii e non secondo l'altrui statuti? perché questi e non quelli possono mantenerlo e bearlo, percioché deve essere attento alla sua comoditade e vita, non a l'altrui. Non è armonia e concordia dove è unità, dove un essere vuol assorbir tutto l'essere; ma dove è ordine et analogia di cose diverse; dove ogni cosa

Moreover, to ensure that I'll complain
Forever, all my hopes absconded, too.

Now to what purpose do my wits remain,
Miserly heaven, my powers, wasted and few,
If not to make of me a precedent,
The stuff of martyrdom and dire torment?

For God's sake, dear progeny
Come, leave my wingéd fire in its place.
And let at least one of you show his face,
Slipped from those stubborn talons' mastery.
Poor me, not one's returning
At long last to relieve me of my yearning.

⸎

Look at poor me, heartless, abandoned by my thoughts, deserted by
the hope I had pinned on them; I have nothing left except the awareness of my own poverty, unhappiness, and misery. And why not have
that desert me as well? Why does death not come to my aid, now that
I have no life? Why should I have my natural powers without their actions? How can I live solely on intelligible species as my intellectual
bread, if my substance is a compound [of both matter and intellect]?
How can I linger among the parts of the dear friendly body that I
have woven around myself, governing them with the symmetry of their
basic qualities, if I have released all my thoughts and emotions, all
bent on foraging for immaterial divine bread? Enough, enough, my
fugitive thoughts, my rebel heart; let sense dine on perceptible things
and intellect on things intelligible. Let the body support itself with a
physical matter and subject, and the intellect will satisfy itself with its
own objects, so that this compound will stay together, so that this machine, in which the spirit keeps the soul united to the body, will not
fall to pieces. How, poor me, could I have foreseen that this horrible
divorce among my parts would take place because of an internal process rather than external violence? Why has the intellect involved itself
in dictating law to the senses and robbing them of their food? And why
do they, on the contrary, resist, and desire to live according to their
own laws rather than those imposed by others?

For it is their own laws, not the laws laid down by the intellect,
which will preserve the senses and make them truly happy: the senses

serva la sua natura. Pascasi dumque il senso secondo la sua legge de cose sensibili, la carne serva alla legge de la carne, il spirito alla legge del spirito, la raggione a la legge de la raggione: non si confondano, non si conturbino. Basta che uno non guaste o pregiudiche alla legge de l'altro, se non è giusto che il senso oltragge alla legge della raggione. È pur cosa vituperosa che quella tirannegge su la legge di questo, massime dove l'intelletto è più peregrino e straniero, et il senso è più domestico e come in propria patria. – Ecco dumque, o miei pensieri, come di voi, altri son ubligati di rimanere alla cura di casa, et altri possono andar a procacciare altrove. Questa è legge di natura, questa per conseguenza è legge dell'autore e principio della natura. Peccate dumque or che tutti sedotti dalla vaghezza de l'intelletto lasciate al periglio de la morte l'altra parte di me. Onde vi è nato questo malencolico e perverso umore di rompere le certe e naturali leggi de la vita vera che sta nelle vostre mani, per una incerta e che non è se non in ombra oltre gli limiti del fantastico pensiero? Vi par cosa naturale che non vivano animale et umanamente, ma divina, se elli non sono dèi ma uomini et animali? È legge del fato e della natura che ogni cosa s'adopre secondo la condizion de l'esser suo: per che dumque mentre perseguitate il nettare avaro de gli dèi, perdete il vostro presente e proprio, affligendovi forse sotto la vana speranza de l'altrui? Credete che non si debba sdegnar la natura di donarvi l'altro bene, se quello che presentaneamente v'offre tanto stoltamente dispreggiate?

> Sdegnarà il ciel dar il secondo bene
> a chi 'l primiero don caro non tiene.

Con queste e simili raggioni l'anima prendendo la causa de la parte più inferma, cerca de richiamar gli pensieri alla cura del corpo. Ma quelli (benché al tardi) vegnono a mostrarsegli non già di quella forma con cui si partiro, ma sol per dechiarargli la sua ribellione, e forzarla tutta a seguitarli. Là onde in questa forma si lagna la dolente:

must worry about their own well-being and life, not those of others. There is no harmony or concord where there is unity, where one being wants to absorb all being; harmony only exists where there is an order and correlation among different things, where every thing serves its own nature. Therefore, let the senses nourish themselves according to the laws of sensible things; let the flesh serve the laws of the flesh, the spirit the laws of the spirit, reason the laws of reason: let them not be confused; let them not upset one another. Suffice it that one not wreck or prejudice the law of the other; if it is unjust for the senses to outrage the laws of reason, it is equally improper for reason to tyrannize the laws of the flesh, especially where the intellect is more of a foreigner and stranger, and the senses are at home in their own homeland.

So, now, my thoughts, it is the same with you: some of you are obliged to stay home to care for the house, and others can be emissaries abroad. This is a law of nature, and hence also a law created by the author and ultimate principle of nature. You err, therefore, now that all of you, seduced by the beauty of the intellect, abandon the other part of me to the risk of death. Where did you get this melancholy and perverse impulse to break the sure and natural laws of the genuine life that is in your hands for an uncertain life that has no existence except in the shadows beyond the limits of imaginative thought? Does it seem natural to you that creatures should not live animally and humanly but divinely, when they are not gods but rather animals and men? It is a law of fate and nature that every thing should operate according to the condition of its being. Why, then, as you chase after the scarce nectar of the gods, do you lose your own present and proper nectar, tormenting yourself over what may be the vain hope of theirs? Do you think that nature will rush to give you another gift, when you stupidly reject the one she already offers you?

> The heavens will withhold a second favour
> From those who fail the first delight to savour.[61]

With these and similar arguments the soul, taking up the cause of the weaker party, strives to recall her thoughts to care for the body. These do appear to her (albeit much later), but no longer in the same form they had at their departure, and only to declare their rebellion, and to compel her, all of her, to follow them. Then she, lamenting, makes her complaint in this form:

ॐ

Ahi cani d'Atteon, o fiere ingrate,
che drizzai al ricetto de mia diva,
e vòti di speranza mi tornate;
anzi venendo a la materna riva,

tropp'infelice fio mi riportate:
mi sbranate, e volete ch'i' non viva.
Lasciami, vita, ch'al mio sol rimonte,
fatta gemino rio senz'il mio fonte.

Quand'il mio pondo greve
converrà che natura mi disciolga?
Quand'avverrà ch'anch'io da qua mi tolga,

e ratt' a l'alt'oggetto mi sulleve;
e insieme col mio core
e i communi pulcini ivi dimore?

ॐ

Vogliono gli Platonici che l'anima, quanto alla parte superiore, sempre consista ne l'intelletto, dove ha raggione d'intelligenza più che
de anima: atteso che anima è nomata per quanto vivifica il corpo e lo
sustenta. Cossì qua la medesima essenza che nodrisce e mantiene li
pensieri in alto insieme col magnificato cuore, se induce dalla parte
inferiore contristarsi e richiamar quelli come ribelli.

CICADA: Sì che non sono due essenze contrarie, ma una suggetta a doi
termini di contrarietade?

TANSILLO: Cossì è a punto; come il raggio del sole il quale quindi tocca la
terra et è gionto a cose inferiori et oscure che illustra, vivifica et accende, indi è gionto a l'elemento del fuoco, cioè a la stella da cui procede,
ha principio, è diffuso, et in cui ha propria et originale sussistenza:
cossì l'anima ch'è nell'orizonte della natura corporea et incorporea,
ha con che s'inalze alle cose superiori, et inchine a cose inferiori. E ciò
puoi vedere non accadere per raggion et ordine di moto locale, ma

Ai, dogs of Actaeon, ungrateful pack
I sent you out to where my goddess hides,
Now, destitute of hope, you're slinking back,
And here, along your mother's riverside

The dreadful news you brought takes me aback;
You tear me into bits, and hope I've died.
Life, leave me; towards the Sun I'll set my course,
You're just a double stream without my source.

And from my heavy weight
Will nature ever grant me my reprieve?
From here when shall I take my final leave

And rise, enraptured, to my lofty fate,
Together with my heart
To live among our fledglings, far apart?

The Platonists maintain that the soul, at least its superior part, always dwells in the intellect, where it is really more intelligence than soul. Now, the soul is named *anima* because it *animates* the body and sustains it. Here, therefore, the same essence that nourishes and keeps the thoughts on a lofty plane, along with the exalted heart, makes the soul's lower part feel sorry for itself, and prompts it to address those thoughts as rebels.

CICADA: And consequently there are not two opposing essences, but one, subjected to two opposing extremes?

TANSILLO: Exactly; just as the Sun's ray, which touches the Earth and penetrates to the dark and inferior things that it illuminates, vivifies, and inflames, at the same time also reaches elemental fire, namely, the star from which it proceeds, has its origin, is diffused, and has its proper and original subsistence. So, too, the soul, which is on the boundary between bodily and bodiless nature, has the means both to raise itself to superior things and to lower itself to things inferior. You

solamente per appulso d'una e d'un'altra potenza o facultade. Come quando il senso monta all'imaginazione, l'imaginazione alla raggione, la raggione a l'intelletto, l'intelletto a la mente, all'ora l'anima tutta si converte in Dio, et abita il mondo intelligibile. Onde per il contrario descende per conversion al mondo sensibile per via de l'intelletto, raggione, imaginazione, senso, vegetazione.

CICADA: È vero ch'ho inteso che per trovarsi l'anima nell'ultimo grado de cose divine, meritamente descende nel corpo mortale, e da questo risale di nuovo alli divini gradi; e che son tre gradi d'intelligenze: perché son altre nelle quali l'intellettuale supera l'animale, quali dicono essere l'intelligenze celesti; altre nelle quali l'animale supera l'intellettuale, quali son l'intelligenze umane; altre sono nelle quali l'uno e l'altro si portano ugualmente, come quelle de dèmoni o eroi.

TANSILLO: Nell'apprender dumque che fa la mente, non può desiderare se non quanto gli è vicino, prossimo, noto e familiare. Cossì il porco non può desiderar esser uomo, né quelle cose che son convenienti all'appetito umano. Ama più d'isvoltarsi per la luta che per un letto de bissino; ama d'unirsi ad una scrofa, non a la più bella donna che produca la natura: perché l'affetto séguita la raggion della specie (e tra gli uomini si può vedere il simile, secondo che altri son più simili a una specie de bruti animali, altri ad un'altra: questi hanno del quadrupede, quelli del volatile; e forse hanno qualche vicinanza, la qual non voglio dire, per cui si son trovati quei che sono affetti a certe sorte di bestie). Or a la mente (che trovasi oppressa dalla material congionzione de l'anima) se fia lecito di alzarsi alla contemplazione d'un altro stato in cui l'anima può arrivare, potrà certo far differenza da questo a quello, e per il futuro spreggiar il presente. Come se una bestia avesse senso della differenza che è tra le sue condizioni e quelle de l'uomo, e l'ignobiltà del stato suo dalla nobiltà del stato umano, al quale non stimasse impossibile di poter pervenire; amarebbe più la morte che li donasse quel camino et ispedizione, che la vita quale l'intrattiene in quel essere presente. Qua dumque quando l'anima si lagna dicendo «O cani d'Atteon», viene introdotta come cosa che consta di potenze inferiori solamente, e da cui la mente è ribellata con aver menato seco il core, cioè gl'intieri affetti, con tutto l'exercito de pensieri: là onde per apprension del stato presente et ignoranza d'ogni altro stato, il quale non più lo stima essere, che da lei possa esser conosciuto, si

must see that this cannot happen by some kind or order of local motion, but only by the drive from one or another power or ability. Just as the senses rise to the imagination, imagination to reason, reason to intellect, intellect to mind, the soul, in the same way, turns itself entirely towards God and inhabits the intelligible world. And alternatively, it descends by conversion to the sensual world by passing through intellect, reason, imagination, perception, down to a vegetative state.

CICADA: To be sure, I have heard that, in order to reach the highest level of divinity, the soul rightly descends into the mortal body, and from there rises again to divine levels, and that there are three levels of intelligence: because in some, the intellectual vanquishes the animal; these are called celestial intelligences, in others, the animal vanquishes the intellectual, and these are human intelligences, and there are others in which each has equal weight, like those of the demons or heroes.[62]

TANSILLO: When the mind is in the process of perceiving, it cannot desire anything but what is near it, neighbouring, known, and familiar. Hence, a pig cannot desire to be a man, nor desire the things that are proper to human desire. It would rather roll around in the mud than in a bed of satin, and would rather couple with a sow than the most beautiful woman ever produced by nature, because its affections fit its species (and you can see the same thing among men; some men are more similar to one species of brute animal, and others to another: some have the essence of a quadruped, some of a bird, and perhaps they have a certain affinity (which I do not want to describe in detail) that makes them have a special affection for certain kinds of animals. Now if the mind (which finds itself oppressed by the soul's link to matter) is able to raise itself high enough to contemplate another level where the soul arrives, then certainly it can distinguish between this lofty state and that material link, and disdain the present for the future's sake. It is as if a beast could perceive the difference between its conditions and those of men, and the ignobility of its state in comparison with the nobility of the human state; and if it reckoned that it might possibly reach the human state, it would prefer the death that might afford it such a path and progress, to the life that detains it in its present existence.[63] So when the soul complains, saying, *Ai, dogs of Actaeon*, she is concentrated entirely in her lower powers; for the mind has rebelled against her, taking the heart along, that is, all the affections, as well as the whole army of her thoughts. Hence, aware of her

lamenta de pensieri li quali al tardi convertendosi a lei vegnono per tirarla su più tosto che a farsi ricettar da lei. E qua per la distrazzione che patisce dal commune amore della materia e di cose intelligibili, si sente lacerare e sbranare di sorte che bisogna al fine di cedere a l'appulso più vigoroso e forte. Qua se per virtù di contemplazione ascende o è rapita sopra l'orizonte de gli affetti naturali, onde con più puro occhio apprenda la differenza de l'una e l'altra vita, all'ora vinta da gli alti pensieri, come morta al corpo, aspira ad alto; e benché viva nel corpo, vi vegeta come morta, e vi è presente in atto de animazione et absente in atto d'operazioni; non perché non vi operi mentre il corpo è vivo, ma perché l'operazioni del composto sono rimesse, fiacche e come dispenserate.

CICADA: Cossì un certo Teologo, che si disse rapito sin al terzo cielo, invaghito da la vista di quello, disse che desiderava la dissoluzione dal suo corpo.

TANSILLO: In questo modo, dove prima si lamentava del core e querelavasi de pensieri, ora desidera d'alzarsi con quelli in alto, e mostra il rincrescimento suo per la communicazione e familiarità contratta con la materia corporale, e dice: «Lasciami vita» corporale, e non m'impacciar «ch'io rimonti» al mio più natio albergo, «al mio sole»: lasciami ormai che più non verse pianto da gli occhi miei, o perché mal posso soccorrerli, o perché rimagno divisa dal mio bene; lasciami, che non è decente né possibile che questi doi rivi scorrano «senza il suo fonte», cioè senza il core: non bisogna (dico) che io faccia doi fiumi de lacrime qua basso, se il mio core il quale è fonte di tai fiumi, se n'è volato ad alto con le sue ninfe, che son gli miei pensieri. Cossì a poco a poco, da quel disamore e rincrescimento procede a l'odio de cose inferiori; come quasi dimostra dicendo: «Quand'il mio pondo greve converrà che natura mi disciolga?» e quel che séguita appresso.

CICADA: Intendo molto bene questo, e quello che per questo volete inferire a proposito della principale intenzione: cioè che son gli gradi de gli amori, affezzioni e furori, secondo gli gradi di maggior o minore lume di cognizione et intelligenza.

present state and ignorant of any other (for she thinks that there can be no state except the one she knows), she bewails the thoughts that, when they finally return to her, have only come to pull her upward rather than stay with her. And because of her shared love for both matter and ideas, she feels torn apart and dismembered, until, in the end, she gives way to the stronger and more powerful drive. Now, if she ascends by the power of contemplation, or is carried beyond the boundary of physical affections, so that with a purer eye she can grasp the difference between her former life and this one, then, conquered by her lofty thoughts, she aspires higher. Although she is alive in her body, she is as motionless as the dead; she is present in the act of living and absent from the act of operation, not because she fails to operate while the body is alive, but because the operations of her compound nature are weak, slack, and – literally – thoughtless.

CICADA: Thus, a certain theologian (who was said to have been taken in a rapture all the way to the third heaven), entranced by the sight of it, said that he wanted his body to dissolve.[64]

TANSILLO: And hence, no matter how much she may have complained at first to her heart and scolded her thoughts, now she wants to raise herself aloft together with them. Now she shows her regret for the familiar connection she had contracted with matter, and she says: physical *Life, leave,* do not keep me from rising to my more native haunts, *towards my Sun.* Leave me now that I no longer shed tears from my eyes, either because I am unable to soothe them, or because I remain divided from what I love; leave me, because it is neither decent nor possible for these two streams to flow without their source, that is, without the heart; there is no need (I say) for me to create two rivers of tears here below, if my heart, which is the source of those rivers, has flown away on high with its nymphs, which are my thoughts. Thus, little by little, from that former disenchantment and regret, she progresses to outright hatred of things below. She reveals this, in effect, by saying: *And from my heavy weight / Will nature ever grant me my reprieve?* and what follows after.

CICADA: I understand this very well, as well as what you want to infer from it about the principal meaning of the sonnet: namely, that there are several levels of love, affections, and frenzies, defined according to their degree of illumination by the light of knowledge and intelligence.

TANSILLO: Intendi bene. Da qua devi apprendere quella dottrina che comunmente tolta da' Pitagorici e Platonici vuole che l'anima fa gli doi progressi d'ascenso e descenso, per la cura ch'ha di sé e de la materia; per quel ch'è mossa dal proprio appetito del bene, e per quel ch'è spinta da la providenza del fato.

CICADA: Ma di grazia dimmi brevemente quel che intendi de l'anima del mondo: se ella ancora non può ascendere né descendere?

TANSILLO: Se tu dimandi del mondo secondo la volgar significazione, cioè in quanto significa l'universo, dico che quello per essere infinito e senza dimensione o misura, viene a essere inmobile et inanimato et informe, quantumque sia luogo de mondi infiniti mobili in esso, et abbia spacio infinito, dove son tanti animali grandi che son chiamati astri. Se dimandi secondo la significazione che tiene appresso gli veri filosofi, cioè in quanto significa ogni globo, ogni astro, come è questa terra, il corpo del sole, luna et altri, dico che tal anima non ascende né descende, ma si volta in circolo. Cossì essendo composta de potenze superiori et inferiori, con le superiori versa circa la divinitade, con l'inferiori circa la mole la qual viene da essa vivificata e mantenuta intra gli tropici della generazione e corrozzione de le cose viventi in essi mondi, servando la propria vita eternamente: perché l'atto della divina providenza sempre con misura et ordine medesimo, con divino calore e lume le conserva nell'ordinario e medesimo essere.

CICADA: Mi basta aver udito questo a tal proposito.

TANSILLO: Come dumque accade che queste anime particolari diversamente secondo diversi gradi d'ascenso e descenso vegnono affette quanto a gli abiti et inclinazioni, cossì vegnono a mostrar diverse maniere et ordini de furori, amori e sensi: non solamente nella scala de la natura, secondo gli ordini de diverse vite che prende l'anima in diversi corpi, come vogliono espressamente gli Pitagorici, Saduchimi et altri, et implicitamente Platone et alcuni che più profondano in esso; ma ancora nella scala de gli affetti umani, la quale è cossì numerosa de gradi come la scala della natura, atteso che l'uomo in tutte le sue potenze mostra tutte le specie de lo ente.

CICADA: Però da le affezzioni si possono conoscer gli animi, se vanno

TANSILLO: You understand me well. Next you need to learn what both the Pythagoreans and the Platonists teach: that the soul's two progressions, upward or downward, according to its devotion to itself or to matter, depend on its own desire for goodness, and on a push from a providential fate.

CICADA: But please, tell me briefly what you think about the world-soul: can it ascend and descend?

TANSILLO: If you are asking about "the world" in its common meaning, that is, the universe, I declare that, because it is infinite and without dimension or measure, it is immobile, lifeless, and formless, even though it is a place that contains infinite mobile worlds within itself, and contains infinite space, in which there are many, many great animals called stars. If you mean "the world" as it is meant by the true philosophers, that is, every globe, every star, like this earth, the body of the Sun, Moon, and the others, I declare that such a soul neither ascends nor descends, but revolves in a circle. It is composed of higher and lower powers, with the higher powers turned towards divinity and the lower towards the mass it infuses with life and keeps within the limits of generation and corruption, at least in connection with the individual things living in these worlds. But it preserves its own life eternally, for the action of divine providence preserves it in its ordinary and changeless essence with unchanging measure and order, with divine heat and light.

CICADA: I have heard enough on this point.

TANSILLO: Now things happen differently to these individual souls; their habits and inclinations are affected by their different degrees of ascent and descent, so that they display different kinds and orders of frenzies, loves, and senses; not only on the ladder of nature, according to the different lives that the soul takes on with different bodies – as the Pythagoreans, Sadduccees, and others hold explicitly, and Plato, along with some others who have studied the matter profoundly, hold implicitly – but also on the ladder of human affections, which has as many rungs as the ladder of nature, for man in all his powers displays all the species of being.

CICADA: Similarly, spirits can be known by their affections: whether they

alto o basso, o se vegnono da alto o da basso, se procedeno ad esser bestie o pur ad essere divini, secondo lo essere specifico come intesero gli Pitagorici, o secondo la similitudine de gli affetti solamente come comunmente si crede: non dovendo la anima umana posser essere anima di bruto, come ben disse Plotino, et altri Platonici secondo la sentenza del suo principe.

Tansillo: Bene. Or per venire al proposito, da furor animale questa anima descritta è promossa a furor eroico, se la dice: «Quando averrà ch'al alto oggetto mi sulleve, et ivi dimore in compagnia del mio core e miei e suoi pulcini?». Questo medesimo proposito continova quando dice:

᭍

Destin, quando sarà ch'io monte monte,
qual per bearm' a l'alte porte porte,
che fan quelle bellezze conte, conte,
el tenace dolor conforte forte

chi fe' le membra me disgionte, gionte,
né lascia mie potenze smorte morte?
Mio spirto più ch'il suo rivale vale,
s'ove l'error non più l'assale, sale.

Se dove attende, tende,
e là 've l'alto oggett'ascende, ascende:
e se quel ben ch'un sol comprende, prende,

per cui convien che tante emende mende;
esser felice lice,
come chi sol tutto predice dice.

᭍

«O destino», o fato, o divina inmutabile providenza, «quando sarà ch'io monte a quel monte», cioè ch'io vegna a tanta altezza di mente, che mi faccia toccar transportandomi quegli alti aditi e penetrali, che mi fanno evidenti e come comprese e numerate quelle «conte», cioè

are proceeding upward or downward, or whether they come from below or above, whether they are on the way to becoming beasts or becoming divine, either according to their specific essence, as the Pythagoreans understood it, or merely by similarity to their affections, as is commonly believed; for the human soul should not become the soul of a brute animal, as Plotinus rightly said, and other Platonists as well, following the teaching of their master.[65]

TANSILLO: Good. Now to get to the point, the soul described here has been promoted from animal frenzy to heroic frenzy if she can say: [*When shall I take my leave*] *And rise, enraptured, to my lofty fate: / Together with my heart / To live among our fledglings far apart?* This same discussion continues when she says:[66]

༣

Ah, Destiny, when shall I mount the mount
That to me kindly relegates the gates
That make the beauties there encountered count
And bring strong solace to my straitened straits?

Who reconnected my disjointed joints
Nor left my powers, however deadened, dead?
My spirit beyond disappointment points
When past the reach of error ahead it heads.

If it attends its ends
And where its high Object ascends ascends,
That goodness which the Sun comprises prizes,

And for its sake revises all its vices,
The benefit is fit,
Just as the future's sole writer has writ.

༣

O *Destiny*, O fate, O divine immutable providence, *when shall I mount the mount*, that is, when shall I arrive at such exaltation of the mind that it will allow me to touch, by transporting me there, those lofty sanctums and secret chambers, that reveal to me, as if they were *counted*

rare «bellezze»? Quando sarà, che «forte» et efficacemente «conforte il mio dolore» (sciogliendomi da gli strettissimi lacci de le cure, nelle quali mi trovo) «colui che fe' gionte» et unite «le mie membra», ch'erano disunite e «sgionte»: cioè l'amore che ha unito insieme queste corporee parti, ch'erano divise quanto un contrario è diviso da l'altro, e che ancora queste «potenze» intellettuali, quali ne gli atti suoi son «smorte», non le «lascia» a fatto «morte», facendole alquanto respirando aspirar in alto? Quando, dico, mi confortarà a pieno, donando a queste libero et ispedito il volo, per cui possa la mia sustanza tutta annidarsi là dove forzandomi convien ch'io emende tutte le mende mie; dove pervenendo il «mio spirito», «vale più ch'il rivale», perché non v'è oltraggio che li resista, non è contrarietà ch'il vinca, non v'è error che l'assaglia? Oh se «tende» et arriva là dove forzandosi «attende»; et «ascende» e perviene a quell'altezza, dove «ascende», vuol star montato, alto et elevato il suo oggetto: se fia che prenda quel bene che non può esser compreso da altro che da uno, cioè da se stesso (atteso che ogn'altro l'have in misura della propria capacità; e quel «solo» in tutta pienezza): all'ora avverrammi l'esser felice in quel modo che «dice chi tutto predice», cioè dice quell'altezza nella quale il dire tutto e far tutto è la medesima cosa; in quel modo che «dice» o fa chi tutto «predice», cioè chi è de tutte cose efficiente e principio: di cui il dire e preordinare è il vero fare e principiare. Ecco come per la scala de cose superiori et inferiori procede l'affetto de l'amore, come l'intelletto o sentimento procede da questi oggetti íntelligibili o conoscibili a quelli; o da quelli a questi.

CICADA: Cossì vogliono la più gran parte de sapienti la natura compiacersi in questa vicissitudinale circolazione che si vede ne la vertigine de la sua ruota.

## DIALOGO QUINTO

I. CICADA: Fate pure ch'io veda, perché da me stesso potrò considerar le condizioni di questi furori, per quel ch'appare esplicato nell'ordine (in questa milizia) qua descritto.

TANSILLO: Vedi come portano l'insegne de gli suoi affetti o fortune. La-

and numbered, the rare *beauties there encountered?* When will he, *who reconnected my joints,* which were disconnected and *disjointed, bring strong* and effective *solace* to my pain (releasing me from the *straitened* bonds of the cares in which I find myself), namely, the love that has knit together as one the parts of my body that were divided as one contrary is divided from another. Who will not leave these intellectual *powers, deadened* in their actions, for *dead* in fact, by granting them some breathing space through lofty aspirations? When, I say, will love entirely comfort me, giving these intellectual *powers* free and quickened flight, through which all my whole substance can make its nest, there where I must make an effort to *revise* all my *vices,* where, when my spirit arrives, it *heads past the reach of error, beyond disappointment points,* because there is no offence that can resist it, no opposition that can conquer it, no error that can assail it? Oh, if it *attends* and arrives to the point where its effort *ends,* and *ascends,* and penetrates to that height where it *ascends,* it wants its Object to be lofty and elevated, set *high;* if it derives that *benefit* which cannot be comprehended by anyone but its own self (for every other soul shall benefit in proportion to its own capacities, whereas this soul alone has the benefit in full measure): then it will be my lot to be happy in the manner that *the future's sole writer has writ,* that is, has decreed from that high place where saying all and doing all are one and the same; in just the way that *the future's sole writer* says or does all, that is, He who is the efficient cause and principle of all things, for whom foretelling and preordaining are the true action and principal beginning. Behold how the affection of love proceeds along the ladder of higher and lower things, just as the intellect or sentiment proceeds from these intelligible or knowable objects to those, or those to these.

CICADA: This is how most sages hold that Nature behaves, in the alternating circulation that can be seen in the whirling of its wheel.

## FIFTH DIALOGUE

**I.** CICADA: Let me see, too; to ponder the conditions of these frenzies for myself, using the marching order of this cavalcade we have here before us.[67]

TANSILLO: You see how they carry the banners of their affections or

sciamo di considerar su gli lor nomi et abiti; basta che stiamo su la significazion de l'imprese et intelligenza de la scrittura, tanto quella che
è messa per forma del corpo de la imagine, quanto l'altra ch'è messa
per il più de le volte a dechiarazion de l'impresa.


CICADA: Cossì farremo. Or ecco qua il primo che porta un scudo distinto
in quattro colori, dove nel cimiero è depinta la fiamma sotto la testa di
bronzo, da gli forami della quale esce a gran forza un fumoso vento, e
vi è scritto in circa AT REGNA SENSERUNT TRIA.

TANSILLO: Per dichiarazion di questo direi che per essere ivi il fuoco che
per quel che si vede scalda il globo, dentro il quale è l'acqua, avviene
che questo umido elemento essendo rarefatto et attenuato per la virtù
del calore, e per consequenza risoluto in vapore, richieda molto maggior spacio per esser contenuto: là onde se non trova facile exito, va
con grandissima forza, strepito e ruina a crepare il vase. Ma se vi è loco
o facile exito d'onde possa evaporare, indi esce con violenza minore a
poco a poco; e secondo la misura con cui l'acqua se risolve in vapore,
soffiando svapora in aria. Qua vien significato il cor del furioso, dove
come in esca ben disposta essendo attaccato l'amoroso foco, accade
che della sustanza vitale altro sfaville in fuoco, altro si veda in forma de
lacrimoso pianto boglier nel petto, altro per l'exito di ventosi suspiri
accender l'aria. – E però dice *At regna senserunt tria.* Dove quello 'At' ha
virtù di supponere differenza, o diversità, o contrarietà: quasi dicesse
che altro è che potrebbe aver senso del medesimo, e non l'have. Il che
è molto bene esplicato ne le rime seguenti sotto la figura:

    Dal mio gemino lume, io poca terra
soglio non parco umor porgere al mare;
da quel che dentr'il petto mi si serra
spirto non scarso accolgon l'aure avare;
el vampo che dal cor mi si disserra
si può senza scemars' al ciel alzare:
con lacrime, suspiri et ardor mio
a l'acqua, a l'aria, al fuoco rendo il fio.

fortunes. We may pass over their names and their clothing; it will be enough to concentrate on the meaning of their emblems[68] and on understanding their mottoes, both the meaning expressed by the form of the body of the image, and what is usually expressed in words by the motto.[69]

CICADA: Let us do exactly that. Now here is the first, which bears a shield divided into four colours. The crest shows a flame beneath a brazen jar; a gust of vapour rushes forth from its opening, and around it is written: BUT THEY SAW THREE KINGDOMS.

TANSILLO: To explain this I would say that because the fire is present, which, as we see, heats the globe full of water, this moist element, thinned and rarefied by the power of heat, and consequently transformed into steam, needs a great deal more space to contain it; hence, unless it finds a convenient exit, it will, with extreme force, impetus, and destructive power, proceed to crack the vessel. But if there is an easy outlet for evaporation, then the steam issues forth with less violence, gradually, and as soon as the water transforms into steam, it evaporates into the air in gusts. This signifies the heart of the frenzied hero, which has been set over the lighted fire of love like meat on a spit: part of its vital substance blazes to ash in the fire, and, as we see, part boils in his breast in the form of tearful weeping, and part inflames the air with its windy sighs.

This is why the motto says: "but they saw three kingdoms." That "but" presupposes differences, or diversity, or opposition, as if to say that there is someone else who might have seen the same thing, but has not. This is very well expressed in the sonnet that appears beneath the image:

From my twin lights, though I'm scant earth at best
I give the sea my generous libation;
From what has been enclosed within my chest
The greedy breezes snatch each exhalation.
The flame my heart releases from my breast
Can touch the heavens without dissipation.
With tears, and sighs, and my ardent desire
I pay tribute to water, air, and fire.

Accogli' acqu', aria, foco
qualche parte di me: ma la mia dea
si dimostra cotant'iniqua e rea,

che né mio pianto appo lei trova loco,
    né la mia voce ascolta,
né piatos'al mi' ardor umqua si volta.

⁂

Qua la suggetta materia significata per la «terra» è la sustanza del furioso; versa dal «gemino lume», cioè da gli occhi, copiose lacrime che
fluiscono al mare; manda dal petto la grandezza e moltitudine de suspiri a l'aria capacissimo; et il vampo del suo core non come picciola
favilla o debil fiamma nel camino de l'aria s'intepidisce, infuma e tra-
smigra in altro essere: ma come potente e vigoroso (più tosto acqui-
stando de l'altrui che perdendo del proprio) gionge alla congenea
sfera.

CICADA: Ho ben compreso il tutto. A l'altro.

II. TANSILLO: Appresso è designato un che ha nel suo scudo parimente
destinto in quattro colori, il cimiero, dove è un sole che distende gli
raggi nel dorso de la terra; e vi è una nota che dice IDEM SEMPER UBI-
QUE TOTUM.

CICADA: Vedo che non può esser facile l'interpretazione.

TANSILLO: Tanto il senso è più eccellente, quanto è men volgare: il qual
vedrete essere solo, unico e non stiracchiato. Dovete considerare che
il sole benché al rispetto de diverse regioni de la terra, per ciascuna,
sia diverso, a tempi a tempi, a loco a loco, a parte a parte; al riguardo
però del globo tutto, come medesimo, sempre et in cadaun loco fa tutto: atteso che in qualumque punto de l'eclittica ch'egli si trove, viene a
far l'inverno, l'estade, l'autunno e la primavera; e l'universal globo de
la terra a ricevere in sé le dette quattro tempeste. Perché mai è caldo a
una parte che non sia freddo a l'altra; come quando fia a noi nel tropico del Cancro caldissimo, è freddissimo al tropico del Capricorno;
di sorte che è a medesima raggione l'inverno a quella parte, con cui a
questa è l'estade, et a quelli che son nel mezzo è temperato, secondo

Water, air, and fire: these three
Take parts of me; but my divinity
Reveals herself as cruel and ruled by spite;

My weeping finds no welcome in her sight
She will not hear my cries,
Nor towards my ardour turn forbearing eyes.

༄

Here the captive matter symbolized by *earth* is the frenzied hero's physical substance; from his *twin lights*, that is, his eyes, he sheds copious *tears* that flow to the sea; from his *breast* he sends forth a great multitude of *sighs* into the capacious air. The fire of his heart is not like some little spark or faltering flame that gathers warmth in the fireplace, turns into smoke, and transmigrates into another state of being; it is powerful and vigorous, engulfing rather than yielding to its surroundings, and thus it penetrates to its own sphere.

CICADA: I have understood it all well. On to the next.

II. TANSILLO: The next insignia has a shield divided into four colours, and on its crest there is a sun spreading its rays over the face of the earth. And there is a motto that says, EVER THE SAME, EVERYWHERE ENTIRE.

CICADA: I see that the interpretation cannot be easy.

TANSILLO: The more excellent the meaning, the less accessible, and you will see that it is single, exclusive, and succinct. Consider the Sun; although its effects differ in different regions of the earth, from time to time, from place to place, from part to part, nonetheless, with respect to Earth's globe itself it is constant: it does what it does at all times and in every single place. Thus, at any point along the ecliptic the Sun creates winter, summer, autumn, and spring, and the whole earthly globe experiences the same four seasons. It is never hot in one part without being cold in another; when we at the Tropic of Cancer are hottest, it is bitter cold at the Tropic of Capricorn. If it is winter down there, for the same reason it must be summer here, and for those who live in between it is temperate, in the direction of either spring or autumn.

la disposizion vernale o autumnale. Cossì la terra sempre sente le piogge, li venti, gli calori, gli freddi; anzi non sarebbe umida qua, se non
disseccasse in un'altra parte, e non la scalderebe da questo lato il sole,
se non avesse lasciato d'iscaldarla da quell'altro.

CICADA: Prima che finisci ad conchiudere, io intendo quel che volete
dire. Intendeva egli che come il sole sempre dona tutte le impressioni a la terra, e questa sempre le riceve intiere e tutte: cossì l'oggetto
del furioso col suo splendore attivamente lo fa suggetto passivo de
lacrime, che son l'acqui; de ardori, che son gl'incendii; e de suspiri
quai son certi vapori, che son mezzi che parteno dal fuoco e vanno a
l'acqui, o partono da l'acqui e vanno al fuoco.

TANSILLO: Assai bene s'esplica appresso:

ᘒ

  Quando declin'il sol al Capricorno,
fan più ricco le piogge ogni torrente;
se va per l'equinozzio o fa ritorno,
ogni postiglion d'Eolo più si sente;
e scalda più col più prolisso giorno,
nel tempo che rimonta al Cancro ardente:
non van miei pianti, suspiri et ardori
con tai freddi, temperie e calori.

  Sempre equalmente in pianto,
quantumqu' intensi sien suspiri e fiamme.
E benché troppo m'inacqui et infiamme,
mai avvien ch'io suspire men che tanto:
  infinito mi scaldo,
equalment' a i suspiri e pianger saldo.

ᘒ

CICADA: Questo non tanto dechiara il senso de la divisa come il precedente discorso faceva: quanto più tosto dice la consequenza di quello,
o l'accompagna.

Thus, the Earth always feels rain, wind, heat, cold; indeed, it could not be moist here if it were not parched somewhere else, and the Sun could not warm this side of the globe if it had not left off warming the other side.

CICADA: Even before you reach your conclusion, I understand what you are saying. He meant that just as the Sun always conveys all its effects to the Earth, and the Earth always receives them, every one of them, entire, so, in the same way, the object of the frenzied hero, with her splendour, actively turns him into the passive subject of *tears*, which are water, of *ardours*, which are fires, and of *sighs*, which are certain vapours in between, for they begin as fire and tend towards water, or begin as water and tend towards fire.

TANSILLO: The next sonnet puts it extremely well:

༄

When into Capricorn the Sun bends low
The rains make every torrent wide and rich;
When through the equinox it comes or goes
We feel the winds that Aeolus's postmen pitch.
It warms the more with each expanding day
As up to fiery Cancer it makes its way.
But my tears, fires, and sighs don't move in time
With earthly chills and heats and tempered climes.

My weeping never alters
No matter how intense my sighs and fires.
Though I'm beset by floods and searing pyres,
It never happens that my sighing falters.
I burn without reprieve;
And with an equal constancy I grieve.

༄

CICADA: Unlike the previous sonnet, this one does not explain the meaning of the emblem so much as predict its consequences, or supplement it.

TANSILLO: Dite megliore, che la figura è latente ne la prima parte, et il motto è molto esplicato ne la seconda; come l'uno e l'altro è molto propriamente significato nel tipo del sole e de la terra.

CICADA: Passamo al terzo.

III. TANSILLO: Il terzo nel scudo porta un fanciullo ignudo disteso sul verde prato, e che appoggia la testa sullevata sul braccio con gli occhi rivoltati verso il cielo a certi edificii de stanze, torri, giardini et orti che son sopra le nuvole, e vi è un castello di cui la materia è fuoco; et in mezzo è la nota che dice MUTUO FULCIMUR.

CICADA: Che vuol dir questo?

TANSILLO: Intendi quel furioso significato per il fanciullo ignudo come semplice, puro et esposto a tutti gli accidenti di natura e di fortuna, qualmente con la forza del pensiero edifica castegli in aria, e tra l'altre cose una torre di cui l'architettore è l'amore, la materia l'amoroso foco, et il fabricatore egli medesimo, che dice *Mutuo fulcimur.* cioè io vi edifico e vi sustegno là con il pensiero, e voi mi sustenete qua con la speranza: voi non sareste in essere se non fusse l'imaginazione et il pensiero con cui vi formo e sustegno, et io non sarrei in vita se non fusse il refrigerio e conforto che per vostro mezzo ricevo.

CICADA: È vero che non è cosa tanto vana e tanto chimerica fantasia, che non sia più reale e vera medecina d'un furioso cuore, che qualsivoglia erba, pietra, oglio, o altra specie che produca la natura.

TANSILLO: Più possono far gli maghi per mezzo della fede, che gli medici per via de la verità: e ne gli più gravi morbi più vegnono giovati gl'infermi con credere quel tanto che quelli dicono, che con intendere quel tanto che questi faccino. Or legansi le rime:

Sopra de nubi, a l'eminente loco,
quando tal volta vaneggiando avvampo,

TANSILLO: Better still, we might say that the insignia is latent in the first part of the sonnet and the motto is quite explicit in the second; just as the former and the latter are most appropriately symbolized in the figures of the Sun and the Earth.

CICADA: Let us pass on to the third.

**III.** TANSILLO: The shield of the third shows a naked boy, reclining in a green meadow, who props his raised head on his arm with his eyes turned heavenward towards certain buildings with chambers, towers, fields, and gardens above the clouds; and there is a castle made of fire. In between them is the motto, which says, WE SUPPORT EACH OTHER.

CICADA: What does this mean?

TANSILLO: As you see, the naked boy represents the frenzied hero as simple, pure, and exposed to all the accidents of nature and fortune, and shows how by the power of thought he builds castles in the air, including a tower whose architect is love,[70] whose material is love's fire, and whose builder is the hero himself, who says, "We support each other," that is, I build you and keep you there with my thoughts, and you sustain me here with hope. You would not exist without my imagination and thought, by which I form you and sustain you, and I would not have survived except for the refreshment and comfort that I receive from you.

CICADA: It is true that there is nothing so vain, no fantasy so chimerical, that it cannot provide more real and genuine medicine for a frenzied heart, than any herb, stone, oil, or other species that nature produces.

TANSILLO: The Magi can do more by faith than the doctors by truth; and with the gravest diseases the sick benefit more from believing what the former tell them than from understanding whatever the latter do. Now let's read the sonnet:

Above the clouds, upon that lofty site,
When, in my vagrant thoughts, I flash and flare,

per di mio spirto refrigerio e scampo,
tal formo a l'aria castel de mio foco:

s'il mio destin fatale china un poco,
a fin ch'intenda l'alta grazia il vampo
in cui mi muoio, e non si sdegn' o adire,
o felice mia pena e mio morire.

   Quella de fiamme e lacci
tuoi, o garzon, che gli uomini e gli divi
fan suspirar, e soglion far cattivi,

l'ardor non sente, né prova gl'impacci:
   ma può 'ntrodurt', o Amore,
man di pietà, se mostri il mio dolore.

༅

CICADA: Mostra che quel che lo pasce in fantasia, e gli fomenta il spirito, è che (essendo lui tanto privo d'ardire d'esplicarsi a far conoscere la sua pena, quanto profondamente suggetto a tal martìre), se avvenesse ch'il fato rigido e rubelle chinasse un poco (perché voglia il destino al fin rasserenargli il volto), con far che senza sdegno o ira de l'alto oggetto gli venesse manifesto, non stima egli gioia tanto felice, né vita tanto beata, quanto per tal successo lui stime felice la sua pena, e beato il suo morire.

TANSILLO: E con questo viene a dechiarar a l'Amore che la raggion per cui possa aver adito in quel petto, non è quell'ordinaria de le armi con le quali suol cattivar uomini e dèi; ma solamente con fargli aperto il cuor focoso et il travagliato spirito de lui; a la vista del quale fia necessario che la compassion possa aprirgli il passo et introdurlo a quella difficil stanza.

IV. CICADA: Che significa qua quella mosca che vola circa la fiamma e sta quasi quasi per bruggiarsi, e che vuol dir quel motto: HOSTIS NON HOSTIS?

TANSILLO: Non è molto difficile la significazione de la farfalla, che sedotta dalla vaghezza del splendore, innocente et amica va ad incorrere

For my spirit's refreshment and delight
I build a fiery castle in the air.

If my life's destiny would but commence
In sublime grace to comprehend the fire
Wherein I die, without rage or offence,
How happily I'd languish and expire!

She of your flames and toils
(O youth), that make gods and humanity
Sigh and surrender to captivity,

Feels neither scorch nor subjugation's coils
And yet (O Love) she'll offer
A kindly hand, if you show how I suffer.

ॐ

CICADA: This shows that what nourishes him in his imagination and warms his spirit is the hope (so reluctant is he to explain himself and reveal his suffering, and how profoundly he is subjected to that martyrdom) that if his stern and rebellious fate were to relax a little (and finally bring some serenity to his face) by making his lofty Object appear to him without inciting disdain or anger, he would not reckon joy to be as happy, or life as blessed, as he would in that case regard his pain as happy and his death as blessed.[71]

TANSILLO: And with this he declares to Love that he desires to enter that breast not by the ordinary means; namely, by the arms with which Love normally captures men and gods, but only by opening up his fiery heart and anguished spirit; at the sight of which compassion must needs make way for him and introduce him into that inaccessible chamber.

**IV.** CICADA: What is the meaning of that insect that flies around the flame and is on the verge of burning itself up, and what does that motto mean: THE ENEMY IS NO ENEMY?

TANSILLO: It is a moth,[72] whose meaning is not so difficult to interpret: seduced by the beauty of the light, it rushes, innocent and friendly,

nelle mortifere fiamme: onde *hostis* sta scritto per l'effetto del fuoco, *non hostis* per l'affetto de la mosca. *Hostis* la mosca passivamente, *non hostis* attivamente. *Hostis* la fiamma per l'ardore, *non hostis* per il splendore.

Cicada: Or che è quel che sta scritto nella tabella?

Tansillo:

꒰꒱

Mai fia che de l'amor io mi lamente,
senza del qual non vogli' esser felice;
sia pur ver che per lui penoso stente,
non vo' non voler quel che sì me lice:
sia chiar o fosch' il ciel, fredd' o ardente,
sempr'un sarò ver l'unica fenice.
Mal può disfar altro destin o sorte
quel nodo che non può sciòrre la morte.

Al cor, al spirt', a l'alma
non è piacer, o libertad', o vita,
qual tanto arrida, giove e sia gradita,

qual più sia dolce, graziosa et alma,
  ch'il stento, giogo e morte,
ch'ho per natura, voluntade e sorte.

꒰꒱

Qua nella figura mostra la similitudine che ha il furioso con la farfalla affetta verso la sua luce; ne gli carmi poi mostra più differenza e dissimilitudine che altro: essendo che comunmente si crede che se quella mosca prevedesse la sua ruina non tanto ora séguita la luce quanto all'ora la fuggirebbe, stimando male di perder l'esser proprio risolvendosi in quel fuoco nemico. Ma a costui non men piace svanir nelle fiamme de l'amoroso ardore, che essere abstratto a contemplar la beltà di quel raro splendore, sotto il qual per inclinazion di natura, per elezzion di voluntade e disposizion del fato, stenta, serve e muore: più gaio, più risoluto e più gagliardo, che sotto qualsivogli'altro piacer

into the deadly flames. Thus, the motto reads *The enemy* for the effect of the fire, and *no enemy* for the affection of the moth. The moth is an *Enemy* in a passive sense, *no enemy* in an active sense. The flame is an *Enemy* for its burning, *no enemy* for its glow.

CICADA: Then what is written on the panel below?

TANSILLO:

৵৲

> O may I never come to rue the love
> Without which I've no wish for happiness!
> Though for its sake I sacrifice to prove
> I've no wish not to wish for its largesse.
> Whether the sky be bright, dark, chill, or hot
> To that one Phoenix I'll be wholly true;
> No destiny or fate can breach the knot
> That even death itself could not undo.
>
> For heart, spirit, and soul
> No joy, liberty, life can offer me
> Laughter, or sustenance, or amity
>
> More sweet, welcome, or soothing to my soul
> Than that grief, yoke, dead weight
> I have by nature, preference, and fate.

৵৲

This image shows the similarity between the frenzied hero and the moth attracted to its flame: but the sonnet stresses difference and dissimilarity rather than likeness. For it is commonly believed that if the moth foresees its own ruin, then it will flee the light rather than follow it, sensing that it is bad to lose its own existence by immolating itself in that hostile fire. But for the frenzied hero, vanishing in the flames of amorous ardour is no less pleasant than being carried off to contemplate the beauty of that rare brilliance under whose dominion, by natural inclination, choice of the will, and disposition of fate, he suffers, serves, and dies, more joyous, more resolute, and more coura-

che s'offra al core, libertà che si conceda al spirito, e vita che si ritrove
ne l'alma.

CICADA: Dimmi, perché dice: «sempr'un sarò»?

TANSILLO: Perché gli par degno d'apportar raggione della sua constanza, atteso che il sapiente si muta con la luna, il stolto si muta come la
luna. Cossì questo è unico con la fenice unica.

V. CICADA: Bene; ma che significa quella frasca di palma, circa la quale
è il motto: CAESAR ADEST.

TANSILLO: Senza molto discorrere, tutto potrassi intendere per quel che
è scritto nella tavola:

᷍

    Trionfator invitto di Farsaglia,
essendo quasi estinti i tuoi guerrieri,
al vederti, fortissimi 'n battaglia
sorser, e vinser suoi nemici altieri.
Tal il mio ben, ch'al ben del ciel s'agguaglia,
fatto a la vista de gli miei pensieri,
ch'eran da l'alma disdegnosa spenti,
le fa tornar più che l'amor possenti.

    La sua sola presenza,
o memoria di lei, sì le ravviva,
che con imperio e potestade diva
dòman ogni contraria violenza.
    La mi governa in pace;
né fa cessar quel laccio e quella face.

᷍

Tal volta le potenze de l'anima inferiori, come un gagliardo e nemico essercito che si trova nel proprio paese, prattico, esperto et acco-
modato, insorge contra il peregrino adversario che dal monte de la
intelligenza scende a frenar gli popoli de le valli e palustri pianure.
Dove dal rigor della presenza de nemici e difficultà de precipitosi fossi

geous than he would be under the influence of any other pleasure that might offer itself to the heart, any liberty that might be conceded to the spirit, or any life that might be found in the soul.

CICADA: Tell me, why does he say: *I'll be wholly true?*

TANSILLO: Because he thinks it honourable to justify his constancy. A wise man does not change with the Moon, whereas a fool changes just like the Moon. And so he is one with the one and only Phoenix.

**V.** CICADA: Fine, but what is the meaning of that palm branch surrounded by the motto CAESAR IS HERE?[73]

TANSILLO: Without going on at length, everything can be understood from what is inscribed on the panel below:

ॐ

Triumphant at Pharsalia you stood;
Your warriors had nearly lost the fight –
But seeing you, revived, your army stood
In strength, and put the haughty foe to flight.
So my good lady, peer of Heaven's good
If once my thoughts have caught her in their sight
Commands them, wearied by the soul's disdain,
More powerful than love, to rise again.

Her very company,
The memory of her, revives them so
That under divine sovereignty they go
Subduing every violent enemy.
She governs me in peace
And lets neither my blaze nor bondage cease.

ॐ

Sometimes the lower powers of the soul, like a brave and hostile army that finds itself in its own country, experienced, expert, and prepared, rises up against the foreign adversary that sweeps down from the mountain of understanding to restrain the peoples of the valleys and swampy plains.[74] There, hard pressed by the enemy and the impassi-

vansi perdendo, e perderiansi a fatto, se non fusse certa conversione al splendor de la specie intelligibile mediante l'atto della contemplazione: mentre da gli gradi inferiori si converte a gli gradi superiori.

CICADA: Che gradi son questi?

TANSILLO: Li gradi della contemplazione son come li gradi della luce, la quale nullamente è nelle tenebre; alcunamente è ne l'ombra; megliormente è ne gli colori secondo gli suoi ordini da l'un contrario ch'è il nero a l'altro che è il bianco; più efficacemente è nel splendor diffuso su gli corpi tersi e trasparenti, come nel specchio o nella luna; più vivamente ne gli raggi sparsi dal sole; altissima e principalissimamente nel sole istesso. Or essendo cossì ordinate le potenze apprensive et affettive de le quali sempre la prossima conseguente have affinità con la prossima antecedente, e per la conversione a quella che la sulleva, viene a rinforzarsi contra l'inferior che la deprime (come la raggione per la conversione a l'intelletto non è sedotta o vinta dalla notizia o apprensione et affetto sensitivo, ma più tosto secondo la legge di quello viene a domar e correger questo), accade che quando l'appetito razionale contrasta con la concupiscenza sensuale, se a quello per atto di conversione si presente a gli occhi la luce intelligenziale, viene a repigliar la smarrita virtude, rinforzar i nervi, spaventa e mette in rotta gli nemici.

CICADA: In che maniera intendete che si faccia cotal conversione?

TANSILLO: Con tre preparazioni che nota il contemplativo Plotino nel libro *Della bellezza intelligibile*. de le quali «la prima è proporsi de conformarsi d'una similitudine divina» divertendo la vista da cose che sono infra la propria perfezzione, e commune alle specie uguali et inferiori; «secondo è l'applicarsi con tutta l'intenzione et attenzione alle specie superiori; terzo il cattivar tutta la voluntade et affetto a Dio». Perché da qua avverrà che senza dubio gl'influisca la divinità la qual da per tutto è presente e pronta ad ingerirsi a chi se gli volta con l'atto de l'intelletto, et aperto se gli espone con l'affetto de la voluntade.

CICADA: Non è dumque corporal bellezza quella che invaghisce costui?

bility of the precipitous gorges, they begin to lose their way, and they would be truly lost if they could not turn towards the splendour of intelligible species through the act of contemplation, which, in the meantime, converts them from lower levels to higher.

CICADA: What are these levels?

TANSILLO: The levels of contemplation are like the levels of light, which is not present at all in darkness, present to some degree in shadow, present to a greater degree in the colours, according to their order, which ranges from one extreme, which is black, to the other, which is white, present still more effectively in the splendour diffused by clear and transparent bodies, as by a mirror or the Moon, present with greater vigour still in the rays shed by the Sun, reaching its most lofty and principal level in the Sun itself. Now the powers of perception and affection are so ordered that every successive consequence is linked to its immediate antecedent, and thus by conversion into the superior force that raises them, they are reinforced against the inferior force that presses them back downward (just as reason, once converted to intellect, is no longer seduced or bound by sensual knowledge, perception, or emotion, but instead tames and corrects them). Thus, when rational desire competes with sensual lust, if that rational desire by act of conversion presents the light of intelligence to the eyes, it will recapture lost virtue, reinforce the nerves, strike fear into the enemy, and rout them.

CICADA: How, as you understand it, is this conversion made?

TANSILLO: By three preparations that the contemplative Plotinus notes in his book *On Intelligible Beauty*.[75] The first of these is to set before oneself the goal of conforming to a divine likeness by diverting the sight from things that are beneath its perfection, and common to the range of inferior species. The second is to apply oneself with complete attention and concentration to the superior species; the third, to subject all of the will and affection to God. Then, beyond any doubt, divinity will exert its influence, which is present everywhere in any case, ready to be absorbed by anyone who turns towards it by an action of the intellect, and offers himself openly with the affection of his will.

CICADA: So it is not some physical beauty that attracts him?

TANSILLO: Non certo, perché la non è vera né constante bellezza, e però non può caggionar vero né constante amore: la bellezza che si vede ne gli corpi è una cosa accidentale et umbratile e come l'altre che sono assorbite, alterate e guaste per la mutazione del suggetto, il quale sovente da bello si fa brutto senza che alterazion veruna si faccia ne l'anima. La raggion dumque apprende il più vero bello per conversione a quello che fa la beltade nel corpo, e viene a formarlo bello: e questa è l'anima che l'ha talmente fabricato e infigurato. Appresso l'intelletto s'inalza più, et apprende bene che l'anima è incomparabilmente bella sopra la bellezza che possa esser ne gli corpi; ma non si persuade che sia bella da per sé e primitivamente: atteso che non accaderebbe quella differenza che si vede nel geno de le anime, onde altre son savie, amabili e belle; altre stolte, odiose e brutte. Bisogna dumque alzarsi a quello intelletto superiore il quale da per sé è bello e da per sé è buono. Questo è quell'unico e supremo capitano, qual solo messo alla presenza de gli occhi de militanti pensieri, le illustra, incoraggia, rinforza e rende vittoriosi sul dispreggio d'ogn'altra bellezza e ripudio di qualsivogli'altro bene. Questa dumque è la presenza che fa superar ogni difficultà e vincere ogni violenza.

CICADA: Intendo tutto. Ma che vuol dire «La mi governa in pace, Né fa cessar quel laccio e quella face»?

TANSILLO: Intende e prova, che qualsivoglia sorte d'amore quanto ha maggior imperio e più certo domìno, tanto fa sentir più stretti i lacci, più fermo il giogo, e più ardenti le fiamme. Al contrario de gli ordinarii prencipi e tiranni, che usano maggior strettezza e forza, dove veggono aver minore imperio.

CICADA: Passa oltre.

VI. TANSILLO: Appresso veggio descritta la fantasia d'una fenice volante, alla quale è volto un fanciullo che bruggia in mezzo le fiamme, e vi è il motto: FATA OBSTANT. Ma perché s'intenda meglior, leggasi la tavoletta:

꒰꒱

Unico augel del sol, vaga Fenice,
ch'appareggi col mondo gli anni tui,

TANSILLO: Certainly not, for it is not a real and constant beauty, and for that reason cannot generate real or constant love. The beauty we see in physical bodies is an accidental and shadowy thing, like other accidental qualities that are absorbed, altered, and wasted by change in a subject, which often may be transformed from beautiful to ugly without any alteration occurring in the soul. Reason perceives a more genuine beauty by converting to what creates beauty in the body, and then forms it into something beautiful: that is, the soul, which has thus formed and figured it. Then the intellect rises still higher, and grasps that the soul is incomparably more beautiful than the beauty that may exist in bodies, but it is not convinced that this beauty of soul is beautiful originally and in itself; otherwise we would not see that difference among souls that makes some wise, amiable, and beautiful, and others stupid, odious, and ugly. Hence, it must rise to the superior intellect that is beautiful in itself and good in itself: that one supreme captain, who by his mere presence before the eyes of the soldiering thoughts will shed light upon them, encourage them, reinforce them, and make them victorious at the expense of every other kind of beauty, repudiating every other kind of good. This, then, is the presence that makes it possible to overcome every difficulty and vanquish every violence.

CICADA: I understand everything. But what does it mean to say: *She governs me in peace / And lets neither my blaze nor bondage cease?*

TANSILLO: It means and proves that for any sort of love, the greater its authority and the more certain its dominion, the tighter its bonds, the firmer its yoke, and the more ardent its flames, unlike ordinary princes and tyrants, who use greater stringency and force whenever they have less authority.

CICADA: On to the next.

VI. TANSILLO: Next we see the figure of a flying Phoenix, to whom a lad turns who is burning in the flames,[76] with the motto THE FATES STAND IN THE WAY. But in order to understand better, let's read the panel:

O lovely Phoenix, sole bird of the Sun,
The years you've spent in Happy Araby[77]

quai colmi ne l'Arabia felice:
tu sei chi fuste, io son quel che non fui;·

io per caldo d'amor muoio infelice,
ma te ravviv'il sol co' raggi sui;
tu bruggi 'n un, et io in ogni loco;
io da Cupido, hai tu da Febo il foco.

   Hai termini prefissi
di lunga vita, et io ho breve fine,
che pronto s'offre per mille ruine,

né so quel che vivrò, né quel che vissi.
   Me cieco fato adduce,
tu certo torni a riveder tua luce.

            ॐ

Dal senso de gli versi si vede che nella figura si disegna l'antitesi de la sorte de la fenice e del furioso; e che il motto *Fata obstant*, non è per significar che gli fati siano contrarii o al fanciullo, o a la fenice, o a l'uno e l'altro; ma che non son medesimi, ma diversi et opposti gli decreti fatali de l'uno e gli fatali decreti de l'altro: perché la fenice è quel che fu, essendoché la medesima materia per il fuoco si rinova ad esser corpo di fenice, e medesimo spirito et anima viene ad informarla; il furioso è quel che non fu, perché il suggetto che è d'uomo, prima fu di qualch'altra specie secondo innumerabili differenze. Di sorte che si sa quel che fu la fenice, e si sa quel che sarà: ma questo suggetto non può tornar se non per molti et incerti mezzi ad investirsi de medesima o simil forma naturale. Appresso, la fenice al cospetto del sole cangia la morte con la vita; e questo nel cospetto d'amore muta la vita con la morte. Oltre, quella su l'aromatico altare accende il foco; e questo il trova e mena seco, ovumque va. Quella ancora ha certi termini di lunga vita; ma costui per infinite differenze di tempo et innumerabili caggioni de circonstanze, ha di breve vita termini incerti. Quella s'accende con certezza, questo con dubio de riveder il sole.

Equal the number that this world has run;
You're who you were, but I'm another me.

In misery from Love's heat I expire;
The Sun, meanwhile, revives you with his rays.
You burn but once; I'm everywhere afire –
For I have Cupid's, you have Phoebus's blaze.

Your terms are set, and give
Long life; my end is destined to be brief;
I'm threatened by a thousand forms of grief.

I know not what I'll be, nor what I've lived –
Blind Fate shows me the way;
You'll certainly return to see your day.

⌇

From the meaning of the sonnet you can see that the insignia contrasts the fate of the Phoenix and the frenzied hero, and that the motto, *The Fates stand in the way*, does not mean that the Fates oppose either the boy or the Phoenix, or both, but rather that Fate's decrees for one are different, indeed contrary, to Fate's decrees for the other. For the Phoenix is what it was, because its same matter renews itself by fire to become the same body of a Phoenix, and the same spirit and soul return to give it form. The frenzied hero is not what he was before, because the kind of man he is now used to be a different species of man in countless respects. We know what the Phoenix was, and we know what it will be, but this young man cannot come back, except by roundabout and uncertain ways, to clothe himself in the same – or even a similar – natural form. The Phoenix, in the face of the Sun, exchanges death for life, but the frenzied hero, in the face of Love, exchanges life for death. Furthermore, the Phoenix lights its pyre on a fragrant altar, but the frenzied hero finds his pyre within himself, and carries it with him wherever he goes. The Phoenix, finally, has a definite and long lifespan, but the frenzied hero, for infinite differences in timing and countless reasons of circumstance, has a brief and uncertain span of existence. The Phoenix catches fire with certainty; the frenzied hero catches fire doubting that he will ever see the Sun again.

CICADA: Che cosa credete voi che possa figurar questo?

TANSILLO: La differenza ch'è tra l'intelletto inferiore, che chiamano intelletto di potenza o possibile o passibile, il quale è incerto, moltivario e moltiforme; e l'intelletto superiore, forse quale è quel che da Peripatetici è detto infima de l'intelligenze, e che immediatamente influisce sopra tutti gl'individui dell'umana specie, e dicesi intelletto agente et attuante. Questo intelletto unico specifico umano che ha influenza in tutti li individui, è come la luna, la quale non prende altra specie che quella unica, la qual sempre se rinova per la conversion che fa al sole che è la prima et universale intelligenza: ma l'intelletto umano individuale e numeroso viene come gli occhi a voltarsi ad innumerabili e diversissimi oggetti, onde secondo infiniti gradi che son secondo tutte le forme naturali viene informato. Là onde accade che sia furioso, vago et incerto questo intelletto particulare; come quello universale è quieto, stabile e certo, cossì secondo l'appetito come secondo l'apprensione. O pur quindi (come da per te stesso puoi facilmente desciferare) vien significata la natura dell'apprensione et appetito vario, vago, inconstante et incerto del senso, e del concetto et appetito definito, fermo e stabile de l'intelligenza; la differenza de l'amor sensuale che non ha certezza né discrezion de oggetti, da l'amor intellettivo il qual ha mira ad un certo e solo, a cui si volta, da cui è illuminato nel concetto, onde è acceso ne l'affetto, s'infiamma, s'illustra et è mantenuto nell'unità, identità e stato.

VII. CICADA: Ma che vuol significare quell'imagine del sole con un circolo dentro, et un altro da fuori, con il motto CIRCUIT?

TANSILLO: La significazion di questo son certo che mai arrei compresa, se non fusse che l'ho intesa dal medesimo figuratore: or è da sapere che quel *circuit* si referisce al moto del sole che fa per quel circolo, il quale gli vien descritto dentro e fuori; a significare che quel moto insieme insieme si fa et è fatto: onde per consequenza il sole viene sempre ad ritrovarsi in tutti gli punti di quello. Perché s'egli si muove in uno instante, séguita che insieme si muove et è mosso, e che è per tutta la circonferenza del circolo equalmente, e che in esso convegna in uno il moto e la quiete.

CICADA: What, do you think, can this emblem depict?

TANSILLO: The difference that exists between the lower intellect, what they call the intellect of potential, or the possible or sensitive intellect, which is uncertain, multifarious, and multiform, and the higher intellect, which is perhaps what the Peripatetics call the lowermost intelligence; it exerts immediate influence upon all the individuals of the human species, and is called the agent or activating intellect.[78] This uniquely, specifically human intellect, which exerts influence over all individuals, is like the Moon, which assumes no other species than one alone, endlessly renewed by its turning towards the Sun, which is the prime and universal intelligence. The human intellect, by contrast, particular and multiple, turns, like the eyes, towards innumerable and utterly diverse objects, so that it is shaped in infinite gradations that follow all the forms of nature. Hence, this particular intellect is frenzied, vague, and uncertain, just as the universal intellect is quiet, stable, and certain, both in its desires and in its perceptions. Alternatively, then (as you can discover easily for yourself), the emblem shows us the various, vague, inconstant, and uncertain nature of perception and desire on the level of the senses, and the definite, firm, and stable idea and desire of the intelligence; that is, the difference between sensual love, which has neither certainty nor discretion in its choice of object, and intellective love, aiming at one object alone, to which it turns, by which its thoughts are enlightened, through which its affections are ignited, by which it catches fire, is pervaded by light, and is maintained in its single consistent state.

**VII.** CICADA: But what is the meaning of that image of the Sun with one circle inside it and one outside, with the motto IT CIRCLES?

TANSILLO: I am sure that I would never have understood the meaning of this had I not heard it from the artist himself. It is essential to know that this *It circles* refers to the Sun's motion along the circle that has been drawn both inside and outside it, to signify that this motion simultaneously creates itself and is created, and consequently the Sun always finds itself at every point of that circle. For if it moves in one instant, it follows that it both moves and is moved, and that it is equally present along the entire circumference of the circle, and that in it motion and rest converge as one.[79]

CICADA: Questo ho compreso nelli dialoghi *De l'infinito, universo e mondi innumerabili*, e dove si dechiara come la divina sapienza è mobilissima (come disse Salomone) e che la medesima sia stabilissima, come è detto et inteso da tutti quelli che intendono. Or séguita a farmi comprendere il proposito.

TANSILLO: Vuol dire che il suo sole non è come questo, che (come comunmente si crede) circuisce la terra col moto diurno in vintiquattro ore, e col moto planetare in dodeci mesi; laonde fa distinti gli quattro tempi de l'anno, secondo che a termini di quello si trova in quattro punti cardinali del Zodiaco; ma è tale, che (per essere la eternità istessa e conseguentemente una possessione insieme tutta e compita) insieme insieme comprende l'inverno, la primavera, l'estade, l'autunno, insieme insieme il giorno e la notte: perché è tutto per tutti et in tutti gli punti e luoghi.

CICADA: Or applicate quel che dite alla figura.

TANSILLO: Qua, perché non è possibile designar il sol tutto in tutti gli punti del circolo, vi son delineati doi circoli: l'un che 'l comprenda per significar che si muove per quello; l'altro che sia da lui compreso per mostrar che è mosso per quello.

CICADA: Ma questa demostrazione non è troppo aperta e propria.

TANSILLO: Basta che sia la più aperta e propria che lui abbia possuta fare: se voi la possete far megliore vi si dà autorità di togler quella e mettervi quell'altra; perché questa è stata messa solo a fin che l'anima non fusse senza corpo.

CICADA: Che dite di quel *Circuit*?

TANSILLO: Quel motto, secondo tutta la sua significazione, significa la cosa quanto può essere significata; atteso che significa che volta e che è voltato: cioè il moto presente e perfetto.

CICADA: Eccellentemente: e però que' circoli li quali malamente significano la circonstanza del moto e quiete tale, possiamo dire che son

CICADA: This is what I have understood in the *Dialogues On the Infinite Universe and Innumerable Worlds*,[80] which declare that Divine Wisdom is exceedingly mobile (as Solomon said),[81] and yet at the same time utterly stable, as is declared and understood by everyone who understands anything. But please continue helping me to understand the motto.

TANSILLO: It means that the artist's Sun is not like ours, which (as is commonly believed) circles the earth with its diurnal motion in twenty-four hours, and with its planetary motion in twelve months, creating the four distinct seasons as, with each term of the year, it finds itself in one of four cardinal points of the Zodiac. His Sun, by contrast, because it is eternity itself, and consequently a possession both entire and complete, at one and the same time contains the winter, the spring, the summer, the autumn, together with day and night, because all of it is present along the whole circuit, and at every individual point and place.[82]

CICADA: Now apply what you have said to the image.

TANSILLO: Here, because it is impossible to depict the Sun entire at every point of the circle, two circles have been drawn: one to signify that the Sun moves through it; the other, which is contained by the Sun, to signify that it is moved by it.

CICADA: But this explanation is neither particularly clear nor fitting.

TANSILLO: Yet it was the clearest and most fitting that he could devise; let that be enough. If you can make a better one, he authorizes you to remove this one and replace it with your own, because this one was placed here just to ensure that its soul would not lack a body.

CICADA: What do you have to say about that *It circles?*

TANSILLO: The motto, in its full meaning, signifies the situation to the extent that it can be signified: it means that this Sun revolves and is revolved, that is, its motion is present, but also completed.[83]

CICADA: Well said. Hence, we can say that those circles, which are so bad at portraying the circumstances of motion and rest, end up, we might

messi a significar la sola circulazione. E cossì vegno contento del suggetto e de la forma de l'impresa eroica. Or legansi le rime.

TANSILLO:

꒜

> Sol che dal Tauro fai temprati lumi,
> e dal Leon tutto maturi e scaldi,
> e quando dal pungente Scorpio allumi,
> de l'ardente vigor non poco faldi;
> poscia dal fier Deucalion consumi
> tutto col fredd', e i corp'umidi saldi:
> de primavera, estade, autunno, inverno
> mi scald' accend' ard' avvamp'in eterno.

> Ho sì caldo il desio,
> che facilment' a remirar m'accendo
> quell'alt'oggetto, per cui tant'ardendo,

> fo sfavillar a gli astri il vampo mio:
> non han momento gli anni,
> che vegga variar miei sordi affanni.

꒜

Qua nota che gli quattro tempi de l'anno son significati non per quattro segni mobili che son Ariete, Cancro, Libra e Capricorno, ma per gli
quattro che chiamano fissi, cioè Tauro, Leone, Scorpione et Aquario:
per significare la perfezzione, stato e fervor di quelle tempeste. Nota
appresso che in virtù di quelle apostrofi che son nel verso ottavo, possete
leggere «mi scaldo, accendo, ardo, avampo»; over, «scaldi, accendi, ardi,
avampi»; over «scalda, accende, arde, avvampa». Hai oltre da considerare che questi non son quattro sinonimi, ma quattro termini diversi
che significano tanti gradi de gli effetti del fuoco. Il qual prima scalda,
secondo accende, terzo bruggia, quarto infiamma o invampa quel ch'ha
scaldato, acceso e bruggiato. E cossì son denotate nel furioso il desio,
l'attenzione, il studio, l'affezzione, le quali in nessun momento sente
variare.

say, only showing the act of circling. And with this I am satisfied with both the subject and the form of this heroic emblem. Now let's read the sonnet.

TANSILLO:

ঔৈ

> Sun, who in Taurus casts a temperate glow,
> In Leo you ripen things and make them boil.
> When shedding light from stinging Scorpio
> Your ardent vigour cracks and splits the soil.
> And then, from proud Deucalion[84] you go
> Consuming world and man in chilly toils.
> Spring, summer, fall or winter it may be:
> I[85] seethe, spark, burn, blaze for eternity.
>
> I have such hot desire
> That I'm alight from simple admiration
> Of my high Object, and my conflagration
>
> Singes the very heavens with my fire.
> The years hold not an instant
> When my insensate labours are not constant.

ঔৈ

Here he notes that the four seasons of the year are symbolized not by the four mobile signs, which are Aries, Cancer, Libra, and Capricorn, but by the four that they call fixed, namely, Taurus, Leo, Scorpio, and Aquarius, to show the perfection, state, and fervour of those seasons. He then notes that the apostrophes that are in the [Italian version of the] eighth line mean that you can read either *I seethe, spark, burn, blaze,* or *you seethe, spark, burn, blaze,* or *He seethes, sparks, burns, blazes.* Observe in addition that these are not four synonyms, but rather four different terms that signify four degrees of fire's effect, for it first heats, then kindles, third burns, and fourth inflames or blazes what it has heated, lit, and burned. In the frenzied hero they signify his desire, his attention, his zeal, and his affection, in which he feels no variation from moment to moment.

CICADA: Perché le mette sotto titolo d'affanni?

TANSILLO: Perché l'oggetto, ch'è la divina luce, in questa vita è più in laborioso voto che in quieta fruizione: perché la nostra mente verso quella è come gli occhi de gli uccelli notturni al sole.

CICADA: Passa, perché ora da quel ch'è detto posso comprender tutto.

VIII. TANSILLO: Nel cimiero seguente vi sta depinta una luna piena col motto TALIS MIHI SEMPER ET ASTRO. Vuol dir che a l'astro, cioè al sole, et a lui sempre è tale, come si mostra qua piena e lucida nella circonferenza intiera del circolo: il che acciò che meglio forse intendi, voglio farti udire quel ch'è scritto nella tavoletta.

᪥

> Lun' inconstante, luna varia, quale
> con corna or vote e tal'or piene svalli,
> or l'orbe tuo bianc' or fosco risale,
> or Bora e de' Rifei monti le valli
> fai lustre, or torni per tue trite scale
> a chiarir l'Austro, e di Libia le spalli.
> La luna mia per mia continua pena
> mai sempre è ferma, et è mai sempre piena.
>
>  È tale la mia stella,
> che sempre mi si togli' e mai si rende,
> che sempre tanto bruggia e tanto splende,
>
> sempre tanto crudele e tanto bella:
>  questa mia nobil face
> sempre sì mi martóra, e sì mi piace.

᪥

Mi par che voglia dire che la sua intelligenza particulare alla intelligenza universale è sempre «tale»: cioè da quella viene eternamente

CICADA: Why does he classify them all as *labours?*

TANSILLO: Because the Object, which is divine light, in this life consists more in laborious devotion than in quiet enjoyment; because our mind responds to that light as the eyes of a night bird respond to the Sun.

CICADA: Proceed, because by now from what has been said I can understand everything.

**VIII.** TANSILLO: The crest of the next emblem shows a full moon with the motto EVER THUS FOR ME AND FOR THE STAR. This means that for the star, that is, for the Sun, and for the frenzied hero, the Moon is always as it is shown here, full and glowing, filling the entire circumference of its circle; to help you understand better, I'd like to have you hear what is written on the panel:

じ

> Inconstant, changing Moon, who in our sight
> First waxes full, then, horned and empty, wanes:
> Your orb, now white, now dark, bestows its light
> Upon Rhipaean vales, where Boreas reigns,[86]
> Returning back along the well-worn flight
> That leads to Auster, and to Libya's plains.[87]
> My Moon, by my own grief's relentless pull,
> Stays still forever and forever full.
>
> And thus my star is active
> Ever eluding me, conceding never,
> Forever fiery, radiant forever,
>
> Forever cruel, and ever so attractive.
> This noble torch I light
> Torments me, and yet brings me such delight.

じ

To me he seems to be saying that his particular intelligence is *ever thus* with respect to the universal intelligence; that is, its entire hemisphere

illuminata in tutto l'emisfero; benché alle potenze inferiori e secondo gl'influssi de gli atti suoi or viene oscura, or più e meno lucida. O forse vuol significare che l'intelletto suo speculativo (il quale è sempre in atto invariabilmente) è sempre volto et affetto verso l'intelligenza umana significata per la «luna», perché come questa è detta infima de tutti gli astri et è più vicina a noi, cossì l'intelligenza illuminatrice de tutti noi (in questo stato) è l'ultima in ordine de l'altre intelligenze come nota Averroe et altri più sottili Peripatetici. Quella a l'intelletto in potenza or tramonta per quanto non è in atto alcuno, or come «svallasse», cioè sorgesse dal basso de l'occolto emispero, si mostra or vacua or piena secondo che dona più o meno lume d'intelligenza; or ha «l'orbe oscuro or bianco», perché talvolta mostra per ombra, similitudine e vestigio, tal volta più e più apertamente; or declina a l'«Austro», or monta a «Borea», cioè or ne si va più e più allontanando, or più e più s'avvicina. Ma l'intelletto in atto con sua continua pena (percioché questo non è per natura e condizione umana in cui si trova cossì travaglioso, combattuto, invitato, sollecitato, distratto e come lacerato dalle potenze inferiori) sempre vede il suo oggetto fermo, fisso e constante, e sempre pieno e nel medesimo splendor di bellezza. Cossì sempre se gli «toglie» per quanto non se gli concede, sempre se gli «rende» per quanto se gli concede. «Sempre tanto lo bruggia» ne l'affetto, come sempre «tanto gli splende» nel pensiero; «sempre è tanto crudele» in suttrarsi per quel che si suttrae, come sempre è «tanto bello» in comunicarsi per quel che gli se presenta. «Sempre lo martóra», perciò che è diviso per differenza locale da lui, come sempre gli «piace», percioché gli è congionto con l'affetto.

CICADA: Or applicate l'intelligenza al motto.

TANSILLO: Dice dumque *Talis mihi semper*, cioè per la mia continua applicazione secondo l'intelletto, memoria e volontade (perché non voglio altro ramentare, intendere, né desiderare) sempre mi è tale, e per quanto posso capirla, al tutto presente, e non m'è divisa per distrazzion de pensiero, né me si fa più oscura per difetto d'attenzione, perché non è pensiero che mi divertisca da quella luce, e non è necessità di natura qual m'oblighi perché meno attenda. *Talis mihi semper* dal canto suo, perché la è invariabile in sustanza, in virtù, in bellezza et in effetto verso quelle cose che sono constanti et invariabili verso lei. Dice appresso *ut astro*, perché al rispetto del sole illuminator de quella

is eternally illuminated by the latter, although depending on the lower powers and the influence of its own actions, it will grow darker or lighter. Or perhaps he means to show how his speculative intellect (which is always invariably in action), is always lovingly turned towards the human intelligence symbolized by the Moon. For just as the Moon is said to be the lowermost of the stars and the nearest to us, so, too, the intelligence that illuminates all of us (in this state) is the least in rank of the other intelligences, as Averroës and the most clever of the other Peripatetics have observed.[88] In the presence of the intellect in potential, this human intellect now *wanes*, because it is not engaged in any action, now *waxes*, as it were, that is, ascends from the depths of the dark hemisphere, and shows itself as empty or full depending on how much light of intelligence it casts; now it is *white*, now *dark*, for sometimes it appears in shadows, likenesses, or traces, sometimes more and more openly; now it descends south to *Auster*, now it ascends north to *Boreas*: that is, it moves farther and farther away, then draws nearer and nearer. But the intellect engaged in action, with its continual suffering (for it is not by nature or the human condition that it finds itself so troubled, conflicted, invited, solicited, distracted, and, as it were, torn by the lower powers), always sees its object as firm, fixed, and constant, always full, and always in the same splendour of beauty. Hence, it always *eludes* him to the extent that it never concedes itself to him, and always surrenders to the extent that it *concedes* itself.[89] It is *forever fiery* in his affections, just as it is *radiant forever* in his thoughts; it is *forever cruel* in subtracting itself, to the extent that it subtracts itself, and is *ever so attractive* in conveying itself through what it presents to him. It *torments* him because it is separated from him in space, just as it brings him *delight* because it is joined to him through affection.

CICADA: Now apply that understanding to the motto.

TANSILLO: Well, it says: *Ever thus for me*, that is, by the continual application of my intellect, memory, and will[90] (because I want to remember, understand, and desire nothing else), my beloved is always like this for me, and insofar as I can understand her, entirely present, and she is not separated from me by the distraction of my thoughts. Neither does she become more obscure to me for the deficiency of my attention, for there is no thought that can divert me from that light, just as there is no natural necessity that can compel me to pay less attention. She is *Ever thus for me* on her part, because she is invariable in substance, in power, in beauty, and in her effect on the things that are constant

sempre è ugualmente luminosa, essendo che sempre ugualmente gli
è volta, e quello sempre parimente diffonde gli suoi raggi: come fisica-
mente questa luna che veggìamo con gli occhi, quantumque verso la
terra or appaia tenebrosa or lucente, or più or meno illustrata et illu-
strante, sempre però dal sole vien lei ugualmente illuminata; perché
sempre piglia gli raggi di quello al meno nel dorso del suo emispero
intiero. Come anco questa terra sempre è illuminata nell'emisfero
equalmente; quantumque da l'acquosa superficie cossì inequalmente
a volte a volte mande il suo splendore alla luna (qual come molti altri
astri innumerabili stimiamo un'altra terra) come aviene che quella
mande a lei: atteso la vicissitudine ch'hanno insieme de ritrovarsi or
l'una or l'altra più vicina al sole.

CICADA: Come questa intelligenza è significata per la luna che luce per
l'emisfero?

TANSILLO: Tutte l'intelligenze son significate per la luna, in quanto che
son partecipi d'atto e di potenza, per quanto dico che hanno la luce
materialmente, e secondo participazione, ricevendola da altro; dico
non essendo luci per sé e per sua natura: ma per risguardo del sole
ch'è la prima intelligenza la quale è pura et absoluta luce come anco
è puro et absoluto atto.

CICADA: Tutte dumque le cose che hanno dependenza, e che non sono
il primo atto e causa, sono composte come di luce e tenebra, come di
materia e forma, di potenza et atto?

TANSILLO: Cossì è. Oltre, l'anima nostra secondo tutta la sustanza è significata per la luna la quale splende per l'emisfero delle potenze superiori, onde è volta alla luce del mondo intelligibile, et è oscura per le
potenze inferiori, onde è occupata al governo della materia.

IX. CICADA: E mi par che a quel ch'ora è detto abbia certa consequenza
e simbolo l'impresa ch'io veggio nel seguente scudo, dove è una ru-
vida e ramosa quercia piantata, contra la quale è un vento che soffia,
et ha circonscritto il motto UT ROBORI ROBUR. Et appresso è affissa la
tavola che dice:

and changeless towards her. He then says, *and for the star*, because by comparison with the Sun, its source of light, the intelligence is always equally luminous, for it is always equally turned towards the Sun, and the Sun, in turn, always and evenly sheds its rays. Just as, physically, this Moon that we see with our eyes may from an earthly standpoint seem now shadowy, now luminous, now more, now less illuminated and illuminating, still, nonetheless, it is always evenly lit by the Sun, for it always absorbs the Sun's rays evenly over the whole surface of its hemisphere. So, too, the Earth is always evenly lit on its hemisphere, although it projects its glow towards the Moon (which we believe is, like countless other stars, another Earth)[91] unevenly from its watery surface; likewise, the Moon casts its glow on the earth, according to the alternation that puts either one or the other closer to the Sun.

CICADA: How does the full Moon symbolize the intelligence?

TANSILLO: All the intelligences are signified by the Moon to the extent that they are participants in action and power, to the extent, I say, that they possess light physically and by participation, receiving it from another source.[92] I mean that they are not lights in themselves, and by their nature, but by reflection from the Sun, the prime intelligence, which is pure and absolute light, just as it is also pure and absolute action.

CICADA: Everything, in other words, that is dependent, and is not the prime action and cause, is composed, as it were, of light and darkness, just as it is composed of matter and form, of potential and action?

TANSILLO: Just so. Furthermore, our soul, in all its substance, is symbolized by the Moon, which shines in the hemisphere of its higher powers, where it is turned towards the light of the intelligible world, and is dark in the region of the lower powers, where it is occupied with the governing of matter.

IX. CICADA: And it seems to me that the emblem I now see on the next shield has a certain consequence and symbolic force in terms of what we have just said; there a gnarled oak with many branches stands rooted, with the wind blowing against it, and around it is inscribed the motto STRENGTH LIKE THE OAK.[93] And next to it is affixed the panel that says:

∽

Annosa quercia, che gli rami spandi
a l'aria, e fermi le radici 'n terra:
né terra smossa, né gli spirti grandi
che da l'aspro Aquilon il ciel disserra,
né quanto fia ch'il vern'orrido mandi,
dal luog' ove stai salda mai ti sferra;
mostri della mia fé ritratto vero
qual smossa mai stran' accidenti féro.

Tu medesmo terreno
mai sempr' abbracci, fai colto e comprendi,
e di lui per le viscere distendi

radici grate al generoso seno:
i' ad un sol oggetto
ho fiss' il spirt', il sens' e l'intelletto.

∽

TANSILLO: Il motto è aperto, per cui si vanta il furioso d'aver forza e robustezza, come la rovere; e come quell'altro, essere sempre uno al riguardo da l'unica fenice; e come il prossimo precedente conformarsi a quella luna che sempre tanto splende, e tanto è bella; o pur non assomigliarsi a questa anticctona tra la nostra terra et il sole in quanto ch'è varia a' nostri occhi: ma in quanto sempre riceve ugual porzion del splendor solare in se stessa. E per ciò cossì rimaner constante e fermo contra gli Aquiloni e tempestosi inverni per la fermezza ch'ha nel suo astro in cui è piantato con l'affetto et intenzione, come la detta radicosa pianta tiene intessute le sue radici con le vene de la terra.

CICADA: Più stimo io l'essere in tranquillità e fuor di molestia che trovarsi in una sì forte tolleranza.

TANSILLO: È sentenza d'Epicurei la qual se sarà bene intesa non sarà giudicata tanto profana quanto la stimano gli ignoranti; atteso che non toglie che quel ch'io ho detto sia virtù, né pregiudica alla perfezzione

⌁

O ancient oak, your branches you extend
Through air, and fix your roots in earth below;
Neither earth's tremors, nor the mighty winds
That Heaven unleashes from harsh Aquilo,
Nor anything that winter's chill may send
Can change the place where steadfastly you grow.
Of my own faith you furnish a true image
That no strange accidents could ever damage.

This very plot of land
You comprehend, embrace, and ever till,
And thence through the Earth's inward parts expand

The roots that such a generous womb fulfil.
Upon one sole Object
I've fixed my spirit, soul, and intellect.

⌁

TANSILLO: The motto is self-evident; in it the frenzied hero claims to
have the robust strength of the oak, just as in that other emblem he
claims to be constant with regard to the one and only Phoenix, and
in the emblem we have just seen he claims to conform himself to the
Moon that always shines so brightly, and is so beautiful – or at least he
claims that he is unlike that anti-Earth that stands between our Earth
and the Sun in its variability to our eyes, but he is like it in absorbing
an unchanging portion of the Sun's radiance. Hence, he will stand
constant and firm against the hot blasts of Aquilo and the tempests of
winter, because of the fixity he finds in his star, where he is implant-
ed by his affection and purpose, just as that deep-rooted plant has its
roots interwoven with the veins of the earth.

CICADA: I prefer being at peace and beyond annoyance to finding myself
in such a hard contest of endurance.

TANSILLO: That is a position taken by the Epicureans, which, if properly
understood, would not be considered as irreverent as the ignorant
suspect it to be. It neither detracts from that constancy which I have

della constanza, ma più tosto aggionge a quella perfezzione che intendeno gli volgari: perché lui non stima vera e compita virtù di fortezza e constanza quella che sente e comporta gl'incommodi: ma quella
che non sentendoli le porta; non stima compìto amor divino et eroico
quello che sente il sprone, freno o rimorso o pena per altro amore,
ma quello ch'a fatto non ha senso de gli altri affetti: onde talmente è
gionto ad un piacere, che non è potente dispiacere alcuno a distorlo
o far cespitare in punto. E questo è toccar la somma beatitudine in
questo stato, l'aver la voluptà e non aver senso di dolore.

CICADA: La volgare opinione non crede questo senso d'Epicuro.

TANSILLO: Perché non leggono gli suoi libri, né quelli che senza invidia
apportano le sue sentenze, al contrario di color che leggono il corso
de sua vita et il termine de la sua morte. Dove con queste paroli det-
tò il principio del suo testamento: «Essendo ne l'ultimo e medesimo
felicissimo giorno de nostra vita, abbiamo ordinato questo con mente
quieta, sana e tranquilla; perché quantumque grandissimo dolor de
pietra ne tormentasse da un canto, quel tormento tutto venea assorbito dal piacere de le nostre invenzioni e la considerazion del fine». Et
è cosa manifesta che non ponea felicità più che dolore nel mangiare,
bere, posare e generare, ma in non sentir fame, né sete, né fatica,
né libidine. Da qua considera qual sia secondo noi la perfezzion de
la constanza: non già in questo che l'arbore non si fracasse, rompa
o pieghe; ma in questo che né manco si muova: alla cui similitudine
costui tien fisso il spirto, senso et intelletto, là dove non ha sentimento
di tempestosi insulti.

CICADA: Volete dumque che sia cosa desiderabile il comportar de tormenti, perché è cosa da forte?

TANSILLO: Questo che dite «comportare» è parte di constanza, e non
è la virtude intiera; ma questo che dico «fortemente comportare» et
Epicuro disse «non sentire». La qual privazion di senso è caggionata
da quel che tutto è stato absorto dalla cura della virtude, vero bene e
felicitade. Qualmente Regolo non ebbe senso de l'arca, Lucrezia del
pugnale, Socrate del veleno, Anaxarco de la pila, Scevola del fuoco,

described as a virtue nor hinders its perfection; indeed, it reinforces the common idea of what such perfection might be. For the frenzied hero does not regard the true, full virtue of firmness or constancy as suffering and bearing setbacks, but as bearing them without feeling them at all. He does not regard as full, divine, and heroic a love that feels the spur, bridle, or bit, or the pain of another love; indeed, it should have no perception of other feelings whatsoever. Hence, he has arrived at such pleasure that there is no displeasure capable of removing or uprooting him in any way. And this is what it means to touch the highest happiness of this human state: to know pleasure without any sense of pain.

CICADA: Most people do not have this sense of what Epicurus said.

TANSILLO: Because they do not read his books, nor do they read the authors who cite his opinions without envy, unlike the people who do read about the course of his life and the circumstances of his death.[94] He dictated the beginning of his testament with these words: "Having arrived at the last, hence happiest day of our life, we have ordered the following with a calm, healthy, and tranquil mind, for however great a pain from kidney stones may have tormented us on the one hand, on the other hand, all that pain was overwhelmed by pleasure in our creations and the contemplation of our end." Clearly, he did not ascribe greater happiness than pain to eating, drinking, resting, and copulation, but rather to *not* feeling hunger, thirst, fatigue, or desire. Consider, then, in what the perfection of constancy must consist: not in the fact that the tree does not shatter, break, or bend, but in the fact that it does not move at all: like it, the frenzied hero keeps his spirit, sense, and intellect fixed where he has no perception of violent assaults.

CICADA: Do you mean, then, that it is desirable to bear torment, because endurance is a sign of strength?

TANSILLO: This endurance you speak of is only one part of constancy, rather than the entire virtue, which is what I call "endurance with strength," and Epicurus called "not feeling."[95] This lack of feeling comes from being wholly absorbed in care about virtue, true goodness, and happiness. Hence, Regulus had no feeling of the box that crushed him, Lucretia of the dagger, Socrates of the poison, Anaxar-

Cocle de la voragine, et altri virtuosi d'altre cose che massime tormentano e danno orrore a persone ordinarie e vili.


CICADA: Or passate oltre.

X. TANSILLO: Guarda in quest'altro ch'ha la fantasia di quella incudine e
martello, circa la quale è il motto AB AETNA. Ma prima che la consideriamo, leggemo la stanza. Qua s'introduce di Vulcano la prosopopea:

ↄↄ

> Or non al monte mio siciliano
> torn', ove tempri i folgori di Giove;
> qua mi rimagno scabroso Vulcano:
> qua più superbo gigante si smuove,
> che contr' il ciel s'infiamm' e stizz' in vano,
> tentando nuovi studii e varie prove;
> qua trovo meglior fabri e Mongibello,
> meglior fucina, incudine e martello.

> Dov'un pett' ha suspiri
> che quai mantici avvivan la fornace,
> u' l'alm' a tante scosse sottogiace

> di que' sì lunghi scempii e gran martìri;
>     e manda quel concento
> che fa volgar sì aspr'e rio tormento.

ↄↄ

Qua si mostrano le pene et incomodi che son ne l'amore, massime
nell'amor volgare, il quale non è altro che l'officina di Vulcano: quel
fabro che forma i folgori de Giove che tormentano l'anime delinquen-
ti. Perché il disordinato amore ha in sé il principio della sua pena;
attesoché Dio è vicino, è nosco, è dentro di noi. Si trova in noi certa
sacrata mente et intelligenza, cui subministra un proprio affetto che
ha il suo vendicatore, che col rimorso di certa sinderesi al meno, come
con certo rigido martello flagella il spirito prevaricante. Quella osserva
le nostre azzioni et affetti, e come è trattata da noi fa che noi vengamo

chus of the mortar, Scaevola of the fire, Cocles of the Tiber's eddies; nor do other persons of virtue fear the greatest torments, that cause horror among ordinary and vile persons.[96]

CICADA: Now let's move on.

**X.** TANSILLO: Look, this emblem contains the design of a hammer and anvil, around which is the motto FROM AETNA. But before we examine it, let us read the sonnet, addressed to Vulcan:

ᦏ

> From your Sicilian mount I'll keep away,
> There where you temper Jupiter's bolts of lightning
> No, rough-edged Vulcan, this is where I'll stay
> Where stirs a Giant prouder and more frightening
> Who frets and rages, plotting some new way
> To storm the skies in vain. Here, that's to say,
> I've better smiths, a better Mongibello,[97]
> A better anvil, hammer, forge, and bellows.
>
> The sighs one breast releases
> Can stoke a furnace; and no anvil knows
> My captive soul's full complement of blows
>
> From this long martyrdom that never ceases;
> They forge the harmony
> That blares my harsh torment and agony.

ᦏ

This shows the pains and inconveniences that accompany love, especially common love, which is nothing else but the forge of Vulcan, the smith who forms Jove's lightning bolts that torment delinquent souls. Disorderly love contains in itself the very origin of its pain, for God is near, is with us, is within us. Within us, a certain consecrated mind and intelligence is served by its own affection, which acts as its own avenger, or at least by the remorse of a certain conscience it beats the wayward spirit like some unyielding hammer. The mind observes our attentions and affections, and however we treat it, it is certain to

trattati da lei. In tutti gli amanti, dico, è questo fabro Vulcano: come
non è uomo che non abbia Dio in sé, non è amante che non abbia
questo dio. In tutti è Dio certissimamente, ma qual dio sia in ciascuno
non si sa cossì facilmente; e se pur se può examinare e distinguere,
altro non potrei credere che possa chiarirlo che l'amore: come quello
che spinge gli remi, gonfia la vela e modera questo composto, onde
vegna bene o malamente affetto. – Dico bene o malamente affetto
quanto a quel che mette in execuzione per l'azzioni morali e contemplazione; perché del resto tutti gli amanti comunmente senteno
qualch'incomodo: essendoché come le cose son miste, non essendo
bene alcuno sotto concetto et affetto a cui non sia gionto o opposto
il male, come né alcun vero a cui non sia apposto e gionto il falso;
cossì non è amore senza timore, zelo, gelosia, rancore et altre passioni
che procedeno dal contrario che ne perturba, se l'altro contrario ne
appaga. Talmente venendo l'anima in pensiero di ricovrar la bellezza
naturale, studia purgarsi, sanarsi, riformarsi: e però adopra il fuoco,
perché essendo come oro trameschiato a la terra et informe, con certo
rigor vuol liberarsi da impurità; il che s'effettua quando l'intelletto
vero fabro di Giove vi mette le mani essercitandovi gli atti dell'intellettive potenze.


CICADA: A questo mi par che si riferisca quel che si trova nel *Convito* di
    Platone, dove dice che l'Amore da la madre Penìa ha ereditato l'esser
    arido, magro, pallido, discalzo, summisso, senza letto e senza tetto: per
    le quali circonstanze vien significato il tormento ch'ha l'anima trava-
    gliata da gli contrarii affetti.

TANSILLO: Cossì è, perché il spirito affetto di tal furore viene da pro-
    fondi pensieri distratto, martellato da cure urgenti, scaldato da fer-
    venti desii, insoffiato da spesse occasioni: onde trovandosi l'anima
    suspesa, necessariamente viene ad essere men diligente et operosa al
    governo del corpo per gli atti della potenza vegetativa. Quindi il cor-
    po è macilento, mal nodrito, estenuato, ha difetto de sangue, copia
    di malancolici umori, li quali se non saranno instrumenti de l'anima
    disciplinata o pure d'un spirito chiaro e lucido, menano ad insania,
    stoltizia e furor brutale; o al meno a certa poca cura di sé e dispreggio
    del esser proprio, il qual vien significato da Platone per gli piedi di-
    scalzi. Va summisso l'amore e vola come rependo per la terra, quando
    è attaccato a cose basse; vola alto quando vien intento a più generose

treat us in the same way. In all lovers, I maintain, there is this smith Vulcan; for, just as there is no person who does not have God within, there is no lover who lacks this god. In everyone God is most certainly present, but it is less easy to know what kind of God is in each of us; and yet to examine the question, I cannot believe that anything could clarify it better than love, which plies the oars, fills the sails, and moderates the composition by which the person is affected for good or ill. I say "affected for good or ill" in reference to what he sets into motion through moral action and contemplation, because otherwise all lovers feel some inconvenience, for all things are mixed and there is no good, whether of idea or affection, for which there is not some evil conjoined or in opposition, just as there is no truth to which falsehood is not also associated and joined. Hence, there is no love without fear, envy, jealousy, rancour, and other frenzies that proceed from its opposite, which perturbs just as its opposite fulfils. Thus, when the soul conceives the thought of recovering natural beauty, it strives to purify itself, heal itself, reform itself; and so it employs fire, because it is like gold mixed with earth and without form, and wants with a certain rigour to free itself of impurity, which comes about when the intellect, the true smith of Jove, puts his hands to work by exercising the actions of the intellective powers.

CICADA: This, it seems to me, is the point of that passage from Plato's *Symposium* that says Love has inherited his appearance from his mother Poverty: arid, lean, pallid, barefoot, abject, bedless and homeless, and these qualities symbolize the soul's torment when it struggles with opposing emotions.[98]

TANSILLO: Exactly so, for the spirit affected by such a frenzy becomes distracted by profound thoughts, hammered by pressing cares, scalded by fervid desires, blasted by frequent turns of fortune; and hence the soul, caught in suspension, necessarily becomes less diligent and industrious in governing the body through actions of its vegetative power. Then the body becomes emaciated, malnourished, exhausted, anemic, with too many melancholic humors that, if they are not made the tools of a disciplined soul or a clear and lucid spirit, lead to insanity, folly, and brutal furore, or at least to inadequate care of oneself and disdain for one's own being, which Plato signifies by bare feet. Love becomes meek and flies almost as if it were creeping along the ground when it is attached to base things; it flies high when it is intent on more

imprese. In conclusione et a proposito: qualumque sia l'amore, sempre è travagliato e tormentato di sorte che non possa mancar d'esser materia nelle focine di Vulcano; perché l'anima essendo cosa divina, e naturalmente non serva, ma signora della materia corporale, viene a conturbarsi ancor in quel che voluntariamente serve al corpo, dove non trova cosa che la contente. E quantumque fissa nella cosa amata, sempre gli aviene che altretanto vegna ad essagitarsi e fluttuar in mezzo gli soffii de le speranze, timori, dubii, zeli, conscienze, rimorsi, ostinazioni, pentimenti, et altri manigoldi che son gli mantici, gli carboni, l'incudini, gli martelli, le tenaglie, et altri stormenti che si ritrovano nella bottega di questo sordido e sporco consorte di Venere.

CICADA: Or assai è stato detto a questo proposito: piacciavi di veder che cosa séguita appresso.

XI. TANSILLO: Qua è un pomo d'oro ricchissimamente con diverse preciosissime specie smaltato. Et ha il motto in circa che dice PULCHRIORI DETUR.

CICADA: La allusione al fatto delle tre dee che si sottoposero al giudicio de Paride, è molto volgare: ma leggansi le rime che più specificatamente ne facciano capaci de l'intenzione del furioso presente.

TANSILLO:

> Venere, dea del terzo ciel, e madre
> del cieco arciero, domator d'ogn'uno;
> l'altra ch'ha 'l capo giovial per padre,
> e di Giove la mogli' altera Giuno;
> il troiano pastor chiaman, che squadre
> de chi de lor più bell' è l'aureo muno:
> se la mia diva al paragon s'appone,
> non di Venere, Pallad', o Giunone.

> Per belle membra è vaga
> la cipria dea, Minerva per l'ingegno,
> e la Saturnia piace con quel degno

noble achievements. To conclude this topic: whatever love may be, it is always anguished and tormented, so that it can never fail to provide material for Vulcan's forge, for the soul (as something divine, and by its nature not the servant but the mistress of physical matter) still distresses itself in its voluntary service to the body, where it finds nothing to content it. However fixed its attention may be on the beloved, it still becomes agitated, drifting on the breezes of its hopes, fears, doubts, envies, pangs of conscience, remorse, obstinacy, regret, and the other torturers who are the bellows, the coals, the anvils, the hammers, the tongs, and the other tools that are to be found in the workshop of the squalid, filthy consort of Venus.

CICADA: We have said quite a lot on this topic. Let's see, please, what follows next.

**XI.** TANSILLO: Here is a golden apple, richly enamelled with different precious gems, and around it is the motto TO THE FAIREST.[99]

CICADA: This allusion to the story of the three goddesses who subjected themselves to the Judgment of Paris is almost a cliché, but read the verses, which should tell us more specifically what our frenzied hero means by it.

TANSILLO:

᷍

Venus, third heaven's goddess and the mother
Of the blind archer, tamer of every heart
And she who had the Jovial head as father
And haughty Juno, Jupiter's counterpart
Call forth the Trojan shepherd to advise
Which beauty should receive the golden prize.
And yet if my own goddess were so tested
Then Venus, Pallas, Juno would be bested.

For pretty limbs the measure
Is Cypria,[100] Minerva for the mind,
For Saturn's daughter, beauty's in the shine

splendor d'altezza, ch'il Tonante appaga;
    ma quest'ha quanto aggrade
di bel, d'intelligenza, e maestade.

〣

Ecco qualmente fa comparazione dal suo oggetto il quale contiene
tutte le circonstanze, condizioni e specie di bellezza come in un suggetto, ad altri che non ne mostrano più che una per ciascuno; e tutte
poi per diversi suppositi: come avvenne nel geno solo della corporal
bellezza di cui le condizioni tutte non le poté approvare Apelle in
una, ma in più vergini. Or qua dove son tre geni di beltade, benché
avvegna che tutti si troveno in ciascuna de le tre dee, perché a Venere
non manca sapienza e maestade, in Giunone non è difetto di vaghezza
e sapienza, et in Pallade è pur notata la maestà con la vaghezza: tutta
volta aviene che l'una condizione supera le altre, onde quella viene
ad esser stimata come proprietà, e l'altre come accidenti communi,
atteso che di que' tre doni l'uno predomina in una, e viene ad mo-
strarla et intitularla sovrana de l'altre. E la caggion di cotal differenza
è lo aver queste raggioni non per essenza e primitivamente, ma per
participazione e derivativamente. Come in tutte le cose dependenti
sono le perfezzioni secondo gli gradi de maggiore e minore, più e
meno. – Ma nella simplicità della divina essenza è tutto totalmente,
e non secondo misura: e però non è più sapienza che bellezza, e maestade, non è più bontà che fortezza: ma tutti gli attributi sono non
solamente uguali, ma ancora medesimi et una istessa cosa. Come nella
sfera tutte le dimensioni sono non solamente uguali (essendo tanta
la lunghezza quanta è la profondità e larghezza) ma anco medesime:
atteso che quel che chiami profondo, medesimo puoi chiamar lungo
e largo della sfera. Cossì è nell'altezza de la sapienza divina, la quale è
medesimo che la profondità de la potenza, e latitudine de la bontade.
Tutte queste perfezzioni sono uguali perché sono infinite. Percioché
necessariamente l'una è secondo la grandezza de l'altra, atteso che
dove queste cose son finite, avviene che sia più savio che bello e buono, più buono e bello che savio, più savio e buono che potente, e
più potente che buono e savio. Ma dove è infinita sapienza, non può
essere se non infinita potenza: perché altrimente non potrebbe saper
infinitamente. Dove è infinita bontà, bisogna infinita sapienza: perché
altrimente non saprebbe essere infinitamente buono. Dove è infinita
potenza, bisogna che sia infinita bontà e sapienza, perché tanto ben

Of lofty rank, the Thunderer's chief pleasure
But she wins for all three:
Beauty, intelligence, and majesty.

ॐ

Look how he compares his beloved, who contains all the circumstances, conditions, and species of beauty as if in a single subject, with others who show no more than one kind of beauty apiece; and all of them,
moreover, in different individuals, as happened in the case of physical beauty, when Apelles could not find all its qualities united in one
young woman, but only scattered among several of them.[101] Now here,
where there are three kinds of beauty, even though all three are to be
found in each one of the three goddesses – for Venus does not lack
either wisdom or majesty, in Juno there is no dearth of attractiveness
or wisdom, and in Pallas both attractiveness and majesty are notewor-
thy along with wisdom – still, one quality exceeds the others, and is
regarded as the special property of that goddess, whereas the other
qualities are regarded as common accidentals, given that of these
three gifts one predominates in each goddess, revealing and crowning
her as sovereign over the other two. The reason for this difference is
the fact that they possess these qualities not in their essence, and from
their origin, but only by participation and derivation. Likewise, in all
dependent things perfections exist only in degrees of greater or lesser,
more or fewer.

But in the simplicity of divine essence everything is totally present,
and not just in a certain measure. Hence, there is no more wisdom than
there are beauty or majesty, there is no more goodness than strength.
All these qualities are not only equal, but indeed one and the same
thing. Likewise, in a sphere all the dimensions are equal (because its
length equals its depth and width), but also identical, for what you call
a sphere's depth you could just as easily define as its length or breadth.
The same is true of the height of divine wisdom, which is identical to
the depth of its power and the breadth of its goodness. All these perfections are equal because they are infinite. Necessarily, then, if one
quality exists in proportion to the measure of another, given that such
things are finite, it follows that one subject will be wiser than beautiful
or good, better and more beautiful than wise, wiser and better than
powerful, more powerful than good or wise. But where there is infinite
wisdom, there can be nothing but infinite power, for otherwise there

si possa sapere e si sappia possere. Or dumque vedi come l'oggetto di questo furioso, quasi inebriato di bevanda de dèi, sia più alto incomparabilmente che gli altri diversi da quello. Come, voglio dire, la specie intelligibile della divina essenza comprende la perfezzione de tutte l'altre specie altissimamente, di sorte che secondo il grado che può esser partecipe di quella forma, potrà intender tutto e far tutto, et esser cossì amico d'una, che vegna ad aver a dispreggio e tedio ogn'altra bellezza. Però a quella si deve esser consecrato il sferico pomo, come chi è tutto in tutto. Non a Venere bella che da Minerva è superata in sapienza, e da Giunone in maestà. Non a Pallade di cui Venere è più bella, e l'altra più magnifica. Non a Giunone, che non è la dea dell'intelligenza et amore ancora.

CICADA: Certo come son gli gradi delle nature et essenze, cossì proporzionalmente son gli gradi delle specie intelligibili, e magnificenze de gli amorosi affetti e furori.

XII. CICADA: Il seguente porta una testa, ch'ha quattro faccia che soffiano verso gli quattro angoli del cielo; e son quattro venti in un suggetto, alli quali soprastanno due stelle, et in mezzo il motto che dice NOVAE ORTAE AEOLIAE; vorrei sapere che cosa vegna significata.

TANSILLO: Mi pare ch'il senso di questa divisa è conseguente di quello de la prossima superiore. Perché come là è predicata una infinita bellezza per oggetto, qua vien protestata una tanta aspirazione, studio, affetto e desio; percioch'io credo che questi venti son messi a significar gli suspiri; il che conosceremo, se verremo a leggere la stanza:

༄

      Figli d'Astreo Titan e de l'Aurora,
      che conturbate il ciel, il mar e terra,
      quai spinti fuste dal Litigio fuora,
      perché facessi a' dèi superba guerra:

would be no infinite knowledge. Where there is infinite good, there must be infinite wisdom, for otherwise there would be no way to be infinitely good. Where there is infinite power there must be infinite goodness and wisdom, for this is how one is able to know and to know that one is able. Now, then, see how the Object of this frenzied hero, almost drunk on the nectar of the gods, is incomparably loftier than others different from itself. Thus, I mean to say, the intelligible species of the divine nectar contains the perfections of all the other species to the greatest possible extent, so that according to his ability to participate in this Form,[102] he will be able to understand everything, and to do everything, and thus become so familiar with one beauty as to hold every other beauty in bored disdain. Thus, the spherical apple should be awarded to her, for she is the one who is all in all: not to lovely Venus, who is exceeded by Minerva in wisdom and by Juno in majesty; not to Pallas, than whom Venus is more beautiful and Juno more magnificent, nor to Juno, who is goddess of neither intelligence nor love.

CICADA: Certainly, then, just as there are levels of natures and essences, likewise there are levels of intelligible species, and levels of magnificence among amorous emotions and frenzies.

**XII.** CICADA: The next [emblem] bears a head with four faces that blow towards the four corners of the heavens; thus, there are four winds in a single subject. Above this are two stars, and in between a motto that says, NEWBORN AEOLIANS. I would like to know what it means.

TANSILLO: It seems to me that the meaning of this emblem follows on the previous one. For just as an infinite beauty is proposed there as beloved object, here a claim is made for a comparable aspiration, zeal, affection, and desire. For I believe that these winds have been used to signify sighs; and we will know for certain, if we read the sonnet:

*Sons of Astraeus and the dawning day*
*Who agitate the heavens, earth and seas,*
*Forth into exile Strife pushed you away*
*For haughty war against the deities*

non più a l'Eolie spelunche dimora
fate, ov'imperio mio vi fren' e serra:
ma rinchiusi vi siet'entr' a quel petto
ch'i' veggo a tanto sospirar costretto.

Voi socii turbulenti
de le tempeste d'un et altro mare,
altro non è che vagli' asserenare,

che que' omicidi lumi et innocenti:
quelli apert' et ascosi
vi renderan tranquilli et orgogliosi.

᠉

Aperto si vede ch'è introdotto Eolo parlar a i venti, quali non più dice
esser da lui moderati nell'Eolie caverne: ma da due stelle nel petto di
questo furioso. Qua le due stelle non significano gli doi occhi che son
ne la bella fronte: ma le due specie apprensibili della divina bellezza
e bontade di quell'infinito splendore; che talmente influiscono nel
desio intellettuale e razionale, che lo fanno venire ad aspirar infinitamente, secondo il modo con cui infinitamente grande, bello e buono
apprende quell'eccellente lume. Perché l'amore mentre sarà finito,
appagato, e fisso a certa misura, non sarà circa le specie della divina
bellezza: ma altra formata; ma mentre varrà sempre oltre et oltre aspirando, potrassi dire che versa circa l'infinito.

CICADA: Come comodamente l'aspirare è significato per il spirare? che
simbolo hanno i venti col desiderio?

TANSILLO: Chi de noi in questo stato aspira, quello suspira, quello medesimo spira. E però la vehemenza dell'aspirare è notata per quell'iero-
glifico del forte spirare.

CICADA: Ma è differenza tra il suspirare e spirare.

TANSILLO: Però non vien significato l'uno per l'altro come medesimo
per il medesimo: ma come simile per il simile.

CICADA: Seguitate dumque il vostro proposito.

No longer in Aeolian caves to stay
Where my command held rein, and lock, and keys.
Instead, you have been shut within that breast
Which I see by so many sighs distressed.

You turbulent satellites
Of all the storms on this and the other shore,
There's nothing apt to pacify you more

Than those two murderous innocent lights,
Which open, or hide their lustre,
To calm you, or excite your gallant bluster.

～ঽ৲

We see clearly that Aeolus has been introduced speaking to the winds; these, he says, are no longer guided by himself in the Aeolian caverns, but by two stars in the breast of that frenzied hero. Here the two stars mean not the two eyes on the beautiful face of the beloved, but the two perceptible species of that infinite splendour: divine beauty and divine goodness. These so influence intellectual and rational desire that they induce him to aspire infinitely, to the full extent that he understands such excellent light to be infinitely great, beautiful, and good. For love, so long as it is finite, fulfilled, and fixed at a certain measure, is not a love of divine beauty, but of another form. When it aspires ever higher and farther, then it can be said to turn towards the infinite.

CICADA: How can respiration symbolize aspiration? What connection do the winds have with desire?

TANSILLO: Whoever of us in this human state aspires, also sighs, and so respires. That is why the vehemence of his aspiration is symbolized by this hieroglyphic of strong blowing.

CICADA: But there is a difference between respiration and blowing.

TANSILLO: But one is not signified by the other as if they were the same thing; rather, one thing is symbolized by something similar.

CICADA: Then continue your explanation.

TANSILLO: L'infinita aspirazion dumque mostrata per gli suspiri, e significata per gli venti, è sotto il governo non d'Eolo nell'Eolie, ma di detti doi lumi; li quali non solo innocente, ma e benignissimamente uccidono il furioso, facendolo per il studioso affetto morire al riguardo d'ogn'altra cosa: con ciò che quelli che chiusi et ascosi lo rendono tempestoso, aperti lo renderan tranquillo; attesoché nella staggione che di nuvoloso velo adombra gli occhi de l'umana mente in questo corpo, aviene che l'alma con tal studio vegna più tosto turbata e travagliata: come essendo quello stracciato e spinto, doverrà tant'altamente quieta, quanto baste ad appagar la condizion di sua natura.

CICADA: Come l'intelletto nostro finito può seguitar l'oggetto infinito?

TANSILLO: Con l'infinita potenza ch'egli ha.

CICADA: Questa è vana, se mai sarrà in effetto.

TANSILLO: Sarrebe vana se fusse circa atto finito, dove l'infinita potenza sarrebe privativa; ma non già circa l'atto infinito, dove l'infinita potenza è positiva perfezzione.

CICADA: Se l'intelletto umano è una natura et atto finito, come e perché ha potenza infinita?

TANSILLO: Perché è eterno, et acciò sempre si dilette, e non abbia fine né misura la sua felicità; e perché come è finito in sé, cossì sia infinito nell'oggetto.

CICADA: Che differenza è tra la infinità de l'oggetto et infinità della potenza?

TANSILLO: Questa è finitamente infinita, quello infinitamente infinito. Ma torniamo a noi. Dice dumque là il motto *Novae partae Aeoliae*, perché par si possa credere che tutti gli venti (che son negli antri voraginosi d'Eolo) sieno convertiti in suspiri, se vogliamo numerar quelli che procedeno da l'affetto che senza fine aspira al sommo bene et infinita beltade.

XIII. CICADA: Veggiamo appresso la significazione di quella face ardente, circa la quale è scritto AD VITAM, NON AD HORAM.

TANSILLO: Infinite aspiration, manifested in sighs, and symbolized by the winds, is under the government, not of Aeolus, from the Aeolian islands, but of those two lights, which kill the frenzied hero innocently, and gently as well, making him die to every other thing for his zealous affection. Furthermore, when closed and hidden they make him tempestuous; open they make him tranquil, for during the season that casts a cloudy veil over the eyes of the human mind in this body, the soul becomes more disturbed and troubled by such longing, just as, torn and buffeted by that same longing, it will become profoundly quiet, quiet enough to fulfil the condition of its nature.

CICADA: How can our finite intellect pursue the infinite?

TANSILLO: With the infinite power that it commands.

CICADA: But this power is useless, if it is never put into effect.

TANSILLO: It would be useless if it had to do with a finite action, where infinite power would mean deprivation, but not in the case of infinite action, where infinite power is positive perfection.

CICADA: If the human intellect is of a finite nature and action, how and why does it have infinite power?

TANSILLO: Because it is eternal, and therefore takes delight forever, and its happiness has neither boundary nor measure; and because although it is finite in itself, it is infinite in its object.

CICADA: What difference is there between the infinity of the object and infinity of power?

TANSILLO: The latter is infinite in a finite way, but the former is infinitely infinite. But let us return to ourselves. Now here the motto says, *Newborn Aeolians*, because it seems we are supposed to believe that all the winds in the honeycombed caverns of Aeolus have been converted into sighs – if we want to put a number to the sighs that proceed from the affections, which aspire without end to the highest good and infinite beauty.

**XIII.** CICADA: Then let us see the meaning of this burning torch, with the inscription around it: FOR LIFE, NOT FOR THE HOUR.

TANSILLO: La perseveranza in tal amore et ardente desio del vero bene, in cui arde in questo stato temporale il furioso. Questo credo che mostra la seguente tavola:

ॐ

> Partesi da la stanz' il contadino,
> quando il sen d'Oriente il giorno sgombra;
> e quand'il sol ne fere più vicino,
> stanch' e cotto da caldo sied' a l'ombra;
> lavora poi, e s'affatica insino
> ch'atra caligo l'emisfer ingombra;
> indi si posa: io sto a continue botte
> mattina, mezo giorno, sera e notte.

> Questi focosi rai
> ch'escon da que' doi archi del mio sole,
> de l'alma mia (com'il mio destin vuole)

> dal orizonte non si parton mai:
>     bruggiand' a tutte l'ore
> dal suo meridian l'afflitto core.

ॐ

CICADA: Questa tavola più vera che propriamente esplica il senso de la figura.

TANSILLO: Non ho d'affaticarmi a farvi veder queste proprietadi, dove il vedere non merita altro che più attenta considerazione. Gli «rai del sole» son le raggioni con le quali la divina beltade e bontade si manifesta a noi. E son «focosi», perché non possono essere appresi da l'intelletto, senza che conseguentemente scaldeno l'affetto. «Doi archi del sole» son le due specie di revelazione che gli scolastici teologi chiamano «matutina» e «vespertina», onde l'intelligenza illuminatrice di noi, come aere mediante, ne adduce quella specie o in virtù che la admira in se stessa, o in efficacia che la contempla ne gli effetti. L'orizonte de l'alma in questo luogo è la parte delle potenze superiori, dove a l'apprensione gagliarda de l'intelletto soccorre il vigoroso appulso de l'af-

TANSILLO: [It signifies] the frenzied hero's perseverance in this love, and his ardent desire for the true goodness: the flames that fire him in this temporal state. The following panel, I believe, will show this:

ॐ

The peasant leaves his chamber as the day's
Unburdening the bosom of the East.
And when the Sun's struck closer with its rays,
Exhausted, broiled, he takes a shady rest.
He labours then, till darkness overlays
The hemisphere in shrouds of inky mist.
At last he sleeps. But I face every blow
That morning, noon, evening, and night bestow.

And every fiery ray
That my own Sun's twin rainbows may emit
Will never (fate has thus desired it)

From my soul's one horizon go astray;
At all hours they ignite
My stricken heart from their meridian's height.

ॐ

CICADA: This caption explains the meaning of the image more truly than precisely.

TANSILLO: I am not going to make the effort of examining the details, when it will require nothing but a little more attentive consideration for you to see the meaning. The rays of the sun are the reasons for which the divine beauty and goodness manifests itself to us. And they are fiery because they cannot be grasped by the intellect unless they also heat the affection. *My Sun's twin rainbows* are the two species of revelation that the scholastic theologians call "morning" and "evening," through which the intelligence that illuminates us, like intervening air, brings us that species, either virtually, to be admired in itself, or in effect, to be contemplated through its effects. Here the *soul's one horizon* is that part of the superior powers where the vigorous drive of the

fetto, significato per il core, che «bruggiando a tutte l'ore» s'afflige; perché tutti gli frutti d'amore che possiamo raccòrre in questo stato non son sì dolci che non siano più gionti a certa afflizzione, quella almeno che procede da l'apprension di non piena fruizione. Come specialmente accade ne gli frutti de l'amor naturale, la condizion de gli quali non saprei meglio esprimere, che come fe' il poeta epicureo:

Ex hominis vero facie pulchroque colore
nil datur in corpus praeter simulacra fruendum
tenuia, quae vento spes captat saepe misella.
Ut bibere in somnis sitiens cum quaerit, et humor
non datur, ardorem in membris qui stinguere possit;
sed laticum simulacra petit frustraque laborat,
in medioque sitit torrenti flumine potans:
sic in amore Venus simulacris ludit amantis,
nec satiare queunt spectando corpora coram,
nec manibus quicquam teneris abradere membris
possunt, errantes incerti corpore toto.
Denique cum membris conlatis flore fruuntur
aetatis; dum iam praesagit gaudia corpus,
atque in eo est Venus, ut muliebria conserat arva,
adfigunt avide corpus iunguntque salivas
oris, et inspirant pressantes dentibus ora,
nequicquam, quoniam nihil inde abradere possunt,
nec penetrare et abire in corpus corpore toto.

Similmente giudica nel geno del gusto che qua possiamo aver de cose divine: mentre a quelle ne forziamo penetrare et unirci, troviamo aver più afflizzione nel desio che piacer nel concetto. E per questo può aver detto quel savio Ebreo, che chi aggionge scienza aggionge dolore, perché dalla maggior apprensione nasce maggior e più alto desio, e da questo seguita maggior dispetto e doglia per la privazione della cosa desiderata; là onde l'epicureo che séguita la più tranquilla vita, disse in proposito de l'amor volgare:

Sed fugitare decet simulacra, et pabula amoris
abstergere sibi, atque alio convertere mentem,

affection lends its help to the valiant grasp of the intellect, signified by the heart that is afflicted by constant burning; for all the fruits of love that we can gather in this present state are not so sweet that they are not also joined to a certain affliction, at the very least the affliction that comes from recognizing that our fulfilment is incomplete. This happens especially with the fruits of natural love, whose condition I could express no better than did Lucretius, the Epicurean poet:[103]

For of the human face, and likewise of beautiful colour,
No more enjoyment is granted the body than grasping at fleeting
Images, which wretched hope often snatches away on the breezes.
Just as in dreams when the thirsty dreamer will seek after water
Only to be denied what would slake all the fire in his members;
Then he pursues the mirage of liquid, and vainly he labours,
Standing and thirsting amid the torrential surge of a river:
This is how Venus in love deceives every lover with figments;
Neither can they ever sate their bodies simply by gazing
Nor can they rub off one bit of a tender limb as they wander,
Hesitantly, with their hands, across every part of their bodies.
Finally, when they enjoy the flower of their youth with their members
Brought in conjunction (already the body's garnered a foretaste of pleasure)
Venus is present as well, for the sowing of womanly furrows,
Greedily now they clamp fast their bodies, and join their saliva
Breathing from mouth to mouth, while bearing down with their nibbles –
Never, however, can they rub more than this much from each other,
Nor penetrate and be gone, totally, body in body.

He makes the same judgment in the case of the pleasure that we can take in divine things, for while we exert ourselves to penetrate and unite ourselves with them, we discover that we have experienced more affliction in our desire than pleasure in the conception. And for this reason that wise Hebrew could have said that whoever adds to his knowledge adds to his pain, because from greater understanding comes greater and loftier desire, and upon this there follow greater dejection and pain for the lack of the thing desired.[104] For this reason the Epicurean, who pursues the more tranquil life, had this to say about vulgar love:

No! it is better to flee figments, and wipe off the gruel
Love serves, diverting your mind away in another direction,

nec servare sibi curam certumque dolorem:
ulcus enim virescit et inveterascit alendo,
inque dies gliscit furor, atque erumna gravescit.
Nec Veneris fructu caret is qui vitat amorem,
sed potius quae sunt sine paena commoda sumit.

CICADA: Che intende per il «meridiano del core»?

TANSILLO: La parte o region più alta e più eminente de la volontà, dove
più illustre, forte, efficace e rettamente è riscaldata. Intende che tale
affetto non è come in principio che si muova, né come in fine che si
quiete, ma come al mezzo dove s'infervora.

XIV. CICADA: Ma che significa quel strale infocato che ha le fiamme in
luogo di ferrigna punta, circa il quale è avolto un laccio, et ha il motto
AMOR INSTAT UT INSTANS? Dite che ne intendete.

TANSILLO: Mi par che voglia dire che l'amor mai lo lascia, e che eterno
parimente l'affliga.

CICADA: Vedo bene laccio, strale e fuoco; intendo quel che sta scritto:
*Amor instat*; ma quel che séguita, non posso capirlo, cioè che l'amor
come istante o insistente, inste: che ha medesima penuria di proposito, che se uno dicesse: «questa impresa costui la ha finta come finta, la
porta come la porta, la intendo come la intendo, la vale come la vale,
la stimo come un che la stima».

TANSILLO: Più facilmente determina e condanna chi manco considera.
Quello *instans* non significa adiettivamente dal verbo *instare*, ma è
nome sustantivo preso per l'instante del tempo.

CICADA: Or che vuol dir che l'amor insta come l'instante?

TANSILLO: Che vuol dire Aristotele nel suo libro *Del tempo*, quando dice
che l'eternità è uno instante, e che in tutto il tempo non è che uno
instante?

CICADA: Come questo può essere se non è tanto minimo tempo che non
abbia più instanti? Vuol egli forse che in uno instante sia il diluvio, la

Nor should you gather a store of cares and of guaranteed sorrow:
This is an ulcer that thrives, growing chronic as soon as you feed it,
Madness that grows over time, adding more weight to its burden.
Nor will avoidance of love make a man lack the bounty of Venus,
Rather, the pleasure is there for the taking, with none of the payment.[105]

CICADA: What does he mean by the *heart's meridian?*

TANSILLO: The loftiest and most eminent part or region of the will; where he is heated more brightly, strongly, effectively, and rightly. He means that affection like this is not at its beginning where it moves, nor at its end when it has grown quiet, but, as it were, in the middle, where it boils up.

**XIV.** CICADA: But what is the meaning of that fiery bolt that has flames in place of a steel point, and around it is a cord, and it bears the motto AN INSTANT LOVE INSISTS. Tell me, what do you make of it?

TANSILLO: I think it means that love will never leave him, and yet at the same time it afflicts him forever.

CICADA: I see the point of the cord, the bolt, and the flame; I understand where the inscription says, *Love insists*, but as for the rest, I cannot understand it, that is, that love, as instant, or insistent, insists: this is the same lack of ingenuity as if someone were to say: "he has devised this emblem as his device," "he carries it as he carries it," "I understand it as I understand it," "it holds as it holds," "I judge it as a judge of it."

TANSILLO: It is easier to assess and condemn it the less you think about it. That *instant* is not an adjective from the verb "insist," but rather it is the noun taken as an *instant* in time.[106]

CICADA: Then what does it mean if love insists as an instant?

TANSILLO: What does Aristotle mean in his book *On Time*, when he says that eternity is an instant, and that all time is no more than an instant?[107]

CICADA: How is this possible unless we are dealing with such a minimal unit of time that it no longer has instants?[108] Does he perhaps mean

guerra di Troia, e noi che siamo adesso? Vorrei sapere come questo instante se divide in tanti secoli et anni; e se per medesima proporzione non possiamo dire chè la linea sia un punto.

TANSILLO: Sì come il tempo è uno, ma è in diversi suggetti temporali, cossì l'instante è uno in diverse e tutte le parti del tempo. Come io son medesimo che fui, sono e sarò; io medesimo son qua in casa, nel tempio, nel campo e per tutto dove sono.

CICADA: Perché volete che l'instante sia tutto il tempo?

TANSILLO: Perché se non fusse l'instante, non sarrebe il tempo: però il tempo in essenza e sustanza non è altro che instante. E questo baste se l'intendi (perché non ho da pedanteggiar sul quarto de la *Fìsica*); onde comprendi che voglia dire che l'amor gli assista non meno che il tempo tutto: perché questo *instans* non significa punto del tempo.

CICADA: Bisogna che questa significazione sia specificata in qualche maniera, se non vogliamo far che sia il motto vicioso in equivocazione, onde possiamo liberamente intendere ch'egli voglia dire che l'amor suo sia d'uno instante, *idest* d'un atomo di tempo e d'un niente: o che voglia dire che sia (come voi interpretate) sempre.

TANSILLO: Certo se vi fussero inplicati questi doi sensi contrarii, il motto sarrebe una baia. Ma non è cossì, se ben consideri, atteso che in uno instante che è atomo o punto, che l'amore inste o insista non può essere: ma bisogna necessariamente intendere l'instante in altra significazione. E per uscir di scuola, leggasi la stanza:

౭

Un tempo sparge, et un tempo raccoglie;
un edifica, un strugge; un piange, un ride:
un tempo ha triste, un tempo ha liete voglie;
un s'affatica, un posa; un stassi, un side:
un tempo porge, un tempo si ritoglie;
un muove, un ferm'; un fa viv', un occide:

that in a single instant there can be the Flood, the Trojan War, and we who exist now? I want to know how this instant is divided into so many centuries and years. And whether, on the same scale, we might not also say that a line is a point?[109]

TANSILLO: Just as time is one, but exists in different temporal subjects, so the instant is one in different parts of time, and in all of them. Just as I am the same person I was, am, and will be, and I myself am here in my house, in church, in the countryside, and everywhere that I am.

CICADA: Why do you think that the instant is all time?

TANSILLO: Because if there were no instant, there would be no time; therefore time in essence and substance is nothing other than the instant. And this should suffice, if you understand it (because I am not here to play the pedant over the Fourth Book of the *Physics*), and hence you will understand what it means to say that love does not stand by him for any less than for all time, because this *instant* does not mean a point in time.

CICADA: This meaning needs to be specified in some way, if the motto is not going to be faulty for its equivocation, so that we can freely understand either that he means that his love is of an instant, that is, of one atom of time and of one nothingness, or that he means (as you interpret it) that it is forever.

TANSILLO: Certainly if these two opposing meanings were both implied, the motto would be a trifle. But it is not so, if you consider it closely, given that in an instant, which is an atom or point, love cannot insist or stand in it; rather, the instant must be understood as meaning something else. And to release us from school, let us read the sonnet:[110]

꒰ꈍ꒱

One season sows, one gathers in the sheaves;
One builds, one topples, one laments, one plays;
One season longs for joy, another grieves;
One toils, one rests; one sits, another stays;
One season gives, another one receives,
One moves, one pauses, one gives life, one slays;

in tutti gli anni, mesi, giorni et ore
m'attende, fere, accend'e lega amore.

Continuo mi disperge,
sempre mi strugg'e mi ritien in pianto,
è mio triste languir ogn'or pur tanto,

in ogni tempo mi travagli' et erge;
tropp'in rubbarmi è forte,
mai non mi scuote, mai non mi dà morte.

ॐ

CICADA: Assai bene ho compreso il senso: e confesso che tutte le cose accordano molto bene. Però mi par tempo di procedere a l'altro.

XV. TANSILLO: Qua vedi un serpe ch' a la neve languisce dove l'avea gittato un zappatore; et un fanciullo ignudo acceso in mezzo al fuoco, con certe altre minute e circonstanze, con il motto che dice IDEM, ITIDEM, NON IDEM. Questo mi par più presto enigma che altro, però non mi confido d'esplicarlo a fatto: pur crederei che voglia significar medesimo fato molesto, che medesimamente tormenta l'uno e l'altro (cioè intentissimamente, senza misericordia, a morte) con diversi instrumenti o contrarii principii, mostrandosi medesimo freddo e caldo. Ma questo mi par che richieda più lunga e distinta considerazione.

CICADA: Un'altra volta. Leggete la rima.

TANSILLO:

ॐ

Languida serpe, a quell'umor sì denso
ti rintorci, contrai, sullevi, inondi;
e per temprar il tuo dolor intenso,
al fredd' or quest' or quella parte ascondi;
s'il ghiaccio avesse per udirti senso,
tu voce che propona o che rispondi,

In every year, month, day, or hour I see
Love wounds, ignites, binds, and abides with me.

Unfailingly he tears me,
Destroys me always, keeps me ever crying;
And my dejected anguish, so undying

In every season assails me, upward bears me,
Such is his bandit's skill, he
Shall never cease to shake me or to kill me.

⟋

CICADA: Now I have understood the meaning very well, and confess that all the elements accord with each other very well. I think it is time to proceed to the next one.

**XV.** TANSILLO: Here you see a serpent that languishes on the snow where a ploughman has thrown it, and a naked boy burning in the middle of a flame, with certain other details and circumstances, and a motto that says, THE SAME, THE VERY SAME, NOT THE SAME. This appears to me more of an enigma than anything else; hence, I hardly trust myself to explain it fully. However, I believe that it means to symbolize the same hostile fate that equally torments both one and the other (that is, intensely, without mercy, and to the death) with different tools or opposing principles, revealing itself as simultaneously cold and hot. But this, it seems to me, requires a longer and more detailed discussion.

CICADA: Some other time. Read the sonnet.

TANSILLO:

⟋

O serpent, languishing on fluid so dense
You writhe, contract, lift up, and undulate,
To give such piercing pain some recompense
Each part in turn from cold you insulate;
But if the ice for hearing had the sense
Or you a voice to reason and debate

credo ch'areste efficaci' argumento
per renderlo piatoso al tuo tormento.

Io ne l'eterno foco
mi dibatto, mi struggo, scaldo, avvampo;
e al ghiaccio de mia diva per mio scampo

né amor di me, né pietà trova loco:
    lasso, per che non sente
quant'è il rigor de la mia fiamma ardente.

❧

Angue cerchi fuggir, sei impotente;
ritenti a la tua buca, ell' è disciolta;
proprie forze richiami, elle son spente;
attendi al sol, l'asconde nebbia folta;
mercé chiedi al villan, odia 'l tuo dente;
fortuna invochi, non t'ode la stolta.
Fuga, luogo, vigor, astro, uom o sorte
non è per darti scampo da la morte.

Tu addensi, io liquefaccio;
io miro al rigor tuo, tu a l'ardor mio;
tu brami questo mal, io quel desio;
n' io posso te, né tu me tòr d'impaccio.

Or chiariti a bastanza
del fato rio, lasciamo ogni speranza.

❧

CICADA: Andiamone, perché per il camino vedremo di snodar questo intrico, se si può.

TANSILLO: Bene.

I think you'd have a forceful argument
To make it sympathize with your torment.

In this eternal blaze
I shudder, vex myself, ignite, and burn.
My lady's ice leaves nowhere else to turn;

There neither love nor pity finds a place.
Alas! She can't admire
The chilly rigour of my ardent fire.

᷂

Ah, snake! You cannot flee, try as you might;
Slink towards your lair; it's lost now to decay.
Summon your strength; you'll find that it's too slight.
Await the sun; dark clouds obscure the day.
Cry to the peasant: how he hates your bite!
Call Fortune; Fool! She's turned her ear away.
Escape, home, strength, stars, man, or destiny:
Not one of them from death can set you free.

You freeze; I liquefy;
I marvel at your chill; you at my fire.
You want this hardship; I want your desire.
We cannot save each other, you and I.

Now well enough aware
Of our fell fate, let's give in to despair.

᷂

CICADA: Let us go, and as we walk discover whether or not we can unravel this riddle.

TANSILLO: Very well.

# SECONDA PARTE

# SECOND PART

# DIALOGO PRIMO

*Interlocutori*: CESARINO, MARICONDO

I. CESARINO: Cossì dicono che le cose megliori e più eccellenti sono nel mondo quando tutto l'universo da ogni parte risponde eccellentemente: e questo stimano allor che tutti gli pianeti ottegnono l'Ariete, essendo che quello de l'ottava sfera ancora ottegna quello del firmamento invisibile e superiore dove è l'altro zodiaco; le cose peggiori e più basse vogliono che abbiano loco quando domina la contraria disposizione et ordine: però per forza di vicissitudine accadeno le eccessive mutazioni, dal simile al dissimile, dal contrario a l'altro. La revoluzion dumque et anno grande del mondo è quel spacio di tempo in cui da abiti et effetti diversissimi per gli oppositi mezzi e contrarii si ritorna al medesimo: come veggiamo ne gli anni particolari, qual è quello del sole, dove il principio d'una disposizione contraria è fine de l'altra, et il fine di questa è principio di quella: però ora che siamo stati nella feccia delle scienze, che hanno parturita la feccia delle opinioni, le quali son causa della feccia de gli costumi et opre, possiamo certo aspettare de ritornare a meglior stati.

MARICONDO: Sappi, fratel mio, che questa successione et ordine de le cose è verissima e certissima: ma al nostro riguardo sempre, in qualsivoglia stato ordinario, il presente più ne affligge che il passato, et ambi doi insieme manco possono appagarne che il futuro, il quale è sempre in aspettazione e speranza, come ben puoi veder designato in questa figura la quale è tolta dall'antiquità de gli Egizzii, che fêrno cotal statua che sopra un busto simile a tutti tre puosero tre teste, l'una di lupo che remirava a dietro, l'altra di leone che avea la faccia volta in mezzo, e la terza di cane che guardava innanzi; per significare che le cose passate affligono col pensiero, ma non tanto quanto le cose presenti che in effetto ne tormentano: ma sempre per l'avenire ne promettemo meglio. Però là è il lupo che urla, qua il leon che rugge, appresso il cane che applaude.

CESARINO: Che contiene quel motto ch'è sopra scritto?

MARICONDO: Vedi che sopra il lupo è IAM, sopra il leone MODO, sopra

# FIRST DIALOGUE

*Interlocutors*: CESARINO, MARICONDO

I. CESARINO: And thus, they say that the best and most excellent things come into the world when every part of the entire universe is in greatest harmony; this occurs, they think, when all the planets are in Aries, for Aries in the eighth sphere[1] occupies the same house as the Aries that belongs to the Zodiac of the invisible upper heaven. The worst and basest things, they believe, take place under the opposite conditions, and this power of alternation creates the radical changes that we see from like to unlike, from one extreme to the other. The revolution of the Great Year is that span of time within which the world, having passed through the most diverse conditions, returns, along divergent and contrasting paths, to the state from which it began.[2] We can see this happening with individual years, like the solar year, where the beginning of one alignment marks the end of its opposite, and the end of the former is the beginning of the latter. But [in our own time], now that we have wallowed in the dregs of knowledge, which have produced the dregs of opinion, which have caused the dregs of morals and actions, we can certainly expect to return to better conditions.

MARICONDO: Know well, brother, that this cycle and sequence of things is as true and as certain as can be; but from our point of view, always, in any ordinary state whatsoever, the present pains us more than the past, and both together can hardly satisfy us as much as the future, which is always a matter of expectation and hope, as this figure well shows, taken from the antiquities of the Egyptians.[3] They made one kind of statue, on which above three identical torsos they placed three different heads: one of a wolf facing backward, another of a lion with its face turned towards the centre, and the third of a dog looking ahead, to signify that things past trouble our thoughts, but not as much as present things, which effectively torment us, but always promise better for the future. Thus, it is the wolf behind who howls, the lion here who roars, and next it will be the dog who applauds.

CESARINO: What does the motto mean that is written above it?

MARICONDO: See: above the wolf is ALREADY, above the lion, NOW,

il cane PRAETEREA, che son dizzioni che significano le tre parti del tempo.

CESARINO: Or leggete quel ch'è nella tavola.

MARICONDO: Cossì farò.

꒰ꕥ꒱

Un alan, un leon, un can appare
a l'auror, al dì chiar, al vespr'oscuro.
Quel che spesi, ritegno, e mi procuro,
per quanto mi si die', si dà, può dare.

Per quel che feci, faccio et ho da fare
al passat', al presente et al futuro,
mi pento, mi tormento, m'assicuro,
nel perso, nel soffrir, nell'aspettare.

Con l'agro, con l'amaro, con il dolce
l'esperienza, i frutti, la speranza
mi minacciò, m'affligono, mi molce.

L'età che vissi, che vivo, ch'avanza
mi fa tremante, mi scuote, mi folce,
in absenza, presenza, e lontananza.

Assai, troppo, a bastanza
quel di già, quel di ora, quel d'appresso
m'hann' in timor, martir, e spene messo.

꒰ꕥ꒱

CESARINO: Questa a punto è la testa d'un furioso amante; quantumque sia de quasi tutti gli mortali in qualumque maniera e modo siano malamente affetti; perché non doviamo né possiamo dire che questo quadre a tutti stati in generale, ma a quelli che furono e sono travagliosi: atteso che ad un ch'ha cercato un regno et ora il possiede, conviene il timor di perderlo; ad un ch'ha lavorato per acquistar gli frutti de l'amore, come è la particular grazia de la cosa amata, conviene il mor-

above the dog, ANON; these inscriptions signify the three parts of time.

CESARINO: Now read what is in the caption.

MARICONDO: So I shall.

⌇

> A wolf, a lion, and a dog shall show
> At dawn, at bright of day, at evening's gloom;
> What I gave out, possess, and shall assume,
> This much was given me, gives, shall bestow.
>
> For what I did, I do, my next creation
> Before, at present, and in days ahead
> I rue, torment myself, assuage my dread
> In loss, in suffering, in expectation.
>
> And with the sour, the bitter, and the sweet
> Experience, the fruits, expectancy
> Scared me, afflict me, makes my cares retreat
>
> The span I lived, live, what remains to me
> Sets me aquiver, shakes me, guides my feet
> In absence, presence, and in scarcity.
>
> Greatly, too much, sufficiently
> What happened then, what now, and what comes next
> Keep me in fear, distress, and hope perplexed.

⌇

CESARINO: This, to be precise, is the head of a frenzied lover; though it could just as well be the head of almost any mortal badly affected in any way whatsoever. For we should not and cannot say that this squares with all states in general, but only with those that were and are distressing. Thus, anyone who has sought a kingdom and now possesses it also suffers the fear of losing it; anyone who has struggled to earn the fruits of love, for instance, the particular favour of the beloved, also earns

so della gelosia e suspizione. E quanto a gli stati del mondo, quando
ne ritroviamo nelle tenebre e male, possiamo sicuramente profetizar
la luce e prosperitade; quando siamo nella felicità e disciplina, senza
dubio possiamo aspettar il successo de l'ignoranze e travagli: come avvenne a Mercurio Trimigisto che per veder l'Egitto in tanto splendor
de scienze e divinazioni, per le quali egli stimava gli uomini consorti
de gli dèmoni e dèi, e per conseguenza religiosissimi, fece quel profetico lamento ad Asclepio, dicendo che doveano succedere le tenebre
de nove religioni e culti, e de cose presenti non dover rimaner altro
che favole e materia di condannazione. Cossì gli Ebrei quando erano
schiavi nell'Egitto e banditi nelli deserti, erano confortati da lor pro-
feti con l'aspettazione de libertà et acquisto di patria. Quando furono
in stato di domìno e tranquillità, erano minacciati de dispersione e
cattività. Oggi che non è male né vituperio a cui non siano suggetti,
non è bene né onore che non si promettano. Similmente accade a
tutte l'altre generazioni e stati: li quali se durano e non sono annihi-
lati a fatto, per forza della vicissitudine delle cose, è necessario da 'l
male vegnano al bene, dal bene al male, dalla bassezza a l'altezza, da
l'altezza alla bassezza, da le oscuritadi al splendore, dal splendor alle
oscuritadi. Perché questo comporta l'ordine naturale: oltre il qual ordine, se si ritrova altro che lo guaste o corregga, io lo credo, e non ho
da disputarne, perché non raggiono con altro spirito che naturale.

MARICONDO: Sappiamo che non fate il teologo ma filosofo e che trattate
filosofia non teologia.

CESARINO: Cossì è. Ma veggiamo quel che séguita.

II. CESARINO: Veggio appresso un fumante turribolo che è sustenuto da
un braccio, et il motto che dice ILLIUS ARAM; et appresso l'articolo
seguente:

ᘐ

> Or chi quell'aura de mia nobil brama
> d'un ossequio divin credrà men degna
> s'in diverse tabelle ornata vegna
> da voti miei nel tempio de la fama?

the bite of jealousy and suspicion. And as for the state of the world, when we find ourselves in darkness and evil, then we can safely predict a future of light and prosperity; when we are happy and wise, we may anticipate that ignorance and trouble will follow without a doubt. This happened to Hermes Trismegistus, when he saw Egypt in such a splendour of wisdom and skill at divination that he thought of mortals as the consorts of demons and gods, and consequently highly religious. He complained to Asclepius, predicting that the darkness of new religions and cults was bound to follow, and that the things of the present would not survive except as tales and matters to be condemned.[4] Likewise the Hebrews, when enslaved in Egypt and banished to the deserts, were comforted by their prophets with the hope of freedom, and the attainment of a homeland. When they had reached the state of sovereignty and tranquillity, they were threatened by dispersion and captivity. Today, when there is no evil and blame to which they are not subjected, there is no goodness or honour that does not hold out its promise.[5] The same thing happens to every other generation and condition: if they last, and are not annihilated in fact by the natural alternation of things, they will necessarily pass from good to evil, from low to high, from high to low, from darkness to light, from light to darkness. This is the order of nature; if there is some order beyond it that might upset or correct it, I am willing to accept it without argument, but I reason with no spirit other than what is natural.

MARICONDO: We know that you are not speaking as a theologian, but as a philosopher, and that you are discussing philosophy, not theology.[6]

CESARINO: Exactly. But let's see what comes next.

**II.** CESARINO: Here I see a smoking censer held up by an arm, and a motto that says, HIS ALTAR,[7] and then this sonnet:

Who'll deem the glow of my desire's flame
Unworthy of a heavenly oblation
If I've enshrined it in the dedication
Of plaques and icons in the shrine of fame?

perch'altr' impres' eroica mi richiama,
chi pensarà giamai che men convegna
ch'al suo culto cattivo mi ritegna
quella ch'il ciel onora tanto et ama?

Lasciatemi, lasciate, altri desiri,
importuni pensier, datemi pace.
Perché volete voi ch'io mi ritiri

da l'aspetto del sol che sì mi piace?
Dite di me piatosi: «Perché miri
quel, che per remirar sì ti disface?

perché di quella face
sei vago sì?». «Perché mi fa contento
più ch'ogn'altro piacer questo tormento».

༄

MARICONDO: A proposito di questo io ti dicevo che quantumque un rimagna fisso su una corporal bellezza e culto esterno, può onorevolmente e degnamente trattenirsi: purché dalla bellezza materiale la quale è un raggio e splendor della forma, et atto spirituale di cui è vestigio et ombra, vegna ad inalzarsi alla considerazion e culto della divina bellezza, luce e maestade: di maniera che da queste cose visibili vegna a magnificar il core verso quelle che son tanto più eccellenti in sé e grate a l'animo ripurgato, quanto son più rimosse da la materia e senso. Oimè (dirà) se una bellezza umbratile, fosca, corrente, depinta nella superficie de la materia corporale, tanto mi piace e tanto mi commuove l'affetto, m'imprime nel spirito non so che riverenza di maestade, mi si cattiva, e tanto dolcemente mi lega e mi s'attira, ch'io non trovo cosa che mi vegna messa avanti da gli sensi che tanto m'appaghe: che sarà di quello che sustanzialmente, originalmente, primitivamente è bello; che sarà de l'anima mia, dell'intelletto divino, della regola de la natura? Conviene dumque che la contemplazione di questo vestigio di luce mi amene mediante la ripurgazion de l'animo mio all'imitazione, conformità e participazione di quella più degna et alta, in cui mi transforme e a cui mi unisca: perché son certo che la natura che mi ha messa questa bellezza avanti gli occhi, e mi ha dotato di senso interiore, per cui posso argumentar bellezza più profonda et incom-

A hero's task may summon me by name,
But why would that increase my hesitation
To stay a captive, rapt in adulation
Of one the heavens cherish and esteem?

Begone, forsake me, every strange desire;
You thoughts that importune me, pray relent.
Why do you now demand that I retire

From basking in the sun of my content?
For pity's sake tell: why do you aspire
Towards what undoes you to such great extent?

Why are you so intent
On that one torch? – Here's why: because I treasure
This torment more than any other pleasure.

✣

MARICONDO: As for this, I told you that so long as a lover is fixed upon a physical beauty and external service, he may linger honourably and worthily, provided that he raises himself above material beauty (which is only a trace and shadow of spiritual form and action) to the contemplation and service of divine beauty, light, and majesty. In that case, he lifts up his heart away from visible things towards those that are all the more excellent in themselves, and more pleasing to the purified spirit, the farther they are removed from matter and perception. "Alas," he will say, "if a beauty that is shadowed, dark, fleeting, and painted upon the surface of physical matter can please me this much, and can so move my emotions, so impress on my spirit some sort of reverence for majesty, so captivate me, bind me so gently, and attract me until I find that no other thing placed before my senses fulfils me so, then what will happen when something is substantially, originally, and primordially beautiful? What will become of my soul, of the divine intellect, of the rule of nature? It is right, therefore, that the contemplation of this trace of light guide me, through the purification of my spirit, to imitate, conforming to, and participating in, something more worthy and exalted, into which I am transformed and with which I unite myself; for I am sure that Nature has put this beauty before my eyes, and has endowed me with this interior sense to perceive a beauty that is

parabilmente maggiore, voglia ch'io da qua basso vegna promosso a l'altezza et eminenza di specie più eccellenti. Né credo che il mio vero nume come me si mostra in vestigio et imagine, voglia sdegnarsi che in imagine e vestigio vegna ad onorarlo, a sacrificargli, con questo ch'il mio core et affetto sempre sia ordinato, e rimirare più alto: atteso che chi può esser quello che possa onorarlo in essenza e propria sustanza, se in tal maniera non può comprenderlo?

CESARINO: Molto ben dimostri come a gli uomini di eroico spirito tutte le cose si converteno in bene, e si sanno servire della cattività in frutto di maggior libertade, e l'esser vinto una volta convertiscono in occasione di maggior vittoria. Ben sai che l'amor di bellezza corporale a color che son ben disposti non solamente non apporta ritardamento da imprese maggiori, ma più tosto viene ad improntargli l'ali per venire a quelle: allor che la necessità de l'amore è convertita in virtuoso studio per cui l'amante si forza di venire a termine nel quale sia degno della cosa amata, e forse di cosa maggiore, megliore e più bella ancora; onde sia o che vegna contento d'aver guadagnato quel che brama, o sodisfatto dalla sua propria bellezza, per cui degnamente possa spregiar l'altrui che viene ad esser da lui vinta e superata: onde o si ferma quieto, o si volta ad aspirare ad oggetti più eccellenti e magnifichi. E cossì sempre varrà tentando il spirito eroico, sin tanto che non si vede inalzato al desiderio della divina bellezza in se stessa, senza similitudine, figura, imagine e specie, se sia possibile: e più se sa arrivare a tanto.

MARICONDO: Vedi dumque, Cesarino, come ha raggione questo furioso di risentirsi contra coloro che lo riprendono come cattivo de bassa bellezza a cui sparga voti e appenda tabelle; di maniera che quindi non viene rubelle dalle voci che lo richiamano a più alte imprese: essendo che come queste basse cose derivano da quelle et hanno dependenza, cossì da queste si può aver accesso a quelle come per proprii gradi. Queste se non son Dio son cose divine, sono imagini sue vive: nelle quali non si sente offeso se si vede adorare: perché abbiamo ordine dal superno spirito che dice *Adorate scabellum pedum eius*. Et altrove disse un divino imbasciatore: *Adorabimus ubi steterunt pedes eius*.

CESARINO: Dio, la divina bellezza e splendore riluce et è in tutte le cose;

deeper and incomparably greater, so that I will yearn to be promoted from this base level to the height and eminence of more excellent species. Nor do I believe that my true divinity, as it reveals itself to me in shadow and likeness, will disdain the fact that I wish to honour it in shadow and likeness, to sacrifice to it, so that my heart and emotions are forever put in order, and to look higher. For who can possibly honour it in its essence and real substance without thus understanding it?

CESARINO: You show very well how, for men of heroic spirit, all things convert to goodness; they know how to use captivity to yield greater freedom, and how to make a defeat the occasion for a greater victory. You know well that the love of physical beauty, for those who are well disposed, need not keep them from greater endeavours; indeed, it supplies the wings to fly towards these greater things, just as the craving for love is converted into virtuous desire; by this the lover exerts himself to achieve what he must in order to become worthy of the thing he loves, and perhaps of something still greater, better, and more beautiful. Hence, he is either content at having attained what he desires, or is satisfied by its particular beauty, which makes him despise the lesser beauty that he has conquered and overcome. Then he may pause quietly, or turn to aspire towards more excellent and magnificent Objects. Thus, the heroic spirit will forever go on striving, until it has risen to the point of desiring divine beauty in itself, without likeness, figure, image, or species, if that be possible, and more, if it knows enough to reach such heights.

MARICONDO: See, then, Cesarino, how this frenzied hero has reason to resent those who rebuke him as a captive of base beauty, to which he pours forth his prayers and affixes his votive plaques. He does these things so that he will not rebel against the voices that summon him to more lofty endeavours, for just as base things derive from those that are lofty and continue to maintain their dependency, so, too from these base things it is possible to gain access to the lofty ones in appropriate stages. These lofty things, if they are not God outright, are divine things; they are His living images. He does not take offense if He sees that they are adored, for we have an order from the supernal spirit that says: *Worship at his footstool.*[8] And elsewhere a divine ambassador says: *We will worship at his footstool.*[9]

CESARINO: God, the divine beauty and splendour, shines forth and has

però non mi pare errore d'admirarlo in tutte le cose secondo il modo
che si comunica a quelle: errore sarà certo se noi donaremo ad altri
l'onor che tocca a lui solo. Ma che vuol dir quando dice «Lasciatemi,
lasciate, altri desiri»?

MARICONDO: Bandisce da sé gli pensieri, che gli apprensentano altri oggetti che non hanno forza di commoverlo tanto; e che gli vogliono
involar l'aspetto del sole, il qual può presentarsegli da questa fenestra
più che da l'altre.

CESARINO: Come importunato da pensieri si sta constante a remirar quel
splendor che lo disface, e non lo fa di maniera contento che ancora
non vegna fortemente a tormentarlo?

MARICONDO: Perché tutti gli nostri conforti in questo stato di contro-
versia non sono senza gli suoi disconforti cossì grandi come magnifici
son gli conforti. Come più grande è il timore d'un re che consiste su
la perdita d'un regno, che di un mendico che consiste sul periglio
di perdere dieci danaii; è più urgente la cura d'un prencipe sopra
una republica, che d'un rustico sopra un grege de porci: come gli
piaceri e delicie di quelli forse son più grandi che le delicie e piaceri
di questi. Però l'amare et aspirar più alto, mena seco maggior gloria
e maestà con maggior cura, pensiero e doglia: intendo in questo stato
dove l'un contrario sempre è congionto a l'altro, trovandosi la massima contrarietade sempre nel medesimo geno, e per consequenza circa medesimo suggetto, quantumque gli contrarii non possano essere
insieme. E cossì proporzionalmente nell'amor di Cupido superiore,
come dechiarò l'epicureo poeta nel cupidinesco volgare et animale,
quando disse:

> Fluctuat incertis erroribus ardor amantum,
> nec constat quid primum oculis manibusque fruantur:
> quod petiere premunt arte, faciuntque dolorem
> corporis, et dentes inlidunt saepe labellis
> osculaque adfigunt, quia non est pura voluptas,
> et stimuli subsunt qui instigant laedere id ipsum,
> quodcunque est, rabies, unde illa haec germina surgunt.
> Sed leviter paenas frangit Venus inter amorem,

His being in all things. Hence, it seems to me no error to admire Him in all things, as He communicates Himself through them. It would be certain error, of course, if we were to ascribe to others the honour that is due to Him alone.[10] But what does the poet mean, when he says: *Begone, forsake me, every strange desire?*

MARICONDO: He banishes the thoughts that present him with other objects that lack the power to move him as much, and might want to steal from him the sight of the Sun, which can present itself to him through this window better than through the others.

CESARINO: As if, nagged by thoughts, he stands constant to admire the splendour that undoes him, by making him content only at the price of tormenting him utterly?

MARICONDO: Because all these comforts of ours in this state of strife bring their own discomforts, which are as great as the comforts are magnificent. Just as the fear of a king is greater, because it consists in fear of losing a kingdom, than that of a beggar, which consists in the danger of losing ten dimes; just as the worries of a prince about a republic are more urgent than those of a peasant over a horde of pigs; so, too, the pleasures and delights of the former are perhaps greater than the delights and pleasures of the latter. Therefore, love and loftier aspiration bring with them greater glory and majesty, along with greater worry, thought, and pain; in this state, I mean, where every extreme is always bound to its opposite, and the greatest opposition is always to be found within the same category, and regarding the same subject, inasmuch as such extremes can never exist together. The same situation obtains, in proper proportion, with love of the higher Cupid, as the Epicurean poet declared about vulgar and animal cupidity, when he said:[11]

Ardour in lovers will wax and wane in directionless drifting;
Should it be through the eyes, or the hands that they first take their pleasure?
Then, when they find what they want, they cling to it hard and it's painful
For the body; and often, their lips bear the imprint of biting
As they pin down their kisses; for nothing is pure in this pleasure:
Under its surface are prods that urge them to hurt what delights them,
Whatever thing that may be, that madness, the source of these feelings.
Lightly, though, Venus will break the force of love's violent anguish;

blandaque refraenat morsus admixta voluptas;
namque in eo spes est, unde est ardoris origo,
restingui quoque posse ab eodem corpore flammam.

Ecco dumque con quali condimenti il magistero et arte della natura fa
che un si strugga sul piacer di quel che lo disface, e vegna contento in
mezzo del tormento, e tormentato in mezzo de tutte le contentezze:
atteso che nulla si fa absolutamente da un pacifico principio, ma tutto
da contrarii principii per vittoria e domìno d'una parte della contrarietade; e non è piacere di generazione da un canto, senza dispiacere
di corrozzione da l'altro: e dove queste cose che si generano e corrom-
pono sono congionte e come in medesimo suggetto composto, si trova
il senso di delettazione e tristizia insieme. Di sorte che vegna nominata
più presto delettazione che tristizia, se aviene che la sia predominante,
e con maggior forza possa sollecitare il senso.

III. CESARINO: Or consideriamo sopra questa imagine seguente, ch'è
d'una fenice che arde al sole, e con il suo fumo va quasi a oscurar il
splendor di quello, dal cui calore vien infiammata; et èvvi la nota che
dice: NEQUE SIMILE, NEC PAR.

MARICONDO: Leggasi l'articolo prima:

ℑ

    Questa fenice ch'al bel sol s'accende,
    e a dramm' a dramma consumando vassi,
    mentre di splendor cint'ardendo stassi,
    contrario fio al suo pianeta rende:

      perché quel che da lei al ciel ascende
    tepido fumo et atra nebbia fassi,
    ond'i raggi a' nostri occhi occolti lassi
    e quello avvele, per cui arde e splende.

      Tal il mio spirto (ch'il divin splendore
    accende e illustra) mentre va spiegando
    quel che tanto riluce nel pensiero,
    manda da l'alto suo concetto fore

Gentle delight mixes in to curb the effects of their biting,
For there is hope in the fact that wherever the flame first arises
That very body may have the power to quench the inferno.

Look, then, at what enhancements, what mastery and art nature uses
to make him destroy himself in the pleasure that undoes him, and to
find contentment in the midst of torment, and torment in the midst
of every contentment. Nothing, in fact, is born from concord; instead,
all things are born from opposing principles, through the victory and
dominion of one side in the struggle. At the extremes, one side cannot take pleasure in creation without the other's displeasure and decay, and hence where these things come into being and decay they
are joined, and indeed compounded, in the same subject; thus, we
find the senses of pleasure and sadness together. Yet if pleasure predominates, then it is called "pleasure" rather than "sadness," and can
awaken the senses with greater force.

**III.** CESARINO: Now let's discuss this next image, of a Phoenix that burns
in the Sun, whose smoke almost succeeds in obscuring the splendour
of that star whose heat has set it afire. The motto alongside it says NEI-
THER LIKE NOR EQUAL.

MARICONDO: First let's read the sonnet:

ᔓ

This phoenix, by the lovely sun ignited,
Each ounce of her devoured by the blaze,
Even as the enclosing flames their splendour raise,
Contrary tribute to her star has plighted.

For what of her in heaven has alighted
Has turned to tepid smoke and smouldering haze;
The fires hidden from our hapless gaze
Obscure the very reason they were lighted.

Thus, my own spirit (by that holy fire
Ignited and illumined) would recall
What scintillates so brightly in my thought;
It makes exalted intellect inspire

rima, ch'il vago sol vad'oscurando,
mentre mi struggo e liquefaccio intiero.

Oimè questo adro e nero
nuvol di foco infosca col suo stile
quel ch'aggradir vorrebb', e 'l rend'umile.

✑

CESARINO: Dice dumque costui che come questa fenice venendo dal splendor del sole accesa, et abituata di luce e di fiamma, vien ella poi ad inviar al cielo quel fumo che oscura quello che l'ha resa lucente: cossì egli infiammato et illuminato furioso per quel che fa in lode di tanto illustre suggetto che gli have acceso il core e gli splende nel pensiero, viene più tosto ad oscurarlo, che ritribuirgli luce per luce, procedendo quel fumo, effetto di fiamme in cui si risolve la sustanza di lui.

MARICONDO: Io senza che metta in bilancio e comparazione gli studi di costui, torno a dire quel che ti dicevo l'altr'ieri, che la lode è uno de gli più gran sacrificii che possa far un affetto umano ad un oggetto. E per lasciar da parte il proposito del divino, ditemi: chi conoscerebbe Achille, Ulisse e tanti altri greci e troiani capitani, chi arrebe notizia de tanti grandi soldati, sapienti et eroi de la terra, se non fussero stati messi alle stelle e deificati per il sacrificio de laude, che nell'altare del cor de illustri poeti et altri recitatori have acceso il fuoco, con questo che comunmente montasse al cielo il sacrificatore, la vittima et il canonizato divo, per mano e voto di legitimo e degno sacerdote?

CESARINO: Ben dici di degno e legitimo sacerdote; perché de gli apposti-ci n'è pieno oggi il mondo, li quali come sono per ordinario indegni essi loro, cossì vegnono sempre a celebrar altri indegni, di sorte che *asini asinos fricant*. Ma la providenza vuole che in luogo d'andar gli uni e gli altri al cielo, sen vanno giontamente alle tenebre de l'Orco: onde fia vana e la gloria di quel che celebra, e di quel ch'è celebrato; perché l'uno ha intessuta una statua di paglia, o insculpito un tronco di legno, o messo in getto un pezzo di calcina; e l'altro idolo d'infamia e vitupe-rio non sa che non gli bisogna aspettar gli denti de l'evo e la falce di Saturno per esser messo giù: stante che dal suo encomico medesimo

A rhyme to shroud that sunlight in a pall
As I torment myself, and melt to nought.

By darkness overwrought
This fiery cloud envelops in its style
What would be grand, and makes it wholly vile.

CESARINO: So he says that just as this Phoenix, ignited by the splendour
of the Sun and accustomed to light and flame, eventually sends up the
smoke that obscures what made it bright in the first place; so, too, an
inflamed and illuminated frenzied hero, with his actions in praise of
the illustrious person who has ignited his heart and shines within his
thoughts, rather than giving her light in return for light, instead wraps
her in the darkness of the smoke that issues forth as an effect of the
flames in which his substance is dissolving.

MARICONDO: Without assessing and comparing his desires, I will repeat
what I said to you the day before yesterday: praise is one of the greatest sacrifices that human affection can make for an object of desire.
And leaving aside the matter of divinity, tell me: who would recognize Achilles, Ulysses, and all the other Greek and Trojan generals;
who would hear tell of all the great soldiers, sages, and heroes of this
earth, if they had not been placed among the stars and deified by the
sacrifice of praise, which lit the flame on the altar of the hearts of illustrious poets and other artists, so that sacrificant, victim, and deity
all ascended into the heavens by the hand and prayer of a legitimate
and worthy priest?

CESARINO: You speak rightly of a worthy and legitimate priest, because
in these times the world is filled with impostors. Usually worthless
themselves, they celebrate the worthless, so that "one ass scratches another."[12] But Providence wills it that instead of both going to Heaven,
they go jointly into the gloom of Hell, and their glory, both of the cel-
ebrator and the one celebrated, is vainglory. For the former has woven
together a statue of straw, or carved a stump of wood, or moulded a
piece of plaster – and the other, as an idol of infamy and blame, is unaware that he has no need to wait for the teeth of time and the sickle
of Saturn to lay him low: he will be buried alive by his very idolater

vien sepolto vivo all'ora all'ora propria che vien lodato, salutato, no-
minato, presentato. Come per il contrario è accaduto alla prudenza
di quel tanto celebrato Mecenate, il quale se non avesse avuto altro
splendore che de l'animo inchinato alla protezzione e favor delle
Muse, sol per questo meritò che gl'ingegni di tanti illustri poeti gli
dovenessero ossequiosi a metterlo nel numero de più famosi eroi che
abbiano calpestrato il dorso de la terra. Gli proprii studii et il proprio
splendore l'han reso chiaro e nobilissimo, e non l'esser nato d'atavi
regi, non l'esser gran secretario e conseglicro d'Augusto. Quello dico
che l'ha fatto illustrissimo, è l'aversi fatto degno dell'execuzion della
promessa di quel poeta che disse:

> Fortunati ambo, si quid mea carmina possunt,
> nulla dies unquam memori vos eximet aevo,
> dum domus Aeneae Capitoli immobile saxum
> accolet, imperiumque pater Romanus habebit.

MARICONDO: Mi sovviene di quel che dice Seneca in certa epistola dove
referisce le paroli d'Epicuro ad un suo amico, che son queste: «Se
amor di gloria ti tocca il petto, più noto e chiaro ti renderanno le mie
lettere che tutte quest'altre cose che tu onori, e dalle quali sei onorato,
e per le quali ti puoi vantare». Similmente arria possuto dire Omero
se si gli fusse presentato avanti Achille o Ulisse, Vergilio a Enea et alla
sua progenia; perciò che, come ben suggionse quel filosofo morale,
«è più conosciuto Domenea per le lettere d'Epicuro che tutti gli me-
gistani, satrapi e regi, dalli quali pendeva il titolo di Domenea, e la
memoria de gli quali venea suppressa dall'alte tenebre de l'oblio. Non
vive Attico per essere genero d'Agrippa e progenero de Tiberio, ma
per l'epistole de Tullio. Druso pronepote di Cesare non si trovarebbe
nel numero de nomi tanto grandi, se non vi l'avesse inserito Cice-
rone. Oh che ne sopraviene al capo una profonda altezza di tempo,
sopra la quale non molti ingegni rizzaranno il capo». Or per venire
al proposito di questo furioso il quale vedendo una fenice accesa al
sole, si rammenta del proprio studio, e duolsi che come quella per
luce et incendio che riceve, gli rimanda oscuro e tepido fumo di lode
dall'olocausto della sua liquefatta sustanza. Qualmente giamai possiamo non sol raggionare, ma e né men pensare di cose divine, che non
vengamo a detraergli più tosto che aggiongergli di gloria: di sorte che
la maggior cosa che far si possa al riguardo di quelle, è che l'uomo in
presenza de gli altri uomini vegna più tosto a magnificar se stesso per

at the exact moment when he is praised, saluted, named, presented. The opposite happened to the prudent and much celebrated Maecenas,[13] who may have had no other splendour than a spirit inclined towards protecting and promoting the Muses, and yet for this alone he deserved to have the talents of so many illustrious poets ensure his place among the most famous heroes ever to tread the broad back of this earth. His own labours and his own splendour have made him illustrious and noble, not his royal ancestry, nor his position as chief secretary and councillor of Augustus. What made him so famous, I tell you, is having made himself worthy to carry out the promise of that poet who said:[14]

> Fortunate we shall be, if my verse can muster the power
> Never a day will pass of our era when you're not remembered.
> So long as the Capitol's rock still welcomes the house of Aeneas
> Motionless, so long, too, will Rome's father keep his dominion.

MARICONDO: I am reminded of what Seneca says in a certain letter of his, in which he quotes the words of Epicurus to one of his friends: "If the love of glory touches your breast, my letters will make you more notable and famous than all these other things that you honour, and by which you are honoured, and on account of which you may pride yourself."[15] Homer could have said the same thing, had Achilles or Ulysses stood before him, or Vergil to Aeneas and his progeny, for, as that moral philosopher suggested so aptly: Idomeneus is better known from the letters of Epicurus than all the great satraps and kings who dangled the title of Idomeneus, and whose memory has been suppressed by the deep gloom of oblivion. Atticus does not live through having been the father-in-law of Agrippa and the grandfather-in-law of Tiberius, but through the letters of Cicero. Drusus, great-nephew of Caesar, would never have appeared among the ranks of such great names unless Cicero had inserted him there. Oh, a deep flood of time washes over our heads, and not many wits will raise their heads above it.[16] Now, to return to the subject of our frenzied hero: when he sees a Phoenix ignited by the Sun, he thinks about his own desires, and laments the fact that, as he receives light and fire from it, so, in return, he sends a dark and tepid smoke of praise from the holocaust of his liquefied substance. Likewise, we can never conceive of, let alone reason about, divine things, without detracting from them rather than adding to their glory; hence, the greatest thing that can be done with

il studio et ardire, che donar splendore ad altro per qualche compita e perfetta azzione. Atteso che cotale non può aspettarsi dove si fa
progresso all'infinito, dove l'unità et infinità son la medesima cosa;
e non possono essere perseguitate dal altro numero, perché non è
unità, né da altra unità perché non è numero, né da altro numero et
unità: perché non sono medesimo absoluto et infinito. Là onde ben
disse un teologo che essendo che il fonte della luce non solamente gli
nostri intelletti, ma ancora gli divini di gran lunga sopraavanza, è cosa
conveniente che non con discorsi e paroli, ma con silenzio vegna ad
esser celebrata.

CESARINO: Non già col silenzio de gli animali bruti et altri che sono ad
imagine e similitudine d'uomini: ma di quelli, il silenzio de quali è
più illustre che tutti gli cridi, rumori e strepiti di costoro che possano
esser uditi.

IV. MARICONDO: Ma procediamo oltre a vedere quel che significa il resto.

CESARINO: Dite se avete prima considerato e visto quel che voglia dir
questo fuoco in forma di core con quattro ali, de le quali due hanno
gli occhi, dove tutto il composto è cinto di luminosi raggi, et hassi in
circa scritta la questione: NITIMUR IN CASSUM?

MARICONDO: Mi ricordo ben che significa il stato de la mente, core, spirito et occhi del furioso; ma leggiamo l'articolo:

> Questa mente ch'aspira al splendor santo,
> tant'alti studi disvelar non ponno;
> il cor, che recrear que' pensier vonno,
> da guai non può ritrarsi più che tanto;
>   il spirto che devria posarsi alquanto,
> d'un moment' al piacer non si fa donno;
> gli occhi ch'esser derrian chiusi dal sonno
> tutta la notte son aperti al pianto.

> Oimè miei lumi con qual studio et arti

regard to them is this: a man, in the presence of other men, should magnify himself for his own striving and daring rather than lend splendour to someone else for some completed and perfect action. Yet this situation cannot obtain in the case of progress towards the infinite, where unity and infinity are the same thing; and they cannot be pursued from another number, because no other number is a unity, nor from some other unity, because it is not number, nor from some other number and unity, because their absoluteness and infinity are not the same. This is why a theologian well said that because the source of light greatly surpasses not only our own intellects, but indeed divine [intellects], it is appropriate to celebrate it not with speeches and words, but with silence.[17]

CESARINO: Not, however, the silence of brute animals, and others created in the image and likeness of human beings, but of those whose silence is more illustrious than all the cries, noises, and commotion of those creatures who can be heard.

**IV.** MARICONDO: But let's move on and see what the rest of it means.

CESARINO: Tell me, have you already seen and pondered the meaning of this heart-shaped fire with four wings, two of which have eyes, and the entire composition is encircled by luminous rays? Around it is inscribed the question DO WE STRIVE IN VAIN?

MARICONDO: I remember well; it symbolizes the state of the mind, heart, spirit, and eyes of the frenzied hero; but let us read the sonnet.

The mind aims upward, towards the holy light
That even deepest study can't reveal;
The heart, which all those thoughts would gladly heal,
Finds only scant protection from its plight.
The spirit, which should pause and take delight,
Denies itself that rest from its ordeal.
These eyes, which sleep should gently close and seal,
Are opened wide with weeping every night.

My eyes, by what art or imagination

tranquillar posso i travagliati sensi?
Spirto mio, in qual tempo et in quai parti
mitigarò gli tuoi dolori intensi?
E tu, mio cor, come potrò appagarti
di quel ch'al grave tuo suffrir compensi?

    Quand' i debiti censi
daratti l'alma, o travagliata mente,
col cor, col spirto e con gli occhi dolente?

Perché la mente aspira al splendor divino, fugge il consorzio de la turba, si ritira dalla commune opinione: non solo dico e tanto s'allontana dalla moltitudine di suggetti, quanto dalla communità de studii, opinioni e sentenze; atteso che per contraer vizii et ignoranze tanto è maggior periglio, quanto è maggior il popolo a cui s'aggionge: «Nelli publici spettacoli» disse il filosofo morale, «mediante il piacere più facilmente gli vizii s'ingeriscono». Se aspira al splendor alto, ritiresi quanto può all'unità, contrahasi quanto è possibile in se stesso, di sorte che non sia simile a molti, perché son molti; e non sia nemico de molti, perché son dissimili, se possibil fia serbar l'uno e l'altro bene: altrimente s'appiglie a quel che gli par megliore. – Conversa con quelli gli quali o lui possa far megliori, o da gli quali lui possa essere fatto megliore: per splendor che possa donar a quelli, o da quelli possa ricever lui. Contentesi più d'uno idoneo che de l'inetta moltitudine; né stimarà d'aver acquistato poco quando è dovenuto a tale che sia savio per sé, sovvenendogli quel che dice Democrito: *Unus mihi pro populo est, et populus pro uno*; e che disse Epicuro ad un consorte de suoi studii scrivendo: *Haec tibi, non multis; satis enim magnum alter alteri theatrum sumus.* – La mente dumque ch'aspira alto, per la prima lascia la cura della moltitudine, considerando che quella luce spreggia la fatica, e non si trova se non dove è l'intelligenza; e non dove è ogni intelligenza: ma quella che è, tra le poche, principali e prime, la prima, principale et una.

Might I grant my poor senses some relief?
My spirit, in what time and situation
Might I make your sharp suffering more brief?
And you, my heart, what form of compensation
Will quite repay the burden of your grief?

When will the soul reprieve
You, battered mind, which suffering abides
Together with my heart, spirit and eyes?

ॐ

Because the mind aspires towards the divine splendour, the frenzied hero flees the company of the masses, and withdraws himself from common opinions: and not only this, I tell you, for he also keeps as great a distance from the plurality of subjects as he does from the commonality of studies, opinions, and judgments; for the danger of contracting vices and ignorance is greater when it affects a greater population.[18] "In public spectacles," said the moral philosopher, "vices are more easily absorbed through pleasure."[19] If he aspires towards the exalted light, let him retire as much as he can to the unity, withdraw himself as much as possible into himself, so that he will not be like the many, because they are many; neither, however, let him be an enemy to the many because they are different – if it is possible, let him keep both benefits, and otherwise let him choose the one that seems better. Let him converse with those whom he can improve, or by whom he can be improved, for the lustre that he may give them or that they may give him. Let him derive greater content from a single worthy man than from the bungling multitude. Nor let him think that he has acquired a small thing by becoming wise unto himself, bolstering himself with what Democritus said: "An individual is as good as a nation to me, and a nation as good as an individual," and what Epicurus said to a companion in his studies: "This is for you, not for the multitude; for each of us is worth as much to the other as a great theatre." The mind that aims high, then, first leaves behind any concern about the multitude, aware that the light it seeks disdains toil and can only be found where there is intelligence; and not every sort of intelligence, but only that intelligence which is rare, principal, and prime, the first principle, the one.[20]

CESARINO: Come intendi che la mente aspira alto? verbigrazia con guardar alle stelle? al cielo empireo? sopra il cristallino?

MARICONDO: Non certo, ma procedendo al profondo della mente per cui non fia mistiero massime aprir gli occhi al cielo, alzar alto le mani, menar i passi al tempio, intonar l'orecchie de simulacri, onde più si vegna exaudito: ma venir al più intimo di sé, considerando che Dio è vicino, con sé e dentro di sé, più ch'egli medesimo esser non si possa; come quello ch'è anima de le anime, vita de le vite, essenza de le essenze: atteso poi che quello che vedi alto o basso, o in circa (come ti piace dire) de gli astri, son corpi, son fatture simili a questo globo in cui siamo noi, e nelli quali non più né meno è la divinità presente che in questo nostro, o in noi medesimi. Ecco dumque come bisogna fare primeramente de ritrarsi dalla moltitudine in se stesso. Appresso deve dovenir a tale che non stime ma spreggie ogni fatica, di sorte che quanto più gli affetti e vizii combattono da dentro, e gli viziosi nemici contrastano di fuori, tanto più deve respirar e risorgere, e con uno spirito (se possibil fia) superar questo clivoso monte. Qua non bisognano altre armi e scudi che la grandezza d'un animo invitto, e tolleranza de spirito che mantiene l'equalità e tenor della vita, che procede dalla scienza, et è regolato da l'arte di specolar le cose alte e basse, divine et umane, dove consiste quel sommo bene. Per cui disse un filosofo morale che scrisse a Lucilio: «non bisogna tranar le Scille, le Cariddi, penetrar gli deserti de Candavia et Apennini, o lasciarsi a dietro le Sirti: perché il camino è tanto sicuro e giocondo quanto la natura medesima abbia possuto ordinare. Non è» dice egli «l'oro et argento che faccia simile a Dio, perché non fa tesori simili; non gli vestimenti, perché Dio è nudo; non la ostentazione e fama, perché si mostra a pochissimi, e forse che nessuno lo conosce, e certo molti, e più che molti hanno mala opinion de lui»; non tante e tante altre condizioni de cose che noi ordinariamente admiriamo: perché non queste cose delle quali si desidera la copia ne rendeno talmente ricchi, ma il dispreggio di quelle.

CESARINO: Bene: ma dimmi appresso in qual maniera costui «Tranquillarà gli sensi», «mitigarà gli dolori del spirito», «appagarà il core» e «darà gli proprii censi a la mente», di sorte che con questo suo aspirare e studii non debba dire *Nitimur in cassum?*

CESARINO: What do you mean by saying that the mind aims high? Does it look towards the stars, for example? Towards the empyrean sky? Beyond the crystalline sphere?

MARICONDO: Certainly not, but by proceeding into the depths of the mind. Hence, there should be no need [for the frenzied hero] to open his eyes to the heavens, raise his hands, enter the temple, shout into the ears of idols the better to be heard; instead, he should withdraw into the most intimate part of himself in the belief that God is near, with him and in him, more than he himself can be: as it were, the soul of souls, the life of lives, the essence of essences. And bearing in mind that what you see above, below, and all around the stars (as you would say) are bodies, formations like this globe on which we stand, and in which divinity is no more or less present than in our own [orb], or in our own selves, then you can see why he must first withdraw from that multitude into himself. Next he should come to the point where he no longer pays any attention to labour, but shrugs it off, so that the more his emotions and vices struggle within, and his vicious enemies oppose him without, the more he should take a deep breath and rise above them, and in one breath (if possible) scale this steep mountain. Here there is no need for any weapons or shields, aside from the greatness of an indomitable courage, and a tolerance of spirit that maintains a balance and tone of life based on knowledge and regulated by that art of reflecting upon things lofty and base, divine and human, which constitutes the highest good. Hence, a moral philosopher who wrote to Lucilius said: "There is no need to swim past Scylla and Charybdis, penetrate the desert of Candavia and the Apennines or leave the Syrtoi behind, for the road is as safe and cheerful as Nature itself could have ordered."[21] "It takes," he says, "no gold and silver to become like God, because God does not make such treasures; no vestments, because God is nude; no fame or ostentation, because He reveals Himself only to a few, and perhaps no one knows Him; furthermore, many, and more than many, will certainly have a bad opinion of Him." Neither does He contain many, many other kinds of things that we ordinarily admire, because it is not these things, which we desire in abundance, that make us so rich, but the disregard of them.

CESARINO: Very well. But tell me, then, how will the frenzied hero grant his poor senses relief, mitigate the pains of his spirit, satisfy his heart and give his mind its due so that, as he aspires and desires, he will not have to say: "Do we strive in vain?"

MARICONDO: Talmente trovandosi presente al corpo che con la meglior parte di sé sia da quello absente, farsi come con indissolubil sacramento congionto et alligato alle cose divine, di sorte che non senta amor né odio di cose mortali, considerando d'esser maggiore che esser debba servo e schiavo del suo corpo: al quale non deve altrimente riguardare che come carcere che tien rinchiusa la sua libertade, vischio che tiene impaniate le sue penne, catena che tien strette le sue mani, ceppi che han fissi gli suoi piedi, velo che gli tien abbagliata la vista. Ma con ciò non sia servo, cattivo, inveschiato, incatenato, discioperato, saldo e cieco: perché il corpo non gli può più tiranneggiare ch'egli medesimo si lasce; atteso che cossì il spirito proporzionalmente gli è preposto, come il mondo corporeo e materia è suggetta alla divinitade et a la natura. Cossì farassi forte contra la fortuna, magnanimo contra l'ingiurie, intrepido contra la povertà, morbi e persecuzioni.

CESARINO: Bene instituito il furioso eroico.

V. CESARINO: Appresso veggasi quel che séguita. Ecco la ruota del tempo affissa, che si muove circa il centro proprio: e vi è il motto: MANENS MOVEOR; che intendete per quella?

MARICONDO: Questo vuol dire che si muove in circolo: dove il moto concorre con la quiete, atteso che nel moto orbiculare sopra il proprio asse e circa il proprio mezzo si comprende la quiete e fermezza secondo il moto retto; over quiete del tutto, e moto secondo le parti; e da le parti che si muoveno in circolo si apprendeno due differenze di lazione, in quanto che successivamente altre parti montano alla sommità, altre dalla sommità descendeno al basso; altre ottegnono le differenze medianti, altre tegnono l'estremo dell'alto e del fondo. E questo tutto mi par che comodamente viene a significare quel tanto che s'esplica nel seguente articolo:

༅

> Quel ch'il mio cor aperto e ascoso tiene,
> beltà m'imprime et onestà mi cassa;
> zelo ritiemmi, altra cura mi passa
> per là d'ond'ogni studio a l'alma viene:
>
> quando penso suttrarmi da le pene,

MARICONDO: By being present in his own body in such a way that the better part of him is absent from it; by making himself bound and joined to divine things as if by an indissoluble sacrament, so that he feels neither love nor hate for mortal things, believing that he is more than a servant or slave to his body, which he should regard as nothing but a prison that confines his liberty, a glue that cements his wings, a chain that binds his hands, fetters that have fastened his feet, a veil that baffles his vision. But in the face of all this he should not be servile, vicious, hampered, chained, disabled, stationary, and blind, because his body cannot tyrannize him any more than he lets it, for spirit has been granted him in the same proportion to his body that the physical world and matter are subjected to divinity and nature. Thus, he will make himself strong in the face of misfortune, magnanimous in the face of injury, intrepid in the face of poverty, disease, and persecution.

CESARINO: The frenzied hero has been well prepared!

**V.** CESARINO: Now let's see what follows. Here stands the wheel of time, rotating around its own centre, and here is the motto I MOVE IN PLACE. What is meant by that?

MARICONDO: This means that it *moves* in a circle *in* a *place* where motion coincides with rest. For circular motion, above its own axis and around its own centre, entails rest and fixity in terms of linear motion; or, rather, rest for the whole and motion for the parts. Furthermore, the parts that move in a circle pull in two different directions: some parts ascend to the top in succession as others descend to the bottom; some occupy the middling levels; others occupy the extremes of high and low. And all of this, it seems to me, is handily shown by the following sonnet:

What my heart both discloses and retires
Beauty inscribes in me, and Worth dispels.
Zeal holds me back, another care impels
Me towards the source of all my soul's desires.

When I resist the pain my quest requires,

speme sustienmi, altrui rigor mi lassa;
amor m'inalz' e riverenz' abbassa
allor ch'aspiro a l'alt' e sommo bene.

Alto pensier, pia voglia, studio intenso
de l'ingegno, del cor, de le fatiche,
a l'ogetto inmortal, divin, inmenso
fate ch'aggionga, m'appiglie e nodriche;
né più la mente, la raggion, il senso
in altro attenda, discorra, s'intriche.

Onde di me si diche:
costui or ch'hav'affissi gli occhi al sole,
che fu rival d'Endimion si duole.

Cossì come il continuo moto d'una parte suppone e mena seco il moto del tutto, di maniera che dal ributtar le parti anteriori sia conseguente il tirar de le parti posteriori: cossì il motivo de le parti superiori resulta necessariamente nell'inferiori, e dal poggiar d'una potenza opposta séguita l'abbassar de l'altra opposta. Quindi viene il cor (che significa tutti l'affetti in generale) ad essere ascoso et aperto; ritenuto dal zelo, sullevato da magnifico pensiero; rinforzato da la speranza, indebolito dal timore. Et in questo stato e condizione si vederà sempre che trovarassi sotto il fato della generazione.

VI. CESARINO: Tutto va bene; vengamo a quel che séguita. Veggio una nave inchinata su l'onde; et ha le sarte attaccate a lido et ha il motto: FLUCTUAT IN PORTU. Argumentate quel che può significare: e se ne siete risoluto, esplicate.

MARICONDO: E la figura et il motto ha certa parentela col precedente motto e figura, come si può facilmente comprendere se alquanto si considera. Ma leggiamo l'articolo:

Se da gli eroi, da gli dèi, da le genti
assicurato son che non desperi;

Hope fosters what her chill resistance quells;
Love lifts me up, but reverence compels
Meekness, when to the summit I aspire.

High thoughts, righteous desire, study intense
Of wit, of heart, and of laborious deed
To the deathless Object, divine, immense
Let me reach forth, take hold, there take my feed;
Nor let my mind, my reason, or my sense
Attend, regard, embrace some other creed.

Let it be said indeed:
Now that he's set his sights upon the Sun
He's sorry to have trailed Endymion.[22]

Just as the continuous motion of one part supposes and carries along with it the motion of the whole, so that the downward plunge of the forward parts brings about the upward pull of the rear; so, too, the motion of the upper parts is necessarily detectable in the lower parts, and the rise of one of two contrary powers entails the fall of its opposite. Thus, the heart (which signifies the emotions in general) is opened and hidden; restrained by zeal, raised up by magnificent thought, reinforced by hope, weakened by fear. And the frenzied hero will continue in this state and condition so long as he finds himself subjected to the fate of reproduction.

VI. CESARINO: Excellent. Let's move on to the next. I see a ship inclined above the waves, its lines attached to the shore, with the motto TEMPEST-TOSSED IN PORT. Present your arguments for what it may mean, and if you have reached a conclusion, please explain it to me.

MARICONDO: Both the figure and its motto have a certain relationship with the preceding motto and figure, as can be easily understood upon some reflection. But let's read the sonnet:

If by the gods, the heroes, and the nations
I'm reassured that I should not despair

né téma, né dolor, né impedimenti
de la morte, del corpo, de piaceri
    fia ch'oltre apprendi, che soffrisca e senti;
e perché chiari vegga i miei sentieri,
fàccian dubio, dolor, tristezza spenti
speranza, gioia e gli diletti intieri.

Ma se mirasse, facesse, ascoltasse
miei pensier, miei desii e mie raggioni,
chi le rende sì 'ncerti, ardenti e casse,

    sì graditi concetti, atti, sermoni,
non sa, non fa, non ha qualumque stassi
de l'orto, vita e morte a le maggioni.

    Ciel, terr', orco s'opponi;
s'ella mi splend', e accend', et èmmi a lato,
farammi illustre, potente, e beato.

~~~

Da quel che ne gli precedenti discorsi abbiamo considerato e detto si
può comprendere il sentimento di ciò, massime dove si è dimostrato
che il senso di cose basse è attenuato e annullato dove le potenze superiori sono gagliardamente intente ad oggetto più magnifico et eroico. È tanta la virtù della contemplazione (come nota Iamblico) che
accade tal volta non solo che l'anima ripose da gli atti inferiori, ma et
oltre lascie il corpo a fatto. Il che non voglio intendere altrimente che
in tante maniere quali sono esplicate nel libro *De' trenta sigilli*, dove
son prodotti tanti modi di contrazzione. De quali alcune vituperosa,
altre eroicamente fanno che non s'apprenda téma di morte, non si
soffrisca dolor di corpo, non si sentano impedimenti di piaceri: onde
la speranza, la gioia, e gli diletti del spirto superiore siano di tal sorte
intenti, che faccian spente le passioni tutte che possano aver origine
da dubbio, dolore e tristezza alcuna.

CESARINO: Ma che cosa è quella da cui richiede che mire a que' pensieri
    ch'ha resi cossì incerti, compisca gli suoi desii che fa sì ardenti, et
    ascolte le sue raggioni che rende sì casse?

Then neither fear, nor pain, nor complications
Of death, of body, or of pleasures' snare
Increase my fear, my suffering, my sensations;
I see the path before me free and clear.
Doubt, pain and sadness face obliteration
As hope, joy, and supreme delight appear.

But if my thoughts, desires, or arguments
She'd notice, grant, take in consideration
(Who makes them wavering, fiery, impotent),

Such welcome ideas, acts, and conversation
Would never know, work, be significant,
Where birth and life and death have their location.

Let Heav'n, Earth, Hell dissent;
If she shine forth, inflame, and stand by me
Then splendid, powerful and blest I'll be.

꒰

On the basis of what we have considered and concluded in the preceding discussions, we may understand the meaning of this, especially
now that we have shown how the perception of base things is weakened or annulled when the superior powers are courageously concentrated upon a more magnificent and heroic object. The power of
contemplation is so great that (as Iamblichus notes)[23] on occasion the
soul does not simply withdraw from baser actions, but actually leaves
the body altogether. I do not mean this to be understood except in the
thirty ways described in the book *On Thirty Seals*, which presents thirty
kinds of contraction.[24] Some of these contractions shamefully, some
heroically, ensure that fear of death is no longer felt, the pain of the
body is no longer suffered, pleasure no longer poses an impediment:
and hence hope, joy, and the delights of the higher spirit become so
intense that they extinguish whatever passions might have originated
in any sort of doubt, pain, or sadness.

CESARINO: But who or what is he asking to *notice* his *thoughts*, which she
makes *wavering*; grant his *desires*, which she makes *fiery*, *take in consideration* his *arguments*, which she makes *impotent*?

MARICONDO: Intende l'oggetto il quale allora il mira, quando esso se
gli fa presente; atteso che veder la divinità è l'esser visto da quella,
come vedere il sole concorre con l'esser visto dal sole; parimente essere ascoltato dalla divinità è a punto ascoltar quella, et esser favorito da
quella è il medesimo esporsegli; dalla quale una medesima et immobile procedeno pensieri incerti e certi, desii ardenti et appagati, e raggioni exaudite e casse: secondo che degna, o indegnamente l'uomo
se gli presenta con l'intelletto, affetto et azzioni. Come il medesimo
nocchiero vien detto caggione della summersione o salute della nave,
per quanto che o è a quella presente, overo da quella trovasi absente;
eccetto che il nocchiero per suo diffetto o compimento ruina e salva la
nave: ma la divina potenza che è tutta in tutto, non si porge o suttrae
se non per altrui conversione o aversione.


VII. MARICONDO: Con questa dumque mi par ch'abbia gran concatena-
zione e conseguenza la figura seguente, dove son due stelle in forma
de doi occhi radianti con il suo motto che dice: MORS ET VITA.


CESARINO: Leggete dumque l'articolo.

MARICONDO: Cossì farò:

      Per man d'amor scritto veder potreste
      nel volto mio l'istoria de mie pene;
      ma tu perché il tuo orgoglio non si affrene
      et io infelice eternamente reste,
         a le palpebre belle a me moleste
      asconder fai le luci tant'amene,
      ond'il turbato ciel non s'asserene,
      né caggian le nemiche ombre funeste.

      Per la bellezza tua, per l'amor mio,
      ch'a quella (benché tanta) è forse uguale,
      rèndite a la pietà (diva) per dio.

      Non prolongar il troppo intenso male,

MARICONDO: He means his Object at the moment when it appears to him; for to see divinity is to be seen by divinity, just as seeing the Sun coincides with being seen by the Sun. Likewise, being heard by divinity is exactly the same as hearing divinity, and being favoured by divinity is the same as opening oneself to it. And from it, unique and immobile, there proceed thoughts both uncertain and certain, desires that are both ardent and satisfied, arguments heard and vain, according to how worthily or unworthily a man presents himself with his intellect, emotions, and actions. Thus, the pilot of a ship will be held responsible for its sinking or safety, to the extent that he is either present or absent as a member of the crew. The pilot, however, either ruins or saves the ship by his deficiency or competence; but divine power, which exists completely in everything, does not extend or withdraw itself, except to the extent that others may turn towards it or turn away.

**VII.** MARICONDO: It seems to me, then, the next emblem is closely connected to it, and indeed follows from it directly; here are two stars in the form of two shining eyes, with a motto that says, DEATH AND LIFE.

CESARINO: Read the sonnet then.

MARICONDO: So I shall.

かわ

You might see written by the hand of love
The history of my suffering on my face
But you, caught in your pride's own headlong race
And I, ever unhappy born to prove,
Permit your lovely lashes to remove
From sight those lights so prodigal of grace
And hence the stormy sky will make no peace
Nor shall the sombre hostile shadows move.

Pray by your beauty, by this love of mine
Which matches it (however great it be)
By God have mercy, o lady divine

From my excessive pain now set me free –

ch'è del mio tanto amar indegno fio:
non sia tanto rigor con splendor tale.

Se ch'io viva ti cale,
del grazioso sguardo apri le porte:
mirami, o bella, se vuoi darmi morte.

☙

Qua il «volto in cui riluce l'istoria de sue pene» è l'anima, in quanto
che è esposta alla recepzion de doni superiori, al riguardo de quali è
in potenza et attitudine, senza compimento di perfezzione et atto: il
qual aspetta la ruggiada divina. Onde ben fu detto: *Anima mea sicut
terra sine aqua tibi.* Et altrove: *Os meum aperui et attraxi spiritum, quia
mandata tua desiderabam.* Appresso, l'«orgoglio che non s'affrena» è
detto per metafora e similitudine (come de Dio tal volta si dice gelosia, ira, sonno): e quello significa la difficultà con la quale egli fa
copia di far veder al meno le sue spalli, che è il farsi conoscere mediante le cose posteriori, et effetti. Cossì copre le luci con le palpebre,
non asserena il turbato cielo de la mente umana, per togler via l'ombra de gli enigmi e similitudini. – Oltre (perché non crede che tutto
quel che non è non possa essere) priega la divina luce che «per la sua
bellezza» la quale non deve essere a tutti occolta, almeno secondo la
capacità de chi la mira, e «per il suo amore che forse a tanta bellezza
è uguale» (uguale intende de la beltade in quanto che la se gli può far
comprensibile), che «si renda alla pietà», cioè che faccia come quelli
che son piatosi, quali da ritrosi e schivi si fanno graziosi et affabili: e
che «non prolonghe il male» che avviene da quella privazione; e non
permetta che il suo «splendor» per cui è desiderata, appaia maggiore
che il suo amore con cui si communiche: stante che tutte le perfezzioni in lei non solamente sono uguali, ma ancor medesime. – Al fine la
ripriega che non oltre l'attriste con la privazione; perché potrà ucci-
derlo con la luce de suoi sguardi, e con que' medesimi donargli vita: e
però non lo lasce a la morte con ciò che le amene luci siano ascose da
le palpebre.

CESARINO: Vuol dire quella morte de amanti che procede da somma
gioia, chiamata da Cabalisti *mors osculi?* la qual medesima è vita eterna,

Of my great love it's but a worthless sign.
This glow should not abide hostility.

And for the life of me
Open the gates of that most gracious gaze
And look upon me, beauty; end my days.

⸎

Here the *face* on which the *history of his suffering* shines forth is the soul,
exposed as it is to receiving superior gifts; in regard to these, he lingers
in a state of potential and aptitude whose fulfilment in perfection and
action awaits the divine dew. Hence, the Psalmist did well to say: *My
soul to you is like earth without water.*[25] And elsewhere: *I opened my mouth,
and panted: for I longed for thy commandments.*[26] Next, *headlong pride* is
expressed as metaphor and simile (just as one speaks on occasion of
God's jealousy, wrath, or slumber) to signify how difficult it is to convince God even to show His back: that is, the revelation of His divinity
by means of consequences and effects. Thus, He covers his lights with
eyelids, and will not calm the troubled sky of the human mind in order
to remove the shadows of its enigmas and likenesses.

Next the frenzied hero (because he does not believe that what does
not exist could not exist) prays to the divine light *by* her *beauty*, which
should not be hidden to one and all, but revealed to its admirers according to their capacities, and *by* her *love*, which may be equal to this
beauty (equal to the extent that it can be made comprehensible), that
she yield to *mercy*, that is, that she do as those who are merciful do,
when, having initially been withdrawn and taciturn, they become gracious and affable; and that she not prolong the *excessive pain* caused
by her removal, and not let her splendour, for which she is desirable,
seem greater than the love that communicates it, for all her perfections are not only equal, but also identical.

Finally, then, he beseeches her no longer to vex him with deprivation, because she can kill him with the light of her glances, and yet
with those same glances give him life; therefore, he begs her not to
leave him to death by keeping those lovely lights hidden behind her
eyelids.

CESARINO: Does this mean that kind of lovers' death that proceeds from
the highest joy, the one the Kabbalists call the Death of the Kiss,[27]

che l'uomo può aver in disposizione in questo tempo, et in effetto
nell'eternità?

MARICONDO: Cossì è.

VIII. CESARINO: Ma è tempo di procedere a considerar il seguente dis-
segno simile a questi prossimi avanti rapportati, con li quali ha certa
conseguenza. Vi è un'aquila che con due ali s'appiglia al cielo; ma non
so come e quanto vien ritardata dal pondo d'una pietra che tien legata
a un piede. Et èvvi il motto: SCINDITUR INCERTUM. E certo significa la
moltitudine, numero e volgo delle potenze de l'anima; alla significazion della quale è preso quel verso:

> Scinditur incertum studia in contraria vulgus.

Il qual volgo tutto generalmente è diviso in due fazzioni (quantumque
subordinate a queste non mancano de l'altre), de le quali altre invi-
tano a l'alto dell'intelligenza e splendore di giustizia; altre allettano,
incitano e forzano in certa maniera al basso, alle sporcizie delle volut-
tadi, e compiacimenti de voglie naturali. Onde dice l'articolo:

ふ

> Bene far voglio, e non mi vien permesso;
> meco il mio sol non è, bench'io sia seco,
> che per esser con lui, non son più meco,
> ma da me lungi, quanto a lui più presso.

> Per goder una volta, piango spesso;
> cercando gioia, afflizzion mi reco;
> perché veggio tropp'alto, son sì cieco;
> per acquistar mio ben, perdo me stesso.

> Per amaro diletto, e dolce pena,
> impiombo al centro, e vers' il ciel m'appiglio;
> necessità mi tien, bontà mi mena;

> sorte m'affonda, m'inalza il consiglio;
> desio mi sprona, et il timor m'affrena;
> cura m'accende, e fa tard' il periglio.

which is itself that eternal life that humankind can attain both in mortal time and in eternity?

MARICONDO: So it is.

**VIII.** CESARINO: Now it is time to proceed to consider the next drawing, similar to those we have just shown, and with which it has a certain connection. Here is an eagle who flies towards heaven on two wings, but is held back, I know not how or why, by the weight of a stone tied to one of its feet. And it has the motto THE UNCERTAIN IS SPLIT. And surely this means the multitude, number, and mob of the soul's powers, and for that meaning it has used the following verse [of Vergil]:[28]

> Now the uncertain mob is split in opposing directions.

This mob of the soul generally divides into two factions (though however allied its members are to one side, they will never entirely desert the other). Some of them beckon to the heights of intelligence and the splendour of justice, whereas the others incite and coerce downward, as it were, down to the filth of the pleasures and satisfaction of natural instincts.[29] Hence, the sonnet says:

ॐ

> I would do good, and yet I am denied;
> I'm with my Sun; my Sun is not with me
> To join him I left my own company,
> Forsook myself, and hurried to his side.
>
> I weep for every pleasure I have tried;
> In search of joy I took on misery;
> Because I look so high I cannot see,
> To gain my love my self is nullified.
>
> For bitter pleasures and delicious pains
> I plummet downward, aiming for the sky
> Good sends me forth, Necessity restrains,
>
> Fate sinks me as good counsel lofts me high,
> Desire spurs me, fear tugs back the reins.
> Though care inflames me, danger makes me shy.

Qual dritto o divertiglio
mi darà pace, e mi torrà de lite,
s'avvien ch'un sì mi scacce, e l'altro invite?

༘

L'ascenso procede nell'anima dalla facultà et appulso ch'è nell'ali,
che son l'intelletto et intellettiva volontade, per le quali essa naturalmente si referisce et ha la sua mira a Dio come a sommo bene e primo
vero, come all'absoluta bontà e bellezza. Cossì come ogni cosa naturalmente ha impeto verso il suo principio regressivamente, e progres-
sivamente verso il suo fine e perfezzione, come ben disse Empedocle;
da la cui sentenza mi par che si possa inferire quel che disse il Nolano
in questa ottava:

Convien ch' il sol d'onde parte raggiri,
e al suo principio i discorrenti lumi;
el ch'è di terra, a terra si retiri,
e al mar corran dal mar partiti fiumi,
et ond' han spirto e nascon i desiri
aspiren come a venerandi numi:
cossì dalla mia diva ogni pensiero
nato, che torne a mia diva è mistiero.

La potenza intellettiva mai si quieta, mai s'appaga in verità compresa,
se non sempre oltre et oltre procede alla verità incomprensibile: cossì
la volontà che séguita l'apprensione, veggiamo che mai s'appaga per
cosa finita. Onde per consequenza non si referisce l'essenza de l'anima
ad altro termine che al fonte della sua sustanza et entità. Per le potenze poi naturali, per le quali è convertita al favore e governo della materia, viene a referirse et aver appulso, a giovare et a comunicar de la sua
perfezzione a cose inferiori, per la similitudine che ha con la divinità,
che per la sua bontade si comunica o infinitamente producendo, *idest*
communicando l'essere a l'universo infinito, e mondi innumerabili in
quello; o finitamente, producendo solo questo universo suggetto alli
nostri occhi e comun raggione. Essendo dumque che nella essenza
unica de l'anima se ritrovano questi doi geni de potenze, secondo che
è ordinata et al proprio e l'altrui bene, accade che si depinga con un
paio d'ali, mediante le quali è potente verso l'oggetto delle prime et
immateriali potenze; e con un greve sasso, per cui è atta e efficace

What path, direct or sly
Grants peace, and takes me from this altercation
Between my exile and my invitation?

ॐ

The ascent proceeds from the soul, on the power and impetus in its wings, which are the intellect and the intellective will; by these the soul naturally refers to herself and aims towards God as the highest good and prime truth, as well as absolute goodness and beauty. Thus, too, every thing naturally has a regressive drive towards its own origins and a progressive drive towards its own end and perfection, as Empedocles well said.[30] It seems to me that from his statement we can infer what the Nolan said in the following stanza:

The Sun rightly revolves back where it's been;
The vagrant stars to their initial place.
All earthly things withdraw to earth again
The sea-born rivers run their seaward race
Desires yearn after their life's origin
As if to seek some ancient godly race.
So, too, the thoughts of my own goddess born
Are charged towards my goddess to return.

The intellective power is never quiet, and never satisfied by a truth it has comprehended, not unless it forever proceeds farther and farther towards the incomprehensible truth; thus, we see that the will engendered by perception can never be satisfied by something finite. Consequently, the essence of the soul does not address itself to any particular Object, but to the source of its substance and being. Then, through the natural powers by which it turns to the benefit and government of matter, it applies itself, as if driven, to assist baser things and communicate its own perfection to them, and this happens because of the similarity is has with divinity, which communicates itself through its goodness, either infinitely, by producing, that is, communicating, its being to the infinite universe and its infinite worlds or, finitely, producing only this universe, subject to our own eyes and our own reason. Now because both these two kinds of powers are found in the single essence of the soul in their ordained proportion, to its own benefit and that of others, it is shown with a pair of wings, which

verso gli oggetti delle seconde e materiali potenze. Là onde procede
che l'affetto intiero del furioso sia ancipite, diviso, travaglioso, e messo
in facilità de inchinare più al basso, che di forzarsi ad alto: atteso che
l'anima si trova nel paese basso e nemico, et ottiene la regione lontana
dal suo albergo più naturale, dove le sue forze son più sceme.

CESARINO: Credi che a questa difficultà si possa riparare?

MARICONDO: Molto bene; ma il principio è durissimo, e secondo che si
fa più e più fruttifero progresso di contemplazione, si doviene a maggiore e maggior facilità. Come avviene a chi vola in alto, che quanto
più s'estoglie da la terra, vien ad aver più aria sotto che lo sustenta, e
consequentemente meno vien fastidito dalla gravità; anzi tanto può
volar alto, che senza fatica de divider l'aria non può tornar al basso,
quantumque giudicasi che più facil sia divider l'aria profondo verso la
terra, che alto verso l'altre stelle.

CESARINO: Tanto che col progresso in questo geno, s'acquista sempre
maggiore e maggiore facilità di montare in alto?

MARICONDO: Cossì è; onde ben disse il Tansillo:

> Quanto più sott' il piè l'aria mi scorgo,
> più le veloci penne al vento porgo:
> e spreggio il mondo, e verso il ciel m'invio.

Come ogni parte de corpi e detti elementi quanto più s'avvicina al
suo luogo naturale, tanto con maggior impeto e forza va, sin tanto
che al fine (o voglia o non) bisogna che vi pervegna. Qualmente dumque veggiamo nelle parti de corpi a gli proprii corpi, cossì doviamo
giudicare de le cose intellettive verso gli proprii oggetti, come proprii
luoghi, patrie e fini. Da qua facilmente possete comprendere il senso
intiero significato per la figura, per il motto e per gli carmi.

CESARINO: Di sorte che quanto vi s'aggiongesse, tanto mi parrebe soverchio.

have the power to lift it towards the goal of the primary and immaterial powers; and with a heavy stone, which enables it to turn fittingly and effectively towards material powers. This is why the emotions of the frenzied hero, taken as a whole, are uncertain, divided, troubled, and more inclined to stoop lower than to force themselves upward, for the soul finds itself in low-lying and hostile territory, and occupies a region far from its more natural habitat, where, however, its forces are weaker.

CESARINO: Do you think there is any way to resolve this situation?

MARICONDO: Very much so, but the beginning is extremely arduous, and only becomes easier and easier with more and more fruitful progress in contemplation. The same thing happens to anyone who flies high, for as he leaves the ground farther and farther behind, more air sustains him from beneath, so that he is bothered less and less by gravity;[31] indeed, he may fly so high that, without the effort of parting the air, he cannot turn downward again, however easy he may reckon it would be to traverse the air in the direction of earth rather than in the direction of the other stars.

CESARINO: So that with progress in this kind of pursuit it becomes easier and easier to fly upward?

MARICONDO: So it is, and hence Tansillo was right to say:

> The thinner the air I see beneath my feet
> The more I spread my wings and swiftly fly,
> Despise the world, and set out for the sky.

In the same way, the parts of physical bodies, and what are called the elements, travel with greater impetus and force as they come nearer their natural places, until at last (willing or unwilling) they must arrive at their goal. What we see happening among parts of the body in relation to whole bodies also holds for intellective matters in relation to their own objects, as if these were their rightful places, homelands, and goals. Hence, you can easily understand the complete meaning signified by the insignia, the motto, and the sonnet.

CESARINO: So much so that anything more would seem superfluous.

IX. CESARINO: Vedasi ora quel che vien presentato per quelle due saette radianti sopra una targa, circa la quale è scritto VICIT INSTANS.

MARICONDO: La guerra continua tra l'anima del furioso la qual gran tempo per la maggior familiarità che avea con la materia, era più dura et inetta ad esser penetrata da gli raggi del splendor della divina intelligenza e spezie della divina bontade; per il qual spacio dice ch'il cor smaltato de diamante, cioè l'affetto duro et inetto ad esser riscaldato e penetrato, ha fatto riparo a gli colpi d'amore che aportavano gli assalti da parti innumerabili. Vuol dire non ha sentito impiagarsi da quelle piaghe de vita eterna de le quali parla la *Cantica* quando dice: *Vulnerasti cor meum, o dilecta, vulnerasti cor meum*. Le quali piaghe non son di ferro, o d'altra materia, per vigor e forza de nervi; ma son freccie de Diana o di Febo: cioè o della dea de gli deserti della contemplazione de la Veritade, cioè della Diana che è l'ordine di seconde intelligenze che riportano il splendor ricevuto dalla prima, per comunicarlo a gli altri che son privi de più aperta visione; o pur del nume più principale Apollo che con il proprio e non improntato splendore manda le sue saette, cioè gli suoi raggi, da parti innumerabili tali e tante che son tutte le specie delle cose, le quali son indicatrici della divina bontà, intelligenza, beltade e sapienza, secondo diversi ordini dall'apprension dovenir furiosi amanti, percioché l'adamantino suggetto non ripercuota dalla sua superficie il lume impresso: ma rammollato e domato dal calore e lume, vegna a farsi tutto in sustanza luminoso, tutto luce, con ciò che vegna penetrato entro l'affetto e concetto. Questo non è subito nel principio della generazione quando l'anima di fresco esce ad esser inebriata di Lete et imbibita de l'onde de l'oblio e confusione: onde il spirito vien più cattivato al corpo e messo in essercizio della vegetazione, et a poco a poco si va digerendo per esser atto a gli atti della sensitiva facultade, sin tanto che per la razionale e discorsiva vegna a più pura intellettiva, onde può introdursi a la mente e non più sentirsi annubilata per le fumositadi di quell'umore che per l'exercizio di contemplazione non s'è putrefatto nel stomaco, ma è maturamente digesto. – Nella qual disposizione il presente furioso mostra aver durato «sei lustri», nel discorso de quali non era venuto a quella purità di concetto che potesse farsi capace abitazione delle specie peregrine, che offrendosi a tutte ugualmente batteno sempre alla porta de l'intelligenza. Al fine l'amore che da diverse parti et in diverse volte l'avea assaltato come in vano (qualmente il sole in vano se dice lucere e scaldare a quelli che son nelle viscere de la terra e opaco

**IX.** CESARINO: Now let us see what is presented us by these two shining arrows above a target, around which is written THE INSTANT WON IN-SISTENT.[32]

MARICONDO: The war continues between the soul of the frenzied hero, which, for a long time, because of the greater familiarity it had with matter, was more resistant, and less apt to be penetrated by the rays of divine intelligence and the appearance of divine goodness. During that time he says that his diamond-coated heart, that is, his resistant affections, unfit to be warmed and penetrated, shielded him from the blows of love, which pressed their assault from countless directions. This means that he has not felt himself wounded by those wounds of eternal life about which the Canticle speaks when it says:[33] *Thou hast ravished my heart, my beloved; thou hast ravished my heart.* Now these wounds are not inflicted by steel, or some other material propelled by a sinew bowstring. These, rather, are arrows of Diana, or Phoebus.[34] Either, then, they come from the goddess of the desert of Contemplation of the Truth, that is, the Diana [i.e., the Moon] who is the order of secondary intelligences that reflect the splendour they receive from the prime intelligence, and convey it to others who lack more open vision, or else they come from the more principal god, Apollo [i.e., the Sun], who with his own pristine splendour sends forth his arrows, that is, his rays, from countless directions, as many and as various as all the kinds of things that indicate divine goodness, intelligence, beauty, and wisdom, to become, according to various orders of understanding, frenzied lovers, so that the subject himself, diamond hard, can no longer reflect the penetrating light from his surface; instead, softened and tamed by heat and light, he eventually makes himself entirely luminous in substance, all light, with what has been introduced into his affections and mind. This does not happen at the moment of conception, when the soul issues forth fresh to become drunk on Lethe [the River of Forgetfulness] and imbued with the waves of Oblivion and confusion.[35] Later, however, the spirit is ever more captivated by the body and pressed into the service of vegetative life, and gradually consumes itself through its sensitivity to the acts of the sensitive faculty, until it passes through the rational and discursive faculties to the more pure intellective faculty, and from here it can introduce itself to the mind and no longer feel clouded by the fumes of that humor that, thanks to the exercise of contemplation, has not putrefied in the stomach, but rather is thoroughly digested.

profondo), per essersi «accampato in quelle luci sante», cioè per aver mostrato per due specie intelligibili la divina bellezza, la quale con la raggione di verità gli legò l'intelletto e con la raggione di bontà scaldògli l'affetto, vennero superati gli «studi» materiali e sensitivi che altre volte soleano come trionfare, rimanendo (a mal grado de l'eccellenza de l'anima) intatti; perché quelle luci che facea presente l'intelletto agente illuminatore e sole d'intelligenza, ebbero «facile entrata» per le sue luci (quella della verità per la porta de la potenza intellettiva, quella della bontà per la porta della potenza appetitiva) «al core», cioè alla sustanza del generale affetto. Questo fu «quel doppio strale che venne» come «da man de guerriero irato», cioè più pronto, più efficace, più ardito, che per tanto tempo innanzi s'era dimostrato come più debole o negligente. Allora quando primieramente fu sì scaldato et illuminato nel concetto, fu quello vittorioso punto e momento, per cui è detto: *VICIT INSTANS*. Indi possete intendere il senso della proposta figura, motto, et articolo che dice:

᷾

Forte a i colpi d'amor feci riparo
quand' assalti da parti varie e tante
soffers' il cor smaltato di diamante;
ond' i miei studi de suoi trionfaro.

Al fin (come gli cieli destinaro)
un dì accampossi in quelle luci sante,
che per le mie sole tra tutte quante
facil entrata al cor mio ritrovaro.

Indi mi s'avventò quel doppio strale,
che da man di guerrier irato venne,

In this disposition the present frenzied hero reveals that he has endured for thirty years;[36] during this time he had not yet achieved enough purity of thought to provide a hospitable dwelling for the wayward species that knock perennially at the door of intellect, offering themselves equally to all. Finally Love, which from various directions and on various occasions had assailed him, seemingly in vain (as the Sun is said in vain to shine upon and warm those things that are in the viscera of the earth and in deep darkness), by having him *chance one day upon a holy pair / Of lights,* that is, by revealing divine beauty through two intelligible species, bound his intellect in truth, and warmed his affections in goodness, so that his material and sensitive desires were vanquished, although on other occasions they had seemed to achieve a triumph of sorts by remaining unaffected (despite the excellence of his soul). For those two lights, by revealing the presence of intellect (the illuminating agent and Sun of the intelligence), made easy entrance through his own lights – [the light] of truth through the gate of intellective power, and [the light] of goodness through the gate of the power of desire. They drove on then to the heart, that is, to the substance of the affections in general. This was that *double arrow / Shot by a warrior's hand in battle-rage,* [a warrior] who has become ready, effective, and enthusiastic, after a long time spent in seeming weak or negligent. The instant when the hero's mind was first illuminated and set on fire is the victorious point and instant signified in THE INSTANT WON INSISTENT. Now you can understand the meaning of the insignia and motto presented here, and of the sonnet, which says:

ॐ

Against Love's blows I built a strong redoubt,
But his assaults struck, countless, everywhere,
Pounding my heart within its diamond lair –
Still, over his my own desires won out.

At last (as was the heavens' plan throughout)
I chanced one day upon a holy pair
Of lights, and through my own lights, then and there
They found an entry to my heart laid out.

Towards me then a double arrow sailed,
Shot by a warrior's hand in battle-rage:

qual sei lustri assalir mi seppe male:

notò quel luogo, e forte vi si tenne,
piantò 'l trofeo di me là d'onde vale
tener ristrette mie fugaci penne.

Indi con più sollenne
apparecchio, mai cessano ferire
mio cor, del mio dolce nemico l'ire.

~

Singular instante fu il termine del cominciamento e perfezzione della
vittoria. Singulari gemine specie furon quelle, che sole tra tutte quante trovaro facile entrata; atteso che quelle contegnono in sé l'efficacia
e virtù de tutte l'altre: atteso che qual forma megliore e più eccellente può presentarsi che di quella bellezza, bontà e verità, la quale è il
fonte d'ogn'altra verità, bontà, beltade? «Notò quel luogo», prese possessione de l'affetto, rimarcollo, impressevi il carattere di sé; «e forte
vi si tenne», e se l'ha confirmato, stabilito, sancito di sorte che non
possa più perderlo: percioché è impossibile che uno possa voltarsi ad
amar altra cosa quando una volta ha compreso nel concetto la bellezza
divina. Et è impossibile che possa far di non amarla, come è impossibile che nell'appetito cada altro che bene o specie di bene. E però
massimamente deve convenire l'appetenzia del sommo bene. Cossì
«ristrette» son le «penne» che soleano esser «fugaci» concorrendo giù
col pondo della materia. Cossì da là «mai cessano ferire», sollecitando
l'affetto e risvegliando il pensiero, le «dolci ire», che son gli efficaci
assalti del grazioso nemico, già tanto tempo ritenuto escluso, straniero
e peregrino. È ora unico et intiero possessore e disponitor de l'anima;
perché ella non vuole, né vuol volere altro; né gli piace, né vuol che gli
piaccia altro, onde sovente dica:

Dolci ire, guerra dolce, dolci dardi,
dolci mie piaghe, miei dolci dolori.

IX. CESARINO: Non mi par che rimagna cosa da considerar oltre in pro-

He'd fought for thirty years and always failed

But now he marked the spot and pressed the siege,
Planted his trophy where he'd first prevailed,
And forced my wayward wings into his cage.

On a more solemn stage
The angers of my sweetest enemy
Will never cease to strike my heart, and me.

ॐ

A single moment marked both the beginning of the victory and its completion. Twin singular species, alone among all the others, found easy *entry*, because they contained within themselves the efficacy and virtue of all the others; for what more excellent and better form can present itself than that of the beauty, goodness, and truth that provide the source for every other truth, goodness, and beauty? *He marked the spot*, he took possession of his affection, noted it, impressed his character upon it, and pressed the siege, then confirmed, established, and consecrated it [by planting *his trophy*] so that he could never again lose it, for it is impossible for him to turn away to love some other thing once he has comprehended divine beauty in his mind. And it is impossible for him not to love it, just as it is impossible for anything but goodness or the appearance of goodness to whet his desire. And therefore desire for the greatest good must be the most fitting desire of all. Hence, the wings that used to be *wayward*, because they rushed downward with the weight of matter, have been *forced into his cage*. Hence, the sweet *angers never cease to strike*, namely, the tremendous *assaults*, which stimulate the affections and reawaken thought, of the *gracious enemy* that had for so long been considered shut out, a foreign stranger. And yet he is now the one and only possessor and governor of his soul, for she desires no other and desires to desire no other; nor does any other please her, nor does she desire for any other to please her, so that she often says:

Sweet are the rages, sweet the war, sweet arrows;
Sweet are my wounds, and sweet the pain I suffer.

**X.** CESARINO: I don't think that there is anything more to consider about

posito di questo. Veggiamo ora questa faretra et arco d'amore, come mostrano le faville che sono in circa, et il nodo del laccio che pende: con il motto che è, SUBITO, CLAM.

MARICONDO: Assai mi ricordo d'averlo veduto espresso ne l'articolo; però leggiamolo prima:

꒜

Avida di trovar bramato pasto,
l'aquila vers' il ciel ispiega l'ali,
facend' accorti tutti gli animali,
ch'al terzo volo s'apparecchia al guasto.

E del fiero leon ruggito vasto
fa da l'alta spelunca orror mortali,
onde le belve presentendo i mali
fuggon a gli antri il famelico impasto.

E 'l ceto quando assalir vuol l'armento
muto di Proteo da gli antri di Teti,
pria fa sentir quel spruzzo violento.

Aquile 'n ciel, leoni in terr', e i ceti
signor' in mar, non vanno a tradimento:
ma gli assalti d'amor vegnon secreti.

Lasso, que' giorni lieti
troncommi l'efficacia d'un instante,
che femmi a lungo infortunato amante.

꒜

Tre sono le regioni de gli animanti composti de più elementi: la terra, l'acqua, l'aria. Tre son gli geni de quelli: fiere, pesci et ucelli. In tre specie sono gli prìncipi conceduti e definiti dalla natura: ne l'aria l'aquila, ne la terra il leone, ne l'acqua il ceto: de quali ciascuno come dimostra più forza et imperio che gli altri, viene anco a far aperto atto di magnanimità, o simile alla magnanimità. Percioché è osservato che il leone, prima che esca a la caccia, manda un ruggito forte che fa

this. Now let's look at this quiver and bow, which belong to Love, as the sparks around them show, and the knot in the hanging cord, with the motto SUDDENLY, SECRETLY.

MARICONDO: I recall very well having seen its meaning expressed in the sonnet, so let's read that first:

The avid eagle, longing for its quarry
Spreads forth its wings beneath the light of day
Alerting every creature long before he
Soars thrice aloft and pounces on his prey.

And when the lion emits his mighty roar, he
Lets fear sound forth from his high-vaulted cave;
Beasts in their lairs anticipate the story
And cower to keep his ravening at bay.

With violence the whale spouts from the deep
Caverns of Tethys, ere he first assails
Proteus's herd of silent ocean sheep.

Eagles in heaven, lions on earth, and whales
Who rule the seas their savage nature keep,
Yet safely hide from all of Love's travails.

Alas, my happy tales
Were stopped by one instant's efficacy
That made a luckless lover out of me.

There are three regions in which animals occur, composed of several elements: earth, water, and air. There are three kinds of these: beasts, fish, and birds. The sovereigns granted and defined by nature are three: in the air the eagle, on earth the lion, and in water the whale; among them, each one, in the very act of demonstrating greater power and dominion than the others, at the same time performs an open act of magnanimity, or what is similar to magnanimity. Thus, it is observed

rintonar tutta la selva, come de l'erinnico cacciatore nota il poetico
detto:


> At saeva e speculis tempus dea nacta nocendi,
> ardua tecta petit, stabuli et de culmine summo
> pastorale canit signum, cornuque recurvo
> tartaream intendit vocem, qua protinus omne
> contremuit nemus, et silvae intonuere profundae.

De l'aquila ancora si sa che volendo procedere alla sua venazione,
prima s'alza per dritto dal nido per linea perpendicolare in alto, e
quasi per l'ordinario la terza volta si balza da alto con maggior impeto
e prestezza che se volasse per linea piana; onde dal tempo in cui cerca
il vantaggio della velocità del volo, prende anco comodità di specular
da lungi la preda, della quale o despera o si risolve dopo fatte tre re-
mirate.


CESARINO: Potremmo conietturare per qual caggione, se alla prima si
presentasse a gli occhi la preda, non viene subito a lanciarsegli sopra?

MARICONDO: Non certo. Ma forse che ella sin tanto distingue se si gli
possa presentar megliore o più comoda preda. Oltre non credo che
ciò sia sempre, ma per il più ordinario. Or venemo a noi. Del ceto o
balena è cosa aperta che per essere un machinoso animale non può divider l'acqui se non con far che la sua presenza sia presentita dal ributto-
to de l'onde: senza questo, che si trovano assai specie di questo pesce
che con il moto e respirar che fanno, egurgitano una ventosa tempesta
di spruzzo acquoso. Da tutte dumque le tre specie de prìncipi animali
hanno facultà di prender tempo di scampo gli animali inferiori: di sorte che non procedeno come subdoli e traditori. Ma l'Amor che è più
forte e più grande, e che ha domìno supremo in cielo, in terra et in
mare, e che per similitudine di questi forse derrebe mostrar tanto più
eccellente magnanimità quanto ha più forza, niente di manco assalta
e fere a l'improvisto e subito.


> Labitur totas furor in medullas,
> igne furtivo populante venas,

that the lion, before he goes out to hunt, lets forth a mighty roar that makes the whole forest resound, as the poem says of the avenging huntress:

> Then did the savage goddess of harm issue forth from her cavern,
> Sought out the harsh rooftops, and from the high eaves of the stable
> Sang out her rustic alarm, and then through the curve of her trumpet
> Sent forth her infernal voice; all of the sacred grove shuddered
> At it, and in response the forest groaned from its depths.[37]

About the eagle, we know that when it wants to proceed with its hunting, it first rises straight up from the nest in a perpendicular line, and usually when it has done this a third time it suddenly swoops down from on high, with greater momentum and speed than if it had been flying in a horizontal line; during the time it spends seeking the advantage of greater speed in flight, it also takes time to observe its prey at length, and either gives up hope or resolves to pursue it after making three circuits.

CESARINO: Can we guess why, if the prey presents itself the first time around, he never seizes it immediately?

MARICONDO: Certainly not. But perhaps even at that moment he is deciding whether or not a better or more accessible quarry might present itself. Furthermore, I do not believe that this always happens, but it does happen ordinarily.[38] Now let us return to the subject. As for the sea monster, or whale, it is well known that because it is a complex organism it cannot part the waters without making its presence felt in the rebounding of the waves, not to mention the fact that many species of this fish spew forth a windy tempest of spurting water by their motion and breathing. All three types of sovereign animals, therefore, allow lower animals time to make their escape; hence, these sovereigns never proceed by stealth or treachery. Love, who is stronger and greater still, with supreme dominion over heaven, earth, and sea, perhaps ought, like these, to show a magnanimity that is as much greater than theirs as his power is greater. But instead he attacks by striking suddenly and without warning.

> Madness now laps in every bit of marrow;
> Crowding the veins with all its furtive fire

>       nec habet latam data plaga frontem;
>       sed vorat tectas penitus medullas,
>       virginum ignoto ferit igne pectus.

Come vedete, questo tragico poeta lo chiama «furtivo fuoco», «ignote fiamme»; Salomone lo chiama «acqui furtive», Samuele lo nomò «sibilo d'aura sottile». Li quali tre significano con qual dolcezza, lenità et astuzia, in mare, in terra, in cielo, viene costui a (come) tiranneggiar l'universo.

CESARINO: Non è più grande imperio, non è tirannide peggiore, non è meglior domìno, non è potestà più necessaria, non è cosa più dolce e suave, non si trova cibo che sia più austero et amaro, non si vede nume più violento, non è dio più piacevole, non agente più traditore e finto, non autor più regale e fidele, e (per finirla) mi par che l'amor sia tutto, e faccia tutto; e de lui si possa dir tutto, e tutto possa attribuirsi a lui.

MARICONDO: Voi dite molto bene. L'amor dumque (come quello che opra massime per la vista, la quale è spiritualissimo de tutti gli sensi, per che subito monta sin alli appresi margini del mondo, e senza dilazion di tempo si porge a tutto l'orizonte della visibilità) viene ad esser presto, furtivo, improvisto e subito. Oltre è da considerare quel che dicono gli antichi, che l'amor precede tutti gli altri dèi; però non fia mestiero de fingere che Saturno gli mostre il camino, se non con seguitarlo. Appresso, che bisogna cercar se l'amore appaia e facciasi prevedere di fuori, se il suo alloggiamento è l'anima medesima, il suo letto è l'istesso core, e consiste nella medesima composizione de nostra sustanza, nel medesimo appulso de nostre potenze? Finalmente ogni cosa naturalmente appete il bello e buono, e però non vi bisogna argumentare e discorrere perché l'affetto si informe e conferme; ma subito et in uno instante l'appetito s'aggionge a l'appetibile, come la vista al visibile.

XI. CESARINO: Veggiamo appresso che voglia dir quella ardente saetta circa la quale è avolto il motto: CUI NOVA PLAGA LOCO? Dechiarate che luogo cerca questa per ferire.

> Yet the wound struck is never quite apparent
> No, it devours within the hidden marrow
> With secret fire it strikes the breast of virgins.[39]

As you see, this tragic poet calls him a *furtive fire*, unknown flames; Solomon calls him "stolen waters": Samuel called him "a still small voice."[40] All three of them show how gently, slowly, and astutely, on sea, on land, and in heaven, he has succeeded in tyrannizing the universe.

CESARINO: There is no greater empire, there is no worse tyranny, there is no greater dominion, there is no power more necessary, there is nothing more sweet and gentle, there is no food to be found that is more severe and more bitter, there is no divinity more violent to be seen, no god more pleasant, no agent more treacherous and false, no author more regal and faithful, and (finally) it seems to me that Love is all, and does all, and about him one can say all, and all can be ascribed to him.

MARICONDO: You express it very well. Love, then (as something that works primarily through vision, which is the most spiritual of all the senses, because it ascends immediately to the known margins of the world, and without delay offers itself to the entire horizon of visibility) can become swift, furtive, sudden, and immediate. Furthermore, it is worth considering what the ancients say, that Love precedes all the other gods, and therefore there is no need to pretend that Saturn shows him the way, unless he does so by following along.[41] In any case, what need is there to see whether Love has made an appearance or provided a glimpse of himself outside ourselves, if his lodging is the soul itself, his bed the very heart, and he is made of the same composition as our own substance, subject to the same drives as our own powers? And finally, if everything naturally seeks after what is beautiful and good, then there is no need to argue and discuss why the affections are informed and confirmed by Love, for desire unites at once with what is desirable, just as sight does with what is visible.[42]

**XI.** CESARINO: Now let's see what the meaning might be of that flaming arrow, with the motto wrapped around it, WHERE THE NEW WOUND? Explain where this arrow seeks to strike.

MARICONDO: Non bisogna far altro che leggere l'articolo, che dice
    cossì:

꙳

Che la bogliente Puglia o Libia mieta
tante spiche, et areste tante a i venti
commetta, e mande tanti rai lucenti
da sua circonferenza il gran pianeta,

quanti a gravi dolor quest'alma lieta
(che sì triste si gode in dolci stenti)
accoglie da due stelle strali ardenti,
ogni senso e raggion creder mi vieta.

Che tenti più, dolce nemico, Amore?
qual studio a me ferir oltre ti muove,
or ch'una piaga è fatto tutto il core?

Poiché né tu, né altro ha un punto, dove
per stampar cosa nuova, o punga, o fóre,
volta volta sicur or l'arco altrove.

Non perder qua tue prove,
per che, o bel dio, se non in vano, a torto
oltre tenti amazzar colui ch'è morto.

꙳

Tutto questo senso è metaforico come gli altri, e può esser inteso per
il sentimento di quelli. Qua la moltitudine de strali che hanno ferito
e feriscono il core significa gl'innumerabili individui e specie de cose,
nelle quali riluce il splendor della divina beltade, secondo gli gradi di
quelle, et onde ne scalda l'affetto del proposto et appreso bene. De
quali l'un e l'altro per le raggioni de potenzia et atto, de possibilità et
effetto, e cruciano e consolano, e donano senso di dolce e fanno sentir
l'amaro. Ma dove l'affetto intiero è tutto convertito a Dio, cioè all'idea
de le idee, dal lume de cose intelligibili la mente viene exaltata alla
unità super essenziale, è tutta amore, tutta una, non viene ad sentirsi
sollecitata da diversi oggetti che la distrahano: ma è una sola piaga,

MARICONDO: There is no need to do anything but read the sonnet, which goes as follows:

୬

That torrid Libya or Apulia might
Have harvested as many ears of grain,
Cast to the winds such chaff, or that the light
Shed by the Sun such countless beams contain

As my soul gathers griefs to its delight
(Rejoicing wretched in delicious pain)
Received as rays from two stars burning bright –
Reason and sense forbid me to maintain.

Why try again, Love, my sweet enemy?
What purpose drives you once again to spear
A heart that's now been hurt entirely?

For you'll not find a single place still clear
To stab, skewer, or drill a cavity;
Turn back, convinced, and train your bow elsewhere.

Don't waste your effort here
Because (O pretty god) you try in vain,
And wrongly seek to kill the dead again.

୬

This meaning is metaphorical, as with the others; and it can be understood in the same sense. Here the *countless beams* that have pierced and pierce the heart signify the innumerable individuals and species of things in which the splendour of divine beauty shines forth, according to their level, and hence it warms the affections for what has been well presented and well understood. Of these affections, each one, in potential and actuality, in possibility and effect, both torments and consoles, tastes of sweetness and smacks of bitterness. But when all affection is entirely turned towards God, that is, to the Idea of Ideas, by the light of intelligible things, the mind is uplifted to the super-essential unity, which is all love, all one, and then the mind no longer

nella quale concorre tutto l'affetto, e che viene ad essere la sua medesima affezzione. Allora non è amore o appetito di cosa particolare che
possa sollecitare, né almeno farsi innanzi a la voluntade, perché non
è cosa più retta ch'il dritto, non è cosa più bella che la bellezza, non è
più buono che la bontà, non si trova più grande che la grandezza, né
cosa più lucida che quella luce, la quale con la sua presenza oscura e
cassa gli lumi tutti.

CESARINO: Al perfetto, se è perfetto, non è cosa che si possa aggiongere:
però la volontà non è capace d'altro appetito, quando fiagli presente
quello ch'è del perfetto, sommo, e massimo. Intendere dumque posso
la conclusione, dove dice a l'amore: «Non perder qua tue prove; perché, se non in vano, a torto» (si dice per certa similitudine e metafora)
«tenti ammazzar colui ch'è morto». Cioè quello che non ha più vita né
senso circa altri oggetti, onde da quelli possa esser «punto» o «forato»;
a che oltre viene ad essere esposto ad altre specie? e questo lamento
accade a colui che, avendo gusto de l'optima unità, vorrebe essere al
tutto exempto et abstratto dalla moltitudine.

MARICONDO: Intendete molto bene.

XII. CESARINO: Or ecco appresso un fanciullo dentro un battello che sta
ad ora ad ora per essere assorbito da l'onde tempestose, che languido
e lasso ha abandonati gli remi. Et èvvi circa lo motto FRONTI NULLA
FIDES. Non è dubio che questo significhe che lui dal sereno aspetto de
l'acqui fu invitato a solcar il mare infido; il quale a l'improviso avendo
inturbidato il volto, per estremo e mortal spavento, e per impotenza di
romper l'impeto, gli ha fatto dismetter il capo, braccia, e la speranza.
Ma veggiamo il resto:

の

Gentil garzon che dal lido scioglieste
la pargoletta barca, e al remo frale
vago del mar l'indotta man porgeste,
or sei repente accorto del tuo male.

feels itself tempted by various objects that distract it. It is one single wound, into which all affection converges, and which comes to be this very affection itself. Then it is no longer love or desire for a particular thing that can stimulate, or make its presence felt to the will, for there is nothing more direct than a straight line, there is nothing more beautiful than beauty, there is nothing better than goodness, there is nothing to be found that is greater than greatness, nor anything more radiant than the light that with its presence obscures and dims all other lights.

CESARINO: If perfection is perfect, there is nothing else to be added to it; and thus the will is not capable of any other desire, once what is perfect, supreme, and greatest has been put before it. At last I can understand the conclusion where he says to Love, *Don't waste your effort here,* for *you try in vain* and *wrongly* (he says in a certain simile and metaphor) *to kill the dead again.* That is, he no longer has life or sensation for other objects, and hence cannot be stabbed or skewered by them; why, then, should he be further exposed to other species? And this lament happens to the person who, once he has a taste for the one ultimate good, would like to be entirely exempted and removed from multitude.

MARICONDO: You understand very well.

**XII.** CESARINO: Now here is a boy in a boat, who is about to be engulfed by stormy waves at any moment, and yet, all languid and inert, he has abandoned his oars. And around him is the motto NO FAITH IN FAC-ES.[43] There is no doubt that this means that he was tempted by the calm appearance of the waters to cleave the unreliable sea, whose face has suddenly turned surly; in extreme and mortal fear, unable to stop the onslaught, he has lost his grip on head, arms, and hope. But let us see the rest of the emblem:

You gentle youth, who set out from the strand
In tiny boat, and to your feeble oar,
Sea-dazzled, put your poor untutored hand,
At last you see what perils lie in store:

Vedi del traditor l'onde funeste
là prora tua, ch'o troppo scend' o sale;
né l'alma vinta da cure moleste,
contra gli obliqui e gonfii flutti vale.

Cedi gli remi al tuo fero nemico,
e con minor pensier la morte aspetti,
che per non la veder gli occhi ti chiudi.

Se non è presto alcun soccorso amico,
sentirai certo or or gli ultimi effetti
de tuoi sì rozzi e curiosi studi.

Son gli miei fati crudi
simili a' tuoi, perché vago d'Amore
sento il rigor del più gran traditore.

✣

In qual maniera e perché l'amore sia traditore e frodulento l'abbiamo poco avanti veduto: ma perché veggio il seguente senza imagine e motto, credo che abbia conseguenza con il presente; però continuamo leggendolo:

✣

Lasciato il porto per prova e per poco,
feriando da studi più maturi,
ero messo a mirar quasi per gioco:
quando viddi repente i fati duri.

Quei sì m'han fatto violento il foco,
ch' in van ritento a i lidi più sicuri,
in van per scampo man piatosa invoco,
perché al nemico mio ratto mi furi.

Impotent' a suttrarmi, roco e lasso
io cedo al mio destino, e non più tento
di far vani ripari a la mia morte:

What deadly waves the traitor can command,
Your prow that falls and rises ever more,
Your soul, beset by care, too weak to stand
Against the turbid swollen billows' roar.

Resign your oars to your fierce enemy
Awaiting death without the anxious fear
That shuts your eyes against what you might see

And should, at last, no friendly help appear,
You'll feel the consequence, undoubtedly,
Of all your cruel and curious career.

My destiny's as clear
As yours; ever since Love beguiled my soul
I feel that utter traitor's cruel control.

ॐ

Just how and why love is treacherous and deceitful we have seen shortly
before this. But because I see that the next sonnet lacks an image and
a motto, I believe that it must be connected to this one, and therefore
let us continue by reading it:

ॐ

I'd barely left the port, just as a test;
From study I indulged a brief vacation
My wanderings began almost in jest
And then I saw my cruel destination.

Engulfed in flames, I've given up the quest
For safer shores amid the conflagration;
No friendly hand responds to my request
To seize me in its merciful salvation.

Unable to escape, exhausted, hoarse,
Surrendering to my fate I cease to try
To find an exit from my deadly course.

facciami pur d'ogni altra vita casso,
e non più tarde l'ultimo tormento,
che m'ha prescritto la mia fera sorte.

Tipo di mio mal forte
è quel che si commese per trastullo
al sen nemico, improvido fanciullo.

MARICONDO: Qua non mi confido de intendere o determinar tutto quel
che significa il furioso: pure è molto espressa una strana condizione
d'un animo dismesso dall'apprension della difficultà de l'opra, grandezza della fatica, vastità del lavoro da un canto; e da un altro l'ignoranza, privazion de l'arte, debolezza de nervi, e periglio di morte. Non
ha consiglio atto al negocio; non si sa d'onde e dove debba voltarsi,
non si mostra luogo di fuga o di rifugio; essendo che da ogni parte
minacciano l'onde de l'impeto spaventoso e mortale. *Ignoranti portum,
nullus suus ventus est.* Vede colui che molto e pur troppo s'è commesso
a cose fortuite, s'aver edificato la perturbazione, il carcere, la ruina,
la summersione. Vede come la fortuna si gioca di noi; la qual ciò che
ne mette con gentilezza in mano, o lo fa rompere facendolo versar
da le mani istesse, o fa che da l'altrui violenza ne sia tolto, o fa che ne
suffoche et avvelene, o ne sollecita con la suspizione, timore e gelosia,
a gran danno e ruina del possessore. *Fortunae an ulla putatis dona carere
dolis?* Or, perché la fortezza che non può far esperienza di sé, è cassa;
la magnanimità che non può prevalere, è nulla, et è vano il studio
senza frutto; vede gli effetti del timore del male, il quale è peggio ch'il
male istesso: *Peior est morte timor ipse mortis.* Già col timore patisce tutto
quel che teme de patire, orror ne le membra, imbecillità ne gli nervi,
tremor del corpo, anxia del spirito; e si fa presente quel che non gli è
sopragionto ancora, et è certo peggiore che sopragiongere gli possa:
che cosa più stolta che dolere per cosa futura, absente, e la qual presente non si sente?

CESARINO: Queste son considerazioni su la superficie e l'istoriale de la
figura. Ma il proposito del furioso eroico penso che verse circa l'imbecillità de l'ingegno umano il quale attento a la divina impresa in

In every state and form, then, let me die;
Do not postpone the last tormenting force
Prescribed to me by savage destiny.

The image I go by
Is his, who cast himself while acting coy
Upon his enemy, the feckless boy.

☙

MARICONDO: Here I am not entirely sure that I can understand or explain everything that the frenzied hero means. Nonetheless, he strongly expresses a strange state of mind, humbled by grasping the difficulty of the enterprise, the greatness of the effort, the vast scale of the work, on the one hand, and on the other his ignorance, artlessness, weakness of nerve and risk of death. He has no plan suitable for the business before him, he knows not whether to turn here or there. No place of escape or refuge offers itself, because the waves of the fearsome and mortal deluge threaten on every side: for the ignorant no wind blows towards port. He sees that he has gone much too far to change his situation, that he has created his own trouble, prison, ruin, and drowning. He sees how fortune plays with us, that whatever she bestows on us gently she either breaks by dashing it from our hands, or ensures that it is taken away by some other act of violence, or makes it suffocate and poison us, or stirs us up with suspicion, fear, and jealousy, to the great damage and ruin of the possessor. *Did you ever think that the gifts of fortune came without trickery?*[44] Now the strength that cannot prove itself is shattered, the magnanimity that cannot prevail is nothing, and the fruitless study is vain; he sees the effects of the fear of evil, which is worse than evil itself. *Worse than death is the very fear of death.*[45] Because of fear, he already suffers everything that he fears he will suffer; horror in his limbs, lassitude in his nerves, quavering in his body, anxiety in his spirit; and he imagines what will happen to him, which is certainly worse than what may actually happen. What could be more foolish than to worry about what may happen but is not happening now, and cannot be felt at present?[46]

CESARINO. These are considerations about the surface and the story of the figure. But the enterprise of the frenzied hero, I believe, turns on the weakness of human wit, which, intent on the divine undertaking,

un subito talvolta si trova ingolfato nell'abisso della eccellenza incomprensibile, onde il senso et imaginazione vien confusa et assorbita, che non sapendo passar avanti, né tornar a dietro, né dove voltarsi, svanisce e perde l'esser suo non altrimente che una stilla d'acqua che svanisce nel mare, o un picciol spirito che s'attenua perdendo la propria sustanza nell'aere spacioso et inmenso.

MARICONDO: Bene: ma andiamone discorrendo verso la stanza, perché è notte.

## DIALOGO SECONDO

MARICONDO: Qua vedete un giogo fiammeggiante et avolto de lacci, circa il quale è scritto LEVIUS AURA; che vuol significar come l'amor divino non aggreva, non trasporta il suo servo, cattivo e schiavo al basso, al fondo: ma l'inalza, lo sulleva, il magnifica sopra qualsivoglia libertade.

CESARINO: Priegovi leggiamo presto l'articolo, perché con più ordine, proprietà e brevità possiamo considerar il senso, se pur in quello non si trova altro.

MARICONDO: Dice cossì:

ॐ

Chi femmi ad alt' amor la mente desta,
chi fammi ogn'altra diva e vile e vana,
in cui beltad' e la bontà sovrana
unicamente più si manifesta;

quell'è ch'io viddi uscir da la foresta,
cacciatrice di me la mia Diana,
tra belle ninfe su l'aura Campana,
per cui dissi ad Amor: «Mi rendo a questa»;

et egli a me: «O fortunato amante,
o dal tuo fato gradito consorte:

all of a sudden finds itself engulfed in the abyss of incomprehensible excellence, and hence his senses and imagination become confused and preoccupied, and, not knowing how to proceed farther, nor how to turn back, nor where to turn, he disappears and loses his being, just like a drop of water that disappears into the sea, or a little breeze that dissipates and loses its own substance in the great and spacious air.

MARICONDO: Very well. But let us continue discussing on the way home, because it is night-time.

## SECOND DIALOGUE

MARICONDO: Here you see a flaming yoke wrapped in cords; around it is written LIGHTER THAN THE BREEZE, which means that divine love does not weigh down its servant, does not transport him, a captive slave, downward to the depths, but raises him, lifts him up, magnifies him beyond any other freedom.

CESARINO: Please, let's read the sonnet now, so that we can consider its meaning more systematically, suitably, and quickly, and see whether there is any other meaning to be found.

MARICONDO: This is what it says:

༄

She who awoke my mind to love's high quest,
Who made all other idols vile and vain,
In whom beauty and sovereign goodness reign
(In her alone so purely manifest),

I spied emerging from the wilderness:
Diana, my own huntress, with her train
Of nymphs, breezing across Campania's plain
"To her I shall surrender," I confessed

To Love, and he replied: "O lucky lover!
Welcomed by destiny as her consort!

che colei sola che tra tante e tante,

quai ha nel grembo la vit' e la morte,
più adorna il mondo con le grazie sante,
ottenesti per studio e per sorte,

ne l'amorosa corte
sì altamente felice cattivo,
che non invidii a sciolt' altr'uomo o divo».

Vedi quanto sia contento sotto tal giogo, tal coniugio, tal soma che
l'ha cattivato a quella che vedde uscir da la foresta, dal deserto, da la
selva; cioè da parti rimosse dalla moltitudine, dalla conversazione, dal
volgo, le quali son lustrate da pochi. Diana splendor di specie intelligibili, è cacciatrice di sé, perché con la sua bellezza e grazia l'ha ferito
prima, e se l'ha legato poi; e tienlo sotto il suo imperio più contento
che mai altrimente avesse potuto essere. Questa dice «tra belle nimfe»,
cioè tra la moltitudine d'altre specie, forme et idee; e «su l'aura Campana», cioè quello ingegno e spirito che si mostrò a Nola, che giace
al piano del orizonte campano. A quella si rese, quella più ch'altra gli
venne lodata da l'amore, che per lei vuol che si tegna tanto fortunato,
come quella che, tra tutte quante si fanno presenti et absenti da gli
occhi de mortali, più altamente adorna il mondo, fa l'uomo glorioso
e bello. Quindi dice aver sì «desta la mente» ad eccellente amore, che
apprende «ogni altra diva», cioè cura et osservanza d'ogni altra specie,
«vile e vana». – Or in questo che dice aver desta la mente ad amor alto,
ne porge essempio de magnificar tanto alto il core per gli pensieri,
studii et opre, quanto più possibil fia, e non intrattenerci a cose basse
e messe sotto la nostra facultade: come accade a coloro che o per avarizia, o per negligenza, o pur altra dapocagine rimagnono in questo
breve spacio de vita attaccati a cose indegne.

CESARINO: Bisogna che siano arteggiani, meccanici, agricoltori, servitori,
pedoni, ignobili, vili, poveri, pedanti et altri simili: perché altrimente

The only one, among so many others,

Who holds both life and death within her heart
Adorning this world with her holy favour –
Your struggles won her, and your fated part

Within her loving court.
Where, held in such sublime captivity
You grudge no god nor man his liberty.

ॐ

You can see what is meant by such a yoke, such a partnership, such a burden, that has made him captive to the vision he saw emerging from the forest, from the desert, from the woods, that is, from places far removed from the multitude, from company, from the crowd, places frequented by only a few. Diana, the splendour of intelligible species, is his *huntress*, because with her beauty and grace she first wounded him and then bound him, and under her dominion she keeps him happier than he could ever have been otherwise. It says that she is among beautiful *nymphs*, that is, among the multitude of other species, forms, and ideas; and wafted on the *Campanian breeze*, that is, on the wit and spirit that was revealed to him in Nola, which lies along the Campanian horizon. To her he *surrendered*, she who *more than any other* received the tribute of his *love*, for through her he believes that he should be held as *lucky*, just as she among all the others who present themselves to, or absent themselves from, the eyes of mortals *adorns this world most nobly*, makes a man glorious and beautiful. Hence, he says that she has so awakened his mind to excellent love, that he holds every other goddess, that is, every other species of solicitude, as low and empty, *vile and vain*.

Now, when he says that he has *awakened his mind to love's high quest*, he provides an example of magnifying his heart through his thoughts, studies, and works to the greatest extent possible, not lingering among things that are base and inferior to our own faculties, as happens to those who through greed, or negligence, or some other pusillanimity, remain attached to unworthy things in this brief span of life.

CESARINO: There must be artisans, mechanics, farmers, servants, footmen, subordinates, cowards, indigents, pedants, and the like, because

non potrebono essere filosofi, contemplativi, coltori degli animi, padroni, capitani, nobili, illustri, ricchi, sapienti, et altri che siano eroici simili a gli dèi. Però a che doviamo forzarci di corrompere il stato della natura il quale ha distinto l'universo in cose maggiori e minori, superiori et inferiori, illustri et oscure, degne et indegne, non solo fuor di noi, ma et ancora dentro di noi, nella nostra sustanza medesima, sin a quella parte di sustanza che s'afferma inmateriale? Come delle intelligenze altre son suggette, altre preminenti, altre serveno et ubediscono, altre comandano e governano. Però io crederei che questo non deve esser messo per essempio a fin che li sudditi volendo essere superiori, e gl'ignobili uguali a gli nobili, non vegna a pervertirsi e confondersi l'ordine delle cose, che al fine succeda certa neutralità e bestiale equalità, quale si ritrova in certe deserte et inculte republiche. Non vedete oltre in quanta iattura siano venute le scienze per questa caggione che gli pedanti hanno voluto essere filosofi, trattar cose naturali, intromettersi a determinar di cose divine? Chi non vede quanto male è accaduto et accade per averno simili fatte «ad alti amori le menti deste»? Chi ha buon senso, e non vede del profitto che fe' Aristotele, che era maestro de lettere umane ad Alessandro, quando applicò alto il suo spirito a contrastare e muover guerra a la dottrina pitagorica e quella de filosofi naturali, volendo con il suo raciocinio logicale ponere diffinizioni, nozioni, certe quinte entitadi et altri parti et aborsi de fantastica cogitazione per principii e sustanza di cose, studioso più della fede del volgo e sciocca moltitudine, che viene più incaminata e guidata con sofismi et apparenze che si trovano nella superficie delle cose, che della verità che è occolta nella sustanza di quelle, et è la sustanza medesima loro? Fece egli la mente desta non a farsi contemplatore, ma giudice e sentenziatore di cose che non avea studiate mai, né bene intese. Cossì a' tempi nostri quel tanto di buono ch'egli apporta e singulare di raggione inventiva, iudicativa e di metafisica, per ministerio d'altri pedanti che lavorano col medesimo *sursum corda*, vegnono instituite nove dialettiche e modi di formar la raggione: tanto più vili di quello d'Aristotele quanto forse la filosofia d'Aristotele è incomparabilmente più vile di quella de gli antichi. Il che è pure avvenuto da quel che certi grammatisti dopo che sono invecchiati nelle culine de fanciulli e notomie de frasi e de vocaboli, han voluto destar la mente a far nuove logiche e metafisiche, giudicando e sentenziando quelle che mai studiorno et ora non intendono: là onde cossì questi col favore della ignorante moltitudine (al cui ingegno son

otherwise there could not be philosophers, thinkers, cultivators of souls, masters, captains, nobles, illustrious men, wealthy men, wise men, and others who are of heroic stature, are like the gods. Is that why we have to force ourselves to corrupt the state of nature, which has divided the universe into greater and lesser things, higher and lower, illustrious and obscure, worthy and unworthy, not only outside ourselves, but also within us, in our very substance, right down to that part of our substance that is held to be immaterial? For among intellects some are subordinate, some pre-eminent, some serve and obey, others command and govern. I should think, however, that this fact should not be used as an example by subordinates who fancy themselves to be superiors, and ignoble persons who think themselves the equal of nobility, confusing and perverting the order of things until at last a certain neutral and bestial equality takes over, as can be found in certain forsaken and uncultured republics.[47] Haven't you seen the disaster that has overtaken the state of knowledge because pedants who style themselves philosophers have pronounced on natural science and taken it upon themselves to opine on divinity? Who can fail to note what harm has come about and continues to come about when minds of this sort are "awakened to love's high quest"? What reasonable person hasn't seen what happened when Aristotle, who was Alexander's teacher of humane studies, "lifted up his spirit" to oppose and declare war on the teachings of Pythagoras and the natural philosophers, thereby hoping, with the help of his logic chopping, to pass off definitions, notions, certain quintessences, and other miscarried spawn of his hallucinating cogitations as the first principles and substance of things? He sought more eagerly for the faith of the vulgar and foolish masses, who are more easily steered and guided by sophistry and external appearances of things, than he did for the truth, which is hidden deep within their substance, and is, in fact, their very substance. He awakened the mind, not to make himself a contemplator, but rather a judge and a proclaimer of opinions about things that he had never studied, nor properly understood. In our own time, then, what small contribution he may have provided, that is, the individual contributions of inventive and critical reasoning, and of metaphysics, has, thanks to the ministrations of other pedants who toil to the same tune of "lift up your hearts,"[48] established new dialectics and disciplines that are as greatly inferior to those of Aristotle as, perhaps, the philosophy of Aristotle is inferior to that of the ancients.[49] The same

più conformi), potranno cossì bene donar il crollo alle umanitadi e raziocinii d'Aristotele, come questo fu carnefice delle altrui divine filosofie. Vedi dumque a che suol promovere questo consiglio, se tutti aspireno al splendor santo, et abbiano altre imprese vili e vane.

MARICONDO:

> Ride si sapis, o puella, ride,
> pelignus (puto) dixerat poeta;
> sed non dixerat omnibus puellis:
> et si dixerit omnibus puellis,
> non dixit tibi. Tu puella non es.

Cossì il *sursum corda* non è intonato a tutti, ma a quelli ch'hanno l'ali. Veggiamo bene che mai la pedantaria è stata più in exaltazione per governare il mondo, che a' tempi nostri; la quale fa tanti camini de vere specie intelligibili et oggetti de l'unica veritade infallibile, quanti possano essere individui pedanti. Però a questo tempo massime denno esser isvegliati gli ben nati spiriti armati dalla verità et illustrati dalla divina intelligenza, di prender l'armi contra la fosca ignoranza, montando su l'alta rocca et eminente torre della contemplazione. A costoro conviene d'aver ogn'altra impresa per vile e vana. – Questi non denno in cose leggieri e vane spendere il tempo, la cui velocità è infinita: essendo che sì mirabilmente precipitoso scorra il presente, e con la medesima prestezza s'accoste il futuro. Quel che abbiamo vissuto è nulla, quel che viviamo è un punto, quel ch'abbiamo a vivere non è ancora un punto, ma può essere un punto, il quale insieme sarà e sarà stato. E tra tanto questo s'intesse la memoria di genealogie, quello attende a desciferar scritture, quell'altro sta occupato a moltiplicar sofismi da fanciulli. Vedrai verbigrazia un volume pieno di:

thing has happened in the case of certain grammarians, who, after spending a lifetime in the posterior analytics – of boys[50] – dissecting words and phrases, have hoped to awaken their minds by creating new systems of logic and metaphysics, passing judgment and pronouncing on things that they never studied and hardly understand now, so that they may, by the favour of the ignorant multitude (to whose wits they are well matched), topple Aristotle's studies and reasoning, just as he in his own time butchered those other divine philosophies. You see, then, what the effect of promoting this advice might be if everyone decides to aspire to the divine splendour, when their other ventures are *vile and vain*.

MARICONDO:

> "Laugh if you're able, lady, laugh," so Ovid
> Said (if I'm right) – the poet of Paelignum.
> He never said it, though, to all the ladies;
> Even if he said it to all the ladies,
> He never spoke to you. You aren't a lady.[51]

"Lift up your hearts," then, is not sung to one and all, but only to those who have their wings. We can see clearly that pedantry has never enjoyed greater favour in the running of the world than it has in our own time: creating as many detours through genuine intelligible species, and objects of the one and only truth, as there are individual pedants. Now, more than ever, noble spirits must be awakened, armed with truth and enlightened by the divine intelligence, to take arms against dismal ignorance, by climbing the high bastion and lofty tower of contemplation. To such as these, every other enterprise will rightly seem *vile and vain.*

These spirits should not spend their time, whose speed is infinite, in trivial and empty things, for the present rushes by with phenomenal quickness, and the future approaches just as fast. The span we have lived is nothing, our life now is a point, what we have yet to live has not even become a point, but could become a point, by which time it will at once be and have been. Amid this congestion, someone has woven the memory of genealogies, another waits to decipher scripts, another multiplies childish sophistries. You will see, for example, a book filled with [riddles like]

«COR» est fons vite,
«NIX» est alba:
ergo «CORNIX» est fons vitae alba.

Quell'altro garrisce se il nome fu prima o il verbo, l'altro se il mare o gli fonti, l'altro vuol rinovare gli vocaboli absoleti che per esserno venuti una volta in uso e proposito d'un scrittore antico, ora de nuovo le vuol far montar a gli astri; l'altro sta su la falsa e vera ortografia, altri et altri sono sopra altre et altre simili frascarie, le quali molto più degnamente son spreggiate che intese. Qua diggiunano, qua ismagriscono, qua intisichiscono, qua arrugano la pelle, qua allungano la barba, qua marciscono, qua poneno l'àncora del sommo bene. Con questo spreggiano la fortuna, con questo fan riparo e poneno il scudo contra le lanciate del fato. Con tali e simili vilissimi pensieri credeno montar a gli astri, esser pari a gli dèi, e comprendere il bello e buono che promette la filosofia.

CESARINO: È gran cosa certo che il tempo che non può bastarci manco alle cose necessarie, quantumque diligentissimamente guardato, viene per la maggior parte ad esser speso in cose superflue, anzi cose vili e vergognose. – Non è da ridere di quello che fa lodabile Archimede o altro appresso alcuni, che a tempo che la cittad andava sottosopra, tutto era in ruina, era acceso il fuoco ne la sua stanza, gli nemici gli erano dentro la camera a le spalle, nella discrezzion et arbitrio de quali consisteva de fargli perdere l'arte, il cervello e la vita; e lui tra tanto avea perso il senso e proposito di salvar la vita, per averlo lasciato a dietro a perseguitar forse la proporzione de la curva a la retta, del diametro al circolo o altre simili matesi, tanto degne per giovanetti quanto indegne d'uno che (se posseva) devrebbe essere invecchiato et attento a cose più degne d'esser messe per fine de l'umano studio.

MARICONDO: In proposito di questo mi piace quello che voi medesimo poco avanti dicesti, che bisogna ch'il mondo sia pieno de tutte sorte de persone, e che il numero de gl'imperfetti, brutti, poveri, indegni e

The heart (cor) is the fountain of life.

Snow (nix) is white.

Therefore, the crow (cornix) is the white fountain of life.

Another babbles about whether nouns or verbs came first; another whether it was the ocean or freshwater springs; another wants to revive obsolete words, used and presented by some ancient writer – now, once again, he hopes that they will be extolled to the stars; another frets about false and true orthography, others still fritter away over similar trivialities, most of which are better disregarded than understood. Some fast, some grow thin, some catch consumption; their skin grows wrinkled, their beards grow long, they rot, they sink their anchor in the highest good, and having done so, they disdain the turns of fortune beneath its shelter, raising their shield against the volleys of fate.[52] With these and other equally trifling thoughts they believe that they have climbed up to the stars, that they are equal to the gods, and that they understand all the goodness and beauty that philosophy promises.

CESARINO: Certainly it is remarkable that time, which can barely spare us enough for the necessities, however carefully we save it, for the most part comes to be spent in superfluous things, indeed for things that are low and disgraceful. There is nothing laughable in what Archimedes is often praised for having done (though some say it was someone else):[53] when his city was turned upside down and everything was in ruins, his house had caught fire, and the enemy hovered behind him in his chamber (an enemy whose discretion and judgment consisted in making Archimedes lose his art, his brain, and his life) [he continued to work unperturbed on a geometric problem until a Roman soldier struck him down]. He, however, had so lost his grip on any instinct to preserve his life that he effectively abandoned it in order to pursue some proportion of curve to straight line, or diameter to circle, or some other such mathematical problem fit for young students and most unfit for someone who (had he been able) should have grown old, to ponder matters more worthy to serve as the goal of human endeavour.

MARICONDO: In this regard I like what you said yourself a while ago: the world must contain every sort of person, the greater number of whom are imperfect, ugly, poor, worthless, and criminal, and – in short –

scelerati sia maggiore: et in conclusione non debba essere altrimente che come è. La età lunga e vechiaia d'Archimede, Euclide, di Prisciano, di Donato et altri che da la morte son stati trovati occupati sopra li numeri, le linee, le dizzioni, le concordanze, scritture, dialecti, sillogismi formali, metodi, modi de scienze, organi et altre isagogie, è stata ordinata al servizio della gioventù e de' fanciulli, gli quali apprender possano e ricevere gli frutti della matura età di quelli, come conviene che siano mangiati da questi nella lor verde edate: a fin che più adulti vegnano senza impedimento atti e pronti a cose maggiori.

CESARINO: Io non son fuor del proposito che poco avanti ho mosso: essendo in proposito di quei che fanno studio d'involar la fama e luogo de gli antichi con far nove opre o peggiori, o non megliori de le già fatte, e spendeno la vita su le considerazioni da mettere avanti la lana di capra o l'ombra de l'asino; et altri che in tutto il tempo de la vita studiano di farsi esquisiti in que' studii che convegnono alla fanciullezza, e per la massima parte il fanno senza proprio et altrui profitto.

MARICONDO: Or assai è detto circa quelli che non possono né debbono ardire d'aver «ad alt' amor la mente desta». Venemo ora a considerare della volontaria cattività, e dell'ameno giogo sotto l'imperio de la detta Diana: quel giogo, dico, senza il quale l'anima è impotente de rimontar a quella altezza da la qual cadìo, perciochè la rende più leggiera et agile; e gli lacci la fanno più ispedita e sciolta.

CESARINO: Discorrete dumque.

MARICONDO: Per cominciar, continuar e conchiudere con ordine, considero che tutto quel che vive, in quel modo che vive, conviene che in qualche maniera si nodrisca, si pasca. Però a la natura intellettuale non quadra altra pastura che intellettuale, come al corpo non altra che corporale: atteso che il nodrimento non si prende per altro fine eccetto perché vada in sustanza di chi si nodrisce. Come dumque il corpo non si trasmuta in spirito, né il spirito si trasmuta in corpo (perché ogni trasmutazione si fa quando la materia che era sotto la forma de uno viene ad essere sotto la forma de l'altro), cossì il spirito et il corpo non hanno materia commune, di sorte che quello che era soggetto a uno possa dovenire ad essere soggetto de l'altro.

the world cannot be other than it is. The long life and venerable old age of Archimedes, Euclid, Priscian, Donatus, and others, surprised by death when they were busy with numbers, lines, diction, agreement, scripts, dialects, formal syllogisms, methods, disciplines, tools of logic, and other such elementary concerns, were ordained for the benefit of young people and children, so that these might learn, and receive from their elders those fruits of maturity that are best eaten by the young and green, so that they may grow up without hindrance, fit and ready for greater things.

CESARINO: I will not be straying from this same point if I note that there are those who endeavour to steal the fame and stature of the ancients by making new, inferior creations, or at least nothing better than what has already been done, and spend their lives in considering whether to study the wool of a goat or the shadow of an ass, and others who strive their whole lives to refine arts that are appropriate for childhood – and for the most part do so to no benefit for themselves or anyone else.

MARICONDO: Now we have spoken at length about who should or should not dare awaken the mind "to love's high quest." Now let us consider the voluntary captivity and the pleasant yoke of obedience to the rule of Diana, the yoke, I would say, without which the soul is powerless to climb back to the height from which it fell, because that yoke makes it lighter and more agile, and the reins make it all the more swift and unrestrained.

CESARINO: Speak then.

MARICONDO: To begin, continue, and conclude in proper order, I hold that every living thing should nourish itself and feed according to the way in which it lives. Hence, for the intellectual nature no food will do but intellectual food, just as nothing will do for the body but bodily food, because nourishment is taken for no other reason than to become the substance of what feeds on it. Thus, just as the body is not transmuted into spirit, nor the spirit transmuted into body (because every transmutation is made when matter in one form takes on another), so, too, the spirit and the body have no common substance, through which what was subject to one could become subject to the other.

CESARINO: Certo se l'anima se nodrisse de corpo si portarebe meglio
dove è la fecondità della materia (come argumenta Iamblico), di sorte
che quando ne si fa presente un corpo grasso e grosso, potremmo
credere che sia vase d'un animo gagliardo, fermo, pronto, eroico, e
dire: «O anima grassa, o fecondo spirito, o bello ingegno, o divina
intelligenza, o mente illustre, o benedetta ipostasi da far un convito a
gli leoni, over un banchetto a i *dogs*». Cossì un vecchio, come appare
marcido, debole e diminuito de forze, debba esser stimato de poco
sale, discorso e raggione. Ma seguitate.

MARICONDO: Or l'esca de la mente bisogna dire che sia quella sola che
sempre da lei è bramata, cercata, abbracciata, e volentieri più ch'altra
cosa gustata, per cui s'empie, s'appaga, ha prò e dovien megliore: cioè
la verità alla quale in ogni tempo, in ogni etade et in qualsivoglia stato
che si trove l'uomo, sempre aspira, e per cui suol spreggiar qualsivoglia fatica, tentar ogni studio, non far caso del corpo, et aver in odio
questa vita. Perché la verità è cosa incorporea; perché nessuna, o sia
fisica, o sia metafisica, o sia matematica, si trova nel corpo; perché vedete che l'eterna essenza umana non è ne gl'individui li quali nascono
e muoiono. È la unità specifica (disse Platone) non la moltitudine
numerale che comporta la sustanza de le cose; però chiamò l'idea uno
e molti, stabile e mobile: perché come specie incorrottibile è cosa intelligibile et una, e come si communica alla materia et è sotto il moto
e generazione, è cosa sensibile e molti. In questo secondo modo ha
più de non ente che di ente: atteso che sempre è altro et altro, e corre
eterno per la privazione; nel primo modo è ente e vero. Vedete appresso che gli matematici hanno per conceduto che le vere figure non
si trovano ne gli corpi naturali, né vi possono essere per forza di natura né di arte. Sapete ancora che la verità de sustanze sopranaturali è
sopra la materia. – Conchiudesi dumque che a chi cerca il vero, bisogna montar sopra la raggione de cose corporee. Oltre di ciò è da considerare che tutto quel che si pasce, ha certa mente e memoria
naturale del suo cibo, e sempre (massime quando fia più necessario)
ha presente la similitudine e specie di quello, tanto più altamente,
quanto è più alto e glorioso chi ambisce, e quello che si cerca. Da questo, che ogni cosa ha innata la intelligenza de quelle cose che apparte-
gnono alla conservazione de l'individuo e specie, et oltre alla perfezion
sua finale, depende la industria di cercare il suo pasto per qualche
specie di venazione. – Conviene dumque che l'anima umana abbia il
lume, l'ingegno e gl'instrumenti atti alla sua caccia. Qua soccorre la

CESARINO: If the soul were really to be nourished by the body, she would thrive best where there is fertility of matter (as Iamblichus says),[54] so that when a large fat body appeared, we would readily believe it to be the vessel of a courageous, steadfast, attentive, heroic spirit, and say: O stout soul, O fertile spirit, O lovely wit, O divine intelligence, O illustrious mind, O blessed incarnation, fit to provide a feast for lions, or a banquet for the dogs.[55] And likewise an old man, seemingly decrepit, feeble, and diminished in strength, would be regarded as correspondingly lacking in wit, discretion, and reason. But continue.

MARICONDO: Now it must be said that the mind's food can only be what she has always longed for, sought out, embraced, and more gladly tasted than anything else, by which she is filled, satisfied, benefited, and improved: truth, to which, at every moment, at every age, in every state in which humankind has found itself, she has always aspired, and for the sake of which she will discount every struggle, try every endeavour, care nothing for the body, and detest life itself. Truth is a bodiless thing, for no truth, be it physical, metaphysical, or mathematical, is to be found in the body; the eternal essence of humanity does not lie in the individuals who are born and die. It is specific oneness, not numerical multitude (Plato said),[56] that gives substance to things: hence, he described Idea as both one and many, stable and mobile, because like an incorruptible species it is a single and intelligible entity; but inasmuch as it communicates itself to matter and is subject to movement and generation, it is perceptible and multiple. In this second case it is more in a state of non-being than of being, for it is changing from one state to another and always rushing after what it lacks. In its first mode it is true being. Next, as you see, mathematicians take it for granted that true [geometric] figures cannot exist in natural bodies, nor could they, either by force of nature or by art. You know as well that the truth of supernatural substances is superior to matter.

We should conclude, then, that whoever seeks the truth must rise above the level of material things. It should also be borne in mind that everything that nourishes itself has a certain mind and memory for its food, and always (especially when the need most arises) remembers the likeness and species of that nourishment, all the more profoundly when the seeker and the nourishment are more lofty and glorious. This fact, that every thing has an innate understanding of what is essential to preservation of the individual and the species and, beyond that, of what is essential to their final perfection, explains the industry

contemplazione, qua viene in uso la logica, attissimo organo alla venazione della verità, per distinguere, trovare e giudicare. Quindi si va
lustrando la selva de le cose naturali dove son tanti oggetti sotto l'ombra e manto, e come in spessa, densa e deserta solitudine la verità suol
aver gli antri e cavernosi ricetti; fatti intessuti de spine, conchiusi de
boscose, ruvide e frondose piante: dove con le raggioni più degne
et eccellenti maggiormente s'asconde, s'avvela e si profonda con diligenza maggiore, come noi sogliamo gli tesori più grandi celare con
maggior diligenza e cura, accioché dalla moltitudine e varietà de cacciatori (de quali altri son più exquisiti e exercitati, altri meno) non
vegna senza gran fatica discuoperta. Qua andò Pitagora cercandola
per le sue orme e vestigii impressi nelle cose naturali, che son gli numeri li quali mostrano il suo progresso, raggioni, modi et operazioni
in certo modo: perché in numero de moltitudine, numero de misure,
e numero de momento o pondo, la verità e l'essere si trova in tutte le
cose. Qua andò Anaxagora et Empedocle che considerando che la
omnipotente et omniparente divinità empie il tutto, non trovavano
cosa tanto minima che non volessero che sotto quella fusse occolta
secondo tutte le raggioni, benché procedessero sempre vèr là dove era
predominante et espressa secondo raggion più magnifica et alta. Qua
gli Caldei la cercavano per via di suttrazzione non sapendo che cosa di
quella affirmare: e procedevano senza cani de demostrazioni e sillogismi; ma solamente si forzaro di profondare rimovendo, zappando,
isboscando per forza di negazione de tutte specie e predicati com-
prensibili e secreti. Qua Platone andava come isvoltando, spastinando
e piantando ripari: perché le specie labili e fugaci rimanessero come
nella rete, e trattenute da le siepe de le definizioni, considerando le
cose superiori essere participativamente, e secondo similitudine speculare nelle cose inferiori, e queste in quelle secondo maggior dignità
et eccellenza; e la verità essere ne l'une e l'altre secondo certa analogia, ordine e scala, nella quale sempre l'infimo de l'ordine superiore
conviene con il supremo de l'ordine inferiore. E cossì si dava progresso dal infimo della natura al supremo come dal male al bene, dalle
tenebre alla luce, dalla pura potenza al puro atto, per gli mezzi. Qua
Aristotele si vanta pure da le orme e vestigii impressi di posser pervenire alla desiderata preda, mentre da gli effetti vuol amenarsi a le cause. Benché egli per il più (massime che tutti gli altri ch'hanno
occupato il studio a questa venazione) abbia smarrito il camino, per
non saper a pena distinguere de le pedate. – Qua alcuni teologi nodriti in alcune de le sette cercano la verità della natura in tutte le forme

with which each creature seeks its nourishment by some kind of hunting.

It is useful, then, for the human mind to be endowed with the light, the wit, and the tools appropriate for its hunt. Here contemplation helps, as does logic, an excellent tool for hunting out the truth, for distinguishing, finding, and guiding. Thus, the mind ranges through the forest of Nature, where so many objects hide beneath a cloak of shadow.[57] As if in a thick, dense, and deserted wilderness, the truth keeps to caves and grottoes, tangled in brambles, screened by dense, luxuriant, and leafy plants, where (together with its most worthy and excellent reasons) it is most wont to hide, veil, and secrete itself, just as we conceal our greatest treasures with the most diligence and care. Hence, the multitude and variety of hunters (of whom some are more refined and experienced, others less) cannot discover her except with great effort.

Pythagoras went into this wilderness, seeking truth by means of the footprints and tracks she had impressed in natural things, that is, numbers, which in a certain way measure our progress, reason, methods, and operations; for truth and being are present in all things in numbered quantity, numbered dimension, numbered timing, and numbered weight. Anaxagoras went there, too, and Empedocles, knowing that the all-powerful and all-begetting divinity fills everything; hence, they could find nothing so small that they could not see truth hidden beneath its surface on all its different levels, although they always tended to go where truth predominated and was expressed in more magnificent and lofty terms. The Chaldeans sought truth in the wilderness by subtraction, not knowing what they could assert about her, and proceeding without the dogs of demonstration and syllogism;[58] indeed, they only strove to penetrate deeper by clearing, cultivating, and removing the forest by force of negation from every species and every attribute, whether comprehensible or secret. Plato went there by a process of circling, uprooting, and replanting hedges, so that the unstable, fleeting species would remain, as it were, in his net, restrained by the hedges of definition, for he thought that higher things existed in lower by participation, in mirror image, and that lower things existed in higher at a higher level of dignity and excellence; hence, truth existed in both one and the other according to a certain analogy, order, and scale, by which the lowest thing on the higher level matched what was highest on the lower level. And by these intermediaries he secured his own progress from the lowest part of nature to

naturali specifiche, nelle quali considerano l'essenza eterna e specifico sustantifico perpetuator della sempiterna generazione e vicissitudine de le cose, che son chiamate dèi conditori e fabricatori, sopra gli
quali soprasiede la forma de le forme, il fonte de la luce, verità de le
veritadi, dio de gli dèi, per cui tutto è pieno de divinità, verità, entità,
bontà. Questa verità è cercata come cosa inaccessibile, come oggetto
inobiettabile, non sol che incomprensibile: però a nessun pare possibile de vedere il sole, l'universale Apolline e luce absoluta per specie
suprema et eccellentissima; ma sì bene la sua ombra, la sua Diana, il
mondo, l'universo, la natura che è nelle cose, la luce che è nell'opaci-
tà della materia: cioè quella in quanto splende nelle tenebre. De molti
dumque che per dette vie et altre assai discorreno in questa deserta
selva, pochissimi son quelli che s'abbattono al fonte de Diana. Molti
rimagnono contenti de caccia de fiere salvatiche e meno illustri, e la
massima parte non trova da comprendere avendo tese le reti al vento,
e trovandosi le mani piene di mosche. Rarissimi dico son gli Atteoni
alli quali sia dato dal destino di posser contemplar la Diana ignuda: e
dovenir a tale che dalla bella disposizione del corpo della natura invaghiti in tanto, e scorti da que' doi lumi del gemino splendor de divina
bontà e bellezza, vegnano trasformati in cervio, per quanto non siano
più cacciatori ma caccia. Perché il fine ultimo e finale di questa venazione è de venire allo acquisto di quella fugace e selvaggia preda, per
cui il predator dovegna preda, il cacciator doventi caccia; perché in
tutte le altre specie di venaggione che si fa de cose particolari, il cacciatore viene a cattivare a sé l'altre cose, assorbendo quelle con la bocca de l'intelligenza propria; ma in quella divina et universale viene
talmente ad apprendere che resta necessariamente ancora compreso,
assorbito, unito: onde da volgare, ordinario, civile e populare, doviene
salvatico come cervio, et incola del deserto; vive divamente sotto quella procerità di selva, vive nelle stanze non artificiose di cavernosi monti, dove admira gli capi de gli gran fiumi, dove vegeta intatto e puro da
ordinarie cupiditadi, dove più liberamente conversa la divinità, alla
quale aspirando tanti uomini che in terra hanno volsuto gustar vita
celeste, dissero con una voce: *Ecce elongavi fugiens, et mansi in solitudine.*
Cossì gli cani, pensieri de cose divine, vorano questo Atteone, facendolo morto al volgo, alla moltitudine, sciolto dalli nodi de perturbati
sensi, libero dal carnal carcere della materia; onde non più vegga
come per forami e per fenestre la sua Diana, ma avendo gittate le mu-
raglia a terra, è tutto occhio a l'aspetto de tutto l'orizonte. Di sorte che
tutto guarda come uno, non vede più per distinzioni e numeri, che

the highest, as from evil to good, from darkness to light, from pure potential to pure action. Here Aristotle, too, boasts that by imprinted footprints and tracks he can stalk his desired prey, and at the same time he claims the ability to track down causes by examining their effects – even though he, more than any of them (especially because all the others have occupied their studies with this hunt), lost his way, because he barely knew how to identify the footprints.

Here in the wilderness some theologians, nourished on the doctrine of certain sects, seek the truth of nature in all the specific natural forms, in which they contemplate the eternal essence and the specific creator of matter, the perpetuator of the eternal reproduction and alternation of things. These are called the founder and creator gods, and above them reigns the form of forms, the source of light, the truth of truths, the god of gods, through whom everything is filled with divinity, truth, being, and goodness. This truth is sought as an inaccessible thing, as an Object that is beyond either objectification or comprehension. None of them, therefore, would ever think it possible to behold the Sun, the universal Apollo and absolute light, belonging as it does to some supreme and most excellent species, but only [to perceive it] in the form of its shadow, its Diana: the world, the universe, the nature that is in things, the light that is in the opacity of matter, that is, light as it shines in the darkness. Of the many, then, who scurry along these paths and many others in this deserted wilderness, there are few indeed who ever encounter the fountain of Diana. Many are content to hunt wild and less illustrious beasts, and most of them never find anything to comprehend, because they have stretched their nets out to the wind, and find their hands full of flies. Rare indeed, I tell you, are the Actaeons whose destiny lets them contemplate the nude Diana, and become one of those who, captivated by the beautiful form of nature's body, and escorted by those twin lights of the twin splendour of divine goodness and beauty, are transformed into a stag, so that they are no longer hunters, but prey. For the final and ultimate purpose of this hunt is to come into possession of that fleeting and wild quarry by which the predator becomes prey, the hunter becomes the hunted. In all the other kinds of hunting in pursuit of particular things, the hunter captures these other things for himself, taking them in by the mouth of his own intelligence; but in that divine and universal hunt he takes such possession that he himself is necessarily possessed, absorbed, joined as one. Hence, from a vulgar, ordinary, civil man of the people he becomes as wild as a stag, a desert dweller, living

secondo la diversità de sensi, come de diverse rime fanno veder et apprendere in confusione. Vede l'Amfitrite, il fonte de tutti numeri, de tutte specie, de tutte raggioni, che è la Monade, vera essenza de l'essere de tutti; e se non la vede in sua essenza, in absoluta luce, la vede nella sua genitura che gli è simile, che è la sua imagine: perché dalla monade che è la divinitade, procede questa monade che è la natura, l'universo, il mondo; dove si contempla e specchia come il sole nella luna, mediante la quale ne illumina trovandosi egli nell'emisfero delle sustanze intellettuali. Questa è la Diana, quello uno che è l'istesso ente, quello ente che è l'istesso vero, quello vero che è la natura comprensibile, in cui influisce il sole et il splendor della natura superiore secondo che la unità è destinta nella generata e generante, o producente e prodotta. Cossì da voi medesimo potrete conchiudere il modo, la dignità, et il successo più degno del cacciatore e de la caccia: onde il furioso si vanta d'esser preda della Diana, a cui si rese, per cui si stima gradito consorte, e più felice cattivo e suggiogato, che invidiar possa ad altro uomo che non ne può aver ch'altretanto, o ad altro divo che ne have in tal specie quale è impossibile d'essere ottenuta da natura inferiore, e per consequenza non è conveniente d'essere desiata, né meno può cadere in appetito.

CESARINO: Ho ben compreso quanto avete detto, e m'avete più che mediocremente satisfatto. Or è tempo di ritornar a casa.

MARICONDO: Bene.

divinely beneath that towering forest, and in the chambers made without art in cavernous mountains, where he admires the headwaters of the great rivers, where he flourishes untouched, pure of all ordinary cravings, where divinity visits more freely: the place to which so many men aspire who have desired to taste the life of heaven on earth, and have said with one voice: *Lo, then would I wander far off, and remain in the wilderness.*[59] Thus, the dogs, who are thoughts of divine matters, devour this Actaeon, making him dead to the crowd, to the masses, freed from the knots of his turbulent senses, freed from the carnal prison of matter, so that he no longer sees his Diana as if through openings and windows, but, having razed to the ground the walls that enclosed him, he is all eyes before the entire horizon. Then he sees everything as if it were one, and no longer by distinctions and numbers, which, according to the diversity of the senses, as if through different apertures, fill seeing and learning with confusion. He sees Amphitrite, the source of all numbers, of all species, of all principles, who is the Monad, the true essence of all being; and if he does not see her in her essence, in absolute light, he sees her in the offspring that is like her: her image. For from the oneness that is divinity there proceeds the oneness that is nature, the universe, the world, where she is contemplated and mirrored, as the Sun is mirrored in the Moon, where he can be found lighting the hemisphere of intellectual substances. This is Diana, the One that is the same being, the being that is the same truth, the truth that is comprehensible nature, upon which the Sun shines and the splendour of superior nature, just as their unity is distinguished into begotten and begetter, or producer and product. Thus, you yourself can draw your own conclusions about the method, the dignity, and the most worthy success of the hunter and of the prey: this is why the frenzied hero boasts that he is Diana's prey, to whom he has surrendered. This is why he believes himself to be her welcome consort, and happier in his captivity and subjugation to her than envious of any other man, for no one can have any more than this. Neither does he envy any god, who might reach a species of happiness that is impossible for an inferior nature to reach – and thus there is no reason for him to desire it, nor shall he develop such a craving.

CESARINO: I have well understood what you have said, and you have more than sufficiently satisfied me. Now it is time to return home.

MARICONDO: Very well.

## DIALOGO TERZO

*Interlocutori*: LIBERIO, LAODONIO

LIBERIO: Posando sotto l'ombra d'un cipresso il furioso, e trovandosi
l'alma intermittente da gli altri pensieri (cosa mirabile), avvenne che
(come fussero animali e sustanze de distinte raggioni e sensi) si par-
lassero insieme il core e gli occhi: l'uno de l'altro lamentandosi come
quello che era principio di quel faticoso tormento che consumava
l'alma.

LAODONIO: Dite, se vi ricordate, le raggioni e le paroli.


LIBERIO: Cominciò il dialogo il core, il qual facendosi udir dal petto
proruppe in questi accenti:

꒰

### *Prima proposta del core a gli occhi*

> Come, occhi miei, sì forte mi tormenta
> quel che da voi deriva ardente foco,
> ch'al mio mortal suggetto mai allenta
> di serbar tal incendio, ch'ho per poco
> l'umor de l'Oceàn e di più lenta
> artica stella il più gelato loco,
> perché ivi in punto si reprima il vampo,
> o al men mi si prometta ombra di scampo?

> Voi mi féste cattivo
> d'una man che mi tiene, e non mi vuole;
> per voi son entro al corpo, e fuor col sole,
> son principio de vita, e non son vivo:
>     non so quel che mi sia
> ch'appartegno a quest'alma, e non è mia.

꒰

## THIRD DIALOGUE

*Interlocutors*: LIBERIO, LAODONIO

LIBERIO: When the frenzied hero was resting under the shade of a cypress, with his soul (remarkably) disengaged from his other thoughts, his heart and his eyes began to speak to one another (as if they were living creatures, entities with distinct powers of reason and sense), each blaming the other for the strenuous torment that now consumed the soul.

LAODONIO: Tell me, if you remember, what they discussed, and what they said.

LIBERIO: The heart began the dialogue, and making himself heard from within the breast, he burst forth in these tones:

### First Proposal of the Heart to the Eyes

How can it be, my eyes, that I'm so racked
By blazes that originate in you?
For never will that flaming grip retract
From this poor mortal victim, in whose view
All Ocean's waters and the iciest tract
Beneath the Arctic pole will never do
To suffocate my inner conflagration
Or grant at least some shade of consolation.

You put me in the thrall
Of a reluctant hand; by you I hide
Within the breast, or join the Sun outside.
I give life, yet I hardly live at all.
Myself I can't define:
I'm subject to this soul that isn't mine.

LAODONIO: Veramente l'intendere, il vedere, il conoscere è quello che
accende il desio, e per consequenza per ministerio de gli occhi vien
infiammato il core: e quanto a quelli fia presente più alto e degno
oggetto, tanto più forte è il foco e più vivaci son le fiamme. Or qual
esser deve quella specie per cui tanto si sente acceso il core, che non
spera che temprar possa il suo ardore tanto più fredda quanto più
lenta stella che sia conchiusa nell'artico cerchio, né rallentar il vampo
l'umor intiero de l'Oceano? Quanta deve essere l'eccellenza di quello
oggetto che l'ha reso nemico de l'esser suo, rubello a l'alma propria,
e contento di tal ribellione e nemicicia, quantumque sia cattivo d'una
man che 'l dispreggia e non lo vuole? Ma fatemi udire se gli occhi
risposero e che cosa dissero.

LIBERIO: Quelli per il contrario si lagnavano del core come quello che
era principio e caggione per cui versassero tante lacrime. Però a l'incontro gli proposero in questo tenore:

꒰꒱

### Prima proposta de gli occhi al core

Come da te sorgon tant'acqui, o core,
da quante mai Nereidi alzar la fronte
ch'ogni giorn' al bel sol rinasce e muore?
A par de l'Amfitrite il doppio fonte
versar può sì gran fiumi al mondo fore,

che puoi dir che l'umor tanto surmonte,
che gli fia picciol rio chi Egitto inonda
scorrend' al mar per sette doppia sponda.

Die' natura doi lumi
a questo picciol mondo per governo;
tu perversor di quell'ordin eterno,
le convertiste in sempiterni fiumi.
   E questo il ciel non cura,
ch' il natìo passa, el violento dura.

꒰꒱

LAODONIO: Truly understanding, seeing, and knowing ignite desire; hence, the heart is inflamed by the service of the eyes; and the more lofty and worthy the object that is presented to them, the stronger the fire shall be, and the more lively its flames. Now what is the species that makes the heart feel itself so fiery that not even the coldest, slowest star enclosed within the Arctic Circle can temper its ardour, nor all the waters of the Ocean slow the spark?[60] How excellent an object must be to turn the heart into an enemy of its own being, a rebel against its own soul, content with such rebellion and enmity despite its imprisonment by a hand that disdains it and lacks all desire for it? But let me hear whether the eyes made reply, and what they said.

LIBERIO: They, for their part, complained that the heart was the origin and reason for which they had shed so many tears. Hence, they addressed him in the following tones:

ॐ

### First Proposal of the Eyes to the Heart

How can you gush as many waters, heart,
As those from which the Nereids raise their heads[61]
At day's rebirth, until the Sun depart?
The mighty rivers Amphitrite sheds
Cannot exceed what these twin fountains start.

The waters mount so high, it might be said
That Egypt's watered by a minor runnel,
For all Nile's seaward rush and sevenfold channel.

Two eyes Nature bestowed
To hold this little world in governance.
You who pervert that ageless ordinance
Transformed them into two eternal flows;
And heaven never heeds
How nature fails and violence succeeds.

ॐ

LAODONIO: Certo ch'il cor acceso e compunto fa sorger lacrime da gli occhi, onde come quelli accendeno le fiamme in questo, quest'altro viene a rigar quelli d'umore. Ma mi maraviglio de sì forte exaggerazione per cui dicono che le Nereidi non alzano tanto bagnata fronte a l'oriente sole, quanta possa appareggiar queste acqui; et oltre agguagliansi all'Oceano, non perché versino, ma perché versar possano questi doi fonti, fiumi tali e tanti, che computato a loro il Nilo apparirebbe una picciola lava distinta in sette canali.

LIBERIO: Non ti maravigliar della forte exaggerazione e di quella potenza priva de l'atto; perché tutto intenderete dopo intesa la conchiusione de raggionamenti loro. Or odi come prima il core risponde alla proposta de gli occhi.

LAODONIO: Priegovi fatemi intendere.

LIBERIO:

✧

### Prima risposta del core a gli occhi

Occhi, s'in me fiamma immortal s'alluma,
et altro non son io che fuoco ardente,
se quel ch'a me s'avvicina, s'infuma,
e veggio per mio incendio il ciel fervente;
come il gran vampo mio non vi consuma,
ma l'effetto contrario in voi si sente?
Come vi bagno, e più tosto non cuoco,
se non umor, ma è mia sustanza fuoco?

Credete ciechi voi
che da sì ardente incendio derivi
el doppio varco, e que' doi fonti vivi
da Vulcan abbian gli elementi suoi,
come tal volt' acquista
forza un contrario, se l'altro resista?

✧

LAODONIO: Certainly the inflamed and smitten heart makes tears well up from the eyes, just as the eyes ignite the flames in the heart, and the heart in turn bathes them in liquid. But I am amazed at the grand exaggeration of their claim that the Nereids do not raise so many dripping heads to the rising sun as their own waters present. And beyond that, they equal themselves to the Ocean, not because their two fountains actually pour forth anything, but because potentially they could pour forth so many mighty rivers that, if they were added together, the Nile by comparison would appear to be a little rivulet divided into seven channels.

LIBERIO: Do not be surprised at such grand exaggeration and this potential without action, for you will understand everything once you have understood the conclusion their conversation reaches. Now hear how the heart responds to the eyes' proposal.

LAODONIO: Please, let me hear it.

LIBERIO:

### First Reply of the Heart to the Eyes

If in me, eyes, a deathless flame's alight
So that I'm nothing but an ardent blaze;
If all that's near me's wreathed in smoky blight
And heaven seethes through my own fiery gaze;
Can my flames not consume you in their might?
(And yet with you the opposite takes place.)
Why are you bathed and not incinerated
When it's of fire – not water – I'm created?

Can't you believe, blind pair
That these two streams were born of blazing fire,
And that the living springs of my desire
Consist of matter forged in Vulcan's lair?
For sometimes one condition
Gains strength from its contrary's opposition.

Vede come non possea persuadersi il core di posser da contraria causa
e principio procedere forza di contrario effetto, sin a questo che non
vuol affirmare il modo possibile, quando per via d'antiperistasi, che
significa il vigor che acquista il contrario da quel che fuggendo l'altro
viene ad unirsi, inspessarsi, inglobarsi e concentrarsi verso l'individuo
della sua virtude, la qual quanto più s'allontana dalle dimensioni, tanto si rende efficace di vantaggio.

LAODONIO: Dite ora come gli occhi risposero al core.

LIBERIO:

✧

### Prima risposta de gli occhi al core

Ahi cor, tua passion sì ti confonde,
ch'hai smarito il sentier di tutt' il vero.
Quanto si vede in noi, quanto s'asconde,
è semenza de mari, onde l'intero
Nettun potrà ricovrar non altronde,
se per sorte perdesse il grand'impero;
come da noi deriva fiamma ardente,
che siam del mare il gemino parente?

Sei sì privo di senso,
che per noi credi la fiamma trapasse,
e tant' umide porte a dietro lasse,
per far sentir a te l'ardor immenso?
Come splendor per vetri,
crederai forse che per noi penétri?

✧

Qua non voglio filosofare circa la coincidenza de contrarii, de la quale ho studiato nel libro *De principio et uno*; e voglio supponere quello
che comunmente si suppone, che gli contrarii nel medesimo geno
son distantissimi, onde vegna più facilmente appreso il sentimento
di questa risposta, dove gli occhi si dicono semi o fonti, nella virtual

See how the heart was unable to persuade itself that a force could proceed from its opposite cause and principle to opposite effect, to the point that it refuses to acknowledge the way in which this might be possible: that is, through antiperistasis, which means the power that one extreme gains from the fact that in fleeing its contrary it ends up unifying itself, reinforcing itself, condensing itself, concentrating itself on the individual substance of its virtue, which gains in effectiveness the more it loses in dimension.

LAODONIO: Now tell how the eyes replied to the heart.

LIBERIO:

༄

### First Reply of the Eyes to the Heart

Ai, heart, your passion's led you far astray
From truth's right path in your bewilderment,
For what you see and what we hide away
Is all the spawn of Ocean; in the event
Here Neptune could recover all his sway,
If he should see his mighty empire spent.
How could we spark a conflagration, we
Who bear, as twins, such kinship with the sea?

Are you so void of sense
As to believe that fire penetrates
And leaves behind it two such fluid gates
To make you feel an ardour so immense?
Like radiance through a glass
Do you believe that through us it might pass?

༄

Here I have no desire to philosophize about the coincidence of opposites, which I have studied in the book *On the Principle and One*.[62] I will simply assume what is commonly assumed, namely, that extremes of the same quality are vastly distant from one another, so that we can understand this reply, in which the eyes declare that they are seeds,

potenza de quali è il mare: di sorte che se Nettuno perdesse tutte l'acqui, le potrebbe richiamar in atto dalla potenza loro, dove sono come
in principio agente e materiale. Però non metteno urgente necessità
quando dicono non posser essere che la fiamma per la lor stanza e
cortile trapasse al core con lasciarsi tant'acqui a dietro, per due caggioni: prima perché tal impedimento in atto non può essere se non
posti in atto tali oltraggiosi ripari; secondo perché per quanto l'acqui
sono attualmente ne gli occhi, possono donar via al calore come alla
luce: essendo che l'esperienza dimostra che senza scaldar il specchio
viene il luminoso raggio ad accendere per via di reflessione qualche
materia che gli vegna opposta; e per un vetro, cristallo, o altro vase
pieno d'acqua, passa il raggio ad accendere una cosa sottoposta senza
che scalde il spesso corpo tramezzante: come è verisimile et anco vero
che caggione secche et aduste impressioni nelle concavitadi del profondo mare. Talmente per certa similitudine, se non per raggioni di
medesimo geno, si può considerare come fia possibile che per il senso
lubrico et oscuro de gli occhi possa esser scaldato et acceso di quella
luce l'affetto, la quale secondo medesima raggione non può essere
nel mezzo. Come la luce del sole secondo altra raggione è nell'aria
tramezzante, altra nel senso vicino, et altra nel senso commune, et
altra ne l'intelletto: quantumque da un modo proceda l'altro modo di
essere.


LAODONIO: Sonvi altri discorsi?

LIBERIO: Sì, perché l'uno e l'altro tentano di saper con qual modo quello contegna tante fiamme, e quelli tante acqui. Fa dumque il core la
seconda proposta:

やる

### Seconda proposta del core

S'al mar spumoso fan concorso i fiumi,
e da fiumi del mar il cieco varco
vien impregnato, ond'è che da voi lumi
non è doppio torrente al mondo scarco
che cresca il regno a gli marini numi,

or fountains, whose virtual power is the sea. Accordingly, if Neptune were to lose all his waters, he could still recover them by activating the potential of the eyes, which are in principle, as it were, agent and material. Hence, they see no urgent necessity when they say that it is impossible for flame to penetrate from their chambers and courts into the heart, leaving behind so many waters, for two reasons: first, because such an impediment cannot exist in action unless outrageous obstacles are put into effect; second, because, to the extent that these waters are actually present in the eyes, they can make way for heat just as they do for light; for experience demonstrates that a ray of light can ignite any material put before it by reflection without warming the mirror itself, and through a glass, crystal, or other vessel full of water the ray can pass to ignite an object put beneath it without heating the dense body in between. Likewise, it is plausible, and indeed true, that it causes dry and burnt-out impressions in the hollows of the deep sea.[63] In the same way, on the basis of a certain similarity, if not for reasons of exactly the same kind, it is possible to consider how the affections can be heated and ignited through the dim and inconstant sensation of the eyes by this same light, an effect that, by these same principles, cannot occur in the space in between. Likewise, the light of the Sun, by another process of reasoning, resides in the intervening air, in one way as immediate perception, in another way as the light of common sense, and in yet another way as the light of the intellect, just as one level of being proceeds from another.

LAODONIO: Are there any further discussions?

LIBERIO: Yes, because each side of the debate tries to discover how the one can contain such flames, and the other such waters. And so the heart makes its second proposal:

꒰

### Second Proposal of the Heart

If rivers rush to reach the foaming sea
And fertilize the Ocean's dark domain
Why, eyes, were you not able to foresee,
A double stream to act as this world's drain
And thus increase the sea gods' majesty –

scemando ad altri il glorioso incarco?
Perché non fia che si vegga quel giorno,
ch'a i monti fa Deucalion ritorno?

   Dove gli rivi sparsi?
Dove il torrente che mia fiamma smorze,
o per ciò non posser più la rinforze?
Goccia non scende a terra ad inglobarsi,
   per cui fia ch'io non pensi
che sia cossì, come mostrano i sensi?

↭

Dimanda qual potenza è questa che non si pone in atto; se tante son l'acqui, perché Nettuno non viene a tiranneggiar su l'imperio de gli altri elementi? Ove son gli inondanti rivi? Ove chi dia refrigerio al fuoco ardente? Dove è una stilla onde io possa affirmar de gli occhi quel tanto che niegano i sensi? Ma gli occhi di pari fanno un'altra dimanda:

↭

### Seconda proposta de gli occhi al core

   Se la materia convertita in foco
acquista il moto di lieve elemento,
e se ne sale a l'eminente loco,
onde avvien che veloce più che vento,
tu ch'incendio d'amor senti non poco,
non ti fai gionto al sole in un momento?
per che soggiorni peregrino al basso,
non t'aprendo per noi e l'aria il passo?

   Favilla non si scorge
uscir a l'aria aperto da quel busto,
né corpo appar incenerit' o adusto,
né lacrimoso fumo ad alto sorge:
   tutt'è nel proprio intiero,
né di fiamma è raggion, sens', o pensiero.

↭

The worldly loss the Ocean's glorious gain?
Why will we never see Deucalion[64] come
To climb the native mountains of his home?

What streams now burst their banks?
Where is the torrent that can quench my flame –
Or will it only reinforce the same?
For not a drop strikes earth to join the ranks.
Why should I not believe
That things occur as sense has us perceive?

❧

It asks: what power is this that does not express itself in action? If the waters are so many, why does Neptune not come to rule over the empire of the other elements? Where are the bursting riverbanks? Where is the person who will offer relief from the burning fire? Where is there a drop that will allow me to confirm about the eyes what the senses deny me? But the eyes in turn present another question:

❧

### Second Proposal of the Eyes to the Heart

If matter when converted into fire
Moves lightly as the state to which it's passed
And rises up, why does it not transpire
That you, more swiftly than a windy blast
(Who suffer so Love's incandescent ire)
Fly instantly to reach the Sun at last?
Why do you linger wandering down there
Not opening our pathway through the air?

No spark as yet appears
Escaping from that breast into the sky
No charred or smouldering bodies do we spy;
No rising smoke has driven us to tears.
All's perfect and entire;
There's neither hint, nor sense, nor thought of fire.

❧

LAODONIO: Non ha più né meno efficacia questa che quell'altra proposta: ma vengasi presto alle risposte, se vi sono.

LIBERIO: Vi son certamente e piene di succhio; udite:

༄

*Seconda risposta del core a gli occhi*

    Sciocco è colui che sol per quanto appare
al senso, et oltre a la raggion non crede:
il fuoco mio non puote alto volare,
e l'infinito incendio non si vede,
perché de gli occhi han sopraposto il mare,
e un infinito l'altro non eccede:
la natura non vuol ch'il tutto pera,
se basta tanto fuoco a tanta sfera.

    Ditemi, occhi, per dio,
qual mai partito prenderemo noi,
onde far possa aperto o io, o voi,
per scampo suo, de l'alma il fato rio,
    se l'un e l'altro ascoso
mai potrà fargli il bel nume piatoso?

༄

LAODONIO: Se non è vero, è molto ben trovato: se non è cossì, è molto
bene iscusato l'uno per l'altro, se stante che dove son due forze de
quali l'una non è maggior de l'altra, bisogna che cesse l'operazion di
questa e quella: essendo che tanto questa può resistere quanto quella
insistere; non meno quella ripugna, che possa oppugnar questa. Se
dumque è infinito il mare et inmensa la forza de le lacrime che sono
ne gli occhi, non faranno giamai ch'apparir possa favillando o isvam-
pando l'impeto del fuoco ascoso nel petto; né quelli mandar potranno
il gemino torrente al mare, se con altretanto di vigore gli fa riparo il
core: però accade che il bel nume per apparenza di lacrima che stille
da gli occhi, o favilla che si spicche dal petto, non possa esser invitato
ad esser piatoso a l'alma afflitta.

LAODONIO: This proposal is neither more nor less effective that the first. But let's go on to the replies, if there are any.

LIBERIO: Certainly there are, and choice ones. Listen:

ॐ

### Second Reply of the Heart to the Eyes

A fool's the only one who would rely
On sense, and not the reasoning behind it.
My fire lacks the power to soar on high;
As for my endless blaze, no one can find it
Submerged beneath an ocean of the eyes
Too infinite for borders to confine it.
Nature wants neither one to disappear,
If such a fire can balance such a sphere.

By God's grace, tell me, eyes:
What choices should the three of us endorse
To show the soul, for its own good, the course
Its reckless fate intends now to devise?
With both of us concealed
How can her divine mercy be revealed?

ॐ

LAODONIO: If it is not true, it ought to be: if it is not so, still each has made an excellent excuse to the other, for where there are two forces, neither one greater than the other, then they must each cease operations, given the fact that each can resist as much as the other insists, no less than each can repel what the other compels. If, then, the ocean is infinite and the power of the tears in the eyes is boundless, then they will never allow the force of the fire hidden in the breast to blaze up or flash forth. Neither, in turn, will they ever be able to send their twin torrents to the sea, if the heart retaliates against them with equal vigour. Hence, the beautiful goddess cannot be invited to take pity on the afflicted soul, either by tears welling up in the eyes or by a spark that flashes in the breast.

LIBERIO: Or notate la conseguente risposta de gli occhi:

꩜

### Seconda risposta de gli occhi al core

> Ahi per versar a l'elemento ondoso,
> l'émpito de noi fonti al tutt'è casso;
> ché contraria potenza il tien ascoso,
> acciò non mande a rotilon per basso.
> L'infinito vigor del cor focoso
> a i pur tropp'alti fiumi niega il passo;
> quindi gemino varco al mar non corre,
> ch'il coperto terren natura aborre.

> Or dìnne, afflitto core,
> che puoi opporti a noi con altretanto
> vigor: chi fia giamai che porte il vanto
> d'esser precon di sì 'nfelice amore,
> s'il tuo e nostro male
> quant'è più grande, men mostrarsi vale?

꩜

Per essere infinito l'un e l'altro male, come doi ugualmente vigorosi contrarii si ritegnono, si supprimeno; e non potrebbe esser cossì, se l'uno e l'altro fusse finito, atteso che non si dà equalità puntuale nelle cose naturali, né ancora sarebbe cossì se l'uno fusse finito e l'altro infinito: ma certo questo assorbirebbe quello, et avverrebe che si mostrarebbono ambi doi, o al men l'uno per l'altro. Sotto queste sentenze la filosofia naturale et etica che vi sta occolta, lascio cercarla, considerarla e comprenderla a chi vuole e puote. Sol questo non voglio lasciare, che non senza raggione l'affezzion del core è detta infinito mare dall'apprension de gli occhi: perché essendo infinito l'oggetto de la mente, et a l'intelletto non essendo definito oggetto proposto, non può essere la volontade appagata de finito bene; ma se oltre a quello si ritrova altro, il brama, il cerca, perché (come è detto commune) il summo della specie inferiore è infimo e principio della specie superiore, o si prendano gli gradi secondo le forme le quali non possiamo stimar che siano infinite, o secondo gli modi e raggioni di quelle, nella

LIBERIO: Now consider the following reply of the eyes:

ॐ

### Second Reply of the Eyes to the Heart

Ai! To pour forth our watery element
We fountains have entirely lost our force;
A countervailing power keeps it pent
Against all downward progress from the source.
The fiery heart's infinite powers prevent
The swollen rivers from their wonted course,
And thus the twofold current cannot run;
For Nature hates what's hidden to the Sun.

Afflicted heart, now prove
How you'd oppose us with an equal vigour;
For who would care to undertake the rigour
Of heralding such an unhappy love,
When your ills and our own,
As they grow greater, are less clearly shown?

ॐ

Because both of these evils are infinite, they restrain and suppress each other as two equally vigorous opposites. This could never happen if each were finite, for precise equality is not granted to natural things; neither would it occur if one were finite and the other infinite: then one would certainly absorb the other, so that either both would emerge, or one, at least, would emerge through the other. As for the natural and ethical philosophy that underlies these conversations, I will let those who are willing and able to do so pursue it, ponder it, and understand it. For the moment, I will note only this: there is good reason to call the heart's affection the infinite sea of the eyes' perception. Because the mind's objective is infinite, it cannot become a definite objective put before the intellect, or satisfy the will with a finite benefit; but if the will looks beyond that finite benefit it will discover something else, desire it, and pursue it, because (as is commonly said) the highest of the lower species is the lowermost of the higher species. We progress step by step, pursuing forms that we cannot believe

qual maniera per essere infinito il sommo bene, infinitamente crede-
mo che si comunica secondo la condizione delle cose alle quali si diffonde: però non è specie definita a l'universo (parlo secondo la figura
e mole), non è specie definita a l'intelletto, non è definita la specie de
l'affetto.

LAODONIO: Dumque queste due potenze de l'anima mai sono, né essere
possono perfette per l'oggetto, se infinitamente si referiscono a quello.

LIBERIO: Cossì sarrebe se questo infinito fusse per privazion negativa o
negazion privativa de finé, come è per più positiva affirmazione de
fine infinito et interminato.

LAODONIO: Volete dir dumque due specie d'infinità: l'una privativa la
qual può essere verso qualche cosa che è potenza, come infinite son
le tenebre, il fine delle quali è posizione di luce; l'altra perfettiva la
quale è circa l'atto e perfezzione, come infinita è la luce, il fine della
quale sarebbe privazione e tenebre. In questo dumque che l'intelletto
concepe la luce, il bene, il bello, per quanto s'estende l'orizonte della
sua capacità, e l'anima che beve del nettare divino e de la fonte de vita
eterna, per quanto comporta il vase proprio; si vede che la luce è oltre
la circunferenza del suo orizonte dove può andar sempre più e più
penetrando; et il nettare e fonte d'acqua viva è infinitamente fecondo,
onde possa sempre oltre et oltre inebriarsi.

LIBERIO: Da qua non séguita imperfezzione nell'oggetto né poca satisfazzione nella potenza; ma che la potenza sia compresa da l'oggetto e
beatificamente assorbita da quello. Qua gli occhi imprimeno nel core,
cioè nell'intelligenza, suscitano nella volontà un infinito tormento di
suave amore, dove non è pena, perché non s'abbia quel che si desidera: ma è felicità, perché sempre vi si trova quel che si cerca; et in
tanto non vi è sazietà, per quanto sempre s'abbia appetito, e per consequenza gusto: acciò non sia come nelli cibi del corpo il quale con la
sazietà perde il gusto, e non ha felicità prima che guste, né dopo ch'ha
gustato, ma nel gustar solamente: dove se passa certo termine e fine,
viene ad aver fastidio e nausea. – Vedi dumque in certa similitudine
qualmente il sommo bene deve essere infinito, e l'appulso de l'affetto
verso e circa quello esser deggia anco infinito, acciò non vegna talvolta

are infinite, or pursuing their methods and principles. In this way, because the highest good is infinite, we believe that it communicates itself infinitely, in the qualities of the things into which it diffuses itself. Therefore, the universe has no definite species (I am speaking about shape and size), the intellect has no definite species, and affection has no definite species.

LAODONIO: Then these two powers of the soul are never, and can never be, perfect for their object, if they refer infinitely to it.

LIBERIO: That would be true if the universe were infinite by negative deprivation or privative negation of an end, but instead it is the positive affirmation of an infinite and boundless end.

LAODONIO: Then you mean to say that there are two species of infinity: one is privative, and regards some potential entity (so darkness is infinite, and it ceases when light appears). The other species of infinity is perfective, and regards action and perfection (so light is infinite; its end would mean deprivation and darkness). In these terms, then, the intellect conceives of light, goodness, beauty, as far as it can broaden its own horizon; and the soul drinks divine nectar from the fountain of eternal life as deeply as its own container permits. Clearly, there is still light beyond the circumference of the intellect's horizons, where it can penetrate more and more deeply; divine nectar and the fountain of living water are also infinitely bountiful, so that the soul can always become more and more intoxicated.

LIBERIO: This will lead neither to imperfection in the object nor to scant satisfaction of potential; instead, potential is taken in by the object and joyously absorbed by it. Here, then, the eyes leave their imprint on the heart, that is, on the intelligence, and arouse in the will an infinite torment of sweet love; yet there is no pain of unfulfilled desire, only joy, for it always finds what it seeks. In the meantime, it is never sated, because there is always appetite, and consequently taste, unlike what happens with the body's food, which loses its taste with satiety.[65] The body has no joy before it tastes, nor after it has tasted, but only as it tastes. And past a certain boundary and limit, it only feels disgust and nausea.

By this simile you can see how the highest goodness must be infinite, and the drive of the affections to and around that goodness

a non esser bene: come il cibo che è buono al corpo, se non ha modo, viene ad essere veleno. Ecco come l'umor de l'Oceano non estingue quel vampo, et il rigor de l'Artico cerchio non tempra quell'ardore. Cossì è cattivo d'una mano che il tiene e non lo vuole: il tiene perché l'ha per suo, non lo vuole perché (come lo fuggesse) tanto più se gli fa alto quanto più ascende a quella, quanto più la séguita tanto più se gli mostra lontana per raggion de eminentissima eccellenza, secondo quel detto: *Accedet homo ad cor altum, et exaltabitur Deus.* – Cotal felicità d'affetto comincia da questa vita, et in questo stato ha il suo modo d'essere: onde può dire il core d'essere entro con il corpo, e fuori col sole, in quanto che l'anima con la gemina facultade mette in execuzione doi uffici: l'uno de vivificare et attuare il corpo animabile, l'altro de contemplare le cose superiori; perché cossì lei è in potenza receptiva da sopra, come è verso sotto al corpo in potenza attiva. Il corpo è come morto e cosa privativa a l'anima la quale è sua vita e perfezzione; e l'anima è come morta e cosa privativa alla superiore illuminatrice intelligenza da cui l'intelletto è reso in abito e formato in atto. Quindi si dice il core essere prencipe de vita, e non esser vivo; si dice appartenere a l'alma animante, e quella non appartenergli: perché è infocato da l'amor divino, è convertito finalmente in fuoco, che può accendere quello che si gli avicina: atteso che avendo contratta in sé la divinitade, è fatto divo, e conseguentemente con la sua specie può innamorar altri: come nella luna può essere admirato e magnificato il splendor del sole. Per quel poi ch'appartiene al considerar de gli occhi, sapete che nel presente discorso hanno doi uffici: l'uno de imprimere nel core, l'altro de ricevere l'impressione dal core; come anco questo ha doi uffici: l'uno de ricevere l'impressioni da gli occhi, l'altro di imprimere in quelli. Gli occhi apprendono le specie e le proponeno al core, il core le brama et il suo bramare presenta a gli occhi: quelli concepeno la luce, la diffondeno, et accendeno il fuoco in questo; questo scaldato et acceso invia il suo umore a quelli, perché lo digeriscano. Cossì primieramente la cognizione muove l'affetto, et appresso l'affetto muove la cognizione. Gli occhi quando moveno sono asciutti, perché fanno ufficio di specchio e di ripresentatore; quando poi son mossi, son turbati et alterati; perché fanno ufficio de studioso executore: atteso che con l'intelletto speculativo prima si vede il bello e buono, poi la voluntà l'appetisce, et appresso l'intelletto industrioso lo procura, séguita e cerca. Gli occhi lacrimosi significano la difficultà de la separazione della cosa bramata dal bramante, la quale acciò non sazie, non fastidisca, si porge come per studio infinito, il quale sempre

must also be infinite, so that it never goes bad, whereas food that is good for the body can become poison if not taken in moderation. This is why the waters of Ocean cannot extinguish that spark, and the chill of the Arctic Circle cannot temper that heat. This is how the heart becomes the captive of a reluctant hand that holds it and does not want it: the beloved holds it because it is hers; she does not want it, because (as if she were fleeing) it becomes more lofty the more it ascends towards her, and the more it pursues her the more distant she seems, by reason of her pre-eminent excellence; as the saying goes: *Both the inward thought of every one of them, and the heart, is deep ... But suddenly God shall shoot at them, and they shall be wounded ... And all men shall fear, and declare the work of God, for they shall wisely consider of his doing.*[66]

Such joy of the affections begins in this life, and in our human condition it has its mode of existence. Hence, the heart can say that it is inside with the body, and outside with the sun, for the soul, with its twin faculties, carries out two duties: one, to give life and activation to the liveable body; second, to contemplate superior things. Thus, the soul is as potentially receptive to influence from above as she is potentially active below in the body. The body is dead and deprived when compared with the soul, which is its life and perfection; and the soul is dead and deprived in comparison with the higher illuminating intelligence by which the intellect is put into its present clothing and actively formed. Hence, the heart is said to be the ruler of life, not to be alive. It is said [to] belong to the life-giving soul, not the soul to it, because it is inflamed by divine love, and is converted at last into flame, which can ignite anything that approaches it; for once it has contracted divinity into itself, it is made divine, and thereafter its appearance can engender love in others, just as the splendour of the Sun can be admired and praised in the Moon.

As for the argument of the eyes, you know that in the present debate they have two duties: one, to leave their impress on the heart, secondly, to receive the heart's impression; just as the heart has its two duties: one, to receive the impressions of the eyes, and the other, to leave its impress on them. The eyes perceive species and propose them to the heart, the heart desires them, and presents its desire to the eyes. These in turn conceive the light, diffuse it, and ignite the flame in the heart; which, heated and ignited, sends its liquid to the eyes so that they will digest it. Hence, knowledge moves the affections first, and then the affections move knowledge. The eyes, when they move, are dry,

ha e sempre cerca: atteso che la felicità de dèi è descritta per il bevere non per l'aver bevuto il nettare, per il gustare non per aver gustato l'ambrosia, con aver continuo affetto al cibo et alla bevanda, e non con esser satolli e senza desio de quelli. Indi hanno la sazietà come in moto et apprensione, non come in quiete e comprensione, non son satolli senza appetito, né sono appetenti senza essere in certa maniera satolli.

LAODONIO: *Esuries satiata, satietas esuriens.*

LIBERIO: Cossì a punto.

LAODONIO: Da qua posso intendere come senza biasimo ma con gran verità et intelletto è stato detto che il divino amore piange con gemiti inenarrabili, perché con questo che ha tutto ama tutto, e con questo che ama tutto ha tutto.

LIBERIO: Ma vi bisognano molte glose se volessimo intendere de l'amor divino che è la istessa deità; e facilmente s'intende de l'amor divino per quanto si trova ne gli effetti e nella subalternata natura; non (dico) quello che dalla divinità si diffonde alle cose: ma quello delle cose che aspira alla divinità.

LAODONIO: Or di questo et altro raggionaremo a più aggio appresso. Andiamone.

## DIALOGO QUARTO

*Interlocutori*: SEVERINO, MINUTOLO

SEVERINO: Vedrete dumque la raggione de nove ciechi, li quali apporta-

because they carry out the work of a mirror, representing an image; when they in turn are moved, they are disturbed and altered, because they carry out the work of a careful executor, for with the speculative intellect the first step is to see what is beautiful and good, and then the will desires it, and next the industrious intellect procures, pursues, and seeks it. The tearful eyes symbolize the difficulty of the separation between the thing desired and the desirer: the thing desired, because it never satiates, and never disgusts, offers itself for an infinite longing that always possesses and yet always seeks. And thus the joy of the gods is described as drinking, not as having drunk, nectar; as tasting, not having tasted, ambrosia, as an unending affection for food and drink, not as repletion or the absence of desire for these things. Hence, their fullness seems to consist in motion and perception, in quiet and comprehension; they are not sated without appetite, nor do they feel an appetite without feeling, in a certain manner, sated.

LAODONIO: "A sated longing, a longing satiation."

LIBERIO: This is exactly what it is.

LAODONIO: From here I can understand how it has been said, not mistakenly, but rather with great truth and insight, that divine love weeps with unspeakable sobs, for in having everything it loves everything, and in loving everything, it has everything.

LIBERIO: But we would need many an explanatory note if wanted to understand the divine love that is deity itself; it is easy enough to understand divine love as it is found in its effects and in subaltern nature – not (I mean) the divinity that is diffused in things, but what, in things, aspires to divinity.

LAODONIO: But about this and other matters we can converse more comfortably later on. Let us be off.


# FOURTH DIALOGUE

*Interlocutors*: SEVERINO, MINUTOLO

SEVERINO: Now you shall see the topic of nine blind men, who introduce

no nove principii e cause particolari de sua cecità, benché tutti convegnano in una causa generale d'un comun furore.

MINUTOLO: Cominciate dal primo.

SEVERINO: Il primo di questi benché per natura sia cieco, nulladimeno per amore si lamenta, dicendo a gli altri che non può persuadersi la natura esser stata più discortese a essi che a lui; stante che quantumque non veggono, hanno però provato il vedere, e sono esperti della dignità del senso e de l'eccellenza del sensibile, onde son dovenuti orbi: ma egli è venuto come talpa al mondo a esser visto e non vedere, a bramar quello che mai vedde.

MINUTOLO: Si son trovati molti innamorati per sola fama.

SEVERINO: Essi (dice egli) aver pur questa felicità de ritener quella imagine divina nel conspetto de la mente, de maniera, che quantumque ciechi, hanno pure in fantasia quel che lui non puote avere. Poi nella sestina si volta alla sua guida, pregandola che lo mene in qualche precipizio, a fin che non sia oltre orrido spettacolo del sdegno di natura. Dice dumque:

꒰꒱

### Parla il primo cieco

Felici che talvolta visto avete,
voi per la persa luce ora dolenti
compagni che doi lumi conoscete.
Questi accesi non furo, né son spenti;
però più grieve mal che non credete
è il mio, e degno de più gran lamenti:
perché, che fusse torva la natura
più a voi ch'a me, non è chi m'assicura.

Al precipizio, o duce,
conducime, se vòi darmi contento,
perché trove rimedio il mio tormento,

nine principles that are the particular causes of their blindness, despite the fact that they have come together for the general cause of a common frenzy.

MINUTOLO: Begin with the first.

SEVERINO: The first of these, although he is blind by nature, nonetheless raises a lover's lament, saying to the others that he cannot convince himself that nature has been more disrespectful to them than to him, for they may not see now, but they have at least known what it is to see; they have experienced the dignity of perception, and the excellence of what is perceptible before going blind, but he has come like a mole into the world, seen but unseeing, to long for what he never saw.

MINUTOLO: Many have fallen in love on hearsay alone.

SEVERINO: They (he says) at least have the joy of keeping that divine image in the mind's eye, so that, even blind, they possess in imagination that which he can never possess at all. Then, in the sestet he turns to his guide, asking to be directed to some precipice, so that he will no longer provide a horrid exhibit of nature's disdain. And so he says:

ॐ

### The First Blind Man Speaks

How happy you who had the chance to see,
Though you bewail your lost illumination!
For you, my friends, know what two lights can be:
My own, unlit, endured no suffocation,
And hence a graver evil falls to me
Than you'd believe, worth louder lamentation.
That nature's dealt more savagely with you
Than with myself, I cannot think is true.

To the abyss, my guide!
Lead me away, if you would now content me;
Relieve me of the evils that torment me,

ch'ad esser visto, e non veder la luce,
  qual talpa uscivi al mondo,
e per esser di terra inutil pondo.

ॐ

Appresso séguita l'altro che morsicato dal serpe de la gelosia, è venuto
infetto nell'organo visuale. Va senza guida, se pur non ha la gelosia
per scorta: priega alcun de circonstanti che se non è rimedio del suo
male, faccia per pietà che non oltre aver possa senso del suo male;
facendo cossì lui occolto a se medesimo, come se gli è fatta occolta la
sua luce: con sepelir lui col proprio male. Dice dumque:

ॐ

### *Parla il secondo cieco*

  Da la tremenda chioma ha svèlto Aletto
l'infernal verme, che col fiero morso
hammi sì crudament' il spirto infetto,
ch'a tòrmi il senso principal è corso,
privando de sua guida l'intelletto:
ch'in vano l'alma chiede altrui soccorso,
  sì cespitar mi fa per ogni via
  quel rabido rancor di gelosia.

  Se non magico incanto,
né sacra pianta, né virtù de pietra,
né soccorso divin scampo m'impetra,
un di voi sia (per dio) piatoso in tanto,
  che a me mi faccia occolto:
con far meco il mio mal tosto sepolto.

ॐ

Succede l'altro il qual dice esser dovenuto cieco per essere repentina-
mente promosso dalle tenebre a veder una gran luce; atteso che essendo avezzo de mirar bellezze ordinarie, venne subito a presentarsegli
avanti gli occhi una beltà celeste, un divo sole: onde non altrimente si

For I never to see, but to be spied
As a blind mole came forth
To be a useless burden on the earth.

Another follows next, who, bitten by the serpent of jealousy, has become infected in his visual organ. He goes without a guide, unless he has Jealousy as his escort. He implores some bystanders, should there be no cure for his infection, at least, out of pity, to take away his awareness of his own misfortune, hiding him from his own self in the same way that his light has become hidden: that is, by burying him together with his own disease. And so he says:

### The Second Blind Man Speaks

Allecto plucked from her repulsive head
The infernal snake, who with its savage bite
My spirit so infected that it spread
To my chief sense, and robbed me of my sight.
My intellect, therefore, has lost its head;
The soul in vain seeks solace for its plight
And how it makes me wander aimlessly!
This ravenously raging jealousy.

No magic incantation
No holy herb, no wonder-working stone,
No godlike helper bids it to be gone.
Has one of you (by God) the inclination
To hide me from my doom?
Inter me in my own untimely tomb!

Another blind man follows, who claims to have gone blind because he was suddenly thrust forth from the darkness to see a great light: for he was accustomed to look upon ordinary beauties, and suddenly a heavenly beauty presented itself before his eyes, a divine Sun. In this and

gli è stemprata la vista e smorzatosegli il lume gemino che splende in prora a l'alma (perché gli occhi son come doi fanali che guidano la nave), ch'accader suole a un allievato nelle oscuritadi cimmerie, se subito immediatamente affiga gli occhi a sole. E nella sestina priega che gli sia donato libero passagio a l'inferno, perché non altro che tenebre convegnono ad un supposito tenebroso. Dice dumque cossì:

❧

*Parla il terzo cieco*

S'appaia il gran pianeta di repente
a un uom nodrito in tenebre profonde,
o sott' il ciel de la cimmeria gente,
onde lungi suoi rai il sol diffonde;
gli spenge il lume gemino splendente
in prora a l'alma, e nemico s'asconde:
cossì stemprate fur mie luci avezze
a mirar ordinarie bellezze.

Fatemi a l'orco andare:
perché morto discorro tra le genti?
perché ceppo infernal tra voi viventi
misto men vo? Perché l'aure discare
sorbisco, in tante pene
messo per aver visto il sommo bene?

❧

Fassi innanzi il quarto cieco per simile, ma non già per medesima caggione orbo, con cui si mostra il primo: perché come quello per repentino sguardo della luce, cossì questo con spesso e frequente remirare, o pur per avervi troppo fissati gli occhi, ha perso il senso de tutte l'altre luci, e non si dice cieco per consequenza al risguardo di quella unica che l'ha occecato; e dice il simile del senso de la vista a quello ch'aviene al senso dell'udito, essendo che coloro che han fatte l'orecchie a gran strepiti e rumori, non odeno gli strepiti minori: come è cosa famosa de gli popoli cataduppici che son là d'onde il gran fiume Nilo da una altissima montagna scende precipitoso alla pianura.

in no other way, his vision was damaged and the twin light that shines on the prow of the soul was snuffed out (for the eyes are like two lamps that guide a ship). This also happens to the people who are reared in the Cimmerian darkness of the far north, if suddenly they should fix their eyes on the Sun.[67] Then, in the sestet, he prays that he be given free passage to Hell, because nothing but darkness is fit for a creature of darkness. And this is what he says:

సా

### The Third Blind Man Speaks

If ever the Great Planet should appear
To those grown up with darkness all around,
Or born beneath Cimmerian skies (for there
The Sun sheds longer rays to reach the ground)
Light douses both the shining lights they bear
On their soul's prow, retreats, and can't be found.
Thus were my lights extinguished, for I knew
No more than common beauty hitherto.

To Hell direct me please;
Why should a dead man keep your company?
Why does the spawn of Hades mingle free
Among the living? What unwelcome breeze
Should I inhale, so blighted
To suffer for that highest good I've sighted?

సా

The fourth blind man presents himself, sightless for a similar, but not identical reason to that of his predecessor, for, like the man blinded by a sudden glimpse of light, this fellow has been blinded by frequent and repeated gazing; that is, he has lost the sense of all other lights for having excessively fixed his eyes on one; hence, he will not declare himself blind as a consequence of this single light that has blinded him. About the sense of sight he says substantially what is said about the sense of hearing, for those who have exposed their ears to great clamours and noises no longer hear lesser commotions, as is famously the case with the Catadupian people, who live where the great river Nile descends to the plain from a precipitous height.[68]

MINUTOLO: Cossì tutti color ch'hanno avezzo il corpo, l'animo a cose più difficili e grandi, non sogliono sentir fastidio dalle difficultadi minori. E costui non deve essere discontento della sua cecità.

SEVERINO: Non certo. Ma si dice volontario orbo, a cui piace che ogn'altra cosa gli sia ascosa, come l'attedia col divertirlo da mirar quello che vuol unicamente mirare. – Et in questo mentre priega gli viandanti che si degnino de non farlo capitar male per qualche mal rancontro, mentre va sì attento e cattivato ad un oggetto principale.

MINUTOLO: Riferite le sue paroli.

SEVERINO:

🙟

### Parla il quarto cieco

Precipitoso d'alto al gran profondo,
il Nil d'ogn' altro suon il senso ha spento
de Cataduppi al popolo ingiocondo;
cossì stand'io col spirto intiero attento
alla più viva luce ch'abbia il mondo,
tutti i minor splendori umqua non sento:
or mentr'ella gli splende, l'altre cose
sien pur a l'orbo volontario ascose.

Priegovi, da le scosse
di qualche sasso, o fiera irrazionale,
fatemi accorto, e se si scende o sale:
perché non caggian queste misere osse
in luogo cavo e basso,
mentre privo de guida meno il passo.

🙟

Al cieco che séguita, per il molto lacrimare accade che siano talmente appannati gli occhi, che non si può stendere il raggio visuale a com-

MINUTOLO: Similarly, all those who have accustomed body and the soul to more difficult and grander enterprises no longer feel irritation at minor difficulties. And this man should not be unhappy with his blindness.

SEVERINO: Certainly not. But he declares that he is a voluntary blind man who is glad that all other things lie hidden, as they would only annoy him by diverting his gaze from what he wants to gaze upon exclusively. At the same time, as he goes on so attentively captivated by one principal object, he begs passersby to preserve him from the harm of some unfortunate encounter.

MINUTOLO: Tell me his words.

SEVERINO:

### The Fourth Blind Man Speaks

In dropping headlong from a lofty station
The Nile suppresses every other sound
For wretches of the Catadupian nation
So I, too, with my spirit wholly bound
To watch the brightest light in all Creation,
Am left unmoved by splendours less profound.
When she beams, every other apparition
Is hidden to me, sightless by volition.

Please warn me whether blow
Of random stone or reckless beast is pending,
And whether I'll be climbing or descending
Lest these poor bones should stumble as they go
Into some lowly hollow
As I press on without a guide to follow.

As for the next blind man, his eyes are so exhausted from frequent weeping that the visual ray can no longer extend as far as any visible

pararsi le specie visibili, e principalmente per riveder quel lume ch'a
suo mal grado, per raggion di tante doglie una volta vedde. Oltre che
si stima la sua cecità non esser più disposizionale ma abituale, et al
tutto privativa; perché il fuoco luminoso che accende l'alma nella pu-
pilla, troppo gran tempo e molto gagliardamente è stato riprimuto et
oppresso dal contrario umore: de maniera che quantumque cessasse
il lacrimare, non si persuade che per ciò conseguisca il bramato vedere. Et udirete quel che dice appresso alle brigate, perché lo facessero
oltrepassare:

꒰ঌ

**Parla il quinto cieco**

Occhi miei d'acqui sempremai pregnanti,
quando fia che del raggio visuale
la scintilla se spicche fuor de tanti
e sì densi ripari, e vegna tale,
che possa riveder que' lumi santi,
che fur principio del mio dolce male?
lasso: credo che sia al tutto estinta,
sì a lungo dal contrario oppressa e vinta.

Fate passar il cieco,
e voltate vostr' occhi a questi fonti
che vincon gli altri tutti uniti e gionti;
e s'è chi ardisce disputarne meco,
è chi certo lo rende
ch'un de miei occhi un Oceàn comprende.

꒰ঌ

Il sesto orbo è cieco, perché per il soverchio pianto ha mandate tante
lacrime che non gli è rimasto umore, fin al ghiacio et umor per cui
come per mezzo diafano il raggio visuale era transmesso, e s'intromet-
tea la luce esterna e specie visibile, di sorte che talmente fu compunto
il core che tutta l'umida sustanza (il cui ufficio è de tener unite ancora
le parti diverse varie e contrarie) è digerita; e gli è rimasta l'amorosa
affezzione senza l'effetto de le lacrime, perché l'organo è stemprato
per la vittoria de gli altri elementi, et è rimasto consequentemente

species, and, especially, see again that light which, to his misfortune
(because of his many sorrows), he once beheld. Furthermore, he believes that his blindness is no longer a matter of disposition but of
habit, and entirely privative, because the luminous fire that ignites the
soul in the pupil has been suppressed for too long and too energeti-
cally by its opposing moisture, so that even if he were to cease his crying, he doubts that he could regain the sight for which he longs. You
shall hear what he says then to the company, so that they will let him
pass:

꒒

### The Fifth Blind Man Speaks

My brimming eyes, forever overflowing,
When will your visual ray again set free
Another spark that sizzles in the going
Forth from your tangled hiding place, for me
To spy again those holy lights aglowing,
The first cause of my sweet calamity?
I fear, alas, that every fire is gone;
Repressed by a contrary force too long.

Now clear the blind man's way!
And to this pair of fountains turn your mind
For they surpass all other springs combined,
And anyone who dares dispute my say
Shall falter by and by,
For I contain an ocean in each eye.

꒒

The sixth blind man is sightless because he has shed so many tears
through overpowering weeping that he has no more moisture left in
him, not even the crystal and humor through which, as through a di-
aphanous membrane, the visual ray was transmitted, and introduced
external light and visible species. His heart was so pierced that all his
moist substance (whose task it is to keep all the different, various, and
opposing parts united) has been digested, and he is left with amorous
affection, but no effect in tears, for the organ of sight has become un-

senza vedere e senza constanza de le parti del corpo insieme. Poi propone a gli circonstanti quel che intenderete:

⁂

### Parla il sesto cieco

Occhi non occhi; fonti, non più fonti,
avete sparso già l'intiero umore,
che tenne il corpo, il spirto e l'alma gionti.
E tu visual ghiaccio che di fore
facevi tanti oggetti a l'alma conti,
sei digerito dal piagato core:
cossì vèr l'infernale ombroso speco
vo menando i miei passi, arido cieco.

Deh non mi siate scarsi
a farmi pronto andar, di me piatosi,
che tanti fiumi a i giorni tenebrosi
sol de mio pianto m'appagando ho sparsi:
  or ch'ogni umor è casso,
vers' il profondo oblio datemi il passo.

⁂

Sopragionge il seguente che ha perduta la vista dal intenso vampo che
procedendo dal core è andato prima a consumar gli occhi, et appresso a leccar tutto il rimanente umore de la sustanza de l'amante, de
maniera che tutto incinerito e messo in fiamma non è più lui: perché
dal fuoco la cui virtù è de dissolvere gli corpi tutti ne gli loro atomi, è
convertito in polve non compaginabile, se per virtù de l'acqua sola gli
atomi d'altri corpi se inspessano e congiongono a far un subsistente
composto. Con tutto ciò non è privo del senso de l'intensissime fiamme; però nella sestina con questo vuol farsi dar largo da passare: ché
se qualch'uno venesse tócco da le fiamme sue, dovenerebbe a tale che
non arrebe più senso delle fiamme infernali come di cosa calda, che
come di fredda neve. Dice dumque:

balanced by the victory of the other elements. Hence, he is left without either sight or equilibrium among all the elements of the body. He then presents what you are about to hear to the bystanders:

**The Sixth Blind Man Speaks**

You eyes and fonts have given up your role;
You've squandered all the liquid by whose art
Soul, breath, and body forged a single whole;
You, visual crystal that, standing apart,
Made known so many objects to the soul
Have been digested by the smitten heart.
Thus, towards the infernal cave to which I'm fated
I trudge along, both blind and desiccated.

Be generous in action
And speed me, by your mercy, on my way
I've shed such rivers every darkling day
Of my own tears, for my own satisfaction,
That every humor's gone;
Now to profound oblivion lead me on.

Now the next blind man appears, who lost his sight from the intense flash that, proceeding from the heart, went on first to consume the eyes and then to lap up all the remaining moisture from the lover's substance, so that, entirely incinerated and turned into flame, he is no longer himself. For from fire, whose property is to dissolve all bodies into their component atoms, he has been converted into a dust that cannot be compacted together; only by the power of water can the atoms of other bodies grow in density and join together to create a compound substance. Despite all this, he is still aware of these searing flames. Therefore, in the sestet he means to clear a path for himself by declaring that anyone touched by his flames will no longer be able to distinguish whether the flames of Hell are something hot or cold as snow. This, then, is what he says:

✧

*Parla il settimo cieco*

La beltà che per gli occhi scorse al core
formò nel petto mio l'alta fornace
ch'assorbì prima il visuale umore,
sgorgand' in alt' il suo vampo tenace;
e poi vorando ogn'altro mio liquore,
per metter l'elemento secco in pace,
m'ha reso non compaginabil polve,
chi ne gli atomi suoi tutto dissolve.

Se d'infinito male
avete orror, datemi piazza, o gente;
guardatevi dal mio fuoco cuocente;
che se contagion di quel v'assale,
crederete che inverno
sia, ritrovars' al fuoco de l'inferno.

✧

Succede l'ottavo, la cecità del quale vien caggionata dalla saetta che
Amore gli ha fatto penetrare da gli occhi al core. Onde si lagna non
solamente come cieco, ma et oltre come ferito, et arso tanto altamente, quanto non crede ch'altro esser possa. Il cui senso è facilmente
espresso in questa sentenza:

✧

*Parla l'ottavo cieco*

Assalto vil, ria pugna, iniqua palma,
punt'acuta, esca edace, forte nervo,
aspra ferit', empio ardor, cruda salma,
stral, fuoco e laccio di quel dio protervo,
che puns' gli occhi, arse il cor, legò l'alma,
e femmi a un punto cieco, amante e servo:
talché orbo de mia piaga, incendio e nodo,
ho 'l senso in ogni tempo, loco e modo.

❧

### The Seventh Blind Man Speaks

Beauty, moving from eyes to heart, first forged
A furnace in my breast as once it passed.
And there the visual humor was absorbed
When first love's spark raised its tenacious blast,
And finally on every drop it gorged
To grant the arid element peace at last.
I'm turned to uncompanionable dust
That melts all things to atoms, as it must.

If infinite dejection
Strikes horror in you, people, I'll not tarry.
Be careful of the scorching fire I carry;
If ever you're attacked by its infection
You'll soon believe that winter
Is to be found in fire at Hell's own centre.

❧

The eighth blind man follows, whose blindness is caused by the arrow that Love has forced to penetrate from the eyes to the heart. Hence, he complains not only as a blind man, but as a man wounded, and burned more deeply, he believes, than any other could be. And the meaning of this is clearly expressed in the following sonnet:

❧

### The Eighth Blind Man Speaks

Vicious assault, rogue battle, conquest foul,
Sharp point, voracious bait, relentless tie,
Harsh wound, impious ardour, savage toll
Ray, fire, and snare of that brash deity.
Who stabbed my eyes, my heart seared, bound my soul
At once to blindness, love, servility.
Blind, I'm aware of wound and fire and prison
At every time and place, for every reason.

Uomini, eroi e dèi,
che siete in terra, o appresso Dite o Giove,
dite (vi priego) quando, come e dove
provaste, udiste o vedeste umqua omei
    medesmi, o tali, o tanti
tra oppressi, tra dannati, tra gli amanti?

Viene al fine l'ultimo, il quale è ancor muto: perché non possendo (per non aver ardire) dir quello che massime vorrebe senza offendere o provocar sdegno, è privo di parlar di qualsivogli' altra cosa. Però non parla lui, ma la sua guida produce la raggione circa la quale, per esser facile, non discorro, ma solamente apporto la sentenza:

**Parla la guida del nono cieco**

Fortunati voi altri ciechi amanti,
che la caggion del vostro mal spiegate:
esser possete, per merto de pianti,
graditi d'accoglienze caste e grate;
di quel ch'io guido, qual tra tutti quanti
più altamente spasma, il vampo late,
muto forse per falta d'ardimento
di far chiaro a sua diva il suo tormento.

Aprite, aprite il passo,
siate benigni a questo vacuo volto
de tristi impedimenti, o popol folto,
mentre ch'il busto travagliato e lasso
    va picchiando le porte
di men penosa e più profonda morte.

Qua son significate nove caggioni per le quali accade che l'umana mente sia cieca verso il divino oggetto, perché non possa fissar gli occhi a quello. De le quali:

Men, heroes, gods who dwell
Upon the earth, with Hades or with Jove
If somewhere, somehow, sometime you can prove
Seeing or hearing such laments, pray tell –
Can their like be discovered
Among the oppressed, the damned, or among lovers?

&#8667;

Finally, the last blind man comes along, who is also mute. He was once unable (for lack of courage) to say what he most wanted to say for fear of offending or provoking disdain, and so he is now unable to speak about anything at all. Therefore, he does not speak himself; instead, his guide presents the discussion, which, to facilitate matters, I shall not describe, but will simply present the sonnet:

&#8667;

### The Guide of the Ninth Blind Man Speaks

You're fortunate, you other sightless lovers
Able to tell what evils you've incurred
By merit of your tears, you may recover
A chaste and gracious welcome, long deferred.
He whom I guide alone among you others
Loves most profoundly, but the spark's interred.
He's dumbstruck for his faltering intent
To make clear to his goddess his torment.

Make way, you milling throng!
Be gentle to this vacant countenance
Remove dire obstacles to his advance,
And let this troubled figure move along
To knock upon the gate
Of death's less painful and deeper estate.

&#8667;

Here we see symbolized nine reasons why the human mind becomes blind to the divine object on which it cannot fix its eyes. Of these:

La prima, allegorizata per il primo cieco, è la natura della propria specie, che per quanto comporta il grado in cui si trova, in quello aspira per certo più alto che apprender possa.

MINUTOLO: Perché nessun desiderio naturale è vano, possiamo certificarci de stato più eccellente che conviene a l'anima fuor di questo corpo in cui gli fia possibile d'unirsi o avvicinarsi più altamente al suo oggetto.

SEVERINO: Dici molto bene che nessuna potenza et appulso naturale è senza gran raggione, anzi è l'istessa regola di natura la quale ordina le cose: per tanto è cosa verissima e certissima a ben disposti ingegni, che l'animo umano (qualumque si mostre mentre è nel corpo) per quel medesimo che fa apparire in questo stato, fa espresso il suo esser peregrino in questa regione, perché aspira alla verità e bene universale, e non si contenta di quello che viene a proposito e profitto della sua specie.

La seconda, figurata per il secondo cieco, procede da qualche perturbata affezzione, come in proposito de l'amore è la gelosia, la quale è come tarlo che ha medesimo suggetto, nemico e padre, cioè che rode il panno o legno di cui è generato.

MINUTOLO: Questa non mi par ch'abbia luogo nell'amor eroico.

SEVERINO: Vero, secondo medesima raggione che vedesi nell'amor volgare: ma io intendo secondo altra raggione proporzionale a quella la quale accade in color che amano la verità e bontà; e si mostra quando s'adirano tanto contra quelli che la vogliono adulterare, guastare, corrompere, o che in altro modo indegnamente vogliono trattarla: come son trovati di quelli che si son ridutti sino alla morte, alle pene et esser ignominiosamente trattati da gli popoli ignoranti e sette volgari.

MINUTOLO: Certo nessuno ama veramente il vero e buono che non sia iracondo contra la moltitudine: come nessuno volgarmente ama, che non sia geloso e timido per la cosa amata.

SEVERINO: E con questo vien ad esser cieco in molte cose veramente, et affatto affatto secondo l'opinion commune è stolto e pazzo.

MINUTOLO: Ho notato un luogo che dice esser stolti e pazzi tutti quelli

The *first*, symbolized by the first blind man, is the nature of one's own species, which, no matter the level at which it finds itself, always aspires to some higher level than it perceives.

MINUTOLO: Because no natural desire is pointless, we can be certain of a more excellent state, more fitting to the soul, outside this body, in which it is possible for him to unite with or approach his object more nobly.

SEVERINO: You have said it well: no potential and natural drive exists without its grand reason; indeed, it is the very rule of Nature, who orders all things. Hence, well-favoured wits recognize it as true and certain that the human spirit (however it may manifest itself while in the body) does indeed appear in this condition, but at the same time it also declares that it is only a wanderer in this [lower] region, for it aspires to the universal truth and goodness, and cannot content itself with what regards or benefits only its present species.

The *second*, symbolized by the second blind man, proceeds from some kind of unbalanced affection, like jealousy in love, which is like a woodworm that has the same subject, enemy, and father, that is, the worm that gnaws away the fabric or wood by which it is generated.[69]

MINUTOLO: This, it seems to me, has no place in heroic love.

SEVERINO: True, at least for the reasons that are observed in vulgar love; but I mean for another reason, appropriate to what happens to those who love truth and goodness; it emerges when they rage at those who try to adulterate, waste, or corrupt the highest good, or treat it in some other unworthy fashion; some of these people are put to death, or reduced to misery and unjust treatment by ignorant peoples and vulgar sects.

MINUTOLO: To be sure, no one can truly love truth and goodness without raging at the masses; just as no one can love in the vulgar way without the beloved making him jealous and timid.

SEVERINO: And thus he comes to be truly blind to many things, and, according to common opinion, entirely foolish and insane.

MINUTOLO: I have noted a passage that declares anyone foolish and in-

che hanno senso fuor et estravagante dal senso universale de gli altri uomini; ma cotal estravaganza è di due maniere, secondo che si va estra o con ascender più alto che tutti e la maggior parte sagliano o salir possano: e questi son gli inspirati de divino furore; o con descendere più basso dove si trovano coloro che hanno difetto di senso e di raggione più che aver possano gli molti, gli più, e gli ordinarii: et in cotal specie di pazzia, insensazione e cecità non si trovarà eroico geloso.

SEVERINO: Quantumque gli vegna detto che le molte lettere lo fanno pazzo, non gli si può dire ingiuria da dovero.

    La terza, figurata nel terzo cieco, procede da che la divina verità, secondo raggione sopra naturale, detta metafisica, mostrandosi a que' pochi alli quali si mostra, non proviene con misura di moto e tempo, come accade nelle scienze fisiche (cioè quelle che s'acquistano per lume naturale, le quali discorrendo da una cosa nota secondo il senso o la raggione, procedeno alla notizia d'altra cosa ignota: il qual discorso è chiamato argumentazione), ma subito e repentinamente secondo il modo che conviene a tale efficiente. Onde disse un divino: *Attenuati sunt oculi mei suspicientes in excelsum.* Onde non è richiesto van discorso di tempo, fatica de studio, et atto d'inquisizione per averla: ma cossì prestamente s'ingerisce come proporzionalmente il lume solare senza dimora si fa presente a chi se gli volta e se gli apre.

MINUTOLO: Volete dumque che gli studiosi e filosofi non siano più atti a questa luce che gli quantumque ignoranti?

SEVERINO: In certo modo non, et in certo modo sì. Non è differenza quando la divina mente per sua providenza viene a comunicarsi senza disposizione del suggetto: voglio dire quando si communica, perché ella cerca et eligge il suggetto; ma è gran differenza quando aspetta e vuol esser cercata, e poi secondo il suo bene placito vuol farsi ritrovare. In questo modo non appare a tutti, né può apparir ad altri che a color che la cercano. Onde è detto: *Qui quaerunt me invenient me*, et in altro loco: *Qui sitit, veniat, et bibat.*

MINUTOLO: Non si può negare che l'apprensione del secondo modo si faccia in tempo.

sane whose sensibility is alien, or extravagant, compared with the universal sensibility of other people. But this extravagance is of two sorts: either it is expressed in climbing higher than everyone else, or at least the great majority climbs or is able to climb – these are the ones who are inspired by divine frenzy – or in descending lower down to join those who have a greater defect of sense or reasoning than the many, the majority, and the ordinary; but a jealous hero would never be found suffering from this kind of insanity, senselessness, and blindness.

SEVERINO: If he is told that too much studying has driven him crazy, he cannot truly say that he has been insulted.

The *third* reason, symbolized by the third blind man, originates on those occasions when divine truth, by supernatural reason, that is, metaphysics, reveals itself to those few to whom it reveals itself. It does not appear with any moderation of movement and time, as happens in the physical sciences (that is, the knowledge we acquire by the natural light of reason, which arrives by discussing something known by sense or reason, to knowledge of some other, unknown, matter; this progress is called argumentation). Instead, it appears immediately and suddenly, as befits its origin. Hence, a divine once said:[70] *My eyes fail from looking upward.* No vain progress of time, exertion of study, and act of inquiry are required to obtain it; it presents itself as quickly as, in proportion, the light of the sun without hesitation makes itself present to anyone who turns and opens himself to it.[71]

MINUTOLO: Do you mean, then, that scholars and philosophers are no more likely to see this light than some ignorant person?

SEVERINO: In a certain sense, no, and in a certain sense, yes. There is no difference, when the divine mind in its providence communicates itself without regard for the subject's disposition; I mean when it communicates itself because it has sought out and chosen its own subject. But there is a great difference when it waits expectantly, longing to be sought, and then, according to its pleasure, makes itself available to discovery. In this way it does not appear to everyone, nor can it appear to any but those who seek it. Hence, it is said: *Who seeks me shall find me.*[72] And elsewhere, *If any man thirst, let him come and drink.*[73]

MINUTOLO: It cannot be denied that perception of the second kind occurs over time.

SEVERINO: Voi non distinguete tra la disposizione alla divina luce, e la apprensione di quella. Certo non niego che al disporsi bisogna tempo, discorso, studio e fatica: ma come diciamo che la alterazione si fa in tempo, e la generazione in instante; e come veggiamo che con tempo s'aprono le fenestre, et il sole entra in un momento: cossì accade proporzionalmente al proposito.

La quarta, significata nel seguente, non è veramente indegna, come quella che proviene dalla consuetudine di credere a false opinioni del volgo il quale è molto rimosso dalle opinioni de filosofi: opur deriva dal studio de filosofie volgari le quali son dalla moltitudine tanto più stimate vere, quanto più accostano al senso commune. E questa consuetudine è uno de grandissimi e fortissimi inconvenienti che trovar si possano: perché (come exemplificò Alcazele et Averroe) similmente accade a essi, che come a color che da puerizia e gioventù sono consueti a mangiar veneno, quai son dovenuti a tale, che se gli è convertito in suave e proprio nutrimento; e per il contrario abominano le cose veramente buone e dolci secondo la comun natura. Ma è dignissima, perché è fondata sopra la consuetudine de mirar la vera luce (la qual consuetudine non può venir in uso alla moltitudine come è detto). Questa cecità è eroica, et è tale, per quale degnamente contentare si possa il presente furioso cieco, il qual tanto manca che si cure di quella, che viene veramente a spreggiare ogni altro vedere, e da la comunità non vorrebe impetrar altro che libero passagio e progresso di contemplazione: come per ordinario suole patir insidie, e se gli sogliono opporre intoppi mortali.

La quinta, significata nel quinto, procede dalla improporzionalità delli mezzi de nostra cognizione al cognoscibile; essendo che per contemplar le cose divine, bisogna aprir gli occhi per mezzo de figure, similitudini et altre raggioni che gli Peripatetici comprendono sotto il nome de fantasmi; o per mezzo de l'essere procedere alla speculazion de l'essenza: per via de gli effetti alla notizia della causa; gli quali mezzi tanto manca che vagliano per l'assecuzion di cotal fine, che più tosto è da credere che siano impedimenti, se credere vogliamo che la più alta e profonda cognizion de cose divine sia per negazione e non per affirmazione, conoscendo che la divina beltà e bontà non sia quello che può cader e cade sotto il nostro concetto: ma quello che è oltre et oltre incomprensibile; massime in questo stato detto «speculator de fantasmi» dal filosofo, e dal teologo «vision per similitudine speculare et enigma»; perché veggiamo non gli effetti veramente, e le vere specie de le cose, o la sustanza de le idee, ma le ombre, vestigii e simulacri

SEVERINO: You are not distinguishing between receptivity to divine light and the perception of it. Certainly I will not deny that receptivity requires time, discussion, study, and effort, and just as we say that alteration happens over time and conception in an instant, and as we see that windows open over time, whereas the Sun enters in a moment, so, too, it happens in the same way with our present case.

The *fourth*, symbolized by the next blind man, is not truly unworthy, unlike the blindness that derives from the habit of believing in the false opinions of the common crowd, which is exceedingly remote from the opinions of philosophers, or derives from the study of vulgar philosophies, which are the more esteemed as true by the masses the closer they come to common opinion. Now this habit is one of the greatest and most powerful obstacles we find, for (as Algazel and Averroës showed)[74] the same thing happens to people who have been accustomed to eat poison from childhood and youth, until they have reached the point where the poison has been converted into sweet and appropriate nourishment; then, on the contrary, they loathe the things that are genuinely good and sweet according to common opinion. This blindness, however, is worthy indeed, because it is based on the habit of looking upon the true light (a habit that cannot become common among the multitude, as we have said). This blindness is heroic, a state in which our frenzied blind man is deservedly content, for he truly has come to despise every other passage and progress of contemplation, where ordinarily ambushes lurk, and mortal obstacles obtrude themselves.

The *fifth* reason, symbolized by the fifth blind man, originates in the lack of proportion between our means of knowing and what can be known; for to contemplate divine matters, the eyes must be opened with the help of symbols, likenesses, and other methods that the Peripatetics classify under the term phantasms,[75] or by proceeding through being to speculation about being, or by proceeding through effects to knowledge about their cause. Now all these methods are so deficient for the pursuit of such an end that it is almost better to regard them as impediments, especially if we mean to believe that the most lofty and profound knowledge of divinity comes by way of negation rather than affirmation. For we know that divine beauty and goodness are not what can and do fall under our categories of thinking; they exist far beyond our comprehension, especially in that state known as "mirroring of phantasms" by the philosopher, and by the theologian as vision by images "through a glass darkly";[76] for we see not the real effects, and the

de quelle, come color che son dentro l'antro et hanno da natività le spalli volte da l'entrata della luce, e la faccia opposta al fondo: dove non vedeno quel che è veramente, ma le ombre de ciò che fuor de l'antro sustanzialmente si trova. – Però per la aperta visione la quale ha persa, e conosce aver persa, un spirito simile o meglior di quel di Platone piange desiderando l'exito da l'antro, onde non per reflessione, ma per «immediata conversione» possa riveder sua luce.

MINUTOLO: Parmi che questo cieco non versa circa la difficultà che procede dalla vista reflessiva: ma da quella che è caggionata dal mezzo tra la potenza visiva e l'oggetto.

SEVERINO: Questi doi modi quantumque siano distinti nella cognizion sensitiva o vision oculare, tutta volta però concorreno in uno nella cognizione razionale o intellettiva.

MINUTOLO: Parmi aver inteso e letto che in ogni visione si richiede il mezzo over intermedio tra la potenza et oggetto. Perché come per mezzo della luce diffusa ne l'aere e la similitudine della cosa che in certa maniera procede da quel che è visto a quel che vede, si mette in effetto l'atto del vedere: cossì nella regione intellettuale dove splende il sole dell'intelletto agente mediante la specie intelligibile formata e come procedente da l'oggetto, viene a comprendere de la divinità l'intelletto nostro o altro inferiore a quella. Perché come l'occhio nostro (quando veggiamo) non riceve la luce del foco et oro in sustanza, ma in similitudine: cossì l'intelletto in qualumque stato che si trove, non riceve sustanzialmente la divinità, onde sieno sustanzialmente tanti dèi quante sono intelligenze, ma in similitudine; per cui non formalmente son dèi, ma denominativamente divini, rimanendo la divinità e divina bellezza una et exaltata sopra le cose tutte.

SEVERINO: Voi dite bene; ma per vostro dire bene non è mistiero ch'io mi ritratte, perché non ho detto il contrario: ma bisogna che io dechiare et expliche. Però prima dechiaro che la visione immediata, det-

real appearances of things, or the substance of ideas, but only their shadows, traces, and images, just like the people [of Plato's allegory][77] who live within the cave and from birth have had their backs turned to the light that enters, and their faces turned to the depths; hence, they do not see what truly exists, but only the shadows of what is found in substance outside the cave.

Hence, for the open vision which he has lost, and knows that he has lost, he weeps, a spirit like or better than Plato's, desiring escape from the cave, so that he can see his light again, not by reflection, but by immediate conversion.

MINUTOLO: It seems to me that this blind man is hindered not by the difficulty that proceeds from seeing in a reflection, but rather by [the difficulty posed by] the intermediary that stands between the power of sight and the object.[78]

SEVERINO: These two ways of seeing, however distinct they may be in sensible perception or ocular vision, still nonetheless merge as one in rational or intellective knowing.

MINUTOLO: I seem to have understood and read that in all vision a medium or intermediary is required between the power to see and the object. The act of seeing is put into effect through the intermediaries of light diffused in the air and the image of the object that in a certain manner proceeds from that which is seen to the seer. In the region of intelligence, where the Sun of the active intellect shines through the intermediary of intelligible species, formed and, as it were, proceeding from the object, our intellect, or another intellect inferior to ours, comes to understand about divinity. For just as our eye (when we see) does not receive firelight or gold in substance, but rather in image, so, too, the intellect, in whatever state it finds itself, does not receive divinity substantially, so that there would be substantially as many divinities as there are intelligences, but in divinity's image and likeness; hence, these images are not gods in a formal sense, but they are divine in a denominative sense. Divinity and divine beauty, however, remain one, exalted above all things.

SEVERINO: Well said, but however well you have spoken, I have no need to retract my own statement, because I have not contradicted you. Still, I need to clarify and explain what I have said. First, then, I declare that

ta da noi et intesa, non toglie quella sorte di mezzo che è la specie intelligibile, né quella che è la luce; ma quella che è proporzionale alla spessezza e densità del diafano, o pur corpo al tutto opaco tramezzante: come aviene a colui che vede per mezzo de le acqui più e meno turbide, o aria nimboso e nebbioso; il quale s'intenderebbe veder come senza mezzo quando gli venesse concesso de mirar per l'aria puro, lucido e terso. Il che tutto avete come esplicato dove si dice: «Spicche fuor di tanti e sì densi ripari». Ma ritorniamo al nostro principale.

La sesta, significata nel sequente, non è altrimente caggionata che dalla inbecillità et insubsistenza del corpo, il quale è in continuo moto, mutazione, et alterazione; e le operazioni del quale bisogna che seguiteno la condizione della sua facultà, la quale è consequente dalla condizione della natura et essere. Come volete voi che la immobilità, la sussistenza, la entità, la verità sia compresa da quello che è sempre altro et altro, e sempre fa et è fatto altri et altrimente? Che verità, che ritratto può star depinto et impresso dove le pupille de gli occhi si dispergono in acqui, l'acqui in vapore, il vapore in fiamma, la fiamma in aura, e questa in altro et altro, senza fine il suggetto del senso e cognizione per la ruota delle mutazioni in infinito?

MINUTOLO: Il moto è alterità, quel che si muove sempre è altro et altro, quel che è tale, sempre altri et altrimenti si porta et opra, per che il concetto et affetto séguita la raggione e condizione del suggetto. E quello che altro et altro, altri et altrimenti mira, bisogna necessariamente che sia a fatto cieco al riguardo di quella bellezza che è sempre una et unicamente, et è l'istessa unità et entità, identità.

SEVERINO: Cossì è.

La settima, contenuta allegoricamente nel sentimento del settimo cieco, deriva dal fuoco dell'affezzione, onde alcuni si fanno impotenti et inabili ad apprendere il vero, con far che l'affetto precorra a l'intelletto. Questi son coloro che prima hanno l'amare che l'intendere: onde gli avviene che tutte le cose gli appaiano secondo il colore della sua affezzione; stante che chi vuole apprendere il vero per via di contemplazione deve essere ripurgatissimo nel pensiero.

immediate vision, as we have discussed and understood it, does not exclude either the intermediary of intelligible species or the intermediary of light; but it does remove the kind of intermediary that stands in our way, whatever its thickness or density, whether it is translucent or totally opaque, that makes us resemble someone who sees through waters that are more or less turbid, or air that is cloudy or foggy; this person may think that he sees immediately, without barriers, as if he is looking through pure, bright, and clean air. All of which you have, as it were, explained where the sonnet says, *Forth from your tangled hiding place.* But let us return to the main track of our discussion.

The *sixth* reason for blindness, symbolized in the next blind man, is caused by nothing other than the weakness and inconsistency of the body, which is in continuous motion, change, and alteration; and whose operations depend on the condition of its faculties, which are contingent upon the condition of its nature and being. How can you think that immobility, consistency, being, truth are contained in something that is forever different, always acts differently, and is differently composed? What truth, what portrait could be painted and imprinted when the pupils of the eyes are dispersed in water, water in vapour, vapour in flame, flame in wind, and this into something else, so that the subject of sensation and cognition is forever travelling the wheel of change?

MINUTOLO: Motion is otherness; what moves is always something else and then something else again. Whatever something is like, it will always behave and operate otherwise, because ideas and affections follow the state and condition of their subject. And anyone who looks upon one thing and then another, looking at it in one way and then in another, must of necessity be absolutely blind to a beauty that is always uniquely one, and is itself unity, being, and identity.

SEVERINO: So it is.

The *seventh* reason, expressed allegorically in the feelings of the seventh blind man, derives from the fire of affection, for the sake of which some render themselves impotent, unable to apprehend what is true, by letting their affections run ahead of the intellect. These are the ones who put loving before understanding; for them, all things appear coloured by their affections; but anyone who wants to gain awareness of truth through contemplation must be extremely pure in thought.

MINUTOLO: In verità si vede che sì come è diversità de contemplatori et
inquisitori per quel che altri (secondo gli abiti de loro prime e fon-
damentali discipline) procedeno per via de numeri, altri per via de
figure, altri per via de ordini ò disordini, altri per via di composizione
e divisione, altri per via di separazione e congregazione, altri per via
de inquisizion e dubitazione, altri per via de discorso e definizione,
altri per via de interpretazioni e desciferazion de voci, vocaboli e dialecti: onde altri son filosofi matematici, altri metafisici, altri logici, altri
grammatici; cossì è diversità de contemplatori che con diverse affezzioni si metteno ad studiare et applicar l'intenzione alle sentenze scrit-
te: onde si doviene sin a questo che medesima luce di verità espressa in
un medesimo libro per medesime paroli, viene a servire al proposito
di sette tanto numerose, diverse e contrarie.


SEVERINO: Per questo è da dire che gli affetti molto sono potenti per
impedir l'apprension del vero, quantumque gli pazienti non se ne
possano accorgere: qualmente aviene ad un stupido ammalato che
non dice il suo gusto amaricato, ma il cibo amaro. – Or tal specie de
cecità è notata per costui, gli occhi del quale son alterati e privi dal
suo naturale, per quel che dal core è stato inviato et impresso, potente
non solo ad alterar il senso, ma et oltre l'altre tutte facultadi de l'alma,
come la presente figura dimostra.

Al significato per l'ottavo, cossì l'eccellente intelligibile oggetto
have occecato l'intelletto, come l'eccellente sopraposto sensibile a
costui ha corrotto il senso. Cossì avviene a chi vede Giove in maestà,
che perde la vita, e per consequenza perde il senso. Cossì avviene che
chi alto guarda tal volta vegna oppresso da la maestà. Oltre quando
viene a penetrar la specie divina, la passa come strale: onde dicono gli
teologi il verbo divino essere più penetrativo che qualsivoglia punta
di spada o di coltello. Indi deriva la formazione et impressione del
proprio vestigio, sopra il quale altro non è che possa essere impresso
o sigillato; là onde essendo tal forma ivi confirmata, e non possendo
succedere la peregrina e nova, senza che questa cieda, consequentemente può dire che non ha più facultà di prendere altro, se ha chi la
riempie, o la disgrega per la necessaria improporzionalitade.

La nona caggione è notata per il nono che è cieco per inconfidenza,
per deiezzion de spirito, la quale è administrata e caggionata pure da
grande amore, perché con lo ardire teme de offendere; onde disse

MINUTOLO: In truth, we see that, just as there are different kinds of contemplators and inquirers, for some (according to the habit of their
primary and fundamental discipline) proceed by way of numbers,
others by way of images, others by way of order or disorder, others
by way of composition and division, others by way of separation and
assembly, others by way of inquiry and doubt, others by way of discussion and definition, others by way of interpretation and decipherment
of words, vocabularies, and dialects; so that some are mathematical
philosophers, others metaphysicians, others logicians, others grammarians, so, too, there is a diversity among contemplators, who with
their different affections set themselves to study and apply their understanding to written phrases, until they reach the point where that
very light of truth, expressed in the same book by the same words,
comes to serve the interests of sects that are numerous, diverse, and
opposed to one another.[79]

SEVERINO: For this reason it is worth stating that the affections are extremely effective at blocking the perception of truth, although the sufferers themselves do not recognize it, like some stupid sick person who
does not say that his taste has grown bitter, but that the food is bitter.

Now this species of blindness is signified by the fellow whose eyes
are altered and deprived of their nature, because of what has been
dispatched and impressed on that nature by the heart, which is able
not only to alter perception, but also all the other faculties of the soul,
as he himself demonstrates.

As for the meaning of the *eighth* blind man, the excellent intelligible
Object has blinded his intellect, just as the excellent perceptible Object that is superimposed on it has corrupted his sight. This is what
happens to anyone who sees Jupiter in majesty; they lose their life,
and consequently their sense. So it happens that anyone who looks
on high is sometimes oppressed by majesty. But when he succeeds in
penetrating the divine appearance, he passes through it like an arrow;
hence, the theologians say that the divine word is more penetrating
than any point of sword or knife.[80] This penetration brings about the
formation and impression of its own imprint, and over it no other
imprint can be impressed or sealed. With this form sealed within him,
which nothing new and fleeting can supersede unless this first imprint
should give way, the blind man declares that he has no ability to take
in anything else, for he has something that entirely fills his sight, or
has dissolved his vision by overpowering it.

la *Cantica: Averte oculos tuos a me, quia ipsi me avolare fecere*. E cossì supprime gli occhi da non vedere quel che massime desidera e gode di
vedere; come raffrena la lingua da non parlare con chi massime brama di parlare, per téma che difetto di sguardo o difettosa parola non
lo avvilisca, o per qualche modo non lo metta in disgrazia: e questo
suol procedere da l'apprensione de l'excellenza de l'oggetto sopra de
la sua facultà potenziale, onde gli più profondi e divini teologi dicono che più si onora et ama Dio per silenzio, che per parola; come si
vede più per chiuder gli occhi alle specie representate, che per aprirli:
onde è tanto celebre la teologia negativa de Pitagora e Dionisio, sopra
quella demostrativa de Aristotele e scolastici dottori.

MINUTOLO: Andiamone raggionando per il camino.

SEVERINO: Come ti piace.

## DIALOGO QUINTO

*Interlocutori*: LAODOMIA, GIULIA

LAODOMIA: Un'altra volta, o sorella, intenderai quel che apporta tutto
il successo di questi nove ciechi, quali eran prima nove bellissimi et
amorosi giovani, che essendo tanto ardenti della vaghezza del vostro
viso, e non avendo speranza de ricevere il bramato frutto de l'amore,
e temendo che tal desperazione le riducesse a qualche final ruina,
partironsi dal terreno della Campania felice, e d'accordo (quei che
prima erano rivali) per la tua beltade giuròrno di non lasciarsi mai sin
che avessero tentato tutto il possibile per ritrovar cosa più de voi bella,
o simile al meno; con ciò che scuoprir si potesse in lei accompagnata
quella mercé e pietade che non si trovava nel vostro petto armato di
fierezza: perché questo giudicavano unico rimedio che divertir le potesse da quella cruda cattivitade. Il terzo giorno dopo la lor sollenne
partita, passando vicini al monte Circeo, gli piacque d'andar a veder
quelle antiquitadi de gli antri e fani di quella dea. Dove essendo gion-

The *ninth* reason for blindness is denoted by the ninth blind man, who is blinded by lack of confidence, by dejection of the spirit, which is inflicted and caused, also, by great love, which he is afraid to offend by his ardour. This is why the Canticle said, *Turn away thine eyes from me, for they have overcome me.*[81] And thus he prevents his eyes from seeing what he most desires and delights in seeing, just as he reins in his tongue so that it will not address the one he most desires to address, for fear that a deficiency in his expression or a defective word will humiliate him, or somehow put him in disgrace. And this happens because perception of the excellence of the object exceeds his potential to perceive it. Hence, the most profound and divine theologians say that God is better honoured by silence than by speech, just as God is better seen with eyes closed to the species that represent Him than with open eyes; and this is why the negative theology of Pythagoras and Dionysius is prized above the demonstrative theology of Aristotle and the scholastic doctors.

MINUTOLO: Let us continue conversing as we walk.

SEVERINO: As you like.

## FIFTH DIALOGUE

*Interlocutors*: LAODOMIA, GIULIA

LAODOMIA: On another occasion, my sister, you will understand what the whole story of these nine blind men means; initially, they were nine handsome and amorous youths, who, ardent for the beauty of your face, lacking all hope of receiving the longed-for fruit of love, and fearing that such desperation would reduce them to some ultimate ruin, departed the happy land of Campania. All together (they who had been rivals at first), they swore by your beauty never to leave each other until they had made every possible effort to discover something more beautiful than you, or at least similar to you. They hoped that they might also discover in her the mercy and pity that they never found in your breast, armoured as it was in pride: this, they judged, was the only remedy that could divert them from their cruel captivity. On the third day after their solemn departure, passing in the vicinity of Monte Circeo, they decided to visit the ancient caves and shrines

ti, dalla maestà del luogo ermo, de le ventose, eminenti e fragose rupi, del mormorìo de l'onde maritime che vanno a frangersi in quelle cavitadi, e di molte altre circonstanze che mostrava il luogo e la staggione, vennero tutti come inspiritati; tra' quali un (che ti dirò), più ardito espresse queste paroli: «Oh se piacesse al cielo che a questi tempi ne si fesse presente, come fu in altri secoli più felici, qualche saga Circe che con le piante, minerali, veneficii et incanti era potente di mettere come il freno alla natura: certo crederei che ella, quantumque fiera, piatosa pur sarebbe al nostro male. Ella molto sollecitata da nostri supplichevoli lamenti, condescenderebbe o a darne rimedio, o ver a concederne grata vendetta contra la crudeltà di nostra nemica». A pena avea finito di proferir queste paroli, che a tutti si presentò visibile un palaggio, il quale chiumque have ingegno di cose umane, possea facilmente comprendere che non era manifattura d'uomo, né di natura: de la figura e descrizzion de la quale ti dirò un'altra volta. Onde percossi da gran maraviglia, e tócchi da qualche speranza che qualche propizio nume (il qual ciò gli mise avanti) volesse definire il stato de la lor fortuna, dissero ad una voce che peggio non posseano incorrere che il morire, il quale stimavano minor male che vivere in tale e tanta passione. Però vi entraro dentro non trovando porta che fermata gli fusse, o portinaio che gli dimandasse raggione; sin che si ritrovaro in una richissima et ornatissima sala, dove in quella regia maestade (che puoi dire che Apolline fusse stato ritrovato da Fetonte) apparve quella ch'è chiamata sua figlia; con l'apparir de la quale veddero sparire le imagini de molti altri numi che gli administravano. Là con grazioso volto accettati e confortati, si fero avanti: e vinti dal splendor di quella maestade, piegaro le ginocchia in terra, e tutti insieme con quella diversità de note che gli dettava il diverso ingegno, esposero gli lor voti alla dea. Dalla quale in conclusione furono talmente trattati, che ciechi, raminghi et infortunatamente laboriosi hanno varcati tutti mari, passati tutti fiumi, superati tutti monti, discorse tutte pianure, per spacio de diece anni; al termine de quali entrati sotto quel temperato cielo de l'isola britannica, gionti al conspetto de le belle e graziose ninfe del padre Tamesi, dopoi aver essi fatti gli atti di conveniente umiltade, et accettati da quelle con gesti d'onestissima cortesia, uno tra loro, il principale, che altre volte ti sarà nomato, con tragico e lamentevole accento espose la causa commune in questo modo:

of the goddess Circe.[82] When they arrived, by the majesty of that deserted place, by the windy, sheer, and jagged rocks, by the murmur of the sea waves that break against those hollows, and by many other circumstances that the place and season offered, they all became, as it were, inspired: and among them one (whom I shall identify for you), the boldest, exclaimed in these words: "Oh, if only it would please Heaven that now, as in happier ages, some sorceress Circe were here, with plants, minerals, potions, and incantations to put the reins on nature! However haughty she might be, still, she would have pity on our distress. She, invoked by our pleading lamentations, would deign to grant us relief, or at least concede us a welcome revenge on the cruelty of our enemy." No sooner had he finished uttering these words, than a palace presented itself to the sight of one and all; anyone with the slightest awareness of human affairs could easily grasp that it was not of human manufacture, nor of nature's; I will tell you about its appearance and describe it on some other occasion.

Then, struck by great wonder, and touched by the slight hope that some favourable deity (the one who had made it appear) might want to hear the state of their fortunes, they said with one voice that they risked nothing worse than death, which they reckoned was a lesser evil than continuing to live with such great passion. And so they entered into the palace, where they found no door closed to them, no doorkeeper to question them. At last they found themselves in an opulent and ornate hall, and there, in majesty as regal as Apollo's when he received Phaethon, Apollo's daughter [i.e., Circe] appeared to them, and when she appeared they saw the apparitions of many deities disappear who had been attending her. There, comforted and accepted with a gracious countenance, they stepped forward, and conquered by the splendour of that majesty, they bent their knees to the earth. All together, with the diversity of tone that their diverse talents dictated, they revealed their prayers to the goddess. In conclusion, this is how she treated them: blind, wanderers, and unfortunate sufferers, they have crossed every river, climbed every mountain, traversed every plain for ten years, until they entered under the temperate sky of the Britannic island, and arrived in the presence of the lovely and gracious Nymphs of father Thames. There, after having made acts of appropriate humility, and having been accepted by those Nymphs with gestures of noble courtesy, one of them, the leader, who will be identified for you on some other occasion, in tragic and woeful tones presented their common cause in this fashion:

· Di que', madonne, che col chiuso vase
si fan presenti, et han trafitt' il core,
non per commesso da natur' errore,
ma d'una cruda sorte
ch'in sì vivace morte
le tien astretti, ogn'un cieco rimase.

Siam nove spirti che molt' anni, erranti,
per brama di saper, molti paesi
abbiam discorsi, e fummo un dì surpresi
d'un rigid' accidente,
per cui (se siete attente)
direte: «O degni, et o infelici amanti».

Un'empia Circe, che si don' il vanto
d'aver questo bel sol progenitore,
ne accolse dopo vario e lungo errore;
e un certo vase aperse,
de le cui acqui insperse
noi tutti, et a quel far giunse l'incanto.

Noi aspettand' il fine di tal opra,
eravam con silenzio muto attenti,
sin al punto che disse: «O voi dolenti,
itene ciechi in tutto;
raccogliete quel frutto,
che trovan troppo attenti al che gli è sopra».

«Figlia e madre di tenebre et orrore
– diss' ogn'un fatto cieco di repente, –
dumque ti piacque cossì fieramente
trattar miseri amanti,
che ti si fero avanti,
facili forse a consecrart' il core?»

Ma poi ch'a i lassi fu sedato alquanto
quel subito furor, ch'il novo caso

These men, Ladies, their vessel sealed tight
Present themselves, each with his skewered heart
Not for an error made on Nature's part
But by a cruel fate
That keeps them in a state
Of living death, for each has lost his sight.

Nine spirits we, who, eager to discover,
Wandered for years, traversing many realms
Until the day when we were overwhelmed
By cruel accident
Of which (if you're intent)
You'll say, "O worthy, o unlucky lovers!"

A faithless Circe, vaunting in her station
(The Sun had been her father, so she'd say)
Received us on our long and varied way
She opened up a vase
And sprinkled all of us
With liquid, as she sang an incantation.

In muted silence, waiting, we stood by
For the procedure's end, wholly enthralled
Until she said, "You sufferers, one and all
Go forth entirely blind
Collect fruit of the kind
That's fit for those who fix their thoughts too high."

"O child and dam of dark and gloomy arts"
(Said all of those now suddenly struck blind)
"Is cruelty the way you had in mind
To treat us wretched swains
Who thus before you came
Prepared, perhaps, to dedicate our hearts?"

But once the sudden fury was sedated
In those poor men, at fortune's revelation

porse, ciascun più accolto in sé rimaso,
mentr' ira al dolor cede,
voltossi alla mercede,
con tali accenti accompagnand' il pianto:

«Or dumque s'a voi piace, o nobil maga,
che zel di gloria forse il cor ti punga,
o liquor di pietà il lenisca et unga,
farti piatosa a noi
co' medicami tuoi,
saldand' al nostro cuor l'impressa piaga;

se la man bella è di soccorrer vaga,
deh non sia tanto la dimora lunga,
che di noi triste alcun a morte giunga
pria che per gesti tuoi
possiam umqua dir noi:
tanto ne tormentò, ma più ne appaga».

E lei soggiunse: «O curiosi ingegni,
prendete un altro mio vase fatale,
che mia mano medesma aprir non vale;
per largo e per profondo
peregrinate il mondo,
cercate tutti i numerosi regni:

perché vuol il destin che discuoperto
mai vegna, se non quando alta saggezza
e nobil castità giunte a bellezza
v'applicaran le mani;
d'altri i studi son vani
per far questo liquor al ciel aperto.

All'or, s'avvien ch'aspergan le man belle
chiumque a lor per remedio s'avicina,
provar potrete la virtù divina:
ch'a mirabil contento
cangiand' il rio tormento,
vedrete due più vaghe al mondo stelle.

Then each of them stood rapt in contemplation
As wrath gave way to pain,
They turned to her again
And cried out as the tears flowed unabated:

"If ever, please, O noble sorceress,
Some arrow of the zeal for glory points you
Or kindly humor softens and anoints you
Be merciful with us
And with your tonics thus
Knit up the wounds within our hearts impressed.

If your sweet hand should long for helpful action
Come! Let there be no harrowing delays
Let some of us meet death along the way
Before we by your acts
Can give away the fact
That pain was less than was the satisfaction."

And she replied, "Now, you inquiring minds,
Receive from me this strangely destined jar
Whose seal my hand has failed to breach so far
And wander all the earth
Deeply and widely, search
In all the many kingdoms you may find:

For destiny decrees that it shall ne'er
Be opened, unless rare sagacity
With beauty joined, and noble chastity
Hands to the task apply;
The others need not try
To open up this liquid to the air.

And when those hands have sprinkled every soul
Who comes to them in order to be healed,
Then shall its holy power be revealed
That makes wondrous content
Of criminal torment
You'll see the two best stars that heaven holds.

Tra tanto alcun di voi non si contriste,
quantumque a lungo in tenebre profonde
quant'è sul firmamento se gli asconde:
perché cotanto bene
per quantumque gran pene
mai degnamente avverrà che s'acquiste.

Per quell' a cui cecità vi conduce,
dovete aver a vil ogn'altro avere,
e stimar tutti strazii un gran piacere;
ché sperando mirare
tai grazie uniche o rare,
ben potrete spreggiar ogni altra luce».

Lassi, è troppo gran tempo che raminghe
per tutt' il terren globo nostre membra
son ite, sì ch'al fine a tutti sembra
che la fiera sagace
di speranza fallace
il petto n'ingombrò con sue lusinghe.

Miseri, ormai siam (bench'al tardi) avisti
ch'a quella maga, per più nostro male,
tenerci a bada eternamente cale;
certo perché lei crede
che donna non si vede
sott' il manto del ciel con tanti acquisti.

Or benché sappiam vana ogni speranza,
cedemo al destin nostr' e siam contenti
di non ritrarci da penosi stenti,
e mai fermando i passi
(benché trepidi e lassi)
languir tutta la vita che n'avanza.

Leggiadre Nimfe, ch'a l'erbose sponde
del Tamesi gentil fate soggiorno,
deh, per dio, non abiate (o belle) a scorno
tentar voi anco in vano

Not one of you should give in to dismay
However long the wait or deep the night
Through which the heavens keep you from all sight
The goodness that you gain
No matter what the pain
Is worth far more than any price you pay.

To reach the goal to which your blindness leads
You ought to hold all other goods as toys
And look upon your agonies as joys
In hopes that you may face
Such rare and peerless grace
Justly despising other lights than these."

Too long, alas! as wandering refugees
Our weary limbs have trod the earthly sphere
Until to each of us it would appear
That she, the clever pest,
Has burdened every breast
With hopes as false as all her flatteries.

Poor mortals, now we know (however late)
That to our greater harm it shall befall
The sorceress to keep us in her thrall.
For surely she must know
No woman here below
Has been observed endowed with gifts so great.

Although we know that every hope's in vain
Let's give in to our fate and be content
To face our miseries without relent
And never cease our trek
(Each one a timid wreck)
Enduring what of life may yet remain.

You gracious Nymphs who make your gentle stay
Along the grassy banks of Thames, we ask
By God, fair ladies, don't disdain the task
Of trying, if you might

con vostra bianca mano
di scuoprir quel ch'il nostro vase asconde.

    Chi sa? forse che in queste spiaggie, dove
con le Nereidi sue questo torrente
si vede che cossì rapidamente
da basso in su rimonte
riserpendo al suo fonte,
ha destinat' il ciel ch'ella si trove.

ॐ

Prese una de le Ninfe il vase in mano, e senza altro tentare, offrillo ad
una per una, di sorte che non si trovò chi ardisse provar prima: ma
tutte de commun consentimento, dopo averlo solamente remirato, il
riferivano e proponevano per rispetto e riverenza ad una sola; la quale
finalmente non tanto per far pericolo di sua gloria, quanto per pietà
e desìo di tentar il soccorso di questi infelici, mentre dubbia lo con-
trattava, come spontaneamente s'aperse da se stesso. Che volete ch'io
vi referisca quanto fusse e quale l'applauso de le Nimfe? Come possete credere ch'io possa esprimere l'estrema allegrezza de nove ciechi,
quando udiro del vase aperto, si sentiro aspergere dell'acqui bramate,
apriro gli occhi e veddero gli doi soli; e trovarono aver doppia felicitade: l'una della ricovrata già persa luce, l'altra della nuovamente
discuoperta, che sola possea mostrargli l'imagine del sommo bene in
terra? Come, dico, volete ch'io possa esprimere quella allegrezza e tri-
pudio de voci, di spirto e di corpo, che lor medesimi tutti insieme non
posseano esplicare? Fu per un pezzo il veder tanti furiosi debaccanti,
in senso di color che credono sognare, et in vista di quelli che non
credeno quello che apertamente veggono: sin tanto che tranquillato
essendo alquanto l'impeto del furore, se misero in ordine di ruota,
dove:

ॐ

Il primo cantava e sonava la citara in questo tenore:
O rupi, o fossi, o spine, o sterpi, o sassi,
o monti, o piani, o valli, o fiumi, o mari,
quanto vi discuoprite grati e cari,

With you own hands so white
To uncover what our vessel hides away.

Who knows? Perhaps it's on this very ground
Surrounded by the Nereids, who see
The river move with such rapidity
Setting an upward course
Recoiling to its source
That heaven has decided she'll be found.

꒰꒱

One of the Nymphs took the vessel in hand, and without making any further attempt, passed it to her companions one by one, in such a way that not one dared to try it first, but all, by common consent, after having done no more than look at it, passed it on and offered it, out of respect and reverence, to one alone, and when she, at last, not so much to meet the challenge to her reputation, but out of pity and desire to help these poor souls, handled it hesitantly, it opened spontaneously, almost by itself. What do you want me to say about the Nymphs' applause, how great it was and how enthusiastic? How can you believe that I could ever express the extreme joy of the nine blind men when they heard the vessel open, felt themselves sprinkled by the longed-for waters, opened their eyes and beheld those two alone; and they discovered that they had a double joy: one, in their recovered sight, and the other in this newly discovered sight that alone could show them the highest good on earth? How, I say, do you want me to convey the happiness, the dance of voices, spirit, and body that they themselves were unable to express? For a while there was nothing to see but the frenzied bacchanal of those who think that they are dreaming when they are awake, and those who behold what they never thought to see openly, until, when the rush of their frenzy had calmed somewhat, they formed themselves into a circle, in which:

꒰꒱

The First sang and played the cithara in this strain:
O crags, O gorges, O thorns, O rocks, O trees,
O mountains, O plains, O valleys, O rivers, O sea!
How dear and welcome now you prove to be

ché mercé vostra e merto
n'ha fatt' il ciel aperto:
o fortunatamente spesi passi.

જી

Il secondo con la mandòra sua sonò e cantò:
O fortunatamente spesi passi,
o diva Circe, o gloriosi affanni;
o quanti n'affligeste mesi et anni,
    tante grazie divine,
     se tal è nostro fine
dopo che tanto travagliati e lassi.

જી

Il terzo con la lira sonò e cantò:
Dopo che tanto travagliati e lassi,
se tal porto han prescritto le tempeste,
non fia ch'altro da far oltre ne reste
    che ringraziar il cielo
     ch'oppose a gli occhi il velo,
per cui presente al fin tal luce fassi.

જી

Il quarto con la viola cantò:
Per cui present' al fin tal luce fassi,
cecità degna più ch'altro vedere,
cure suavi più ch'altro piacere;
    ch'a la più degna luce
     vi siete fatte duce:
con far men degni oggetti a l'alma cassi.

જી

Il quinto con un timpano d'Ispagna cantò:
Con far men degni oggetti a l'alma cassi,
con condir di speranza alto pensiero,
fu chi ne spinse a l'unico sentiero,

For by your grace and merit
Our heaven we inherit;
O fortunate the footsteps that were these!

৵

The Second, with his mandolin, played and sang:
O fortunate the footsteps that were these!
O divine Circe! O glorious tears!
How sore you plagued me over months and years
Yet what a blessed state
If this should be our fate
After such labours and such miseries.

৵

The Third, with the lyre, played and sang:
After such labours and such miseries
Is this the port our tempests shall ordain?
Then let no other task to us remain
Than raising to the skies
Our thanks for veiled eyes:
The light has made its presence known through these.

৵

The Fourth, with the viola, sang:
The light has made its presence known through these;
Hence, blindness is more praiseworthy than sight.
Care's sweeter far than any fair delight.
This great illumination
You made our destination,
As lesser goals now fail the soul to please.

৵

The Fifth, with a Spanish tambourine, sang:
As lesser goals now fail the soul to please
By leavening our lofty thought with hope,
You pushed us up the one and only slope

per cui a noi si scuopra
de Dio la più bell'opra:
cossì fato benigno a mostrar vassi.

༯

Il sesto con un laùto cantò:
Cossì fato benigno a mostrar vassi;
perché non vuol ch'il ben succeda al bene,
o presagio di pene sien le pene;
 ma svoltando la ruota,
 or inalze, ora scuota:
com'a vicenda il dì e la notte dassi.

༯

Il settimo con l'arpa d'Ibernia:
Come a vicenda il dì e la notte dassi,
mentr' il gran manto de faci notturne
scolora il carro de fiamme diurne:
 talmente chi governa
 con legge sempiterna
supprime gli eminenti, e inalz' i bassi.

༯

L'ottavo con la viola ad arco:
Supprime gli eminenti, e inalza i bassi,
chi l'infinite machini sustenta:
e con veloce, mediocre e lenta
 vertigine dispensa
 in questa mole immensa
quant'occolto si rende e aperto stassi.

༯

Il nono con una rebecchina:
Quant'occolto si rend'e aperto stassi,
o non nieghi, o confermi che prevagli
l'incomparabil fine a gli travagli
 campestri e montanari

That held the revelation
Of God's highest creation
And thus our bitter fate began to ease.

※

The Sixth, with a lute, sang:
And thus our bitter fate began to ease
Not wanting what begins well to end well,
Nor evil only evil to foretell;
Fate set the wheel's rotation,
Its plunge and elevation,
As day and night grant mutual release.

※

The Seventh, with an Irish harp:
As day and night grant mutual release
When night's star-spangled mantle steals away
The colour from the chariot of day
Our ruler thus secures
His Law that e'er endures:
Toppling the lofty as the low increase.

※

The Eighth, with a violà da braccio:
Toppling the lofty as the low increase,
The keeper of the infinite machines
By spinning quickly, slowly, in between,
Arranges to dispense
Within this world immense
What hides away, and everybody sees.

※

*The Ninth, with a rebec.*[83]
What hides away, and everybody sees:
Deny it not; confirm that it prevails,
And marks the peerless end to our travails
Through mountain, countryside,

de stagni, fiumi, mari,
de rupi, fossi, spine, sterpi, sassi.

ॐ

Dopo che ciascuno in questa forma singularmente sonando il suo in-
strumento ebbe cantata la sua sestina, tutti insieme ballando in ruota
e sonando in lode de l'unica Nimfa con un suavissimo concento can-
tarono una canzona, la quale non so se bene mi verrà a la memoria.

GIULIA. Non mancar (ti priego, sorella) di farmi udire quel tanto che ti
potrà sovvenire.

LAODOMIA:

ॐ

### Canzone de gl'illuminati

«Non oltre invidio, o Giove, al firmamento,»
dice il padre Oceàn col ciglio altero,
   «se tanto son contento
per quel che godo nel proprio impero»;

   «Che superbia è la tua?» Giove risponde,
«alle ricchezze tue che cosa è gionta?
   o dio de le insan' onde,
perché il tuo folle ardir tanto surmonta?»

   «Hai,» disse il dio de l'acqui, «in tuo potere
il fiammeggiante ciel, dov'è l'ardente
   zon', in cui l'eminente
coro de tuoi pianeti puoi vedere.

   Tra quelli tutt' il mondo admira il sole,
qual ti so dir che tanto non risplende
   quanto lei che mi rende
più glorioso dio de la gran mole.

   Et io comprendo nel mio vasto seno
tra gli altri quel paese, ove il felice

Pond, river, ocean wide,
Through crags and gorges, thorns and rocks and trees.

ॐ

After each one, in this form, individually playing his instrument, had sung his own sestet, then all together, dancing in a circle and sounding forth the praises of the one and only Nymph, they sang a song in sweetest harmony; I do not know if I shall remember it all.

GIULIA: Please, sister, do not fail to let me hear whatever you recall of it.

LAODOMIA:

ॐ

### Song of the Enlightened

"O Jove, I envy not your firmament,"
Said father Ocean, with his haughty glance,
"For I am well content
With such delights as my own empire grants."

"What arrogance is this?" Great Jove replied.
"What's added to the riches that you know?
God of the raging tide
Why does your crazy daring overflow?"

"You have," the briny god said, "in your hands
The flaming heaven, where the Zodiac
Bears on its burning back
The chorus of the planets in their dance.

The Sun earns universal admiration
Among them, but I tell you that it pales
Before her who regales
Me with the brightest light in all creation.

And I within my vasty breast contain
That land among all others whence the Thames,

> Tamesi veder lice,
> ch'ha de più vaghe ninfe il coro ameno.
>
> Tra quelle ottegno tal fra tutte belle,
> per far del mar più che del ciel amante
> te Giove altitonante,
> cui tanto il sol non splende tra le stelle»;
>
> Giove responde: «O dio d'ondosi mari,
> ch'altro si trove più di me beato
> non lo permetta il fato;
> ma miei tesori e tuoi corrano al pari.
>
> Vagl' il sol tra tue ninfe per costei;
> e per vigor de leggi sempiterne,
> de le dimore alterne,
> costei vaglia per sol tra gli astri miei».

Credo averla riportata intieramente tutta.

GIULIA: Il puoi conoscere, perché non vi manca sentenza che possa appartener alla perfezzion del proposito; né rima che si richieda per compimento de le stanze. Or io, se per grazia del cielo ottenni d'esser bella, maggior grazia e favor credo che mi sia gionto: perché qualumque fusse la mia beltade, è stata in qualche maniera principio per far discuoprir quell'unica e divina. Ringrazio gli dèi, perché in quel tempo che io fui sì verde, che le amorose fiamme non si posseano accendere nel petto mio, mediante la mia tanto restia quanto semplice et innocente crudeltade, han preso mezzo per concedere incomparabilmente grazie maggiori a'C miei amanti, che altrimente avessero possute ottenere per quantumque grande mia benignitade.

LAODOMIA: Quanto a gli animi di quelli amanti, io ti assicuro ancora, che come non sono ingrati alla sua maga Circe, fosca cecitade, calamitosi pensieri et aspri travagli, per mezzo de quali son gionti a tanto bene: cossì non potranno di te esser poco ben riconoscenti.

GIULIA: Cossì desidero, e spero.

That happy river, stems,
Whose lovely nymphs gambol in pleasant train.

And one among them beams with such a light
As ought to make you, Thunderer on high,
Love sea better than sky.
Your Sun can't so outshine the starry night."

Jove answered: "God who rules the bounding sea,
My happiness can never be exceeded,
For so Fate has decreed it,
But we may share our riches equally.

Among your nymphs the sun shall take the station
She held, and by the laws that regulate
Our kingdoms alternate
She'll shed her glow among my constellations.

꒰꒱

I believe that I have remembered it all.[84]

GIULIA: You can see so yourself: for there is no sentence lacking from the perfection of the argument, nor rhyme missing from the completion of the stanzas. Now, if I have obtained Heaven's favour in being beautiful, I believe that I have also obtained still greater grace and favour because, whatever my beauty may have been, it has also been in some wise a beginning from which to discover that unique and divine beauty. I thank the gods, that at the time when I was so green that amorous flames could not be lit in my breast, through my stubborn, simple, and innocent cruelty, they made use of this means to grant incomparably greater grace to my lovers than they would otherwise have been able to obtain through some great kindness of mine.

LAODOMIA: As for the spirits of those lovers, I assure you again that, just as they are not ungrateful to their sorceress Circe, gloomy blindness, calamitous thoughts, or harsh travails, because through these they have arrived at such sovereign goodness, so, too, they cannot but owe you no small gratitude.

GIULIA: So I desire, and so I hope.

# Notes

## The Nolan's Argument of the Heroic Frenzies

1 See, e.g., the *Merriam-Webster Dictionary*, s.v. *argument*: "4: an abstract or summary especially of a literary work."

2 As Shakespeare would soon have his Jacques say, "All the world's a stage." (*As You Like It*, 2.7). The "theatre of the world" is an important Renaissance trope that precedes both Bruno and Shakespeare, and this line is only one of several passages in the *Eroici furori* that seem to have evocative echoes in the Bard's work; see Hilary Gatti, *The Renaissance Drama of Knowledge: Giordano Bruno in England* (London and New York: Routledge, 1989); Gilberto Sacerdoti, *Sovranità e sacrificio. Teologia e politica nell'Europa di Shakespeare e Bruno* (Turin: Einaudi, 2002). A more difficult question to answer, but an intriguing one, is the extent to which English writers like Sir Philip Sidney have echoes in Bruno.

3 A fever that recurred every four days; probably malaria.

4 In Homer's *Odyssey*, the enchantress Circe serves a potion to the companions of Odysseus that turns them all into animals. In ancient times her realm was already associated with the Italian promontory north of Naples and south of Rome now known as San Felice Circeo; hence, for Bruno she was a local heroine as well as an evocative mythological figure. He was particularly fascinated by her ability to reveal the essential animality of human beings, and here her spell is certainly one that brings out the animal side of sexuality. Later in the dialogue, Bruno will deepen and complicate Circe's significance.

5 Bruno's idea of who might be "qualified to pass judgment and render an opinion" can be gathered by his remarks to his Inquisitors late in his seven-year trial for heresy, when they had ordered him to recant eight proposi-

tions drawn from his work. As they wrote: "You replied that if the Holy See
and the Holiness of Our Lord had declared eight propositions as defini-
tively heretical, or that His Holiness knew them to be such, or that they had
been so defined by the Holy Spirit, then you were disposed to revoke them."

6 In Greek and Roman myth, the Rhipaean Mountains (Bruno, whose knowledge of Greek was probably spotty, spells it "Riphaean") stood in perpetual
snow on the boundary between the known world and the land of the fabu-
lous, highly civilized Hyperboreans (people "Beyond the North Wind").
The snows of the Rhipaean mountains resembled feathers, and the range
was patrolled by fierce griffins who stood guard over pots of gold. The origin of the Rhipaean mountains may have been the Urals, just as the myth of
the Hyperboreans may have been inspired by reports in early Greek times
of the Chinese.

7 Wisdom 11:21.

8 This remark is usually taken as a more pointed denunciation than Bruno's
usual sallies against "pedant-asses" and pompous priests. The most immediate target for his ire may have been the dons of Oxford, who, on his visit
there, had laughed at his Italian-accented Latin and accused him of plagiarism. He had lampooned them memorably in his first English dialogue, *The
Ash Wednesday Supper*, published in 1584. His next dialogue, *On the Cause,
Principle and One*, published shortly after *The Ash Wednesday Supper* in 1584,
laments that he has become a prisoner within the French embassy because
of the hostility his remarks about Oxford dons and Cockney rabble have
aroused among the English.

9 Song of Songs 4:1–5, 11:

   1 Behold, thou art fair, my love; behold, thou art fair; thou hast doves'
eyes within thy locks: thy hair is as a flock of goats, that appear from
mount Gilead.

   2 Thy teeth are like a flock of sheep that are even shorn, which came up
from the washing; whereof every one bear twins, and none is barren
among them.

   3 Thy lips are like a thread of scarlet, and thy speech is comely: thy temples are like a piece of a pomegranate within thy locks.

   4 Thy neck is like the tower of David builded for an armoury, whereon
there hang a thousand bucklers, all shields of mighty men.

   5 Until the day break, and the shadows flee away, I will get me to the
mountain of myrrh, and to the hill of frankincense.

   ...

  11 Thy lips, O my spouse, drop as the honeycomb: honey and milk are
under thy tongue; and the smell of thy garments is like the smell of
Lebanon.

10 Cythereis was apparently the "real" name of the courtesan celebrated as
   Lycoris in the love elegies of the first-century Roman poet Cornelius Gallus
   (which no longer survive). Doris was a passing flame of the Roman poet
   Sextus Propertius, and Cynthia the chief subject of his love elegies. Valerius
   Catullus addressed his love poetry to Lesbia, Ovid to Corinna, and Petrarch,
   twelve centuries later, to Laura.
11 Bruno is referring to a myth from Plato's dialogue *Phaedrus*, in which the
   soul, burning with love, takes on wings and flies back to the transcendent
   world of Ideas.
12 Anaxagoras lived in Athens at the time of his friend Pericles.
13 Bruno is referring, as he does incessantly in this dedication, to Petrarch.
14 Here Bruno is thinking of the description of Britain given by the Roman
   poet Vergil: "the Britons, divided off from the whole world," *Eclogue* I, 66.
15 The Inquisition would draw pointed attention to the several occasions on
   which Bruno likened Elizabeth, a Protestant queen, to a goddess. Bruno, in
   turn, noted that such extravagant praise was a customary form of flattery in
   Elizabethan England and should not be taken literally.
16 "Act" and "potential" are the two categories by which Aristotle described the
   workings of the soul in his *On the Soul* (*De Anima*).
17 Bruno uses the term "articoli," which can sometimes mean a poem, but
   here probably means the combination of verse and explanation. In fact
   there are eight sonnets in part 1, and this description applies to the first five
   of them.
18 Literally, "cognitive and apprehensive powers."
19 Song of Songs 2:9.
20 Ibid. 1:6.
21 Bruno uses the term *vicissitudine*, but because "vicissitude" in English has
   come to connote "misfortune" rather than Bruno's idea of a strict alternation between extremes of every kind, the translation uses "alternation." This
   principle of alternation or succession forms one of the pillars of the Nolan
   philosophy.
22 Song of Songs 2:10–12, paraphrased.
23 The term "gas" had not yet been invented for vapours; that would come
   with Lavoisier in the eighteenth century.
24 Proverbs 25:27.
25 Giordano Bruno, *Summa terminorum metaphysicorum* (*Summa of Metaphysical
   Terms*, Zürich 1595), s.v. *modus*: "The modes of a being are the terms for
   whatever is in beings that cannot be strictly termed substances or accidents,
   like the essence of a thing, the existence of a thing, or the degree in a quality such as heat or cold. Existence is the mode of essence, material causality
   is the mode of matter, which is a thing.

26 Aristotle and his school were called "wanderers," *peripatetikoi*, because they travelled extensively (as, in fact, did Plato's students).

27 Bruno's Dominican education looked to Aristotle for the foundations of philosophy in all its various aspects, from natural philosophy to metaphysics.

28 This separate heading is Bruno's, probably because the fifth dialogue of the second part represents the climax and final revelation of the *Eroici furori*.

29 Bruno acknowledges here that his view of women's capacities has been limited by the strictures of his own Neapolitan society (and his Dominican convent) rather than the society of Elizabethan England. For Bruno's misogyny, see the Introduction, xix–xxii.

30 In other words, the nine men are the heavenly bodies, each guided by angels as they are in Dante's *Divine Comedy*. The number nine was traditional; in addition to Earth, Moon, Mercury, Venus, Sun, Mars, Jupiter, Saturn, it included the sphere of the Fixed Stars. Bruno no longer believed that the stars were fixed on a sphere, but he still did believe in numerology, the idea that individual numbers were endowed with special individual qualities, and nine endowed with more special qualities than most.

31 Vergil, who was also regarded as a poet with a "naturally Christian soul." The citation comes from *Aeneid* 6.748–9, 751; as often with Bruno's citations, it is paraphrased rather than exact.

32 Revelation 20:1–3:
   1 And I saw an angel come down from heaven, having the key of the bottomless pit and a great chain in his hand.
   2 And he laid hold on the dragon, that old serpent, which is the Devil, and Satan, and bound him a thousand years,
   3 And cast him into the bottomless pit, and shut him up, and set a seal upon him, that he should deceive the nations no more, till the thousand years should be fulfilled: and after that he must be loosed a little season.

33 As Bruno observes, the time that it takes each planet to make a complete revolution of the Sun is different; therefore the length of the "year" varies from individual planet to individual planet, and the length of the solar year applies only to the Sun. (The same reasoning would apply, of course, to an Earth-centred cosmos.) His own view that the universe was infinite in extent, and was made up of hot "suns" orbited by cold "earths," simply compounded the number of individual planetary "species" to be found there. The relationship between time and the planets was one of urgent interest in Bruno's day. In the 1570s, as Bruno began his European wanderings, Pope Gregory XIII commissioned a reform of the calendar, entrusting the project's technical aspects to the Jesuit Christoph Clavius, the famous

professor of mathematics (which then included astronomy) at the Jesuits' Roman college. The resulting "Gregorian" Calendar, the same one we use today, was finally presented in 1583. Bruno had been a neighbour of Clavius in Rome in 1576, for the Dominican convent of Santa Maria sopra Minerva was located next to the Jesuits' lodgings. There is no evidence, however, that the two men ever met.

By presenting the idea of a different rhythm for stellar time Bruno also suggests a potential solution to the looming problem that motion poses within an infinite universe. The traditional Aristotelian-Ptolemaic cosmology required the entire universe to revolve around the earth every 24 hours, evidently at incredible speed; by having Earth move around the Sun, Copernicus envisioned a far more efficient cosmic machine. Bruno's infinitely larger universe required the stars and planets to traverse infinitely larger distances, with implications for the speed at which the heavenly bodies moved.

34 This passage has been compared to several passages in Plotinus, including *Enneads* 2.3, 3.4.6, and 3.4. But Bruno also read Plotinus as filtered through Neoplatonists like Marsilio Ficino (Giovanni Aquilecchia compares Ficino, *In Plotinum* 4.8.2), and Giles of Viterbo. He was, in any case, a selective reader.

35 Bruno's reading of Origen, like his reading of Plotinus, came on several levels: reading Origen's original texts, reading what Neoplatonists like Ficino and Giles of Viterbo had to say about Origen (which was a great deal), and selective sifting of what he had read.

36 Bruno uses "shadow" and "footprint," *ombra* and *vestigio*, Latin *umbra* and *vestigium*, in a specific philosophical sense: to mean traces of divinity in the physical world that reflect divinity in their beauty and harmony, but do not look like God. (A more direct image of God can be found in the human soul, made, according to Genesis, in God's "image and likeness.") The terms themselves go back to Plato, but they were extensively developed by Marsilio Ficino in the fifteenth century and the Augustinian prelate Giles of Viterbo in the sixteenth. Bruno's thoughts here show surprisingly extensive parallels to Giles, whose work Bruno would have known through his first teacher of logic, the Augustinian friar Teofilo da Vairano.

37 Here Bruno declares that Circe is not simply a mythological figure, but a cosmological one, and her relationship with the nine blind men, which seems to occur on the human plane, is also occurring among heavenly bodies in infinite space.

38 See dialogue 2.5, p. 343.

39 See dialogue 2.5, p. 345.

40 "Whose seal my hand has failed to breach so far," dialogue 2.5. p. 345.

41 The waters above the firmament (*mayim b'shamayim*) appear in Genesis 1:6–
7: "And God said, Let there be a firmament in the midst of the waters, and
let it divide the waters from the waters. And God made the firmament, and
divided the waters which were under the firmament from the waters which
were above the firmament, and it was so." Bruno's interpretation reflects, as
so often in this passage, his readings of Ficino and Christian Neoplatonists
like Giles of Viterbo.

42 This triad will be embodied in the myth of the Judgment of Paris in dialogue 1.5, where Venus represents beauty, Minerva wisdom, and Juno just
authority. Fifteenth- and sixteenth-century Neoplatonist writers like Marsilio
Ficino and Giles of Viterbo played with different kinds of divine trinities,
always with reference to the Holy Trinity. Bruno seems to accept the idea
of Plato and Plotinus that God may be considered under three different
aspects, but he rejected the Holy Trinity per se, as he told the Inquisition in
Venice.

43 John 4:14: "But the water that I shall give him shall be in him a well of water
springing up into everlasting life." John 6:38: "He that believeth on me, as
the scripture hath said, out of his belly shall flow rivers of living water."

44 Vergil, *Eclogue* I.66. Bruno has already referred to the line once in this dedication (see above, note 14), and used it also in *On the Cause, Principle, and
One.*

45 Here Bruno means to refer to the Thames, but the Thames in turn is
praised as if it were a river of Paradise.

46 Bruno's extravagant praise for Queen Elizabeth would not sit well with the
Inquisition, for he was not only praising a Protestant, but also calling her a
goddess and therefore practising idolatry.

47 By making Elizabeth epitomize truth and beauty, Bruno is likening her to
God, and preparing his later troubles with the Inquisition.

48 In other words, Bruno has made his very style of writing conform to his vision of the cosmos.

49 The changes from "we" to "I" throughout this sonnet are Bruno's own.

### First Part of the Heroic Frenzies

1 The decorative elements that appear in the dialogue were placed by Bruno
himself. They "frame" each poetic interlude.

2 The victors in ancient Greek poetry contests were rewarded with crowns
woven of plants. As Bruno will explain shortly, myrtle, sacred to Venus,
symbolized lyric poetry, and laurel, the plant symbolic of Apollo, patron of
poetry, also more specifically denoted epic.

3 The mountain is Helicon, part of the Parnassus range and home of the Muses (the goddesses). The fountainhead is the Hippocrene, the "horse spring" that sprang forth on Helicon when the winged horse Pegasus struck his hoof against its rock.

4 Bruno, unlike Plato, likes to begin his dialogues rather abruptly *in medias res*, as here, where we are not exactly clear who "he," the subject under discussion and the subject of the sonnet, might be. It will emerge gradually that "he" is what Bruno will call the frenzied hero.

5 The couplet, a vernacular paraphrase of a Latin epigram by the Roman poet Martial (*Epigrams* 8.56 [55], 6) is addressed to Horace (whose full name was Quintus Horatius Flaccus). It makes the point that so long as poets can depend on patrons like Gaius Cilnius Maecenas, friend of Augustus and generous sponsor of Horace, Vergil, and Propertius (among others), there will continue to be poets.

By the time Bruno wrote the *Eroici furori* he was well aware that his own patron, Michel de Castelnau, was in an extremely precarious financial state, and continuing to serve as French ambassador in London because he had no money to go elsewhere. By dedicating this dialogue to Sir Philip Sidney, Bruno hoped to gain the Englishman's sponsorship, and thus avoid having to return to Paris with Castelnau's entourage. His hopes would remain unfulfilled.

6 *Species* as a term of restrictive classification goes back to ancient Rome (Cicero and Vitruvius are first to use it); the word means "appearance."

7 Normally, *ingegno* is translated "wit," but here there is an echo in Bruno's Italian with *geni* and *ingegni*, as well as a context that makes "genius" appropriate.

8 Fescennine verses, one of the ancient Romans' native poetic forms, probably derived originally from an ancient Italic fertility ritual; hence the obscenity of these traditional songs combined entertainment with a solemn religious purpose.

9 The lines come from a ribald poem by Pietro Aretino (1492–1556), "All'Albicante." Bruno, as his vernacular dialogues show, was an avid reader of comic verse.

10 Here Tansillo is making the Platonic distinction between the transcendental world of Ideas and the material world. By the time that Bruno wrote the *Eroici furori*, he no longer believed that there was transcendental reality lying beyond the infinite universe. Tansillo is therefore explaining not a final version of Bruno's philosophy, but rather an intermediate stage that will be deepened in the second half of the work. Like Plato's Socrates, he is an outstanding man of the previous generation who has almost reached full enlightenment, but not quite.

11 Although there must be a line missing, the poem's sense is complete as is.

12 This curious rhyme scheme is Tansillo's own.

13 The Greek physician Hippocrates (in the essay *Airs Waters Places*) and the ancient Roman architect Vitruvius (in book 5 of his *Ten Books on Architecture*) both wrote about the effect of geographical position and climate on human populations, each concluding, not surprisingly, that his own homeland was the best of all places for human habitation. Bruno follows Vitruvius in asserting that northerners, because of their thicker blood, are slow-witted, sluggish, and brave in a somewhat stolid manner; by the time he wrote he had amassed a good deal of evidence for such differences as he passed from Naples through northern Italy and France on to England. The first dialogue he wrote in England, *The Ash Wednesday Supper*, includes a bitter denunciation of London's lower classes as well as a blast at the pedants of Oxford, which concludes that he, the Nolan, has better manners because he was born under "a more benign Heaven."

14 By using the phrase *la cosa amata*, "the thing he loves," Bruno makes it clear that such transcendent love does not have a human object.

15 Wisdom 11:21 (see also the Dedication to Sir Philip Sidney, p. 9.

16 The Apulian poet is Horace, who was born in the mountains of southern Italy in Venusia (present-day Venosa); Bruno gives a vernacular translation of the three opening lines from Horace's *Epistles*, 1.1.1–3.

17 Literally, Love turns "images of absent things into real presences," that is, in Platonic terms, Love transforms the recollected image of the beloved into a real presence by propelling the lover into the realm of Ideas, so that what the lover contemplates is no longer the individual beloved thing, but the absolute beauty and goodness of which that thing is an earthly representation.

18 Here, as often, Bruno is dividing human nature into threes, following the Italian Neoplatonists in exploring endless ramifications of Augustine's division of the human soul into memory, intellect, and will (see note 82 below). Augustine and Italian Neoplatonists like Ficino and Giles of Viterbo associated these triads with the Holy Trinity; Bruno associates them instead with the relationship between divine unity and the multiplicity of the infinite universe.

19 Thetis, mother of the hero Achilles, was a water nymph (a Nereid, one of the daughters of Nereus, the Old Man of the Sea); Vulcan, the blacksmith of the gods.

20 Bruno assumes that all earthly things are compounds rather than pure elements.

21 Vergil, *Aeneid* 6.733–4.

22  Bruno published this dialogue in 1585, just before publishing the *Heroic Frenzies.*

23  Ecclesiastes 1:18.

24  Iamblichus, writing in Greek, professed Platonic philosophy in the last years of the Roman Empire, but Bruno is actually quoting the comments of another Neoplatonist, Proclus, on Plato's dialogue *Alcibiades.* Both the *Egyptian Mysteries* of Iamblichus and the commentary of Proclus were translated from Greek to Latin by Marsilio Ficino, and they appear one after the other in the 1576 Basel edition of Ficino's *Opera omnia*, the edition Bruno must have been using when he made this slightly (but informatively) mistaken reference.

25  In Greek myth, Ixion was fettered to a wheel as punishment for trying to rape Hera (Roman Juno), the queen of the gods. Unlike an earthly wheel, however, on which common criminals (after having being beaten until their bones were broken, usually by the heavy wheel itself) were hoisted and exposed to the elements until they died, Ixion's wheel rotated eternally in the heavens as a constellation, with Ixion spread-eagled on it, his limbs intact.

26  Here "to the left," *a sinistra*, has properly sinister connotations; the Latin *laevus*, "left-handed," could also mean "crazy."

27  In Plato's dialogue *Symposium*, Socrates reports that the priestess Diotima told him how philosophers, in loving pursuit of higher truth, eventually "bring forth ideas in beauty" rather than begetting living children.

28  The structure of the sonnet takes to its extreme a favourite conceit of the late fifteenth-century popular singer Serafino Aquilano (d. 1499): the poetic dialogue. Serafino's usually involved a lover and death, as well as the wordplay that Bruno has mastered here with equal virtuosity. See Introduction.

29  The whole sonnet from which this couplet is taken appears in part 1, dialogue 5.

30  Here Bruno is referring to Plato's *Republic*, with its three-part division of the population of the ideal city-state into philosophically aware Guardians, courageous Warriors, and the undistinguished mass of the general populace.

31  The poet from Ferrara is Ludovico Ariosto (1474–1533). The couplet comes, appropriately, from his epic *Orlando furioso*, in which the knight Orlando goes temporarily insane for love. Bruno quotes the same line, *Orlando furioso*, 24.1, in his Latin work *De vinculis in genere.*

32  Erasmus included the image of the "ass carrying the sacraments" in his *Adages*, 1101: "Asinus portans mysteria." This passage is yet another instance of Bruno's fascination with *asinità*, a kind of divine stupidity to which he had dedicated his previous dialogue, *The Kabbalah of the Horse Pegasus.* His idea

of *asinità* was ultimately modelled on the silly, but eventually enlightened Lucius, who becomes the Golden Ass in the novel of Apuleius.

33 Nemesis.

34 As Bruno has warned us, in his dedication, Circe is a cosmic figure as well as a mythological one: she causes souls to follow their baser instincts and mix with matter. Proteus, the Old Man of the Sea, lives off the coast of Egypt and has to be wrestled before he will give up his secrets; he fights his adversaries by changing shape all the time. In Homer's *Odyssey*, clever Odysseus outsmarts both Circe and Proteus, and so, Bruno suggests, will anyone well armed by philosophy.

35 The speech of Pausanias in Plato's *Symposium* does indeed maintain that there are two kinds of Aphrodite, the heavenly goddess (*Ourania*) and the common (*Demotike*). Marsilio Ficino's *Commentary on the Symposium of Plato*, 2.7 simply states that Plato "names two kinds of Venus." But it is not Plato who "names two kinds of Venus" – rather, Pausanias says so, and Apollodorus, who reports on the speech, notes that Pausanias did not develop his point adequately! Bruno is a more acute reader and writer of dialogue than Ficino, and appropriately puts this statement early in his own dialogue, at a comparably basic stage in the development of his own philosophy – that is, he pays attention, as Ficino did not, to the original statement's context.

   Mention of Penelope takes the dialogue back once again to Homer's *Odyssey*, and the shrewd wife of Odysseus, who refused to marry anyone else despite the fact that her husband had been absent for twenty years. Both the suitors and the maidservants who slept with them would die when Odysseus returned, the men shot with bow and arrow, the women hanged from the roof beams.

36 Literally, the passage says: "contemplate the shadows of divine beauty (when he cannot see it in a mirror)," mindful of St Paul's words in 1 Corinthians 13:12: "But now we see through a glass, darkly; but then face to face: now I know in part; but then shall I know even as also I am known."

37 The word "cattivo" can mean either "captive" or "bad" (with the understanding that captivity is a debasing condition in itself). When he means "captive," Bruno normally uses the preposition *de/di* (as he uses "cattivo de amore" in 2.5). Here, "cattivi alla generazione" implies the idea "bad *for* reproduction" as well as "captive *with respect to* reproduction."

38 The strange meter and rhyme scheme are Bruno's own.

39 Contraction is the technical term that Bruno uses to describe God's descent into individuals. See Leo Catana, *The Concept of Conctraction in Giordano Bruno's Philosophy* (Aldershot: Ashgate, 2005).

40  Plotinus, *Ennead* 4.2.24, which Bruno probably read in Marsilio Ficino's translation.

41  David. The citation is from Psalm 42:2.

42  The line is from Isaiah 38:14, but Psalm 69:3 is similar: "Mine eyes fail while I wait for God."

43  In his introduction to Aristotle's *Physics*, Averroës wrote: "The substance of man is perfect and he can become perfect through speculative knowledge; and this state of things for him is happiness and eternal life"; as cited in Latin from the *Opera omnia* of Aristotle (Venice, 1574), vol. 4, p. 1H. For this information and an excellent bibliography, see the note by Miguel Angel Granada, ed., *Giordano Bruno, Oeuvres complètes, vol. VII, Des fureurs héroïques* (Paris: Les Belles Lettres, 1999, rev. ed., 2008), 535 n. 47.

44  Plato's allegory of the winged soul in *Phaedrus* exploited the contrast between rigorous philosophical exercise and the impetuous, undisciplined Icarus, unable to fly successfully on the wings of wax and feathers fashioned for him by his father Daedalus.

45  Plato's cave: An extended allegory in Plato's *Republic* likens normal human consciousness to life inside a cave, where the flickering shadows cast by firelight on the cave's walls represent what most people take for reality; true reality lies outside, in the light of the sun, but for any cave-dweller who ventures forth from the cave (that is, begins through philosophy to learn about higher realities) the initial impact of pure sunlight will be blinding.

46  In this statement, Bruno paraphrases Marsilio Ficino's commentary on Plotinus, *Ennead* 4.4.19.

47  Satan and the rebellious angels were believed to have rebelled against God by their own will.

48  Again, Bruno's reference comes not directly from Plotinus, but from Marsilio Ficino's commentary on Plotinus, *Ennead* 4.4.5.

49  For Pythagoras the letter *upsilon* represented what Robert Frost's "The Road Not Taken" represents for English-speaking readers: the place where "two roads diverged in a lonely wood," and the traveller must make a choice between them. (Frost himself made full use of his poem's ancient Greek pedigree.) For Frost, the two roads are similar, although the one he took "has made all the difference"; for the Pythagorean tradition, one is rocky and uphill, and leads to virtue; one is easy, and leads to vice.

50  For the waters above the firmament, see above, p. 29.

51  Bruno may simply be citing "the Chaldeans" here because the ancient Neoplatonists Proclus and Iamblichus praised these ancient Mesopotamian sages. His first-hand knowledge may extend no further than Marsilio Ficino's translations of these two Greek writers.

52 Unlike the word single word species, used as a term of classification, "intelligible species" comes from Thomas Aquinas: it means the essence of a form that the intellect has abstracted from its material embodiment in an individual.

53 Luke 17:21: "For behold, the kingdom of God is within you." Bruno's choice of the word "reform" cannot be casual here; his most favourable views on the Protestant Reformation applied to Elizabeth's Anglican "compromise."

54 The sonnet draws from two very different sources: the image of the "solitary sparrow" (known in English as the blue rock thrush) comes from a verse of the penitential Psalm 102 (101 Vulgate): "I watch, and am as a sparrow alone upon the house top" (*vigilavi et factus sum sicut passer solitarius in tecto*). The melancholy sparrow contrasts with the joyous image of the winged soul, drawn from Plato's *Phaedrus*.

55 This sonnet, with some slight changes, also appears in Bruno's earlier dialogue, *On the Infinite Universe and Worlds*. It shows several verbal echoes of a fifteenth-century *strambotto*, or popular song, by Serafino Aquilano, although its tone is entirely different (Vatican Library, MS Vat. Lat. 5170, 19v): "A solitary man, I stood apart / No flame of love had put me to the test / But she, with ingenuity and art / Inflamed the frozen heart within my breast. / Now that I've seen my spirit from me part / She's changed, and treats my sorrow as a jest. / And now it's Cupid's help that I invoke / To make that ingrate, too, go up in smoke."

56 Here Bruno slightly changes the text of his sonnet, which makes the "if" in its first version less ambiguous – as Tansillo explains it, the lonely sparrow is definitely gone, and although the sonnet began by calling him "my lonely sparrow," by the end he is no longer "mine." Bruno's Italian is particularly elegant; the first and last words of the sonnet are "mio." In effect, the poem beautifully demonstrates his principle of alternation.

57 After his scathing denunciation of Petrarch in his dedication, it may not be surprising that Bruno is slightly coy about naming the poet here. On the other hand, the Nolan's English and Italian readers would have recognized these lines immediately as *Canzoniere* 276, line 14, with its echo of Psalm 37:11.

58 For the biblical passage, Bruno substitutes part of the sestet of a sonnet. The original reads (in the King James version): "Let him kiss me with the kisses of his mouth; / Stay me with flagons, / For I am sick of love."

59 Here *forma* can either mean the noun "form" or the verb "forms." See CIRCUIT in the next dialogue, p. 164.

60 At this point in the dialogue, Tansillo's understanding is beginning to leave Cicada's behind, just as Bruno's own insights in the second half of the dia-

logue are intended to surpass Tansillo's. The misunderstanding between
Tansillo and Cicada comes about here because Tansillo is speaking about
things too lofty to convey in words; here on earth, they must remain mysteries. Miguel Angel Granada, in his commentary on the passage, notes the
similarities to Plotinus, *Ennead* 6.9.8.

61 The lines are taken from Tansillo's early poem "The Vintner" (*Il Vendemm-
miatore*), stanza 20.

62 Like most people of his day, Bruno believed in demons. In his experience,
they were mostly irritating little beings, who threw stones at passersby and
rummaged through personal effects, misplacing precisely what their victims
were looking for.

63 Bruno believed in reincarnation, as he will shortly explain more fully, p.
139.

64 2 Corinthians 12:2: I know a man in Christ who fourteen years ago was
caught up to the third heaven – whether in the body or out of the body I do
not know – God knows.

65 For Neoplatonists like Ficino, Pico della Mirandola, and, here, Cicada, the
descent of human souls into animal bodies was more a figure of speech
than a literal event; for Bruno, by contrast, the possibility was real. See Miguel Angel Granada's commentary on this dialogue, p. 549, nn. 68 and 69.

66 The doubling of words at the end of the line is a technique that Serafino
Aquilano used in his *strambotti*; this is another occasion when Bruno seems
to be inspired by fifteenth-century Italy's most popular and clever vernacular songwriter.

67 Tansillo and Cicada seem to be looking at a "festival book." Sixteenth- and
seventeenth-century festivities, like coronations, formal entries, religious
processions, weddings, funerals, and tournaments, were often recorded in
extreme detail by written descriptions, and less frequently by drawings or
engravings, with the marching order progressing from less important to
most important. Here Bruno's two soldier-poets seem to be looking at the
written description of a cavalcade of knights – by far the most usual format
for a sixteenth-century festival book.

68 Bruno uses the word *imprese* (for the definition, see above, p. xxvii); strictly
speaking, these are not emblems, but English makes no specific distinction
between emblem and *impresa*.

69 Emblems reached their most complex, and formalized, development in
the sixteenth century, when they were structured as an image (the body
or *corpus*), a motto or *inscriptio*, and an accompanying sonnet or *subscriptio*.
This is the three-part form in which Bruno presents his own total of twenty-
eight *imprese* (emblems with riddling images). The image of knights ranged

under their banners prompted Frances Yates to note that Bruno may well have seen the jousts that were mounted on 17 November 1584 to celebrate the anniversary of Queen Elizabeth's accession, "Elizabethan Chivalry: The Romance of the Accession Day Tilts," in Frances A. Yates, *Astraea: The Imperial Theme in the Sixteenth Century* (London: Routledge and Kegan Paul, 1975), 88–110. Miguel Angel Granada notes that in fact Bruno, who did not include engravings of his images in the published *Eroici furori*, concentrates most of his attention on the mottoes and sonnets, *Des fureurs héroïques*, 550. He made simple illustrations for many of his books, but these complex images would have required a professional experience that Bruno lacked. Furthermore, most contemporary descriptions of knights in marching order, as in festival books, were written texts without illustration.

70 The ultimate source for the image of an architecture of love is St Paul's Letter to the Ephesians, 2:19–22: "Now therefore ye are no more strangers and foreigners, but fellow citizens with the saints, and of the household of God; And are built upon the foundation of the apostles and prophets, Jesus Christ himself being the chief cornerstone; In whom all the building fitly framed together groweth unto an holy temple in the Lord; In whom ye also are builded together for an habitation of God through the spirit"; and, from the same letter, 4:14–16: "That we henceforth be no more children, tossed to and fro, and carried about with every wind of doctrine ... But speaking the truth in love, may grow up into him in all things, which is the head, even Christ: From whom the whole body fitly joined together and compacted by that which every joint supplieth ... maketh increase of the body unto the edifying of itself in love." Most of Bruno's biblical quotations are drawn from the Psalms, Ecclesiastes, and the Song of Songs, but Paul's Neoplatonic imagery fits well with the Neoplatonic cast of the *Eroici furori*.

71 This is the same philosophy of detachment that Bruno's father is said to have professed in the second dialogue; see above, p. 67.

72 Bruno does not seem to be much of an entomologist; in most of this discussion he uses the word mosca, "fly," to refer to what is clearly a moth – at one point, the moth/fly changes species twice in the space of three sentences. *Mosca* may simply mean "flying insect."

73 Bruno's image is probably drawn from an ancient Roman coin. The anecdote refers to the decisive battle at Pharsalus in Thessaly between Julius Caesar and Pompey (Gnaeus Pompeius) in 48 BC. Caesar, although greatly outnumbered (Pompey mustered 45,000 foot and 7000 horse against Caesar's 22,900 foot and 1000 horse), managed to mount a surprise attack on Pompey's cavalry and turn the battle into a rout. "Pharsalia" is actually the name of the epic written about the battle by the Roman poet Lucan

rather than the battle itself; Bruno's feats of memory may have been phenomenal, but his command of facts was not infallible.

74 This image of the invading army in the plain may be drawn significantly from life, if not from Bruno's experiences with his father, the professional soldier, then from the time he spent in France. Violent conflict between Catholics and Protestants drove him from his position at the University of Toulouse in 1582, and then from Paris to London in 1583.

75 Plotinus, *Ennead* 5.8.

76 Bruno's burning boy sounds like an early version of a cult that would become immensely popular in Naples: the souls in Purgatory (*Anime nel Purgatorio*), naked, with flames up to their waists if they are normal sinners, and with flames up to their shoulders if their sins are great. Often the figures wear bishops' mitres or other signs of high status; their nakedness and the flames show that in the end all human souls must answer to divine judgment. The first confraternity officially devoted to the *Anime* was founded in Naples in 1604, but the cult, with roots in pagan antiquity, must have taken form much earlier. Bruno's flames, of course, are caused by love in this life rather than by sin in the afterlife.

77 Arabia Felix was the ancient Roman name for the southwest regions of the Arabian peninsula (modern Yemen), and the legendary home of the Phoenix, which was consumed by fire every five hundred years and reborn from its own ashes. The best-known classical source for the story is Pliny the Elder, *Natural History*, 12.42, but the bird was proverbial in the Italian Renaissance. This sonnet, like the two in dialogues 3 and 4, also seems to look back to a *strambotto* by Serafino Aquilano (Vatican Library, MS Vat. Lat. 5170, 23r): "I burn my life away in lingering phases, / And never dare to beg for some reprieve / For fear that I must leave these burning blazes, / Far sweeter than you others might believe. / When I lose heart, I ask of Love what praises / Such spotless dedication should receive; / So though I burn, I hope by burning fast / That, Phoenix-like, I'll be reborn at last."

78 Bruno's basic source is Aristotle, *De Anima* 3.5.

79 In other words, the Copernican cosmic system, like the Ptolemaic system, is only a model; the motions of the universe occur on a far larger scale than either the heliocentric or geocentric systems, which have a single centre..

80 Bruno's dialogue of the previous year, normally known as *On the Infinite Universe and Worlds*.

81 Wisdom 7:24: "For wisdom is more moving than any motion: she passeth and goeth through all things by reason of her pureness."

82 Compare Bruno's description of infinity in dialogue 4 (p. 117): "It is appropriate and natural that infinity, being infinite, should be infinitely pursued

(by a kind of pursuit that has no physical motion, but rather a certain meta-physical motion – not from imperfection to perfection; instead, it circles through the degrees of perfection, to arrive at the infinite centre, which is neither formed, nor form itself."

83  In Bruno's sixteenth-century Latin, the word *circuit* could probably mean either "It circles" or *circuivit,* "it has circled."

84  Deucalion, who with his wife Pyrrha survived the great primeval flood, was therefore associated with the sign of Aquarius; Bruno's classical source would have been Hyginus, *Astronomia* 2.29.

85  Like most Italian words, the verbs in this line end in vowels, which have been elided by apostrophes to make it perfectly ambiguous whether the subject of the sentence is the Sun, the frenzied hero, or some third character. Bruno emphasizes the fact, but then proceeds to interpret the line as it is translated here, as a self-description of his own actions by the frenzied hero.

86  See the dedication, note 6.

87  Auster is the south wind; "Libya" is often a synonym in the ancient world, especially in ancient Greece, for Africa (as in Herodotus).

88  Bruno is thinking of Averroës's Commentary on Aristotle's *On the Soul* (*De Anima*), book 3, text 36.

89  In the sonnet itself, however, the Moon "never" surrenders itself.

90  According to Augustine (*De Trinitate* xiv), these are the three components of the human soul, which reflect the Holy Trinity. Bruno, who began to doubt the Trinity as a Dominican novice of eighteen, nonetheless preserves the soul's tripartite structure.

91  From the Neapolitan philosopher Bernardino Telesio (whose house on the Via Medina Bruno must have visited when they both lived in Naples), Bruno accepted the idea that the universe was composed of hot "stars" and cold "earths" (what we call stars and planets).

92  This discussion derives from Marsilio Ficino, *Platonic Theology,* 10.2.

93  Bruno's motto plays on the fact that in Latin the word for strength and the word for oak tree were the same, *robur;* the image comes from Vergil, who uses it to describe the beleaguered but steadfast hero Aeneas in *Aeneid* 4.441ff., but Bruno's more immediate source is a sonnet by Tansillo.

94  The following passage is a rather free translation from Diogenes Laertius's *Lives of the Philosophers,* 2.22.

95  *Ataraxia* really means "lack of agitation."

96  Bruno lists a series of people from the ancient world who demonstrated contempt for fear in defence of principle. Marcus Attilius Regulus was a Roman consul and general of the mid-third century BC who fought the

Carthaginians in North Africa. Captured after a battle, he was sent back to Rome to negotiate a treaty between the two powers. Rather than save his own life, he urged the Romans to reject the Carthaginians' terms, and returned to Carthage, where Roman legend had it that he was tortured and executed. Lucretia, a Roman matron of the late sixth century BC, was raped by her husband's friend Sextus Tarquinius in about 509 BC. After revealing what had happened to her husband and father, she stabbed herself ather than live with her dishonour, thereby bringing on the Romans' rebellion against the dynasty of Etruscan kings who had ruled the city, and the subsequent foundation of the Roman Republic. Socrates, condemned to death by an Athenian jury in 399 BC for "corrupting the young and introducing strange gods," preferred to carry out the sentence rather than escape from prison. Anaxarchus of Abdera, a philosopher and follower of Democritus who regarded happiness as the highest human aspiration, showed courageous defiance when he was condemned to death by the tyrant Nicocreon of Cyprus. During the siege of Rome by the Etruscan warlord Lars Porsenna in 509 BC, Mucius Scaevola made an unsuccessful attempt to assassinate Porsenna. When the Etruscan chieftain threatened to torture him with hot coals, Scaevola (which means "Left-handed") thrust his right hand into the brazier, telling Porsenna that there were a hundred more Romans like him ready to strike; if he had failed, one of his companions would succeed. Horatius Cocles, during the same siege, stood his ground on the wooden bridge that connected Rome to Porsenna's camp on the opposite bank, fighting off the Etruscan troops as his companions demolished the bridge under his feet. According to Livy (*History of Rome*), he was able to swim to safety despite his heavy armour; other Roman historians reported that his was a suicide mission, and Bruno must be following this version of the story. (Modern historians, like some ancient Roman historians, believe that Porsenna's invasion of Rome was successful). Bruno takes these examples from Seneca, *Letters to Lucilius*, and Cicero, *De finibus*, as well as the irresistibly entertaining Livy. The presence of Lucretia on the list may reflect Bruno's acute consciousness of Queen Elizabeth as a potential reader of his work, although the virtuous Roman matron was also a favourite subject for Italian Renaissance artists, including Raphael and Tintoretto.

97 Mongibello was the medieval name for Etna, a combination of the Italian "monte" and the Arabic word for mountain, *gebel.* Beneath the mountain the giant Typhon lay trapped as punishment for his attempt to invade Mount Olympus.

98 Plato, *Symposium* 203 C–D.

99  This is the famous golden apple that Strife threw down among the goddesses of Olympus, causing three of them, Juno, Minerva, and Venus, to
compete in a beauty contest judged by the Trojan shepherd prince, Paris.
Each of the goddesses bribed him with a promise: Juno of power, Minerva
of wisdom, and Venus of the world's most beautiful woman for his wife.
Unfortunately, that woman, Helen, was already married; her elopement
with Paris and her husband's attempt to take her back are what started the
Trojan War.

100  Venus was born in the sea near Cyprus.

101  The anecdote is from Cicero's *De inventione*, and involves the painter
Zeuxis rather than Apelles. It was taken up by Renaissance Neoplatonists to
exemplify the contrast between earthly beauty and absolute beauty.

102  The Italian and Latin *forma*, like the Platonic *idea*, are feminine nouns, and
hence easily personified to become the "She" who wins over the three goddesses who competed in the Judgment of Paris.

103  Lucretius, *De rerum natura* 4.1084ff.

104  Ecclesiastes 1:18: "For in much wisdom *is* much grief: and he that increaseth knowledge increaseth sorrow."

105  Lucretius, *De rerum natura*, 4.1055–6, 4.1059–61, 4.1065–6.

106  The pun does not quite work in English (nor do Bruno's grammatical
terms); in Latin *instans* can be either a participle (what Bruno calls an adjective) or a noun.

107  *On Time* was the common name in Bruno's day for the fourth book of Aristotle's *Physics*.

108  The infinite size of Bruno's universe is balanced on the other end of the
scale by the infinite smallness of atoms. Atomism was the last part of the
Nolan philosophy to fall into place, and this dialogue represents one of his
early attempts to describe infinitely small particles. His inspiration, both
poetic and philosophical, is the ancient Roman poet Lucretius.

109  Bruno's thoughts on infinitesimals indicate lines of thought that would
lead in the subsequent century to the simultaneous invention of calculus
by Leibniz and Newton, and in the nineteenth to the invention of non-
Euclidean geometry by Riemann. See esp. Hilary Gatti, "Bruno, Keplero
e la geometria," in Ornella Pompeo Faracovi, ed., *Aspetti della geometria
nell'opera di Giordano Bruno*, Studi del Centro Studi Enriques 8 (Lugano:
Agorà & Co., 2012), 29–52.

110  The sonnet clearly draws its inspiration from the famous passage in Ecclesiastes 3:1–8, "To every thing there is a season; And a time to every purpose
under heaven." This was a biblical book that Bruno cited with particular
frequency.

### Second Part of the Heroic Frenzies

1  That is, the sphere of the fixed stars.
2  Ancient astronomers calculated the Great Year as the time it took for the sphere of the fixed stars to make a complete revolution: 36,000 years. Because modern astronomers believe that the universe is constantly expanding, the Great Year is impossible.
3  The figure is that of Serapis in his temple at Alexandria, and probably taken from the description in Macrobius, *Saturnalia* 1.20.13–15: "They add the statue of a three-headed animal to his image, which shows in its largest and central head the likeness of a lion, while on the right grows the gentle head of a friendly dog, while the left neck ends in a ravening wolf ... Hence, the lion represents the present time, because its condition in the present moment between past and future is strong and eager. And the past is signified by the head of a wolf, because our memory of things we have done is snatched away and carried off. And the image of a friendly dog represents the future's outcome, because our hope in it, although it is uncertain, soothes us."
4  One of the most famous passages from the writings attributed to the Egyptian sage Hermes Trismegistus was a section of the dialogue *Asclepius* known as the Lament for Egypt, which Bruno had cited and translated in his *Expulsion of the Triumphant Beast*: "Do you not know ... that Egypt is the image of heaven, and to state it more clearly, the colony of all things that are governed and exercised in heaven? To tell the truth, our land is the temple of the world. But, alas, the time will come when Egypt will seem to have been the pious worshipper of divinity all in vain, for divinity, returning to heaven, will leave Egypt deserted, and this throne of divinity will become widowed of all religion, piety, law, and creed. O Egypt, Egypt, of your religions only the tales will remain, unbelievable to future generations, and they will have no one to tell of your pious deeds except the letters carved in stone, which will not speak to gods and men (for the latter will be dead, and deity transmigrated to heaven), but to Scythians and Indians, or other savages. Darkness shall prevail over light, death shall be judged more useful than life, the religious person shall be judged insane, the impious prudent, the madman strong, the worst man good." When Cesarino speaks here of "matters to be condemned," he may mean condemnation by the Christians as well as the "savages" of the Hermetic text.
5  The characters in Bruno's dialogues express different attitudes towards the Jews of his own time, from rabid anti-Semitism (Sophia in *Expulsion of the Triumphant Beast*) to respect and sympathy (Saulino in *Expulsion*; Cesarino here).

6   The Inquisition allowed greater liberty for philosophical speculation than it did for pronouncements on theology; here Bruno seems to be insisting on the purely philosophical nature of his discussion in order to limit the potential risk of discussing ideas such as the infinity of the universe, the existence of atoms, and the possibility of reincarnation.

7   The phrase *illius aram* comes from line 8 of Vergil's first eclogue, and refers to Octavian, the future Augustus, of whom the shepherd Tityrus asserts that a sacrificial lamb will often stain *his altar* in the future with its blood, Tityrus's thank-offering, for Octavian is a god to him.

8   Psalm 99 [Vulgate 98]:5: "Exalt ye the Lord our God, and worship at his footstool; for he is holy."

9   Psalm 132 [Vulgate 131]:7: "We will go into his tabernacles; we will worship at his footstool."

10  Here Bruno ensures that no one will confuse his insistence on God's immanence in all things with advocating idolatry.

11  Lucretius, *De rerum natura* 4.1077–87.

12  This is a loose translation of one of the *Adages* of Erasmus (795): *Mutuum muli scabunt*, "Mules scratch each other." As Erasmus says, "It is hard to see this saying as taken in anything but a negative sense, as when an ignorant person praises an ignorant person and vice versa, an ugly person praises another ugly person, a fool another fool."

13  Gaius Cilnius Maecenas, descended from the Etruscan rulers of Aretium (Arezzo), was a close associate of the emperor Augustus. An acute judge of literature, he sponsored the poets Vergil, Horace, and Propertius, making him the leading literary patron of Rome's "Golden Age."

14  Vergil, *Aeneid* 9.446–9.

15  Seneca, *Letters to Lucilius* 21.

16  Bruno, as often, makes a slapdash translation of this passage from Seneca's *Letters to Lucilius* 21, which in fact says: "It was of no advantage [to Atticus] to have Agrippa as a son-in-law and Tiberius as a grandson-in-law and Drusus Caesar as a grandson; among such great names he would have been passed over in silence had Cicero not addressed letters to him."

17  Bruno refers here to the "doctrine of silence" professed by the Neoplatonic mystic whose writings were identified with the Greek converted by St Paul in Athens, Dionysius the Areopagite; he is hence known to classicists as the Pseudo-Dionysius. Marsilio Ficino translated these works into Latin. Ironically, Bruno devotes a great deal of attention to the doctrine of silence in this, the wordiest of all his dialogues.

18  This is an example of how differently Bruno thought in an age when algebra was not yet taken for granted; we would automatically say, implicitly making an algebraic equation, "danger increases with population."

19 All of these citations are taken from Seneca, *Letters to Lucilius* 7.

20 Bruno is referring here to his previous dialogue *On the Cause, Principle, and One.*

21 This whole passage is taken from Seneca, *Letters to Lucilius* 31. Scylla and Charybdis were the monsters guarding the Straits of Messina who appear in Homer's *Odyssey*: Charybdis was the straits' tricky tide and Scylla a monstrous embodiment of the Etruscan pirates who lay in wait on the sea cliffs. The desert of Candavia was in present-day Albania, and the Syrtoi lived in modern Libya. Again Bruno's translation is loose: Seneca refers not to the Apennines but to the Dinaric Alps.

22 Endymion was a shepherd loved by the Moon, Diana, who came to him at night in his sleep. The frenzied hero, once he has seen the pure light of the Sun, has no more interest in the lesser, reflected light of the Moon.

23 Iamblichus, *On the Mysteries of the Egyptians* 3.3. Bruno probably knew Iamblichus through the translation of Marsilio Ficino.

24 Bruno is referring to his Latin work *The Seal of Seals* (Paris, 1583).

25 Psalm 143 [Vulgate 142]:6: "My soul thirsteth after thee, as a thirsty land."

26 Psalm 119 [Vulgate 118]:131: "I opened my mouth, and panted: for I longed for thy commandments."

27 Bruno knew this Kabbalistic doctrine first through Pico della Mirandola, although he was also clearly familiar with the *Dialogues on Love* of Leone Ebreo and the Christian Neoplatonic writings of Giles of Viterbo. The kiss, deadly in its joy, is an image of union with divinity.

28 Vergil, *Aeneid* 2.39; an image of heroic conduct for the frenzied hero.

29 Bruno carefully contrasts the genteel persuasion of the higher powers and the agitating, driving force of the lower.

30 Bruno may well take this information about Empedocles from Pico della Mirandola's *Oration on Human Dignity*.

31 Bruno's observations on gravity and the thinning of the atmosphere with altitude show that he could be an acute observer of nature; he always insisted that his philosophy was also a "natural and physical discourse."

32 This motto, like motto 14 in dialogue 1.5, plays on the Latin word *instans*, which can mean either "instant" or "insistent."

33 *Song of Songs* 4:9: "Thou hast ravished my heart, my sister, my spouse; thou hast ravished my heart."

34 Bruno's *Song of Circe* (*Cantus Circaeus*, Paris, 1582), provides long invocations of the gods and their various names and powers. Here, Diana is the Moon, basking in the reflected light of Apollo, the Sun. For the sixteenth-century Neoplatonist Giles of Viterbo, Diana embodied the human soul and Apollo embodied Christ. Bruno, however, presents the soul's search for God without Christ's mediation.

35 Bruno's account of the soul's descent into a living body after being bathed
   in the waters of Lethe is taken in its essentials from the Myth of Er at the
   end of Plato's *Republic* (book 10), and from Marsilio Ficino's *Platonic Theology* 28.10.

36 This passage shows that the *Eroici furori* traces Bruno's own philosophical
   biography as much as that of some abstract frenzied hero. In 1578, when
   he turned thirty, Bruno was wandering through northern Italy, with short
   stops in Venice, Brescia, Bergamo, Milan, and Turin; this may be the moment when he decided to pursue philosophy rather than the priesthood
   for which his Dominican training had prepared him. Before arriving in
   England, he made an unfortunate stay in Geneva, where he was excommunicated as a Calvinist in 1579, and then spent an unusually fortunate two-
   year term as a professor at the University of Toulouse, eventually travelling
   to Paris, and finally to London in April 1584. The end of the *Eroici furori*,
   with its English nymphs providing revelation, makes it clear that Bruno felt
   that he had only arrived at the full development of his philosophy after the
   experience in England.

37 Vergil, *Aeneid* 7.511–15.

38 Ancient naturalists may have reported that the eagle flew upward three
   times before pouncing, but Bruno is not certain that they always do so. This,
   then, is another occasion where the philosopher reveals his close attention
   to nature, by this time conditioned by close experience of watching eagles
   in the Alps, the Apennines, and the volcanic mountains around Naples.

39 Seneca, *Phaedra* 279–82, 293.

40 Proverbs 9:17: "Stolen waters are sweet, and bread eaten in secret is pleasant." 1 Kings 19:11–12: "And behold, the Lord passed by, and a great and
   strong wind rent the mountains, and brake in pieces the rocks before the
   Lord, but the Lord was not in the wind; and after the wind an earthquake;
   but the Lord was not in the earthquake; And after the earthquake a fire: but
   the Lord was not in the fire: and after the fire, a still small voice."

41 According to ancient Greek myth (which could actually be adjusted by any
   poet who cared to retell the old tales), Kronos, Latin Saturn, was supposedly
   the oldest of the gods. However, the fact that Saturn was born of the loving
   union between Ge and Ouranos, Earth and Heaven, provided evidence that
   Love must be older still – in fact, Ouranos would not stop coupling with his
   wife long enough for their children to emerge from her womb, and so the
   impatient Kronos castrated him.

42 For the physiology of sight, see the Introduction.

43 Juvenal, *Satire* 2.8–9: "There's nothing to trust in a face; for what street
   doesn't abound in grim and obscene ones?"

44 Paraphrased from Vergil, *Aeneid* 2.43–4.

45  Paraphrased from Seneca, *Thyestes* 572.

46  When Bruno wrote these words, he had spent time in a Swiss prison in Geneva and made several other narrow escapes. He would be arrested again in Venice in 1592, and remain in prison until his execution on 17 February 1600. His ability to maintain his Stoicism showed in his response to his Inquisitors when they sentenced him to death: "Perhaps you are more afraid to read me that sentence than I am to receive it."

47  Are these noble savages in the Americas, or Geneva? In any case, Bruno will change his mind about the desirability of enlightened monarchy after his further wanderings among the monarchies of northern Europe and finally opt, in his final works, for a universe that is a republic of stars.

48  In the liturgy of the Mass, when the priest invites his congregation to "Lift up your hearts," *sursum corda*; the congregation answers, "We lift them up unto the Lord" as preparation for the consecration of the Host and wine. Needless to say, Bruno means to shock.

49  That is, the Ionians, Pythagoras, and the Egyptians.

50  The pedophile grammar school teacher was a comic cliché in Bruno's era, but his hatred of these men, expressed in several of his works, is virulent enough to suggest some traumatic experience in his youth.

51  Martial, *Epigrams* 2.41.

52  The parallel with Hamlet's "slings and arrows of outrageous fortune" extends even to the mixing of metaphors. Although the subject is hotly debated among scholars, Bruno seems to have had some influence on Shakespeare; see esp. Hilary Gatti, *The Renaissance Drama of Knowledge: Giordano Bruno in England* (London: Routledge, 1999).

53  Plutarch tells the story that Archimedes died at the hands of a Roman soldier in the siege of Syracuse, when he was too preoccupied with finishing a mathematical proof to run for his life, *Life of Marcellus* 19.

54  Bruno's discussion follows that of Marsilio Ficino, *Platonic Theology* 2.8.

55  Bruno uses the English word for dogs here, writing "i dogs" rather than "i cani."

56  Here, as above, Bruno is following Ficino's *Platonic Theology* 2.8.

57  See Giles of Viterbo, *Sententiae ad mentem Platonis*, MS Vat. Lat. 6325, 37v: "[Plato] declares that the soul is happy in Heaven, rejoicing not in realities, that is, in created things, but in pure Essence, which belongs to God alone. For this reason he teaches that beauty is hunted out from the Forest of Matter, pure beauty, which exists without any mixture or composition ... But come, let us track the hidden understanding from this Forest with the help that we can find in the human soul as nets and snares."

58  This is an image from Plato, taken up by Marsilio Ficino, but developed in the sense that Bruno means here by Giles of Viterbo, *Sententiae ad mentem*

*Platonis*, ibid.: "Sometimes, however, the footprints are so hidden that the power of human intelligence cannot reach them. For this reason we seek help from another source, and bring in experienced dogs so that with their help we may obtain our quarry. Now we are chasing something about God out into the open from its hiding places in Nature, something that we could never succeed in capturing with Nature alone as our guide, not unless we use the demonstrations of dialectic as our dogs, and the study of philosophy as our nets. These dogs cannot track hidden quarry except by means of footprints, clear traces of the feet, or by odours. Thus, in this Forest of Matter divine footprints lie hidden, but when we take notice of them by means of reason, and consider them well, then we hunt out the hiding places of the divine light. Plato assents to this in the third book of the Laws, when he teaches that one should track down musical harmonies in the manner of experienced dogs."

59 Psalm 55:7 [Vulgate 54:3].

60 Bruno was aware that the Pole Star had shifted between antiquity and the present, and therefore refers to the Arctic region of the heavens rather than to Polaris itself. He describes the Pole Star as "slow" because it is sluggish from the northern chill.

61 The Nereids have already appeared in dialogue I.2, see p. 65 above.

62 This is, of course, the dialogue that Bruno published under the title *On the Cause, Principle, and One.*

63 The Age of Exploration brought back every kind of tale about what happened beneath the sea; here Bruno must be referring to undersea volcanoes or trenches, ideas that would lead the German Jesuit Athanasius Kircher, in the succeeding century, to formulate the first theory of plate tectonics.

64 The story of Deucalion, who survived the Great Flood with his wife Pyrrha, is told in its most entertaining version by Ovid in *Metamorphoses* 1.313–415. We have already seen him associated with the sign of Aquarius in dialogue 1.5.

65 Ecclesiasticus 24:29 (Douai-Rheims): "They that eat me, shall yet hunger: and they that drink me, shall yet thirst."

66 Bruno uses the wording of the Latin translation directly from the Hebrew psalms ("Accedet homo ad cor altum") rather than the Latin translated from the Greek Septuagint ("Accedet homo et cor altum") for this citation of Vulgate Psalm 63:6–7. In English, the Douai-Reims version makes the same choice for Psalm 63:7–8: "Man shall come to a deep heart, and God shall be exalted." The King James Version, in which the psalm is numbered 64, is much different: "They accomplish a diligent search: both the inward

thought of every one of them, and the heart, is deep. But God shall shoot
at them with an arrow; suddenly shall they be wounded," and hence, excep-
tionally, that version is not used here.

67 Ovid tells about a cave hidden deep in the mountains of Central Asia where
some of the local people, the Cimmerians, lived in perpetual darkness;
*Metamorphoses* 11.492–6.

68 *Katadoupos* is Greek for waterfall; the word means "downward crashing." In
classical antiquity, the Katadoupoi (in Latin, Catadupi), lived in Egypt in
the region of the First Cataract, and are mentioned by several ancient authors, including Ptolemy, Ammianus Marcellinus, and Bruno's most likely
source, Cicero's *Dream of Scipio*.

69 Bruno believed, like nearly all his contemporaries, in spontaneous generation; indeed, the Nolan philosophy provided him with an excellent explanation of how it occurred. It was not until the later seventeenth century, when
the Florentine Francesco Redi invented a microscope powerful enough to
see fly eggs in dung, that the argument was finally put to rest.

70 Isaiah 38:14.

71 Bruno shows here that he understood the basic point of Plato's *Symposium*;
there is ultimately no course of study, including the Nolan philosophy, that
can guarantee enlightenment; study can only improve the odds that enlightenment will occur.

72 Jeremiah 29:13: "And ye shall seek me, and find me, when ye shall search
for me with all your heart."

73 John 7:37: "In the last day, that great day of the feast, Jesus stood and cried,
saying, If any man thirst, let him come unto me, and drink."

74 Arabic commentators on Aristotle were often confused in the manuscript
tradition, with the result here that Bruno attributes the conviction of Averroës that philosophy should be kept separate from religion to the Muslim
traditionalist Algazel (Al-Gazali, 1058–1111). See Miguel Angel Granada,
*La cena de las cenizas* (translation with commentary of Bruno's *Ash Wednesday Supper*) (Madrid, 1994), 154; F. Papi, *Antropologia e civiltà nel pensiero di
Giordano Bruno* (Florence, 1968), 298ff.

75 The discussion of *phantasmata* is taken from Aristotle, *On the Soul* 3.3.

76 1 Corinthians 13:12: "For now we see through a glass, darkly; but then face
to face: now I know in part; but then shall I know even as also I am known."

77 This is Plato's famous Allegory of the Cave from *Republic* 7.

78 This discussion about the forest is another passage with strong similarities to
Giles of Viterbo's manuscript *Sententiae ad mentem Platonis*. See Introduction,
p. xxix, and nn. 58 and 59, above.

79 Bruno is clearly thinking of the Bible without saying so explicitly.

80  Hebrews 4:12: "For the word of God is quick, and powerful, and sharper
    than any twoedged sword, piercing even to the dividing asunder of soul and
    spirit, and of the joints and marrow, and is a discerner of the thoughts and
    intents of the heart."
81  Song of Songs 6:5.
82  Bruno may well have visited Monte Circeo during the first half of his life; he
    certainly passed through the area en route to Rome.
83  A three-stringed bowed viol.
84  Thus, Bruno's Art of Memory compensates for Platonic forgetfulness.

# Bibliography

The most exhaustive modern edition of the *Eroici Furori* (and one to which this translation is profoundly indebted) is that of Miguel Angel Granada et al., *Giordano Bruno, Oeuvres complètes, VII, Des Fureurs Heroïques*, text by Giovanni Aquilecchia, introduction and notes by Miguel Angel Granada, translation by Paul-Henri Michel, revised by Yves Hersant, Paris: Les Belles Lettres 1999, revised edition 2008. Eugenio Canone's Italian text is a slightly revised version of *Giordano Bruno. De gli Eroici Furori*, edited with an introduction and commentary by Eugenio Canone., Biblioteca dell'Utopia, Milan: Silvio Berlusconi Editore, 2011. The periodical *Bruniana & Campanelliana* provides an annual list of recent publications ("Schede") on Bruno. What follows is a selection.

## On Bruno and His English Experience

Aquilecchia, Giovanni. "Giordano Bruno in Inghilterra (1583–1585)." *Bruniana & Campanelliana* 1 (1995): 21–42.

Canone, Eugenio, ed. *Giordano Bruno, 1548–1600, Mostra storico documentaria, Roma, Biblioteca Casanatense, 7 giugno-30 settembre 2000*. Florence: Leo S. Olschki, 2000.

Canone, Eugenio, ed. *Il dorso e il grembo dell'eterno: Percorsi della filosofia di Giordano Bruno*. Pisa and Rome: Istituti Editoriali e Poligrafici, 2003.

Canone, Eugenio, ed. *Magia dei contrari. Cinque studi su Giordano Bruno*. Pisa and Rome: Edizioni dell'Ateneo, 2005.

Ciliberto, Michele. *Giordano Bruno*. Rome and Bari: Laterza, 1990; 2nd edition 1992.

Ciliberto, Michele. *Giordano Bruno: Il teatro della Vita*. Milan: Arnoldo Mondadori, 2007.

Ciliberto, Michele. *L'occhio di Atteone: Nuovi studi su Giordano Bruno*. Rome: Edizioni di Storia e Letteratura, 2002.

Ciliberto, Michele. *La ruota del tempo: Interpretazione di Giordano Bruno*. Rome: Editori Riuniti, 1986, 1992.

Ciliberto, Michele, and Nicholas Mann, eds. *Giordano Bruno, 1583–1585: The English Experience*. Florence: Leo S. Olschki, 1997.

Feingold, Mordechai. "Bruno in England Revisited." *Huntington Library Quarterly* 67, no. 3 (2004): 329–46.

Gatti, Hilary. *Giordano Bruno and Renaissance Science*. Ithaca, NY: Cornell University Press, 1999.

Gatti, Hilary, ed. *Giordano Bruno, Philosopher of the Renaissance*. Aldershot: Ashgate, 2002.

Gatti, Hilary. *The Renaissance Drama of Knowledge: Giordano Bruno in England*. London: Routledge, 1989.

Granada, Miguel Angel. *Giordano Bruno, Universo infinito, unión con Dios, perfección del hombre*. Barcelona: Herder, 2002.

Michel, Paul-Henri. *The Cosmology of Giordano Bruno*. Trans. R.E.W. Maddison. Ithaca, NY: Cornell University Press, 1973.

Ordine, Nuccio, *La Cabala dell'Asino: Asinità e conoscenza in Giordano Bruno*. Naples: Liguori Editore, 1987.

Provvidera, Tiziana. "On the Printer of Giordano Bruno's London Works." *Bruniana & Campanelliana* 2 (1996): 361–8.

Ricci, Saverio. *Giordano Bruno nell'Europa del Cinquecento*. Rome: Salerno, 2000.

Rowland, Ingrid D. *Giordano Bruno, Philosopher/Heretic*. New York: Farrar, Straus & Giroux, 2008.

Spampanato, Vincenzo. *Vita di Giordano Bruno*, reprint of *Messina: Giuseppe Principato*, 1922, with an afterword by Nuccio Ordine. Rome: Gela Editrice, 1988.

Wyatt, Michael. *The Italian Encounter with Tudor England: A Cultural Politics of Translation*. New York: Cambridge University Press, 2005.

Yates, Frances. *Giordano Bruno and the Hermetic Tradition*. London: Routledge and Kegan Paul, 1964.

Yates, Frances. *The Art of Memory*. London: Routledge and Kegan Paul, 1961.

### On the Eroici furori

Bönker-Vallon, Angelika. "Unità nascosta e autoconoscenza. La presenza della tradizione del neoplatonismo negli Eroici furori." *Bruniana & Campanelliana* 9, no. 2 (2003): 281–94.

Canone, Eugenio. "Le 'due luci.' Il concerto finale degli *Eroici Furori*." *Bruniana & Campanelliana* 9, no. 2 (2003): 295–318.

Canone, Eugenio, and Ingrid D. Rowland, eds. *Alchemy of Extremes: The Laboratory of the Eroici Furori of Giordano Bruno*. Rome and Pisa: Accademia Editoriale, 2007.

Granada, Miguel Angel. "Digges, Bruno, e il copernicanesimo in Inghilterra." In *Giordano Bruno 1583–1585: The English Experience*, ed. Michele Ciliberto and Nicholas Mann, 125–55. Florence: Leo S. Olschki, 1997.

Granada, Miguel Angel. Introduction to Miguel Angel Granada et al., *Giordano Bruno, Oeuvres complètes, VII, Des fureurs heroïques*, text by Giovanni Aquilecchia, introduction and notes by Miguel Angel Granada, translation by Paul-Henri Michel, revised by Yves Hersant. Paris: Les Belles Lettres, 1999.

Granada, Miguel Angel. "'Quel che viviamo è un punto': Nota sobre el uso de Séneca por Giordano Bruno en *De li eroici furori*." In M.A. Granada, *La reivendicación de la filosofia en Giordano Bruno*, 259–77. Barcelona: Herder, 2005.

Ingegno, Alfonso. "L'unità dell'opera bruniana e il significato degli 'Heroici Furori.'" In Nuccio Ordine and Davide Bigalli, eds, *Il dialogo filosofico nel' 500 europeo*: Atti del convegno di Studi, Milano, 28–30 maggio 1987, 229–43. Milan: Angeli, 1990.

Maggi, Armando. "The Language of the Visible: The *Eroici furori* and the Renaissance Philosophy of *Imprese*." *Bruniana & Campanelliana* 6, no. 1 (2000): 115–44.

Nelson, John Charles. *Renaissance Theory of Love: The Context of Giordano Bruno's Eroici furori*. New York, London: Columbia University Press, 1958.

**On Luigi Tansillo**

Rubino, Ciro. *Tansilliana: La vita, la poesia e le opere di Luigi Tansillo*. Naples: Istiuto Grafico Editoriale Italiano, 1996.

Tansillo, Luigi. *Luigi Tansillo: Il Canzoniere edito ed inedito*. Reprint, annotated by Tobia Toscano (Naples: Liguori editore, 1996) of Erasmo Pércopo, ed. Naples: Tipografia degli Artigianelli, 1926.

**Emblems**

Glasgow University Library owns the Stirling Maxwell Collection of Emblem Books, the largest collection of its kind in the world, and manages an extensive website devoted to emblem studies, an excellent starting place for any researcher in this field: http://www.emblems.arts.gla.ac.uk/.

# Index